# East
## of
# Existentialism

# TITLES OF RELATED INTEREST

# East
# of
# Existentialism

## The Tao of the West

Ray Billington

London
**UNWIN HYMAN**
Boston    Sydney    Wellington

Published by the Academic Division of

**Unwin Hyman Ltd**
15/17 Broadwick Street, London W1V 1FP, UK

Unwin Hyman Inc.,
8 Winchester Place, Winchester, Mass. 01890, USA

Allen & Unwin (Australia) Ltd
8 Napier Street, North Sydney, NSW 2060, Australia

Allen & Unwin (New Zealand) Ltd in association with the
Port Nicholson Press Ltd,
Compusales Building, 75 Ghuznee Street, Wellington 1, New Zealand

First published in 1990

---

**British Library Cataloguing in Publication Data**

Billington, Ray
　　East of existentialism : the Tao of the West
　　1. Man – Philosophical perspectives
　　I. Title
　　128

　　ISBN　0–04–445542–9
　　ISBN　0–04–445543–7 pbk

---

**Library of Congress Cataloging-in-Publication Data**

Billington, Ray.
　　East of existentialism : the Tao of the West /
Ray Billington.
　　　p.　cm.
　　Includes bibliographical references.
　　ISBN 0–04–445542–9. — ISBN 0–04–445543–7
(pbk.)
　　　1. Philosophy. 2. East and west. 3. Philosophy,
Oriental.
　　I. Title.
　　B53.B435　1990
　　190—dc20　　　　　　　　　　　　89–77649
　　　　　　　　　　　　　　　　　　　　CIP

---

Typeset in 10 on 12 point Bembo
Printed by The University Press, Cambridge

To Shelagh

– who suffereth long, and is kind

# Contents

# Acknowledgements

Acknowledgement is due to the copyright holders for their kind permission to reprint the following extracts: 'The Newt' by R. P. Lister is reproduced by permission of *Punch*; extracts from Philip Rawson's *Oriental Erotic Art* are reproduced by permission of John Calmann & King Ltd and Quartet Books Ltd; extracts from John Hospers' *An Introduction to Philosophical Analysis*, 3e(© 1988, pp. 280–83) is adapted by permission of Prentice Hall Inc. Englewood Cliffs, New Jersey; lines from T. S. Eliot's 'Morning at the Window' from *Collected Poems 1909–1962* is reproduced by permission of Faber & Faber Limited and Harcourt Brace Jovanovich Inc.; Patrick Lewin's article 'Death and the Self', originally published in the *Guardian* newspaper, is reproduced by permission of Patrick Lewin; extracts from Melanie Phillips' column for the *Guardian* are reproduced by permission of Melanie Phillips; extracts from Mike Page's article, originally appearing in the *Guardian*, are reproduced by permission of Mike Page.

Vast indeed is the Ultimate Tao
Spontaneously itself, seeming not to act;
End of all ages, beginning of all ages,
Existing before earth, existing before heaven,
Silently embracing the whole of time
Continuing uninterrupted through all aeons;
In the East it taught Father Confucius,
In the West it converted the Golden Man.
Taken as pattern by a hundred kings,
Transmitted by generations of wise men,
It is the ancestor of all doctrines
The Mystery beyond all mysteries.
(Ming inscription)

# Foreword

The basic thesis of this book springs from two underlying convictions. The first is that philosophy is, quite simply, the supreme guide to life. Unlike other areas of inquiry, it is unlimited in its scope; and unlike (for instance) religion, it has no special axe to grind. So – although this is sometimes more a hope than a realization – one may expect philosophy to be undertaken without the blinkers of prejudice and with a respect for facts which should eliminate any kind of special pleading. It should not be possible to state truthfully of any philosopher: 'Well, he would say that, wouldn't he.'

The second conviction is that Western philosophy is incomplete without its Eastern counterpart. Western philosophers have healthily reminded us for two-and-a-half millenniums that we must rise above generalities and generalizations because things are not always what they seem. Philosophy has opened the eyes of countless generations to the eternal problems arising from issues metaphysical, epistemological and ethical, and has instilled a healthy scepticism into our inquiries and findings in these fields. Whether we are students of science, history, the human psyche, or the arts, Western philosophy has enabled us to explore more comprehensively than we could have done without it.

But inevitably the exploration has been undertaken in a Western milieu and with Western tools. Nothing wrong with that, it may be argued; the context is broad, and the tools expertly made. Yes: provided one is content to keep one's horizons limited, to stick only to well-trodden and familiar paths. And there's the rub; in recent years, for a variety of reasons, we in the West have been inexorably drawn into a closer relationship with a world whose thought patterns and underlying assumptions, especially in the area of metaphysics, are greatly different from those with which the West is familiar: the 'mysterious East' as it was described when I was a boy, but whose mystery is being increasingly revealed to others. This means, among other things, that the West has had to take account of very different approaches to philosophy – especially to metaphysics – than it has generally found along the familiar Western paths of empirical inquiry and linguistic analysis; to reflect on the possibility that *homo sapiens* may be more than *sapiens*, that 'the heart also has its reasons'.

In what follows I am making an initial foray into this fallow – I had almost written virgin, but it is not quite that – field. Like its predecessor, *Living Philosophy*, it is in three parts (my training as a preacher of three-decker sermons has stuck with me). In all three the pivotal issue is human nature and destiny – who or what are we, and where are we going? In Chapters 2–4 some of the major Western contributions to this theme are considered and – on the whole – discarded. In the central section, Chapters 5–7, the basic connection apropos of these issues is made between existentialism in the West and certain dominant philosophical schools in India and China. It is from this section that the book's title originates. I have space to discuss these schools only briefly, and I know that proponents of any one of them will feel that more has been left unsaid than said about them; but enough, I hope, has been presented to at least suggest the possibility that there is a rich vein to be explored, once the East–West connection has been made.

How rich this vein may be is suggested in the final chapters of the book. In these chapters the implications of the synthesis are outlined not only for philosophical theory but also for moral and social dilemmas, and for practical living generally. These are the chapters which test my conviction that philosophy is for the market-place, not just the ivory tower.

The readership I have in mind is that large and often silent (because frustrated?) body of people who are ready to reflect on metaphysical matters a little more deliberately than is normally required of them; their interest in the subject has never been fostered, so they have remained closet philosophers. This body will include students, of course, but that category embraces many more people than those formally enrolled on philosophy or other academic courses. In fact I'm constantly astonished, as I address meetings at different levels on philosophical matters, how widespread is the interest in the issues – an interest often stifled by philosophical presentations in both the written and spoken word. I hope that whether what I have to say is agreed with or not, at least readers will know precisely what it is that they are either agreeing or disagreeing *with*.

I hope also that neither students nor teachers nor general readers will be deterred from what follows because it is, however inadequately, expressing something bordering on a new idea in philosophy. It would seem to me odd indeed if, in philosophy of all areas, a statement were rejected in obedience to Cornforth's law: Nothing should ever be said for the first time. It is precisely because schools of philosophy have for decades been avoiding the making of precedents that signs of stagnation have been appearing at their edges.

The feeling among many of those who are sympathetic to the basic aims of philosophy – to seek wisdom and an understanding of the universe – is that, after several decades in the doldrums, it is beginning to rediscover and assert itself. In the fields of moral and political philosophy, for instance, journals are appearing which indicate that these fields relate to issues which can actually touch the pulse of humanity. And the same goes for metaphysics: in the West we are slowly beginning to realize that this basic philosophical subject need not be tied to theological assumptions which came into being before the revolution in the human spirit, represented by the Renaissance, the Enlightenment, and the French and other revolutions, made theology (at least in its fundamentalist forms) redundant. In the East, of course, metaphysics was never so beholden to theology as in the West – hence the direction taken in this book.

There is, I suppose, a fair amount of personal reflection in the following pages. This seems to me inevitable if I'm to discuss the nature of Being from my own perspective: how can one be objective about *Being*? My field of Being is what it is because of the path that I myself have trodden – which has included a fair share of hazards and near-disasters. It seems natural that these experiences should be reflected in this book, though I hope that what I've written is not seen to be just a personal testimony. So far as I know, nobody else has made the link between existentialism and Taoism which I present here but, surely, only a pedant would condemn the idea on that ground alone. My hope is that people – students and scholars – from both West and East will find some of the ideas here to be creative, opening a door, perhaps, to new avenues for exploration.

As in my earlier *Living Philosophy*, I have included a number of case studies at the end of each chapter. Perhaps the title 'case study' is pretentious for some of the examples, where the material offered is little more than supplementary to the main text. But some of the 'hypotheticals' should fit more comfortably into the idea of a case study, and even those which are less provocative should allow readers to reflect at their leisure on specific issues raised in the text. This reflection can be undertaken alone, of course, but it is best suited for discussion with fellow-students or like-minded friends and neighbours (if one is lucky enough to have these).

My indebtedness to thinkers of both the East and the West will be plain from these pages, but nobody other than myself can be either praised or blamed for the extrapolations that are made. I should point out, however, that the initial impulse to pursue the combination of ideas presented here arose when I was called to teach a course on 'Philosophy East and West' during my year as exchange professor of Philosophy at the State University of California in Chico. It was my colleagues there, particularly Brooke Moore, the head of department, and James Luyirika-Sewagudda, the overseas students officer at that campus, who encouraged and motivated me to write. The supreme accolades, however, must go to Eric Pearson of that city, for he it was who agreed to hear the entire manuscript read through, and made many pertinent and encouraging comments on it. If the examples I use are more frequently chosen from the British than from the American scene (and I'm not sure that this is the case), this is the accident of current proximity, not of greater relevance to the issues discussed.

I am grateful to Ananda Shakti (her spiritual name) for providing the material on yoga in case study 28; and to one of my students, John Smith, for some of the material used in the section on Hinduism. But my most lasting gratitude must be to the many students over the years who have provided – and still provide – me with the enthusiasm to pursue the issues tackled in this book. The extent to which these issues are taken out of the ivory tower (the graveyard of real philosophy as of the elephant) and confronted as part of the challenge of normal living is the extent of the realism which their presence brings. It is one of the few signs of hope in the current Western scene that young people are willing to resist in their swarms political pressures to study 'useful' subjects like banking and estate management and opt instead to spend their time reflecting on the ancient wisdoms. Thus is the pure flame of civilization kept kindled.

*Ray Billington*
Bristol, August 1989

# 1  Prologue: the tunes of philosophy

Imagine, if you will, that you are attending an orchestral concert in some great city hall. You have been considerably inconvenienced to get there: parking was a nightmare; the ticket was expensive. You regard all this with indifference, however, since the central feature of the concert is the appearance of Vladimir Ashkenazy as piano soloist. You're not sure what concerto he'll be playing, since it was not stated on the programme, but the choice is irrelevant; it will be enough for you simply to sit back and hear the world's leading genius at the keyboard express his own inimitable art.

The overture completed, Ashkenazy ascends to the rostrum. As the applause fades away, he sits at the Steinway, and 3,000 people become totally silent. As his hands hover over the keys, you hold your breath. Then the first notes resound through the hall: a beautiful run up and down the white notes – the key of C. You don't recall either a piano concerto or a sonata which begins in this way, but assume that it must be a new piece, perhaps Ashkenazy's own. A pause: and again the hands move rhythmically and with infinite felicity up and down the piano. This time there is a greater sadness in the playing: it is the key of C minor. From joy to sorrow, you think: the essence of romantic music. Again a pause, and again up and down seven octaves, this time beginning on a higher note – the key of D, you imagine. But by now you're beginning to feel bewildered, and those sitting around you seem to be sharing the feeling. Still the scales continue, major and minor, up a tone, down a semitone, played with every nuance of touch that might be expected of a maestro.

After some twenty minutes of this, Ashkenazy indicates that he has concluded this part of the concert, and comes forward to take his bow beside the conductor. There is spasmodic and perfunctory applause. The conductor then informs the audience that after the interval Ashkenazy will entertain with his own rendition of the arpeggios. A feeling of anger now creeps alongside that of bewilderment: had you paid good money just to hear scales and arpeggios? You note that the final item is one of the

more schmaltzy symphonies of the – in your view – highly overrated
Tchaikovsky. You make a mental note to demand your money back the
next day, and decide to surprise those at home with your early return.
Judging from the enormous queue waiting to leave the hall's car park,
you are not alone in making this decision.

As you drive home, seething and incredulous, you recall your earliest
days of learning the piano, and how firmly your tutor had instilled into you
the necessity of practising scales in order to give the fingers the suppleness
needed for all the works you would learn to play, and the arpeggios so that
your hands would judge unerringly the musical intervals. You know even
years later when you play the piano passably that such practice, boring
though it may be both to the performer and to any involuntary audience,
remains a necessary preliminary to the rendering of tunes, as training is
before the excitement of a game of football.

But, you reflect, scales and arpeggios are merely a means to an end, not
an end in themselves – hence the absurdity of listening to anyone, even
Ashkenazy, performing them. You learned the piano not to play scales
but to play tunes: the piano was made for the Moonlight Sonata, not for
the scale of E minor.

This may seem a strange way to begin a book on philosophy, but the
lesson I want to draw from it colours the approach to the subject which I
shall take throughout its chapters. Philosophy in the Western world has for
much of this century been so engrossed in the technique of faultlessly playing
scales and arpeggios that it has allowed the art of playing tunes to fall into
abeyance. The philosophy I was taught in the early 1950s, and which is still
taught in many of our institutions of higher education, was so absorbed in
the issue of *method* that it had lost – or nearly lost – any *content*. Over the past
decade there have been increasing indications of the dissatisfaction of both
teachers and students of philosophy with this methodological approach, but
the problem remains, and still causes disenchantment among potentially
sound and imaginative students. I shall return to this stricture later, but in
order to give it substance let me first explain the path I took in philosophy,
and how my convictions were formed as to what the subject really entails.
Why, if my criticism is justifiable, should anyone read philosophy any more
than they would go to hear a concert pianist playing scales?

I was lucky enough to begin my readings in the subject with **Bertrand
Russell**'s★ *The Problems of Philosophy* (still, significantly, in print) and,
although limited in its number of themes (it is, after all, almost as old as this
century, so unsurprisingly did not include, for instance, existentialism, one
of the philosophical schools which will loom large in this book), it opened
my eyes to a new way of looking at the world – a process which 'tuneful'
philosophy has always inculcated. It encouraged me to respond more deeply

---

★ see glossary for names and terms appearing in bold type.

to the world around me than is possible through the medium of the five senses alone. This is not to say only that there is more to awareness than can be attained solely through the senses, though that realization is of course significant. Having read Russell, I am never likely to be unconscious of the 'true' situation (inverted commas because, as Russell clearly illustrated, the word is meaningless in the world of perception) when I describe a table-top as 'flat', my shirt as 'green', or the grass in my garden, home for a myriad of spiders and other 'tiny' creatures, as 'short'. To understand the problems of perception is to realize that every judgement we make about what we perceive is relative to *our* perspective.

But for me this was just the beginning of the philosophical experience. The process of looking below the surface led me next to ask questions about human behaviour. Having been raised in a Methodist manse, it had become customary to me to categorize sections of people as 'good' or 'bad' according to certain aspects of this behaviour. Among those who achieved condemnation on these grounds were all who drank alcohol, swore, smoked, mated before marriage, or did their washing on the Sabbath. (If it had been discovered that, say, Adolf Hitler had been a total abstainer, several of my relatives would have revised their opinion of him.) With the inevitable widening of experience over the years came the realization that behaviour cannot be so glibly categorized, and the safe **absolutism** of my youth (safe because, having accepted the generalities, there was no call to agonize over the specifics) was perforce replaced by the more dangerous moral **relativism**, with its appreciation that each problem for the moral agent needs individual examination and a separate commitment.

This realization led to even more searching questions. How can anyone be *sure* of the rightness or wrongness of their behaviour? Right or wrong in what context? From whose perspective? The **Lutheran** theological students with whom I first entered a bar when I was studying in Germany were as dumbfounded at my hesitation to enter what I had believed to be the gateway to perdition as I was in finding those inside to be no more redolent of wickedness than might be found in any convivial group meeting outside. I noted too that those who did not indulge in any of the so-called weaknesses of the flesh were often censorious, cruel with their tongues; I came to perceive that goodness and evil could not be so easily distinguished as I had assumed: whether people were on the side of darkness or of light showed itself to be infinitely more difficult to resolve than I had earlier imagined.

Yet the basic problem remained: decisions were called for, situations continually arose in which I as an individual moral agent was obliged to say 'yes' or 'no'. Reading moral philosophy increased my awareness of the scope and ramifications of the dilemma. Should one's moral stance be established on the basis of a principle, such as **Kant**'s concept of duty, and damn the consequences? Or should one, following the path of **John Stuart Mill** and the **utilitarians**, look at the end in view and leave principles for the preachers? Is there a golden strand running through human experience which will indicate more or less unerringly what is right – the Good as described by **Aristotle**, say, or Natural Law after **Aquinas**? If so, how did this strand come about, and how is one to react to a person who interprets it in a way diametrically different from one's own? If there is no such thread, does that mean that every human being is a law unto him- or herself, with all the concomitant dangers of this for a harmonious society or even, following **Hobbes**'s pessimistic line about human nature, with every man at war with his fellows?

This led to a further question: why bother with goodness anyway? – a question which itself begs and leads to another even more basic question. Should one view the universe, including human behaviour, **teleologically**, that is, purposively? Is there a goal to which all life is moving? If so, who or what has established that goal, and how can anyone know with confidence what it is? Or should we rather accept Russell's own expressed view that the universe came about by chance and will eventually come to nothing so that, with nothing to perceive it, it will be as though it had never been? If so, why the agony of moral decision-making while we are in existence? If the universe was not intended, why do people spend so much time and energy in interpreting it otherwise? If it *was* intended, who or what intended it? And can we learn and be sure of what that intention is? And if there is to be no final resolution of these issues, is it worthwhile pursuing them? Should we not then simply drop altogether from our vocabulary phrases like 'ultimate reality' and 'the meaning of life'?

We are here embarking on the area of philosophy known as metaphysics, a word with which few beginners in the subject are likely to feel at ease. It has a ring of the occult or supernatural about it, and the connotation in the minds of many is that of a pseudo-science like psychoanalysis or the paranormal. In fact the word is quite pedestrian and originated in a very matter-of-fact way. After the death of Aristotle in 322 BC, his editors were arranging his voluminous writings, beginning with those which Aristotle called natural philosophy, and which they termed physics. (In those days 'philosophy' embraced all the subjects in the educational curriculum.) After this they placed the works on what Aristotle called 'first philosophy' but which they termed '*ta meta ta physika*', 'the [writings] after the physics'. Over the centuries the question of whether there is any reality beyond the physical has provided a deeper meaning to the original phrase: the study of the underlying principles of things – which was, in fact, what was in Aristotle's mind in the first place. Is there a single essence or entity in the universe – the material – or is there more than one – the 'spiritual' (for lack of a better term) besides the material? What do we mean when we use the word 'mind'? Are we simply describing the brain from a particular perspective, or should the mind and the brain be viewed and described separately? Is there any part of the human person that is indestructible – call it psyche, soul, mind, or what you will? Is there a God, and does it matter whether or not you believe in Him/Her/It?

These issues, while they can be ignored (as they have been by many philosophers this century), refuse to go away. They affect the way many people approach their work, treat other people, prioritize uses of their time, or even – perhaps especially – how they spend their money. Other areas of reflection could of course be added to these; among these are the theory of beauty and the nature of a work of art (see case study 2). But enough examples have been given to provide substance to my original point: it is in discussion of these issues, more, I feel, than of any others (though others are not excluded) that we discover the *tunes* of philosophy. They have brought countless people over the centuries to view philosophy as the guide of life, the steersman amid its turbulent waters. It is because of the fact that philosophers like Plato and Aristotle, Descartes and **Spinoza**, Hobbes, Kant, **Hume**, **Locke**, **Marx**, **Bradley**, **Schopenhauer**, **Russell**, **Bergson**, Heidegger and Sartre turned their minds to these fundamental questions that our understanding of the universe, and the place in it of *homo sapiens*, has been fostered and nourished. These philosophers and others like them have tackled the problem of the human condition and those who have listened to them have developed a maturity in their reflections without which they may well have remained no more than adolescent in their appreciation of life in general and their own lives in particular.

However, all the philosophers I have named have one significant factor in common: *they are all dead.* Their messages, or tunes, live on, of course, but these need new expression with each new generation. The madrigals of yesteryear will hardly top the charts in the 1990s. So what contributions are today's philosophers making to this human inquiry? What tunes are they playing?

The answer, I feel, is – nothing like enough. There is a fair amount of original and sometimes arresting work taking place in the fields of moral, political and social philosophy, but aesthetics and metaphysics have, on many philosophy syllabuses, been relegated to a secondary role. Their place has been taken, in the main, by the analysis of language: **semiology** and **semantics, linguistics** and the theory of meaning, have forced metaphysics into the role of Cinderella. Some schools have dropped the word philosophy from their courses, on the spurious grounds that the word is elitist or (tell it not in Gath) question-begging. So Communication Studies have become the order of the day, and philosophy is reduced to **philology**. The trouble is that the practitioners in these areas, while capable of developing linguistic analysis to a super-refined state, have not, as I view them, been able to say much of significance. They have become technicians rather than creative thinkers, providing tools but leaving others (novelists, poets, painters, architects sometimes) to do the job. They are like those who can speak a dozen languages fluently but can say little worthwhile in any one of them.

Ideally placed to be guides amid life's conundrums, these philosophers have contented themselves with an editorial role. They have become Ashkenazys playing scales.

I acknowledge that the situation today is not as bad as it was when I first read philosophy. Logical positivism, which flourished before the Second World War, has long since taken its place in the history of (inadequate?) ideas, but the influence of this school can still be felt. Its central theme was that, just as scientific inquiry could proceed only on the basis of what could be verified, so philosophy, and in particular any form of philosophical speculation, must undergo similar scrutiny for it to be valid. The most famous exponent of this school of thought in the English-speaking world was **A. J. Ayer**, who expounded positivism in his masterpiece *Language, Truth and Logic* (1936). The final paragraph vividly sums up the positivist position:

> What we would rather do is to distinguish between the speculative and the logical aspects of science and assert that philosophy must develop into the language of science. That is to say, we distinguish between the activity of formulating hypotheses, and the activity of displaying the logical relationship of these hypotheses and defining the symbols which occur in them. It is of no importance whether we call one who is engaged in the latter activity a philosopher or a scientist. What we must recognise is that it is necessary for a philosopher to become a scientist, in this sense, if he is to make any substantial contribution towards the growth of human knowledge.

It would be difficult to imagine the issue being expressed with greater clarity or pungency. *Language, Truth and Logic* has one of those qualities rare among twentieth-century philosophical writings: it is readable, and is a perfect example of the philosophical discipline which it sets out to inculcate. Ayer had every right to advise his readers to do not only as he said but what he did.

Ayer changed his views radically over the years after writing that book. (In fact, when asked on a BBC TV programme in the series *Men of Ideas* what criticism he would make of the positivists, he replied rather whimsically, 'Only that they were completely wrong.') He was elected president of the Society for Applied Philosophy whose journal, on the whole, is attempting to break away from the general strictures I've made. But I still hear Ayer's book described by colleagues as 'the point in philosophy beyond which we cannot go'. Even **ethics** has been subjected to this method. I have before me a textbook in that field which is divided into sections whose titles indicate the analytical approach to the subject: the referential theory, the verificationist theory, the causal theory, meaning as use, intuitionism, emotivism, prescriptivism, and so on. I have for years recommended the book's use to students of moral philosophy, yet it is difficult to counter the plea of one student after reading it: 'Can philosophers do no more with human behaviour than reduce it to linguistic analysis?'

The great authority in this field, which I have personally carried around for a decade, is John Hospers's *Introduction to Philosophical Analysis* – another book which can be recommended to beginners without fearing that it will deter them for life from the subject because of stylistic obscurity. It includes admirably witty and perceptive discussions on many of the issues I shall pursue in this book, but it is, as the title suggests, a gateway rather than a path. Having decided, for example, what the problems are when contemplating the survival, in some form, of the human personality after death, the discussion forthwith ends. (See case study 4.) Hospers would no doubt argue – justly – that further speculation was superfluous to his brief, and that others must proceed from the point where he left off. The trouble is that too many have taken to heart the last sentence of Wittgenstein's *Tractatus Logico-Philosophicus*: 'Whereof we cannot speak, thereof let us be silent.' And for many years of his life Wittgenstein was silent, believing that philosophy had no more to contribute to human inquiry.

The dominance of Wittgenstein (1889–1951) over Western philosophy for some decades is undeniable, and understandable. He was, quite simply, a genius. Even Russell, not noted for humility in the presence of his fellow-philosophers, acknowledged his pre-eminence. In the recently published *Philosophy in Britain Today* (Shanker, 1986) he is discussed directly on 87 of the 307 pages (Russell merits only 14, which wouldn't have pleased him). As one for whom words are the only usable tools, I have been captivated by the man and his writings, and recognize his abiding influence. Wittgenstein is the philosophers' philosopher, the subject of papers read at learned societies, the source of many a PhD. But inasmuch as the issues which engrossed him bore little relation to the challenge of existence, he must, I believe, be deemed to have been a technological rather than a purely creative genius. Wittgenstein challenges us – uniquely – to sharpen up our sense of what we *mean* when discussing metaphysical issues, but he leaves it to others to engage themselves in the riskier processes of exploration and, possibly, commitment in these fields.

The fact is that human beings do speculate on matters which offer no final verification. The great metaphysical problems still confront people everywhere, even though many people would not recognize them by that name. Why I am here? Where did I come from? Have I a soul? Is there a purpose in life? How do I know right from wrong? Is there life after death? And, perhaps most fateful of all, who or what am I? On this matter **Carl Gustav Jung** gave a clear admonition: 'We need more understanding of human nature, because the only real danger that exists is man himself.' Before Jung, F. H. Bradley (1846–1924) had written, 'It is good to know what a man is, and also what the world takes him for.

But you do not understand him until you have learnt how he understands himself.'

Logic is certainly, then, a tool in human inquiry which we abandon at our peril; but there are some inquiries for which additional tools are needed. Among these are issues raised in this book: the nature of man, and the meaning and purpose of existence. In a word, we are concerned with *ontology*.


ONTOLOGY

Since this word will appear frequently in these pages, it may be as well to attempt a brief definition right at the start. It is derived from the Greek *ontos*, present participle of the verb *einai*, to be, and *logos*, that rare and comprehensive word which may be translated simply as 'word' but which reflects the way in which words create understanding, and may be interpreted as referring to the underlying meaning of things, as in John's Gospel (1.1): 'In the beginning was the word [*logos*].' Being is the 'to be' of anything or anybody, the common feature of all that exists. But from one perspective being is more than this, since it includes things, creatures, that don't actually exist except in our imagination. The American philosopher **William James** (1842–1910) wrote: 'Even things which do not really exist have being insofar as they are objects of thought – things remembered which once existed, things conceivable which have the possibility of being, things imaginary which have being at least in the mind that thinks them.'

I know that the analytical school of philosophy refuses to accept this concession, and insists that 'having existence' be included in the definition of 'being'. James's approach seems to me, however, more realistic. Hallucinations, for example, do not (presumably, or even by definition) *exist*; but their influence and effect on those who experience them are verifiably real and sometimes calamitous. To such people the hallucinations certainly have being: and they will continue to do so even if their unreality is eventually recognized and they survive only as a cautionary memory.

It is a major contribution to philosophy that any glibly held distinction between 'having being' and 'existing' should be exposed: and one is grateful to the analytical philosophers for this stricture. I'm aware that a trap exists (or, since that begs the entire question, has being!) but within my chosen terms of reference the distinction seems to me valid.

Being is the most universal of predicates and the highest abstraction. All other names, whether of an inanimate object, a member of a lower species, or of a *human* being, add something above the idea, or fact, of being: a chair, an armchair, a short armchair, a short red armchair, or a human, a female human, a tall female human, a tall, old female human, and so on. These epithets limit the universality related to the simple fact of being. Viewed from a different perspective, however, being is the very least that can be thought about anything. To be told about anything or anybody only that it is, or that she is, is not to learn much about that thing or person. We need to know whether we are discussing a living or a spiritual being, a real or an imaginary being, an animate or an inanimate being, before we can proceed with any meaningful discourse. So on the one hand we have the fact that when every other trait peculiar to a thing is removed, its being remains – the fact that it *is* in some sense; and on the other hand the fact that, abstracted from everything else, 'being' has only the positive meaning of excluding 'non-being'.

I shall return specifically to this when dealing with a number of major questions relating to the theme of this book: the ontological argument for God's existence; the relationship between existence and being; being and becoming; the ground of being; and so on. At this point I wish to affirm quite simply that ontology is at the heart of metaphysics and at the heart of philosophy. Those who argue (and I could name many philosophers who do so, frequently and publicly) that philosophy no longer possesses its own independent curriculum (independent, that is, of all other academic areas of study) are simply overlooking ontology. With the exception of physics, no other discipline, whether in the arts or the sciences, is directly concerned with the nature of being. It is the central question faced by anyone who goes beyond physics (or natural philosophy, as it is still called in older universities). It may not be asked explicitly when discussing the nature and destiny of man, but it is implicit in every such discussion and, I guess, in many of the after-hours discussions engaged in by thoughtful persons with inquiring minds.

My own reading and thinking on the subject has led me to conclude that two areas of philosophy in particular have made or are making valuable contributions to our understanding of being in modern times (though many of the ideas they express originated in centuries past, of course). The first of these is existentialism, a philosophy somewhat out of vogue since its popularity a generation ago. Few schools of philosophy have been so maligned as this: sneered at by political philosophers because of its inadequacy as a political theory (which it doesn't claim to be); held in contempt by many English philosophers because of its lack of linguistic analysis (a fair criticism of method, but taking no account of content – rather like refusing to pay any attention to Marx because he didn't write in one's native tongue); and dismissed as a 'pose' rather than a philosophy by numerous professional philosophers. My own experience is that no other school of philosophy has come anywhere near holding the interest of students as much as this, and if existentialism cannot be included in that area of study known as philosophy, then philosophy has truly ceased to matter. I shall not be accepting as gospel all that the existentialists had to say, and shall be critical of some of their emphases and expressions. But running through their (admittedly often verbose) utterances are insights which have helped to shape the person I am, and I shall want to outline these.

The second area which I choose for attention is hardly a school, but many schools, summed up under the generic term 'Eastern philosophy'. To try to encapsulate in a sentence or two what this means would be as futile as summing up in that space of words what we mean by 'Semitic thought' or 'the outlook of the ancient Greeks'. My aim will therefore be to pinpoint those areas which illuminate the problem in my own mind, without, I hope, too much of the distortion which must inevitably follow the transferring of a philosophy from its native to an alien culture. This culture is actually more alien than it need have been, for the simple reason that Westerners have spent a despressingly small part of their time over the centuries reflecting on expressions of Eastern thought. The insularity of Western philosophers towards their Eastern counterparts (no doubt reflected in reverse) is to be both rebuked and regretted.

What has particularly drawn my attention in recent years is the amount of common ground to be found between existentialism and Eastern thought. In some respects, of course, this is nonsense: certain expressions of existentialism seem to be pulling diametrically away from the central theme of, for example, Taoism; and the Buddhist reverence for a state beyond desire (opting out?) does not easily accommodate itself with the existentialist espousal of commitment (opting in?). I shall be suggesting that perhaps the most comprehensive being lies in a union, or merger, or balance of both. I have not seen this viewpoint advocated anywhere else, and it represents the basic *raison d'être* of this book. At least there is enough in common between the two schools to justify a second look at some of the ideas expressed, as was hinted at by William Barrett in his first-rate introduction to existentialism, *Irrational Man*. The reader must decide for him- or herself how far it is possible to harmonize the viewpoints expressed in the two schools, and how far one should take the safer course of choosing strands from each as elements in a personal philosophy of life. If the amalgam I present through the crucible of my own experience has anything positive to contribute, with perhaps a new twist, to the age-old questions under discussion, that might help to justify the cutting down of a tree to make this book.

As we struggle to find a way by which to live and, in the process, a consciousness of who we really are, we need all the insights we can get, including those from the most unlikely of sources. For this reason alone we simply cannot afford to ignore, on the one hand, a philosophy which has affected, if not given a totally new and positive view on life to, countless people in the West; or, on the other hand, a perspective on human nature and destiny (that is, an ontological perspective) which has been the mainstay of millions over three millennia in India, China and beyond. The one may not meet the demands of the linguistic analysts, and the other may reflect ideas and beliefs which are exotic, if not outrageous, to Western minds. But as a simple matter of fact they *are* and they won't go away. Ideas are not only stronger than their defenders, they're stronger than their detractors too.

On this 'spaceship earth', as it was dubbed by the environmentalists a generation ago, even to survive is a challenge, and to survive in any form which includes 'quality of life', however that phrase be interpreted, is the supreme challenge to *homo sapiens*. At the age of 89, in 1961, Bertrand Russell wrote his short book *Has Man a Future?* (1962). It concludes with these words:

> The new liberation of the human spirit may be expected to lead to new splendours, new beauties, new sublimities impossible in the cramped and fierce world of the past. . . No limit can be set to what Man [*sic*] may achieve in the future. I see, in my mind's eye, a world of glory and joy, a world where minds expand, where hope remains undimmed, and what is noble is no longer condemned as treachery to this or that paltry aim. All this can happen if we will let it happen. It rests with out generation to decide between this vision and an end decreed by folly.

The main fear which dominated the last years of his life, however, was that the human race would destroy itself with nuclear weapons. That fear remains, and who knows what intensity of psychological stress it has engendered. But other fears have been added since then: the pollution of the planet, the running-out of resources, overcrowding, violence and loss of identity. All these threaten all of us, and are already a living reality and nightmare to many. Amid the rival claimants to the gift of prophecy, the philosopher, with no personal axe to grind, and enabled by training to speak without ignorance, prejudice, or bigotry, should have the right to be heard. *And if a philosopher spoke with authority that right would be accorded.*

That, at any rate, is how I view the role of the philosopher and the function of philosophy. It is a role which has been laid aside for too long by too many, and a function that has rusted with neglect. Let this small effort, then, move at least beyond the secure world of scales and arpeggios and attempt to play a few tunes. False notes may well be struck in the process, but those with ears to hear may find some ground for rejoicing.

## Case study 1
### Expressions of Western philosophical thought

Here is a series of well-known statements by outstanding philosophers of the West. Ask yourself the following questions about each in turn:

1   What does the author mean?
2   How relevant are his words, (a) to me personally; (b) to the present time?

**3**   Has he stated the whole case, or is there an alternative point of view needed if it is to be complete and comprehensive?

**4**   How helpful a guide to living is the statement?

Can you put the statements in an order of importance for the theme of this book? (See also case study 30, pp. 288.)

(1)   'There will be no end to the troubles of states, or indeed, my dear Glaucon, of humanity itself, till philosophers become kings in this world, or till those we now call kings and rulers really and truly become philosophers.'

(Plato (429–347 BC): *The Republic*)

(2)   'Poetry is something more philosophical and more worthy of serious attention than history.'

(Aristotle (384–322 BC): *Poetics*)

(3)   'Every being, to the extent that it is a being at all, must have, simply as a being, the attribute of goodness. So when we say that a flawed being is an evil being, we appear to say that what is good is evil: and that nothing can be evil save what is good, since every being has the attribute of goodness, nor could anything be evil unless the thing which was evil was some sort of being. So nothing can be evil except something good.'

(St Augustine of Hippo (AD 354–430): *Encheiridion*)

(4)   'The condition of man . . . is a condition of war of everyone against everyone . . . No arts; no letters; no society; and which is worst of all, continual fear and danger of violent death; and the life of man, solitary, poor, nasty, brutish, and short.'

(Thomas Hobbes (1588–1679): *Leviathan*)

(5)   'New opinions are always suspected, and usually opposed, without any other reason but because they are not already common.'

(John Locke (1632–1704): *An Essay Concerning Human Understanding*)

(6)   'If we take in our hand any volume; of divinity or school metaphysics, for instance; let us ask, *Does it contain any abstract reasoning concerning quantity or number?* No. *Does it contain any experimental reasoning, concerning matter of fact and existence?* No. Commit it then to the flames: for it can contain nothing but sophistry and illusion.'

(David Hume (1711–76): *An Enquiry Concerning Human Understanding*)

(7)   'Nature abhors a vacuum.'

(Baruch Spinoza (1632–77): *Ethics*)

(8)   'What experience and history teach is this – that people and governments never have learned anything from history, or acted on principles deduced from it.'

(G. W. F. Hegel (1770–1831): *Philosophy of History*)

(9)  'Capitalist production begets, with the inexorability of a law of nature, its own negation.'

(Karl Marx (1818–83): *Das Kapital*)

(10)  'The thing is to find a truth that is true for *me*, to find the idea for which I can live and die.'

(Søren Kierkegaard (1813–55): *Journals*)

(11)  'The creed which accepts as the foundation of morals, Utility, or the Greatest Happiness Principle, holds that actions are right in proportion as they tend to promote happiness, wrong as they tend to produce the reverse of happiness. By happiness is intended pleasure, and the absence of pain; by unhappiness, pain, and the privation of pleasure.'

(J. S. Mill (1806–73): *Utilitarianism*)

(12)  'Now this connection or adaptation of all created things with each, and of each with all the rest, means that each simple substance has relations which express all the others and that consequently it is a perpetual living mirror of the universe.'

(Gottfried Wilhelm Leibniz (1646–1716): *Monadology*)

(13)  'The thing-in-itself, the will-to-live, exists whole and undivided in every being, even in the tiniest; it is present as completely as in all ever were, are, and will be, taken together.'

(Arthur Schopenhauer (1788–1860): *Parerga and Paralipomena*)

(14)  'If there were a verb meaning "to believe falsely", it would not have any significant first person, present indicative.'

(Ludwig Wittgenstein (1889–1951): *A Certain World*; quoted from W. H. Auden)

*Case study 2*
*What is a work of art?*

Among the subject areas which were excluded from philosophical discussion by the logical positivists on the grounds that they were not susceptible to any kind of verification was aesthetics – the theory of beauty. (The others were ethics – the theory of right and wrong conduct – religion and politics.) You may think that this exclusion removed from philosophy most of the interesting areas of discussion. The fact is that these issues are discussed with great animation and at great length; and the tang in such discussions springs precisely from the fact that they *cannot* be verified: there can be no proof, acceptable to scientists along lines suggested by Ayer, that one point of view is 'right' and another 'wrong'. If this were possible there would be no point in discussing the issues.

This case study allows you to delve into one of these imponderable questions. It is not the central theme of this book, but it is one which relates to this at many points. If you can, discuss the questions in a group, and see if the discussion increases your appreciation of the nature of art (by which is meant all the arts, of course – music, drama, literature, sculpture and so on, as well as painting).

1 Who decides what constitutes a 'work of art'?
   (a) The artist himself: but can he or she be the best judge of his or her own efforts?
   (b) Public opinion: but (i)   this is notoriously fickle.
                           (ii)  it is easily manipulated.
                           (iii) it often (usually?) rejects innovation; cf. contemporary views of Beethoven and Van Gogh.
                           (iv)  what percentage of the public qualifies as 'opinion'? Paul McCartney's songs sell in millions: Schumann's *Lieder* in – thousands? hundreds?
                           (v)   are we speaking of today's opinion or tomorrow's – or next century's? They may differ enormously.
   (c) Experts, or critics: but (i)   experts have often made blunders (eg (b) (iii)).
                               (ii)  they don't always agree.
                               (iii) this implies that there are hierarchies of opinion about works of art. Is this valid? Isn't my opinion as good as yours, or the critic's?

2 What distinguishes art from rubbish: poetry from doggerel, painting from daubing, music from mere sound?
   (a) Is it the time spent on the work? (Schubert composed 'Hark, hark, the lark' between courses in a restaurant; Whistler could paint a picture in minutes.)
   (b) Is it the effort involved? (Many an architectural folly has required effort; and does this exclude work done in an artist's relaxed moments?)
   (c) Is it seriousness of purpose? (What about Haydn's Toy Symphony, or the novels of P. G. Wodehouse?)
   (d) Is it 'message'? (What is the message of *Twelfth Night*? Does one have to accept the Christian message in order to appreciate *The Messiah*?)

(e) Is it originality? (Is a two-year-old's painting of his mum more a work of art than a painting by a mature person imitating somebody else's style?)

(f) Is it creativity? (How is this to be defined? One person's creativity may be another's chaos. Is jazz more creative than Bach's chorales, action painting than still life pictures?)

(g) Is it durability? (How long, then, must we wait before we can affirm that a contemporary production is a work of art?)

(h) Is it self-discipline rather than self-indulgence? (Must a line always be drawn here in the world of the arts?)

('Every artist is either a plagiarist or a revolutionary.' Paul Gauguin)

3 Must art be beautiful?

(a) Is there an objective standard for beauty? Doesn't it lie in the eye of the beholder, or in the ear of the listener?

(b) Is there no 'ugly' art? How about Bacon's screaming popes, Fellini's film *Satyricon*, or Stockhausen's music?

(c) Cannot descriptions or depictions of physical violence or sexual crudity be judged 'art'? Both are found in many famous 'works of art', including Shakespeare.

4 Can an object made primarily with a utilitarian purpose be termed a work of art – a Rolls Royce engine, a cut-glass tumbler, the Golden Gate Bridge, and so on? Or is this watering down the concept to the state of being virtually meaningless? Has it any meaning in any case except as an expression of a person's approval?

In favour of the utilitarian view:
Darwin suggested that all human behaviour is motivated by the basic instinct of survival, and that the arts came about because they helped to relieve boredom, which is a non-survival element in life (suggested in the phrase 'deadly dull'). Motorway bridges have been deliberately constructed with a variety of designs in order to give drivers occasional changes of image before their eyes. Is art a life-saver?

Against (or beyond) the utilitarian view:
Many people view art as man's response to the 'numinous' (see pages 32–3). Through the arts, it is suggested, we touch a deeper chord than happens in the normal round of things, reaching, perhaps, towards the 'ground of our being' (to be explained later). Is this too pompous a way of looking at a poem, a song, or a statue?

'Art and religion first; then philosophy; lastly science. That is the order of the great subjects in life, that's their order of importance.'

(Muriel Spark: *The Prime of Miss Jean Brodie*)

Do you agree?

**5**   Which of the following would you describe as a work of art?

(a)   a performance of *King Lear* by the Royal Shakespeare Company at Stratford-upon-Avon: magnificently produced, staged and performed

(b)   The same play in the village hall by the local amateur company: casually produced, cheaply staged, performed by people who seem to have landed in the wrong play – but keeping faithfully to the original script

(c)   as (a) but following Nahum Tate's version of *Lear* with a happy ending.

# 2 *The dualistic view of human nature: dichotomous man*

Of all the theories about human nature expressed through the centuries, the dualistic theory must be the oldest and, I guess, has probably been the most widely held. Read through the world's literature, imaginative or critical, and you will find it abounding with references to spirit and matter, soul and body. 'I am the captain of my soul', 'The spirit is willing but the flesh is weak', 'Keeping body and soul together': these and other common sayings reflect this common dichotomy (without, of course, indicating that the speaker has necessarily taken a dualistic stance – see case study 5, p. 39).

The application of the theory to the universe in general is not the central concern of this book, though inevitably it will bear upon the view taken about human nature. Metaphysical debate between philosophers over the centuries has thrown into relief the two sides of the argument. On the one side is the view that we should hold a **monistic, materialistic** interpretation of the universe, seeing it purely as matter in motion, a blind (in the sense of non-purposive) mechanical force. On the other is the view that we should understand matter rather as containing within itself some vital principle or element (spirit, mind, life force, call it what you will) which animates all matter. The division between so-called **mechanists** on the one hand and so-called **vitalists** on the other has important implications for our main discussion, as will be especially apparent in Chapters 4 and 7. My own view is that the kind of ontological perspective which I hope to develop makes much of this debate redundant.

The general concept behind the dualistic view of human nature is that man or woman is a combination of two elements: the body and the soul. The body is physical and tangible, doomed, as we can freely observe, to death and decay. The soul is immaterial and ethereal, held not to be limited by the laws of matter or, ultimately, by time and space: it is independent of the change to which matter is naturally subject, and reaches above and beyond the confines of the physical and material which can make of life a state of restriction and frustration. As the poet Lovelace wrote,

> Stone walls do not a prison make,
> Nor iron bars a cage. . .
> If I have freedom in my love,
> And in my soul am free!

The soul is normally held by dualists to be indestructible by nature and endless in its destiny. There have been conflicting views about its origin: whether it has been eternally in existence, or came into being only with the creation of the body, for instance; but, whatever the precise view, the body is consistently seen by dualists as no more than a shadow, a temporary physical dwelling-place for the soul. The body, in the words of Plato, is a tomb: 'soma sema', as the Greek has it. As a person may use a car until it is fit only for the scrap-heap, so the soul uses the body. John Brown's body may lie a-mouldering in the grave, but his soul goes marching on.

This image has a strong hold on the human mind. It is as if we need to assure ourselves of the undying nature of our consciousness. The thought that this will cease and that we – you and I – will no longer exist has been the cause of much terror in people's minds. *How can I, who am, not be?* Superstitions abound about the intervention of the world of souls into the material world; it is difficult for even the most sceptical not to be gripped by a ghost story. We may disparage as primitive or immature those who wholeheartedly accept these ideas in some form, but the fact is that beliefs relating to the soul's existence are to be found universally, both geographically and historically. Even the music-hall would be bereft without the idea of an immortal soul: how long is it since you last heard a comedian tell a joke about someone arriving at the pearly gates? Perhaps this concept is best summed up in a fascinating brief poem by the Emperor Hadrian (demonstrating perhaps that in his case the pen *was* mightier than the sword). It is entitled, simply, 'On the soul':

> Odd little comrade, comfortable guest,
> Capricious, elfin puff of air:
> You're off? But where? And when you've left my breast,
> Tense little traveller, pale and bare,
> Will you find anything to laugh at there?

## PLATO

It would be impossible to state with confidence when the idea of dualism as an interpretation of human nature was first expressed. J. B. Watson, the psychologist, wrote at the beginning of his book *Behaviourism*:

Nobody knows how the idea of a soul or the supernatural started. It probably had its origin in the natural laziness of mankind.

You may or may not be sympathetic to this suggestion, but if you are it is worth bearing in mind that the Western philosopher who pioneered this dualistic emphasis was Plato (427–347 BC). He has been accused of many vices, from **elitism** to **philistinism**, but never, so far as I am aware, of laziness in his thinking. In fact, even if it is not the case that the whole of Western philosophy has been, in the words of the philosopher A. N. Whitehead (1861–1947), 'no more than a series of footnotes to Plato's philosophy', it is nearer the truth than could be said of any other philosopher.

The work of Plato which most comprehensively outlines his theory is one of the most famous books in the world's literature, *The Republic*. If you haven't read it, put this book aside and read it now. If you haven't a copy in your possession go out and buy, borrow, or – if we can accept for the moment that the end justifies the means – steal one. Taking it into your system could mark a new stage in your life.

The central concern of *The Republic* is the basis and **modus vivendi** of a just society, and its final words sum up its author's perspective:

> Wherefore my counsel is that we hold fast ever to the heavenly way and follow after justice and virtue always, considering that the soul is immortal and able to endure every sort of good and every sort of evil. Thus shall we live dear to one another and to the gods, both while remaining here and when . . . we receive our reward. And it shall be well with us both in this life and in the pilgrimage of a thousand years which we have been describing.

In the process of arriving at this point, which he had presented as an imaginary dialogue between his teacher, Socrates, and a number of disciples or questioners (as in a well-conducted seminar discussion, perhaps) Plato outlines his famous theory of Ideas, or Forms. This word 'Forms' sounds odd today, and needs some delineation. According to the theory, the world we inhabit is simply the shadow of the *ideal* world, the world of Ideas, or of Forms. Everything we see around us, and every value we hold within us, is no more than an imperfect representation of that ideal: hence one meaning (among many in philosophy) of the word 'idea': the 'idea' or Form of a rose is the perfect rose, of which any earthly specimen is an imperfect copy. More important for our discussion, the idea or Form of any virtue – benevolence, say, or fortitude – is infinitely superior to any worldly manifestation of this. The supreme ideal is justice, which has arguably been the dominant theme of Western philosophy. Plato can of course offer no scientific proof that this ideal world exists, but his

theory and everything that follows from it is built on the inevitability
of this.

The word 'exists' in this context begs an enormous question in any
case. If we apply the verificationist principle of the positivists (see the
quotation from Ayer, p. 6), the whole concept of Forms must be barred
from any philosophical discussion, on the ground that there is no way of
determining their reality to the satisfaction of the scientific inquirer. But
if we take the ontological perspective put forward in the Prologue, then
among those things which may be described as having being are not only
those for which the five senses provide plenty of evidence but also things
remembered, things imaginary and – as in this case – things conceivable.
The fact is that people do have an idea of justice in their minds, even
though they may never have seen this expressed in the activities and
verdicts of the courts, and even though they would find it well-nigh
impossible to define what they mean by justice (try this for yourself if
you think it's easy). In that sense there *is* a world of Forms.

Plato argued that it is the soul, the eternal element in man, which gains
knowledge of the Forms. That is to say, while our bodies are a part of
the transient world of matter, due for decay and destruction (*soma sema*,
as already noted) our souls are incorruptible and are open, or capable of
being opened, to the insights which flash upon us from that ideal world
as through a distorted mirror. The person who most fully understands
what justice means will be the one most awakened to the revelations which
illuminate us from the ideal world. Such a person will seek reality rather
than appearance; will look for the Form rather than the feeble copy; will
be, in a word (Plato's word), an idealist. This person will have reached
a higher state.

The process of arriving at this state is described by Plato in Book VII
of *The Republic* in the famous allegory of the cave. In this allegory, we
are asked to imagine that men are chained from birth in a dark cave,
unable to see the entrance and the light. There is a fire and a kind of
stage behind them, along which figures and objects pass, but the cave's
inhabitants can see only the shadows cast by these on the wall of the cave.
Since they have never known real things, they mistake these shadows for
reality.

Imagine now that one of the chained men were released and free to turn
towards the fire and the stage (we're not asked to discuss who releases this
person, and why him rather than another, though these are interesting
questions). He would be blinded by the light, and bewildered by the figures
he saw, since, as we have seen, his experience had led him to believe that
their shadows were the only reality. But, says Plato, even these figures are
themselves mere images: for reality to be truly perceived by this imaginary
freedman we must picture him leaving the cave altogether and perceiving
the real world outside. This would be an excruciatingly painful experience,

since his eyes had never known light; but having once adjusted to the new light and the real world, he would perceive the unreality of the world he had just left behind, the world of the cave. So it is, said Plato, with the seeker after truth, the 'idealist': by gaining knowledge of the Forms, he leaves behind the artificial bliss of ignorance and experiences the pleasure – and the pain – of enlightenment. For having reached this state he faces a terrible dilemma: should he remain in his newly discovered world and revel in the light, or should he commit himself to the service of his fellows who remain convinced that their shadowy world is the only reality, and are unwilling to be led from it, screaming, into the light? For Plato, philosophy was not just the 'love of wisdom', as the word **etymologically** implies, but 'a taste for every sort of knowledge' (Book V) and a commitment to the sharing of insights with those who had not experienced them. Philosophers were to be the rulers, or guardians, of the state. (See case study 3.)

Intellectual inquiry, then, is the chief means whereby we may come to appreciate the Forms. Plato was a scholar rather than a religious man (these two are not necessarily in conflict of course!) and even though he refers to 'the gods' in the passage quoted earlier they play little or no part in the exposition of his views on human nature and destiny, including, in particular, the immortality of the soul (more of this in Chapter 3). It is important to note that the Greek word for soul is *psyche*, and that this can be translated into two quite different English words: 'soul' and 'mind'. The connotations of these two words are also quite different, illustrating, perhaps, the assertion of Wittgenstein that the *usage* of words brings about their *meaning*. The soul refers to the essential person, the whole character, emotional as well as intellectual; the mind, in contrast, refers solely to the powers of reason, the thinking qualities. We may describe a person as playing the piano 'without any soul' but hardly 'without any mind', while the phrase 'to lose one's soul' differs radically in meaning from 'to lose one's mind'. A dog may have a 'soulful' rather than a 'mindful' expression; I, on the other hand, am mindful of the desire not to bore you, body and/or soul, with this discussion.

For Plato it was the intellectual element in man which initiated him into the ideal world, the world of Forms. He argued that the soul consists of three parts: the appetite, the reason and the spirit. The appetite gives us our physical desires (for shelter, food, love and so on); the reason makes possible the intellectual control of our lives, including control of the appetite; the spirit represents our enthusiasm and self-assertion. In modern parlance we might say that these three represent our bodily needs, our intellect and our will-power.

Plato recognized that the healthiest person would be one who kept all three elements in balance. Such a person would, again in modern speech, be well adjusted: not just a prey to physical passions, or a dreamer overlooking the practicalities of life, or a person so overwhelmed with ambition as to ride rough-shod over friends or colleagues. However, Plato had no doubt about which should be the dominant one of the three. This harmony of life would be possible only if reason were in ultimate control. It alone, he believed, could subdue the excesses of bodily lusts, and modify the selfishness of the will. For Plato, what was morally good was behaviour in tune with reason. Knowledge, wisdom, understanding (all have different connotations, of course, but illustrate the direction of his argument): these were for him the key to insight, the means of escaping from the cave.

You may well feel this last emphasis in Plato to have been unfortunate, since by making it he pioneered an approach to philosophy which has dominated the West ever since: the virtual ignoring of insights which reach us through channels other than the intellect. 'Nous', the Greek word for sense (or even 'common sense') is certainly one way by which we may seek enlightenment, but there are others to which considerable testimony has been given over the centuries. We shall see in Chapter 7 that there are schools of philosophy which hold the view that on some matters the reason, while necessary, is not sufficient.

## CARTESIAN DUALISM

Plato's dualistic philosophy, with its emphasis on reason as the gateway to immortality, was given a vivid (though different in emphasis) re-expression two millenniums later by the French philosopher René Descartes (1596–1650). He is known as 'the father of modern philosophy', which he would have considered an exaggeration, but his defence of reason as the supreme human value and 'intimation of immortality' certainly made a springboard from which numerous successors were to take off.

In his early years, he developed four principles which could serve as a useful paradigm for any student:

(1) Never accept anything as true unless you can prove it to be so.

(2) The most difficult problem should be divided into as many parts as possible before you proceed to solve it.

(3) Begin with the simplest part of the problem and then proceed step by step until you have resolved the most difficult parts of it.

(4) Your notes and observations must be complete: no detail should be omitted.

The meaning of the word 'prove' in the first principle begs a number of questions which will be pursued throughout this book, not least being 'to whose satisfaction?' These principles are important tools for any would-be scholar, but the ontological explorations on which we are embarking, while not excluding them, will, as we shall see, require additional tools.

Descartes began his working life as a soldier and his earlier piece of writing was a treatise on swordsmanship ('Cartesian *duellism*'?). He then progressed (if that does not also beg questions) to philosophy and in particular applied his strict rules to the question *Of what can I be absolutely certain?* He left a vivid record of his way of grappling with this question in what are known as the *Meditations*. Their full title is *Meditations on the First Philosophy in which the Existence of God and the Distinctions between Mind and Body are Demonstrated'*. Our concern here is with the latter part of this title, but it is worth noting that the Cartesian (from his Latin name, Cartesius) argument for the existence of God, the so-called ontological argument first spelt out by St Anselm (1033–1109), is one of the great classical arguments for His existence, and will be discussed in the next chapter.

In seeking to assure himself about what he could be certain of, Descartes described in his *Meditations* how his thinking proceeded step by step according to his own rules. He began by facing the matter-of-fact view, which would have been presented to him by any matter-of-fact sort of person, that he could surely be certain of the evidence of his senses – what he observed around him and, in particular (since they were always with him, playing a continuous role in his daily life), his own physical parts – his arms, and legs, and so on. But then he reflected that often in dreams he had been convinced of many such certainties, only to awaken and find that these apparent certainties had been no more than figments of his imagination.

> At this moment it does indeed seem to me that it is with eyes awake that I am looking at this paper; that this head which I move is not asleep, that it is deliberately and of set purpose that I extend my hand and perceive it . . . But in thinking over this I remind myself that on many occasions I have in sleep been deceived by similar illusions, and . . . I see so manifestly that there are no certain indications by which we may clearly distinguish wakefulness from sleep that I am lost in astonishment . . . such that it is almost capable of persuading me that I now dream.
>
> (Meditation I)

Very well, says Descartes; we can't be sure about the tangible things around us, but what about the intangible certainties? We may doubt, for example, the evidence presented to our senses by physics, astronomy and other sciences, but how can we deny the arithmetical and mathematical *principles* on which the observable data of science are based? 'For whether I am awake or asleep, two and three together always form five, and the square can never have more than four sides' (ibid.). Yes, *I* may indeed be convinced of the absoluteness of these principles, though the second example should rather be termed as *analytical* because the characteristic of four-sidedness is contained in the *definition* of a square (if a square had more, or fewer, than four sides, it would be called something else – pentagon, triangle, etc.); by using the word 'principle' here, Descartes is using **prescriptive** language where **descriptive** is all that is required. However, where any apparently irrefutable principle is concerned (like the logical principle that a thing cannot both exist and not exist at the same time) how can I be sure (asks Descartes) that I am not the victim of a massive act of deception on the part of a superior Being – God Himself? Such a Being would certainly have the power to treat mortal creatures like us exactly as He pleased. It would mean rejecting the image of a loving God in which Descartes had believed: such a God would hardly practise deceit in so full-frontal a way; but Descartes acknowledged that the idea was quite consonant with an alternative to this God – 'some evil genius not less powerful than deceitful who has employed his whole energies in deceiving me'.

Having thus acknowledged that he had grounds for doubting all that he had learned and experienced throughout his life, Descartes, still following the argument through step by step, reached the heart of the matter in the Second Meditation. He might indeed doubt the absolute certainty of all of which he was conscious, but he still *knew* that he was engaging in the act of doubting. Who then was this person behind the doubts, the denials, the hopes and certainties? Who was it that was doing the rejecting or the affirming? The fact was that though he could not be certain of *what* he affirmed or denied, he could be certain *that* he affirmed or denied.

> I find here that thought is an attribute that belongs to me; it alone cannot be separated from me. I am, I exist, that is certain. But how often? Just when I think. . .
>
> I am not more than a thing which thinks, that is to say a mind or a soul or an understanding or a reason . . . a thing which doubts, understands, conceives, affirms, denies, wills, refuses, which also imagines and feels.
>
> (Meditation II)

You may have recognized that we are here in the midst of the argument which culminated in what may well be the most famous sentence in philosophy: '*Cogito ergo sum*' 'I think therefore I am.'

It is not my purpose to discuss the validity of the Cartesian argument here. The soundness of its deduction has been challenged, particularly in the light of increasing knowledge of the mind, and how the memory, storing up within one person or self the infinite number of ideas and experiences which come its way, creates a sense of personal identity, the 'ghost in the machine' as the philosopher Gilbert Ryle described it: the '*cogito*' of Descartes. It has therefore been argued that this sense of identity, which was crucial to the Cartesian argument, could be described in terms of all the accumulated content of that consciousness which, as Descartes himself had acknowledged, could not be affirmed absolutely as true, or 'real'.

Cartesian dualism lays greater stress on the whole person in interpreting the word 'soul' than is to be found in the Platonic form. '*Cogito*' is normally translated as 'I think', which admittedly suggests that, like Plato, Descartes held human intellect to be the highest human quality; but '*cogito*' can also be translated as 'I experience', and any reading of the *Meditations* lends force to this interpretation. Descartes included the imagination and the feelings in his '*cogito*', an emphasis which aligns his thinking more closely than Plato's with the main concerns of this book. There is a further important difference in emphasis between the two. Descartes followed Plato in positing the view that man is an imperfect copy of a perfect original: but for him the perfect original was God. The imperfections in man did not, as Plato had held, come about through the watering-down process which occurred when the original Ideal was made tangible in physical, human form, but because of the folly of man in disobeying the will of God, which was morally perfect. At this point we are shifting from the Platonic view and are entering the world of theism, which is the subject of the next chapter.

Descartes posited two further ideas which, while supplementary to his central theme, are none the less interesting, if only as a historical point. First, he claimed to have discovered the part of the brain in which the soul is to be found – in the small pineal gland at the back. Not every philosophy student knows that Descartes was a noted anatomist in his day, and, among other things, explained the defensive mechanism of the eye wink. Perhaps his suggestion about the pineal gland was intended to inspire a case study in that research.

Secondly, he got himself into considerable trouble with many of his religious contemporaries by propounding the view that animals don't have souls. He could find no evidence to convince himself that they were subjects of conscious experience which was, as we have seen, for him the essential nature of the soul. **Epistemologists** affirm how difficult it is in the world of perception to be certain that even other human beings have minds, or souls; the problem is even tougher when the issue is related to the animal world, and I am not going to attempt it here. For the moment, this modern comment may suffice:

Said Descartes, 'I extol
Myself because I have a soul
And beasts do not.' (Of course
He *had* to put Descartes before the horse.)

For Descartes, then, the revelation he received and outlined in the
*Meditations* was the basis of his dualistic beliefs. The psyche was one
side of this; the body, and all that accompanied it, was the other. 'My'
body, 'my' brain, 'my' limbs, all belong to that side; the 'me' who
perceives all these and can reflect freely about them is the immortal
soul (though you should note that I can still refer to 'my' immortal soul
and leave unanswered the question of who this owner, the ghost of the
'ghost in the machine', may be). At any rate, Descartes has presented us
with a clear-cut, consistent philosophy, and his last words reflect this:
'My soul, thou hast long been held captive; the hour has come for thee
to quit thy prison, to leave the trammels of this body; suffer, then, this
separation with joy and courage.' (An interesting comparison may be
made between these sentiments and those expressed by the materialist
Hobbes as his last words: 'I am about to take my last voyage, a great
leap in the dark.' Clearly we should choose our last words with care.)

## BERKELEY'S **IMMATERIALISM**

Descartes belonged to the Age of Enlightenment (*die Aufklärung*). This
was the period in Europe following the Renaissance; it was the age of
Newton, an age of radical advancement in science, with its consequent
challenge to almost everything that people had believed about the world
they inhabited and their place in it. The cosy 'three-decker' universe which
had been taken for granted for 2,000 years, had been vanquished. In place of
the image of the earth as the centre of the universe, with the sky as a ceiling
and God in His heaven above it, was a much more fearful image of a vast,
unfathomable space filled with stars and planets and moons, with our sun
a tiny representative, and earth in comparison a minuscule speck.

One consequence of this change was that the concept of the law of God in
the universe was replaced, in the minds of many, by that of natural law. The
universe, under this natural law, was increasingly viewed and interpreted
on a mechanistic basis, that is, that it was thought to function according
to certain fixed patterns and processes. Many scientists were accepting
a materialistic philosophy, rejecting any belief in spiritual intervention
in the universe, whether on the part of God or any other being. The
English philosopher Hobbes went so far as to assert that even human
decisions were inevitably controlled by this process, so that the concept
of freedom of choice could no longer be accepted as a true interpretation of
human decision-making (see Chapter 4). Less extreme, but equally linking
their ideas with the new cosmology, were those philosophers who adopted

a form of scepticism concerning human experience, and argued that the only knowledge available to us is what is derived from experience gained through the five senses. This philosophy is known as *empiricism*; it affirms, as the word suggests, that the only knowledge of which we can be sure is what we gain from scientific observation, experiment and experience. The two most famous protagonists of this view were the English philosopher Locke and the Scot, David Hume. Their beliefs contrasted with the *rationalism* of Descartes (so called because he had affirmed that some knowledge is innate and can be arrived at through reason and intuition alone – a view also held by the Dutch philosopher Spinoza).

Within this debate, an Irish philosopher, **Bishop Berkeley** (1685–1753), contributed a new and highly individualistic viewpoint. His argument was that the material world exists only in the minds of those who perceive it: 'To be,' he said, 'is to be perceived', '*Esse est percipi.*' He denied the existence of matter independently of perception, claiming that 'all the choir of heaven and furniture of the earth, in a word all those bodies which compose the mighty frame of the world, have not any subsistence without a mind': an unperceived object is a 'manifest contradiction'. This was Berkeley's way of tackling the materialists and sceptics, who had argued, against the rationalism of Descartes, and later Spinoza and Leibniz, that if we know only our own ideas then we cannot prove that the real world outside them is truly like them – a view which must lead inexorably to the conclusion that no knowledge based on observation alone is possible.

Berkeley's way of dealing with this suggestion was to call attention to the meaning of the word 'exist' – a word which will become increasingly central as the explorations undertaken in this book proceed. When we say that a table exists, he argued, what are we saying more than that we are aware of its colour, shape, size and so on? Have we any evidence of its consciously existing? The thought is absurd. Objects exist only in our senses perceiving them: they have colour because of our perception of colour, taste because of our perception of taste, and similarly smell, sound, texture and the rest.

Locke agreed with Berkeley up to this point, but argued that there were certain 'primary' qualities, such as motion, number, solidity and so on, which exist independently of being perceived; these were the objects of true knowledge because they occur in the real, objective world around us. Berkeley denied this: because we don't experience these 'primary qualities' independently of objects which exemplify and express them ('motion', for instance, is meaningless except in terms of things that move) and these latter objects exist only because and when they are perceived, then, he suggested, the primary qualities are also empirically unknowable: we can know only our own ideas. In his *Treatise Concerning the Principles of Human Knowledge* he wrote:

It is indeed an opinion, strangely prevailing amongst men, that houses, mountains, rivers, and in a word all sensible objects, have an existence, natural or real, distinct from their being perceived by the understanding . . . [but] what are the aforementioned objects but the things we perceive by sense? And what do we perceive besides our own ideas and sensations? And is it not plainly repugnant that any one of these, or any combination of them, should exist unperceived?

(We are entitled, I think, to ask ourselves a pertinent question to which Berkeley's argument points us: accepting, with Berkeley, that we cannot prove the *existence* of primary qualities, do we really *need* them anyway, either for the theory or the practice of living? Our concern is with things which move, not with motion *per se*; with things that are solid, not with solidity *per se*. Berkeley has provided us with an example of Ockham's razor – a process which dispenses with the idea that there must be a generality of which each individual object is a specific example.)

One obvious question to ask apropos of Berkeley's basic proposition relates to the world, or alleged world, before the arrival of *homo sapiens*. If we grant (which we certainly cannot logically refute) that everything around us exists only because and when we perceive it, doesn't it follow that until we human beings evolved – which on the biological time-scale was extremely late in the day – nothing in fact existed?

Berkeley's reply was to present the God whose Being is eternal, who is, was and always will be. Nothing therefore has existed unperceived by this God, the Creator and Sustainer of all. Two famous limericks reflect this argument, the first certainly and the second probably by the Catholic priest and scholar, Ronald Knox (1888–1957):

> There once was a man who said 'God
> Must think it exceedingly odd
> If he finds that this tree
> Will continue to be,
> When there's no one about in the Quad.'

> 'Dear Sir, Your astonishment's odd:
> *I* am always about in the Quad.
> And that's why the tree
> Will continue to be,
> Since observed by, Yours faithfully, God.'

It may be felt that Berkeley has made of God something of a *deus ex machina* in this context. If he had expressed himself in more general ontological terms, such as that only through Being can anything be perceived, his ideas would have been less open to challenge (though one might then have been tempted to ask what specifically was being said). The argument must be considered within the context of theological, rather than dualistic, discourse (Chapter 3), though it is worth mentioning that from the behaviourist perspective (see Chapter 4) Berkeley's theory is self-defeating. If it is the case that *esse est percipi*, and the eternal process of perceiving on the part of God is posited as the vindication of this view in the sense of rendering it comprehensive, then we are entitled to ask who perceives God. The whole debate, it seems to me, has been (and is being) conducted from the wrong premises, but one further question may be posed from this perspective. If, as Berkeley asserts, there are (exist) no external objects to cause us sensations, where do these sensations originate? Berkeley's answer is to present the 'Author of Nature', God, who produces the sensations in us. This seems to me an odd *modus operandi* on God's part. If we're going to have the sensations anyway as part of our daily experience, why should He involve Himself continuously and universally in creating them when, by one comprehensive act of creation (quite within the bounds of possibility for an almighty Being) He could provide for all time in the objects themselves the ongoing source of sensations?

The **immaterialism** of Berkeley is akin to the idealism of Plato in the sense that both agree that (1) there are two worlds of experience, the visible and tangible and the incorporeal or spiritual/mental; and (2) the real world is the world of mind, or soul, or spirit, since without this world the other would either have no existence at all (Berkeley) or no meaning (Plato). Berkeley's theory is normally described as 'immaterialism' rather than dualism, but the questions he raises are not irrelevant to this present account of human nature. His rigorous methods of inquiry foreshadowed those of the twentieth-century linguistic analysts, which for me is both his strength and his weakness: it is strong because of the mental honesty required; it is weak because it uses logic as the *sole* tool of inquiry.

ASSESSING DUALISM

The dualistic account of human nature has, then, been widely held over the centuries though this does not mean that those who have professed it have always given it careful thought. The actress who said to the bishop, for instance, 'You have possessed my body but you will never possess my soul' was hardly likely to be commended for her philosophical know-how. However, the charge of laziness made by Watson seems unfair, if only because the implication behind that charge is that those who hold the alternative, monistic or single-substance view are more likely than the dualists to have thought the matter through. It is surely just as lazy an argument to state something like 'I can't see any soul or spirit but I can see the material world so that must be all that reality contains' as to say 'Well, there must be more in human beings than just dying matter, else what's the point of anything?' The comment of the Russian cosmonaut who claimed to have failed to find God after he had explored the heavens was just as banal as that of a teacher with whom I once engaged in radio debate who affirmed that God must exist because he regularly conversed with Him.

## THE SOUL

There is, then, a good deal of sloppy thinking on this subject, and we need to give it a little critical examination. In trying to give a hint as to the place of the *idea* of the soul in the thinking of this book, let me first try to clear a little ground. The major problems, as I see them, relate to the issues of (1) the origin, (2) the destiny and (3) the present implications of the possession of a soul.

**Origin**    Assuming I possess a soul, where and when did it originate? We may answer that either it is eternal, uncreated, indestructible, or it was created along with my body. If it is eternal, where was it before my experience of this present life? To this I can answer either 'in the world of souls' (the world of Forms, the ideal world, Heaven) or 'in another body'. Both these answers are open to the question of why we cannot recall any earlier existence. Plato, in reply to this, stresses the fact that if our eyes are 'open' we do 'see' reflections of the ideals which we experienced in this former stage, and Wordsworth in (for instance) his 'Ode on the intimations of immortality' suggests that some memory of that idyllic past occasionally flashes on what he elsewhere terms 'the inward eye' (see case study 5).

If we take the reincarnational view, I must accept as true the belief that my soul occupies (if that is the right word) my body – *this* body, whose fingers (two of them) are tapping the keys of a typewriter – as one of a series of occupancies. If this is the case it is surely not inapposite to want to know in what other bodies my soul has resided. It seems strange that I have absolutely no recall of any previous incarnation; nor am I encouraged to be more sympathetic towards this view by those who claim to have such recall. Judging from their evidence, the souls of Napoleon and various Indian chiefs have been incredibly busy over the centuries, while those of illiterate, maltreated peasants seem to have retired into obscurity. There is also the logistical problem of the enormous increase in the number of souls over the past century, the period of the so-called population explosion. Have all these billions of new souls, hitherto deprived of bodies because until recently there simply weren't enough to go round, been hanging about for millions of years waiting for this explosion? (The doctrine of karma is a discrete issue in this context, and will be considered in some detail when discussing Indian philosophy in Chapter 7).

If on the other hand we state that the soul is created with each new body, there then arises the problem of determining the point at which the soul's creation occurs. This may sound a trivial issue, but for many people it has implications, about both the law of the land and human behaviour, which are, to put it mildly, contentious and affect decisions on such mortal questions as abortion, experiments on human embryos and (above all) contraception. (Case study 6 relates to these issues.) Let us not, then, deceive ourselves by thinking that these are matters only for late-night discussion. There are powerful, conscientiously committed organizations set up to foster opposition to all the above practices and any others like them. It would not be unfair to describe these organizations as 'soul protectors', representative of the dualist view of human nature. The issues they raise cannot be ignored – in fact I know of no comparable issues which are anything like as certain as these are to rouse uncontrollable passion among those who fight to uphold or to abolish the varied practices.

**Destiny** The same kind of problems arise when contemplating the *destiny* of the soul. The questions that need to be asked in this context have been admirably presented by Hospers and the relevant passage, witty and perceptive, along with questions for consideration, will be found under case study 4.

**Implications** A third problem relating to the concept of the immortality of the soul is its implication for and relevance to the life we are leading here and now. Are we more, or less, likely to become, in the phrase of the existentialist Nietzsche, 'otherworldsmen', indifferent to the needs of the world, as we cultivate our souls and prepare them for the next life? Or are we, as many believers in the immortality of the soul have evinced in their styles of life, *more* likely to give ourselves to these worldly needs because this existence is viewed as a training-ground for the next? Alternatively, looking at the matter from the receiving end, so to speak, are we more, or less, likely to be able to endure deprivation, suffering, mental and physical torture, the threat of death, if we hold no belief in the soul's existence? Much of the debate in the case studies may involve a fair amount of speculation, but that speculation relates to existence as it is currently experienced by millions of people.

THE NUMINOUS

The discussion so far has ranged around questions to which there are no verifiable answers. We may argue about them till Domesday but we are unlikely to make any worthwhile progress towards resolving them. Even the evidence that a belief 'works' in practice doesn't make this a true belief. So unless the evidence presented by the **spiritualists** (or **spiritists**) and other devotees of the paranormal be accepted as scientifically verifiable, the protagonists either way seem doomed to remain in perpetual alienation from each other. Surely the popularity of dualism, in whatever form it has been held, points to some kind of widespread human experience?

One major explanation of the doctrine's popularity has been the basic urge for survival. It is a logical impossibility for an existing, conscious being to imagine non-existence or unconsciousness, even though we effectively experience this state when we sleep dreamlessly (one of the four states of Advaita, as we shall see in Chapter 7). If I were to try to imagine the world going on its rounds without me, I should do so, willy-nilly, with the implication that I was still somehow around to observe the deluge that followed my demise. The doctrine of the immortality of the soul is one easy escape route from this dilemma.

However, I don't think the popularity of the doctrine can be explained merely in terms of a psychological escape mechanism. There is, I believe, an area in our lives which hints that there is more to experience and reality than can be obtained by logical reasoning – that is an uncontentious issue – but also more than can be conveyed directly by the channel of the five senses. Wordsworth's famous couplet illustrates what I am trying to describe:

> To me the meanest flower that blows can give
> Thoughts that do often lie too deep for tears.

And perhaps too deep to describe: what he was exemplifying is what I shall term experience of the *numinous*.

This word is not easy to define except ostensively; that is, by offering a series of instances of its occurrence. It is derived from the Greek *noumenon*, meaning something known by the mind as against the senses. Kant used the word to mean a thing-in-itself, the essence of a thing, as opposed to *phenomenon* which is the thing as it confronts us. My table, for instance, has a particular size, shape and colour: these are the phenomena of the table; but it would still be a table if these were radically different – noumenally it would still be a table. The issue has profound implications for the abortion debate, for there we have the **phenomenon** of a foetus but – so it is argued – the **noumenon** of a human being.)

Kant's usage points in the direction I intend, but this was given greater clarity by the philosopher of religion, Rudolph Otto (1869–1937) in his seminal work *The Idea of the Holy* (*Das Heilige*, 1917). Here the word denotes the elements of a non-rational and amoral kind (that is, beyond right and wrong in both the intellectual and ethical senses). The numinous includes feelings of awe and even self-abasement (**mysterium fascinans** and **mysterium tremendens** as Otto described them). Otto interpreted the numinous in a broadly religious sense, as basically man's response to the deity, or to some manifestation of the supernatural. But the experiences to which he refers can be interpreted on a purely secular, that is to say a non-supernatural (or, simply, natural) basis. The numinous is a reality to me, but it is what I experience as a human being like other human beings in moments of deepest emotion and aesthetic awareness. People throughout the ages have testified to this experience as both a reality and a unique source of enrichment. To link it solely with religious experience, such as the worship involved in the eucharist among Christians, is in my view both pusillanimous and presumptuous. If it were true, we should have to conclude that many people (non-believers in the religious sense) have never been in a condition to encounter the numinous, and this is manifestly false.

The contexts of the numinous, if we are to accept as genuine the testimonies of those who have described it, have been numerous and varied. Many have encountered it in *nature*; others through the *arts*. 'I heard flowers that sounded and notes that shone,' wrote the French philosopher Saint-Martin. The sense of *history* can provide a similar depth of awe, as past and present become one: I recall this experience vividly as I stood (illegally, but perhaps I may be forgiven) in **Savonarola**'s fifteenth-century pulpit in San Gimignano. So many people have testified to the power of contemplation and meditation to lead them into this dimension that those who have not experienced it must in all honesty maintain only an attitude of agnosticism. Even the experience of sex, with its occasional power to provide a sense of timelessness and spacelessness, can, I think, be included in the contexts of the numinous, and orgasmic rapture described as a mystical experience. (See case study 25 for further exploration in this area.)

There is, I feel, sufficient universal testimony to the experience of the numinous as thus described to lead me to conclude that it cannot be ignored in any ontological discussion. But this is not at all the same as affirming a belief in the soul as the *only* recipient of the experience, even less a belief in God as the sole provider of it. When we turn to the central ontological perspective of this book it will be seen that the whole topic of the origin and destiny of the soul is in fact redundant. But, as we shall see, in that respect it is not alone.

*Case study 3*
*Screaming from the cave*

Part of the homespun philosophy on which many of us were raised is that 'ignorance is bliss'. 'What you don't know won't hurt' must have been in the mind of many an adulterous spouse concerning his/her partner; and doctors sometimes decide not to tell patients, and perhaps even the relatives, the truth about their fatal illnesses on the grounds (justifiable or otherwise) that this knowledge would cause them unnecessary distress.

Plato's allegory of the cave, however, relates not just to temporary disease but to permanent awareness of truths which may, because these embrace a wider and perhaps more intimidating perception of reality than they had been accustomed to, cause considerable anxiety to people who had previously been quite happy with their more limited perceptions. Is it (1) never, (2) always, or (3) sometimes right to shatter such people's illusions on the grounds that 'the truth must out' or, perhaps (taken somewhat out of context), 'the truth shall make you free'? Consider the following situations with these issues in mind. All the examples are real: none is concocted for this exercise.

(1) A remote tribe in South America worship a crashed aeroplane, believing it to be a heavenly messenger, and that by pinning their faith on it they will ensure beatitude for themselves or for their descendants. They have never developed any means of communicating with the world outside their location, and are discovered by a party of Western anthropologists.

(2) Another tribe believe that their god lives on top of the local mountain, and that if they perform an annual ritual this god will bring them seasonal weather.

(3) A woman believes that the spirit of her uncle, who has been dead for twenty years, visits her regularly whenever she needs advice. The 'advice', judging from the woman's subsequent behaviour, is usually quite sound.

(4) A man's life is going to pot because of his addiction to alcohol. He refuses to accept that he is an alcoholic.

(5) There has been a major nuclear disaster, known to many heads of government. They agree not to release any information about this, on the grounds that there will almost certainly be widespread panic among the populace.

(6) A pious family, who are good friends and kind neighbours to all, have a sincere faith in the literal accuracy of the Bible. Major discrepancies in these narratives could be pointed out to them, but this information could mar the happiness of their 'simple' faith.

(7) The school thief is believed by his doting parents to be the model of rectitude. The truth about their child would cause them profound anguish. He could be punished without their having to know.

(8) The Church decides to censor information about the universe following the discovery of the telescope, on the ground that the

destruction of the earlier cosy image of the universe would bring about many suicides.

(9)   A wimp asks you whether you think he has an inferiority complex. You believe he just is inferior.

(10)  A friend believes fervently in the effect of his/her zodiacal sign, and has read avidly all the 'expert' descriptions of people born under this sign. He/she is convinced that this has determined his/her character and life situation, and acts accordingly. You are aware that there are something like 400 million other people in the world who were born under this same sign.

(11)  Your aunt is intensely superstitious. She touches wood when expressing a hope, prepares for a visitor whenever she drops a spoon, crosses herself when facing a problem and starts with 'Please God' when stating her mundane plans.

(12)  An old lady is being systematically embezzled by her unscrupulous grandson. He is the apple of her eye and the basic motivation for her staying alive.

The following poem, 'The newt', presents the allegory of the cave in a new and original way. How far does it encourage you to agree or disagree with John Stuart Mill's aphorism: 'Better to be Socrates dissatisfied than a fool satisfied; better a dissatisfied man than a satisfied pig'?

I spoke of sunrise to a protean newt
That lived in darkness and had lost his eyes;
He was a creature of a wide repute
And he replied (and he was very wise):
'Your fancied legends, sir, I must refute;
There is no sun. Therefore it cannot rise.

I am a newt; they say I cannot see –
I cannot see, indeed. No more can they.
No visionary fool can dazzle me
With mystic tidings of the light of day;
When they come prating of this mystery
I do not answer them; I swim away.'

And so he swam away, and I was left
Amazed at my temerity that I –
I who of all my senses am bereft
Save only five – should in my folly try
To teach an even more insensate eft
Of the sun's glories and the morning sky.

*Case study 4*
*Survival after bodily death*

The following passage is extracted from John Hospers, *An Introduction to Philosophical Analysis*. Read it through and ask yourself the questions that follow.

In what way might a person survive his bodily death? He might live in another body, or he might lead an entirely disembodied existence. Let us examine both these possibilities.

**(1)  Life in another body**   When they attempt to picture a person's post-mortem existence, most religious traditions imagine the person as having a new and resurrected body . . . When we try to imagine people now dead continuing to exist, we usually imagine them as having bodies similar to the ones they had when we knew them, as well as memory, intelligence, and other features sufficiently similar to the ones they had in this life for them to be recognisable by others as the same person. The widow who wants to be reunited with her dead husband imagines him as being very much as he was before he died: doing similar things, looking as he did (if his face and form were very different she might not care for him any more) . . . It is in this way that she wants to rejoin him, not as a disembodied spirit or as having a body so different from the one she knew that she could not recognise him. Of course, there would be problems: if he was a cripple in this world, would he still be one in a better world? Would he be without fault (if that can be imagined), even the faults she loved him for? Would he still belong to the male sex? How much of the man she loved would still exist? This might well make some difference in her attitude toward him . . . Change enough characteristics, and she might not even care to rejoin him: what she wants is a continuation – with improvements, of course – of her present existence with him. . .

Moreover, if he has a *new* body, presumably that body will also have a brain, and his personality in his new form would depend to a very large extent on the nature of this brain – whether he was quick-witted or slow, whether he was lethargic or mercurial, and so on. Would he still have that mole on his cheek? Would he still prefer his steak rare? Would he still be cheerful yet sometimes depressed? (This would depend on things like the supply of oxygen reaching his brain-cells.) Would he have the body of a man of a certain age, say the age at which he died, and remain forever at this age? Or would his new body grow older and die in turn, to be replaced by still another? Most people have not made at all clear to themselves what kind of immortality they have in mind, even when they fix all their hopes on the truth of this hypothesis.

**(2)    Disembodied existence**   Let us try now to imagine an entirely disembodied existence – consciousness continuing entirely in the absence of a body. You have no physical body, but you still think thoughts, have feelings and memories, even sense-experiences (if you like) of seeing, hearing, etc., but (since you lack a body) without the sense-organs that in this life are the empirically necessary condition of having these experiences. Let us try to imagine what it would be like, even in this present life, to awaken and find that you no longer have a body. You go to bed one night, turn out the light, go to sleep and then wake up some hours later to see sunlight streaming in the window, the clock pointing to eight, the mirror near the foot of the bed. You see the bed, but you do not see your own body in it – in fact you see the sheets directly under the places where you thought your limbs were. Startled, you look into the mirror, but your face and body are not visible there either; you see reflected there the entire unin-terrupted expanse of the headboard behind you. 'Have I become invisible?' you ask yourself; and thinking of H. G. Wells's invisible man, who could not be seen but could still be touched, you try to touch yourself, but there is nothing there to be touched any more than to be seen. A person coming into the room would not be able to see you or touch you: he would not know you existed unless you could utter sounds (though you have no organ to utter them with) or communicate with him in some other way. He could run his hands over the entire bed without ever com-ing in contact with a body, visible or invisible. You are now thoroughly alarmed at the idea that no one will know you exist. You try to walk toward the mirror, but of course you have no feet. Nevertheless you find the objects near the mirror increasing in apparent size and the objects behind you apparently becoming smaller just *as if* you were walking toward the mirror: all the experiences are the same, except that of seeing and touching your body. . .

Now, it may be thought, we have imagined a clear case of disembodied existence. But have we? There are some implicit references to body even in this brief description. You see – with eyes? No, you have no eyes, since you have no body. But we may let that pass, as long as you have experiences such as you would ordinarily have by means of eyes. But if you *look* in one direction and then in another, how do you do this? By turning your head? But you have no head to turn. Let us say that you have the experience you *would* ordinarily get by turning your head. This may not pass muster, but let us try the next step. You find that you can't touch your body because no body is there, just the bed and the covers. How do you find this out? Do you reach out with your fingers to touch the bed? But you have no fingers, since you have no body. What would you touch (or try to touch) with? You move, or seem to move, toward the mirror – but what moves? Not your body, since you have none. Nevertheless things seem to get larger in front of you and smaller behind you, as if you were moving. In front of or behind what? Your body? But once again you have none. So how is this apparent motion to be conceived?

Every step along the way is riddled with difficulties. It is not just that we are accustomed to think of people as having bodies and can't get out of the habit. This makes things more difficult, but it is only part of the story. The fact is that you can't imagine doing things like looking in a different direction without turning your head, which is usually the result of a decision to do this – and of course you can't turn your head if you have no head to turn; and if you *decide* to turn your head, you can't carry out this decision in the absence of a head, so how can the fact that you see now the mirror and now the window be the result of your decision? There seem to be many difficulties, not merely technical but logical, constantly embedded in the attempted description.

(John Hospers: *An Introduction to Philosophical Analysis* 3e, pp. 280–3)

1   Is this a full analysis of the options available? Are there other possibilities which Hospers ignores?

2   Is it a fair analysis? Are there any verbal tricks, or devious statements? Is Hospers being totally honest with his readers?

3   How far is this kind of analysis relevant to metaphysical discussion (in this case relating to the immortality of the soul)?

4   How would you react to a person who said, 'I can't answer the problems which Hospers raises, but I still believe in the immortality of the soul'; or 'We can't be expected to know everything since we are imperfect creatures. God is all-knowing and He will have a way. "The foolishness of God is wiser than men."?'

5   From a reading of this passage, would you say that discussion like this, entailing speculation about matters totally outside our

experience, is as pointless as discussing colour with people born blind.?

*Case study 5*
*The soul in literature*

In the following quotations the word 'soul' is used in a variety of contexts and with a range of different emphases. In your reflections on them, ask yourself these questions:

**1**   Is the soul here referred to as effectively the basic, 'real' self? If so, is the passage in any way relevant to the dualism debate?

**2**   Is it referred to as an alternative self to that represented by the physical body? If so, are these passages implicitly accepting the dualist view?

**3**   Does it just mean a human being – no more no less? If so, does this imply that even the use of apparently dualistic language can disguise a basically monistic philosophy?

(1)   'To be rooted is perhaps the most important and least recognised need of the human soul. It is one of the hardest to define. A human being has roots by virtue of his real, active and natural participation in the life of a community which preserves in living shape certain particular treasures of the past and certain particular expectations for the future.'

(Simone Weil: *The Need for Roots*)

(2)                 'Our birth is but a sleep and a forgetting:
                The Soul that rises with us, our life's Star,
                Hath had elsewhere its setting,
                And cometh from afar. . .
                . . . trailing clouds of glory do we come
                From God, who is our home. . .
                Hence in a season of calm weather
                Though inland far we be,
                Our souls have sight of that immortal sea
                Which brought us hither.'

(William Wordsworth:
'Ode on the intimations of immortality')

(3)   'Live with the gods. And he does so who constantly shows them that his soul is satisfied with what is assigned him.'

(Marcus Aurelius: *Meditations*)

(4)   'Man has no Body distinct from his Soul; for that called Body is a portion of Soul discerned by five Senses, the chief inlets of Soul in this age.'

(William Blake: *The Marriage of Heaven and Hell*;
the voice is that of the Devil)

(5)   'No coward soul is mine.'

(Emily Bronte: 'Last lines')

(6)   'The British postgraduate student is a lonely, forlorn soul.'

(David Lodge: *Changing Places*)

(7)   'The voice of the sea speaks to the soul. The touch of the sea is sensuous, enfolding the body in its soft, close embrace.'

(Kate Chopin: *The Awakening*)

(8)   'Two souls dwell, alas! in my breast.'

(J. W. von Goethe: *Faust*)

(9)   'I am aware of the damp souls of housemaids
Sprouting despondently at area gates.'

(T. S. Eliot: 'Morning at the window')

(10)   'To me education is a leading out of what is already there in the pupil's soul.'

(Muriel Spark: *The Prime of Miss Jean Brodie*)

*Case study 6*
*The soul and medical ethics*

The following is a transcript of a discussion between two colleagues. It is their last discussion on this subject, and rumour has it that they haven't spoken to each other since. Follow the debate through, and see if you can discuss the issues raised with anyone who takes the opposite view from your own.

A
You can't discuss medical ethics without bringing in the soul. Billions of people believe in its existence, and that it's immortal. It's bound to affect their views on things like abortion and euthanasia.

Because I believe there's a right moment decreed for the soul to leave the body.

B
I don't see why. Even if you believe that everyone has an immortal soul, how can it be affected just because the date of death has been brought forward a bit by euthanasia?

Decreed by whom?

By God, of course. He made the
soul in the first place, and has
His plan for its destiny.

I don't know. Maybe the travails
of dying are a preparatory test
for the soul's future. And in any
case, it means taking God's
authority away from Him if
human beings presume to take
death into their own hands.

Because once you start interfering with the natural processes
things start getting out of control.
You're obviously talking about
euthanasia for the very old,
which may not change the date
of death radically; but what
about the very sick who're not so
old? And what about the killing
off of handicapped babies that is
going on? Nobody takes *their*
newly formed souls into account,
and I think it's a horrible blas-
phemy.

Of course God would have a
plan. But what I think is wrong

Couldn't that plan contain the
possibility that other creations of
His speed things up a bit? After
all, the motive behind
euthanasia is to alleviate the
sufferings of the dying. This God
of yours surely can't be opposed to
that?

I can't see that at all.
All developments in medicine
and surgery, such as the
life-enhancing discovery of
anaesthetics, are human
interventions in the course of
nature, which is
presumably what you see as the
will of God. So where does His
will end and man's intervention
begin? You presumably allow the
soul to continue in this body by
the use of pain-killing drugs, or
antibiotics: why not other drugs,
one side-effect of which is death?

I'm not going to argue with
you about the purely ethical
considerations of letting mal-
formed infants die: this raises all
sorts of questions about the value
of life, which is a separate issue.
We're talking about the soul.
Assuming that the handicapped
infant has a soul, what's wrong
in releasing it straightaway from
its handicapped body and letting
it develop or exist in better
circumstances? After all, if the
soul is immortal nothing can
destroy it, so God must have a
plan that can be adopted for it.

Well I find your image of God
horrendous. Not even an

is that by killing off infants in that way we're constantly causing Him to have to change His plans. He wouldn't have brought them into the world in the first place if He hadn't planned it. I believe we're bringing His wrath on ourselves by usurping His rights.

No, I don't. It's human beings who make mistakes in their assessment of situations. Because we don't understand, we try to change things, and the worst example of all, which I notice you've kept quiet about, is abortion, which is not only legalized murder, a human matter, but playing a game with immortal souls, acting like Satan.

No. We're acting like prisoners who take over their gaol, or children who take over their school – going way beyond our authority. Only in an infinitely bigger way. We're taking upon ourselves the role of God, which is to commit the unpardonable sin. And the supreme example is experimenting on human embryos.

Of course. The moment the sperm fertilizes the egg the soul is formed. That's how God has ordered things.

Because it's obvious. It's the supreme moment of creation, and God's plan can be seen quite clearly.

ignorant human being would deliberately create a cretin. And you can hardly say that an omnipotent God makes mistakes.

But, once again, how does the act of abortion affect the immortal soul? Assuming it *has* a soul at the time it is aborted – and even those who believe in it disagree as to *when* it is united with the body – you could still say that all that happens when a pregnancy is terminated is that we're allowing God, who has an infinite range of options at His disposal because He's omnipotent, the chance to work on these.

Well, sin or not, I think this is a responsibility we have as human beings, and one that you religious people have so far prevented us from fully assuming. But are you suggesting that a few cells, brought about perhaps as a result of a casual sexual encounter which neither partner may have given a second thought about, have a soul?

How do you know?

I think it's just as likely – assuming there is a soul at all, which I think is a misconception on mankind's part – that it enters the body at the moment of quickening. Then the cells at the early stage can be treated just as cells, even by those who believe in the soul.

That's just so that you can go on playing your science-fiction games with a clear conscience. Using human beings as though they were bottled chemicals. Like taking the foetus of a human and implanting it in another just to cure him of some illness. This is like the Nazi experiments in their extermination camps; it's utterly, utterly evil.

I think you're becoming irrational. For one thing, you're forgetting the point I made about euthanasia – the end in view is the greater happiness of mankind. Anyway, the cells used in experiments on embryos would be simply destroyed otherwise, so what's the difference in the end? And if some are used to help a person with Parkinson's disease, say, why is that so wrong? The motive is good, and I'm sure God can cope with the rest.

It's the likes of you – supporting these evil experiments – who are bringing disaster on the human race. You're as wicked as the scientists.

Well, I think the consequences of your views are evil. It's you and your sort who have fought every development in science as against the will of God. You seem totally indifferent to human pain, or misery, or deprivation.

You've become so unprincipled that you no longer recognize real charity, based on God's laws, when you see it.

And you've allowed your holier-than-thou principles to get in the way of Christian charity.

None of the issues raised allows for any compromise: you cannot *half* abort, or go halfway towards terminating life by euthanasia.

How far do you think that the consequence of this is that there can be no *modus vivendi* between those whose opposition to these forms of bringing about death is based on a belief in the immortal soul, and those who don't believe in the soul?

If not (that is, if you think some kind of working arrangement is possible), what do you suggest is the common ground?

How can these two points of view coexist in a single community?

Can 'agreement to differ' happen where mortal issues like these are concerned?

# 3 Theism and human destiny: God's obedient servants

Theism (from the Greek *theos*, 'God') is the doctrine that there exists a perfect Being (I shall follow normal usage and use capitals in this context) who has been given a variety of names by different races but in the Western world is generally known as God. Among the attributes which comprise God's perfection are: omnipotence, or the ability to do anything He wills; omniscience, or knowledge of everything; omnipresence, or being in all places at once; immutability, or constancy (being unchanging) in both His powers and His nature; and eternity: He had no beginning and will have no end. To these impersonal qualities theists add a belief in His personal concern for the universe He has created, and for the creatures – His creatures – who inhabit it. As their Creator, it is His desire that they should worship Him, love Him and perform His will. His nature therefore includes both justice and mercy; the God of theism is both stern and compassionate.

I have used the male pronoun in this description, question-begging though it is, because it is the one adopted by the major theistic religions of the world – Judaism, Christianity and Islam. (It is becoming common to include **Zoroastrianism** in this list: in fact, this Persian religion is viewed by many theologians as containing the earliest expression of theistic belief.) This male pronoun is significant for two reasons. First, its use in preference to the neuter pronoun 'it' distinguishes theism from another doctrine of God, pantheism. This, as the word suggests (*pan*, 'all') is the view that God exists as a spiritual force or essence in all things. Some pantheistic faiths include in this description only living things, such as human beings, animals, fish, birds, insects, plants and so on, while others also include inanimate things such as rocks, rivers, clouds, springs and so on (though these religions would normally be listed under the title **'animism'**). The personal pronoun in theistic writings emphasizes that God is a personal God, separate from the creatures He has made, but capable (and in some expressions of the belief desirous) of communicating with them. Because

He is not only all-powerful but also all-loving, God is presented in a way quite different from pantheism. The same goes for another school of thought known, rather vaguely, as 'deism' (Latin *deus*, 'God'). There have been several schools of deism, but its dominant emphasis is its acceptance of the impersonal attributes of God expressed in theism – omnipotence, omniscience and so on; but it stops short of attributing to God personal feelings like love, mercy, or compassion. In effect, deism portrays God as an almighty Being who, having created the universe, has, so far as its inhabitants are concerned, retired for a well-earned rest lasting for the remainder of eternity. Deism presents us with a **deus ex machina**, a God who is outside the world of human existence and experience.

The second explanation for the male pronoun has more to do with sociology than theology. The Semites, among whom theism was uniquely expressed, were strongly male-dominated people. If we study the Middle East, where all theistic religions were fostered, we see communities in which the role of women was in virtually all respects subservient to that of men; it was a world in which male strength more than female gentleness was needed for survival, where death could be sudden and life was cheap – hence the prime role of the male as both propagator and defender of the species. It was the primitive raw world of the desert, demanding the expression of the Yang rather than the Yin, two words which will later be discussed at length but which can be loosely defined here as the active, aggressive element normally (though not exclusively, of course) associated with the male, and the passive, reflective element normally (again, concessionary) associated with the female. I shall therefore continue to use the male pronoun in this context, recognizing that to some people this is offensive, but at a loss to know how to avoid this without either begging other questions by using the female pronoun, giving the wrong line of thought by using the neutral 'it', or boring any reader with the laborious 'He/She/It' structure.

## GROUNDS FOR BELIEF IN GOD

The philosophical arguments for the existence of God can be perused in any introduction to metaphysics (one book with that title by C. H. H. Whiteley, Harvester Press, can be recommended), but a brief summary of them here should prove not irrelevant to the main theme of this book.

### *The ontological argument*

This is especially true of the first argument, which is the most philosophical of all (in fact some would say that it is the basic argument, from which all others flow): the *ontological argument*. We have already seen (p. 8) that ontology relates to being, and this argument builds on the statement *being is* (which is **analytically** true) by suggesting that God, as expressed in theistic thought (omnipotent, benevolent and so on) is logically necessary. The two names most closely associated with this argument are St Anselm and Descartes.

In its Cartesian form, the argument proceeds along these lines: I have in mind (for the sake of the discussion) an image of a perfect Being whom I call God. If that Being did not exist, it could hardly be called perfect, since how can anything be perfect if it doesn't even exist? It would then be possible to describe even a tree as greater than God, since at least that tree exists. More to the point, it would consequently in theory be possible for another being to exist possessing all the attributes of this (non-existent) God, plus existence. But we began by saying that we hold an image of a *perfect* Being, and we are now speaking of perfection plus another quality (existence). You cannot have anything more perfect than perfect: therefore God exists.

St Anselm (1033–1109) described God as '*aliquid quo nihil maiorum coqitare est*', 'that Being, a greater than which cannot be conceived of'. If another, greater, Being could be conceived of, then the first Being would lose its status as the greatest; and so on *ad infinitum*. Eventually a point is reached beyond which no amount of conceptualizing can develop the image further.

In assessing this argument, it is necessary to clear our minds at the beginning about the distinction between being and existence. The two words are often used interchangeably, but they are in fact quite distinct. We have seen (pp. 8–9) that something or someone can be said to be even when it is to be found only in our memory or our imagination. Thus we may say that there are unicorns, because we have seen them in drawings, and can describe them with great accuracy; but, of course, unicorns don't exist. In the lives of most of us, there are probably people long dead who *are* a constant present influence, so that an expression of their being – the 'to be' of them – remains with us still: but they don't exist any more (at any rate, not unless we fall back on ideas discussed in the previous chapter). The difference here is, I think, brought out by the German distinction between '*es ist*' and '*es gibt*', both of which being usually translated as 'there is'. But the former literally means 'there is' while the latter means 'there exists'. The example I was given at school to explain this was '*Es ist ein Mann im Monde; es gibt aber keinen Mann im Monde*', 'There *is* a man-in-the-moon, but no man exists in the moon'. (I didn't understand this in my school-days, but at that time I had not begun to study ontology, and neither had my German teacher, though he was an excellent bassoon player.)

At this level it is possible to say there is a God because so many people have an image of Him in their minds, and are powerfully influenced by the idea. But the ontological argument proceeds from this to state that God's *existence* is also necessarily true, since God is the ground, or source, of (all) being, or, alternatively expressed, is the infinite Being whose essence involves its existence and which causes finite beings, which do not necessarily exist of themselves, to exist. We are here left with two views of God and the universe of being: in the former all being is viewed as a unity, while in the latter there is a dualism of being: that which exists of itself, and that which is caused to exist. The former is the view of the Dutch philosopher, Spinoza (1632–77). He argued that 'there cannot be any substance excepting God, and consequently none other can be conceived'. From this, he argued, 'whatever is is in God, and nothing can be or be conceived without God'.

This view is, I think, closer to the pantheistic than to the theistic view of God. It amounts to the identification of God with being *per se*. Spinoza is quite direct about this: 'If there were any substance besides God, it would have to be explained by some attribute of God, and thus two substances would exist possessing the same attribute', which is impossible.

While then it may be helpful to some to equate 'being' generally with 'God', this is not what the majority of theists have proposed, since being is neutral on matters about which God in theistic thought has been committed (on perfect *behaviour*, for instance: we have already seen that one attribute of the theistic God is benevolence). The existence of *this* Being as posited by the ontological argument was rebutted by Immanuel Kant (1724–1804). He argued that existence is not a predicate of a thing in the world of reality (though, as we have seen, such words as existence or non-existence may be relevant in the world of the imagination or the memory). When describing something – say, a town or an exotic plant – to a friend who hasn't seen it, I wouldn't have to add 'and it exists' to its list of attributes. The same would be true of God if the ontological argument were sound, and the fact that we *do* argue about His existence exposes the fallacy of the argument. Since being is logically necessary (being cannot not be, by definition – a point to be pursued later), and if we follow Spinoza and others and equate God with being, then He is also logically necessary. But the moment we begin, as theists do, to add attributes to the understanding of God, we find ourselves in need of other arguments. As Hamlet, or Utopia, or the ideal spouse *is*, so God is: but this is not what we are discussing. We are discussing whether the God of the theists *exists*: the God of mercy and of wrath, the God of Moses, and St Paul, and Muhammad: and that is a totally different matter.

## THE COSMOLOGICAL ARGUMENT

The second major argument for the existence of God is based on our understanding of the **cosmos**, however that word be translated, and is called the *cosmological* argument. Numerous philosophers have presented the case based on this argument, most of them living in the period of what is generally called 'Catholic Philosophy': the period between the end of classical Rome and the Renaissance. During this millennium, the Catholic Church was the main authority in the Western world, and philosophical inquiry reflected issues relevant to Christian metaphysics. The two most famous of these philosophers, St Anselm and St Thomas Aquinas (1225–74), were in fact both in holy orders.

Perhaps the most comprehensive exposition of this argument was made by Aquinas in his massive *Summa Theologica*. His basic argument is that the universe as we perceive it requires, logically, an instigator, or initiator. He expresses this viewpoint from five angles or perspectives. First, the fact that all things in *motion* depend on the motion of something else in order themselves to be set in motion logically requires an original motion independent of any other. Secondly, the fact that everything that occurs in the universe was *caused* by some other factor or factors suggests an original uncaused first cause. Thirdly, since every living being eventually passes out of existence, there must be an original Being whose existence is eternal. Fourthly and fifthly, (somewhat akin to Plato's theory of Forms) since the expression of goodness and powers of knowledge in human beings are always imperfect, they suggest that there is a totally benevolent and omniscient Being, of whose goodness and wisdom the human expressions are an inadequate reflection, but after which they aspire.

From this wide-ranging argument let us concentrate on the second emphasis, causation, which seems pivotal in Aquinas's presentation. The issue is basically straightforward: our observation of the world indicates to us that, without exception, everything that happens or comes into being does so as a result of some antecedent cause. Nothing happens spontaneously, even though our knowledge is sometimes so inadequate that we cannot give a complete scientific account of certain happenings. We may describe an idea as coming to us 'out of the blue', or a person's fear of mice or of men as 'irrational', but we may feel confident that eventually the causes of these will be known, that these causes are discoverable. (I am deliberately avoiding as too complex and wide-ranging for this discussion the *chaos* theory in physics – the notion of a-causality.)

If, then, we agree (as surely we must) that, say, footprints don't just 'appear' in the sand, isn't it just an extension of this observation to reflect in the same way about the universe around us? By the logical extension of the argument, someone or something must have been responsible for its coming into existence. The philosophers I've named, along with

many others, offer 'God' as the (shorthand, if you like) answer to that
conundrum. He is the cause of its coming into existence, whenever or
however this happened. In the words of the first verse of the Bible: 'In
the beginning God created the heavens and the earth.'

In a way, this is an extension of the ontological argument, since it is
positing the view that God, or whatever we call Him, is logically necessary
(and you may have spotted in Aquinas's third mode a point very close to
that later made by Descartes). Even the most simple of minds demands
an answer something like this, whether this demand be expressed by a
child who asks 'Who made the stars?' or 'Where did I come from?' or by
a humble peasant who finds it natural to hold an unsophisticated belief in
an all-powerful Creator.

One problem with the cosmological argument is that it suffers from
over-simplification in its terms of reference. 'The universe' is too vague a
term to handle, since we are in fact dealing with three quite distinct questions. (1) How did matter originate? (2) How did life begin? (3) How did
the human mind (the psyche) come into being? The quotation from Genesis
just given refers to the first of these questions (which is fundamental, since
the other two follow from it, chronologically if not logically) and declares
that matter, 'the heavens and the earth', came into being out of nothing
through the agency of the Almighty who, being omnipotent, can perform
whatever He wills. (I leave aside any discussion of whether this includes the
'impossible', such as making a square ring, or two twos into five, except to
say that if a square ring were made we should simply call it a square, and
if two twos made five then we should use the word 'five' to mean what
we presently mean by 'four'.) The obvious next step in the cosmological
argument is to ask: who made God? since we began by accepting as
true the statement that nothing comes into being without a cause.

Here the apologists for the argument close the discussion, and theology
takes over from philosophy. Quite simply, God *is*: nothing caused Him –
he is 'the uncaused First Cause'. In the words of St Anselm, which sound
marvellous in Greek: *Ou'k e'n pote o'te ou'k e'n, kai ou'k e'sthe pote o'te ou'k
e'sthe*, 'There never was a time when He was not and there never will
be a time when He will not be.' Here we can only throw up our hands,
whether in despair or surrender, since we have arrived at an issue beyond
the confines of the human mind: the meaning of space and time.

Our unchanging experience of these is one of limitation. For us, things
have a beginning, a middle and an end, whether we are speaking
geographically or chronologically. The idea that something, whether
matter or spirit, never had a beginning is simply unfathomable. The
'steady state' theory of the universe, expounded by Professor Fred Hoyle
in his 1950s book *The Nature of the Universe*, in which he argued the case
for 'continuous creation' and the eternal existence of matter in some form,
is just as 'impossible' as is the argument of St Anselm. This point was

expressed by Kant in his *Critique of Pure Reason*. In it, he indicated what he believed to be the fallacy of our equating our subjective experience of space, matter and time with their actual reality – a process which, he argued, leads us to accept two quite contradictory accounts of these at once. We can, for instance, argue equally conclusively and equally logically either that matter had no beginning or that it had a beginning; equally logically, both of these are impossible. Nothing can be made from nothing, therefore matter must have always existed; but if it always existed, where did it come from? Matter *must* have had a beginning – everything does – but it *cannot* have had a beginning – where were its elements before it began? Aristotle expressed the dilemma succinctly: 'What comes to be must do so either from what is, or from what is not, both of which are impossible.' Equally, 'God' is both essential and impossible.

At this stage I'm going to call a halt to this discussion and turn elsewhere. If you follow this line for too long, you're likely to find yourself becoming deeply uneasy if not totally disoriented – and the contributions made by the quantum theory of physics, which seems to require us to abandon even the comforting security of our interpretation of the nature of matter ('matter is neither created nor destroyed in the course of a chemical reaction') and of logic ('a thing cannot both be and not be at the same time'), have naught for our comfort. When we turn to consider Eastern approaches to ontology (and so reorientate ourselves, perhaps) we shall discover that they found little of value in such discussion, simply because it led to this dead end.

## THE TELEOLOGICAL ARGUMENT

An argument which, on the face of it, seems open to debate without stretching the mind beyond its limits is the argument from design – the so-called *teleological* argument (from *telos*, meaning 'end', or 'purpose'). As we observe the universe, so the argument goes, and as we perceive humanity's existence on this planet, the picture presented to us is one of order, not chaos, purposiveness, not aimlessness. There are certain laws of nature which are constant, and certain elements in *homo sapiens* which suggest the completion of a plan. For example, so far as matter is concerned, the laws of motion ensure that a body will move constantly in a particular direction until affected by an encounter with another body, and the law of gravity ensures that bodies attract each other: so the speeds of light and sound remain constant, and the solar system, with its fixedness of planetary orbits around the sun, ensures that we on earth are unlikely to be either frozen or fried in the near future. On the microscale this impression of design is equally strong. Even, say, the eye of a moth contains millions of cells working together co-operatively to ensure that the creature receives the light it needs for its particular existence; and the infinitely greater complexity of human parts must, when reflected on (and familiarity discourages us from doing this very often), create in us an even greater sense of awe. The evidence of such design suggests, so the argument goes, the existence of a designer, in the sense both of a craftsman and of One with an end in view. The universe, in short, looks as though it was planned; the implication of that is that someone planned it; and the teleological argument offers God as the One who intended it all.

At first sight this is a strong argument which common sense suggests we can accept without undue misgivings. There are, however, three cautionary considerations to be pondered on before taking the teleological plunge. First, the question arises of whether, in speaking of the order in the universe and the consistency of the 'laws' of nature, we are doing any more than simply *describing* matter. After all, by the very fact of existing it must have certain properties; that is to say, there must be certain ways in which it characteristically behaves. It has, for example, mass and energy, which relate to each other in a particular way. If it didn't possess *these* properties it would have others, so that we should be perceiving a different universe (one in which we should again be able to perceive order, though a different kind of order). It would be odd, even absurd, if matter existed but had no properties: in fact it would not just be odd but self-contradictory, equivalent to saying that matter did not exist at all in the sense that we are using the word 'exist' in this context (that is, it is empirically observable). That bodies tend to attract one another is a property of bodies; if it were not so, then there would be no interconnecting, coherent universe. The phrase 'laws of nature', which some describe as 'laws of God' (an important point to which I shall return later), should therefore be seen as as *description* of how matter behaves. One may, if one wishes, proceed from that to take a *prescriptive* stance and present the hypothesis of a lawgiver but one could also say, with an equal amount of justification, that matter possesses these properties simply by being: its being and its properties are one, even though they can be discussed separately.

The second cautionary consideration concerns the alleged complexity of life, even in its humblest forms. Since Darwin and the study of evolution this argument has decreased in force, except among those who hold a creationist view of life (that is, they believe that all that exists was created by a unique expression of omnipotence at one identifiable point in time). The evolutionary theory presents the view that as differing species developed gradually over millions of years they underwent a constant process of modification: no single offspring was or is exactly like its parents. In this process, the features most likely to be reproduced in the offspring were those which gave them most chance of survival in their particular environment – speed in an antelope, sight in a hawk, and so on. (Those less endowed with these features would be easy prey to predators, and therefore likely to have less opportunity to reproduce their kind.) One might describe this process in teleological terms and state that the 'end' in view was survival: but this would not be using the word 'end' as elsewhere in the teleological argument, since the process did not involve any conscious choice by the parents of what should be passed on to the offspring. The end product, like, say, the eye of an octopus, may justly be described as miraculous (literally, something to wonder at) but the miracle can be appreciated just as fully and just as reasonably from a natural as from a supernatural perspective: there is no need to introduce 'the hand of God'. In fact it may well be viewed as being as dubious in this context as was its use by the Argentinian forward, Maradona, to explain the illegal goal he got away with in the 1986 world football cup finals ('The head was the head of Maradona, but the hand was the hand of God!').

The third consideration is effectively to question whether the evidence confronting us, in both the world in general and humanity in particular, gives us genuine grounds for upholding a theory of a perfect Creator with a divine plan. It seems difficult, even on logical grounds, to conceive of a perfect Being's making or doing anything imperfect: yet this the universe and *homo sapiens* manifestly are. No human being is physically perfect at any point in life, still less intellectually so; and what faculties a human being does possess decline with age. Furthermore, if we start with the premiss, which I discussed earlier, that this Being is not only omnipotent but also all-loving (a central feature of theistic thought), we are then faced with the problem of explaining, as opposed to explaining away, the evil that is to be found in His creation: the diseases which wrack and destroy body and mind, the natural disasters which abruptly terminate lives without respect of persons, the wholesale manifest injustice which pervades this so-called product of love.

Apologists for the theistic view of God have suggested all manner of reasons to straighten out this apparent anomaly: humanity has brought evil on itself by its own free choices, evil forces are constantly at work seeking to undermine God's will, suffering is a test of character, and so on. The most frequently presented apologia is that evil seems evil only because of humanity's blinkered perspective: if it could see as God sees, it would understand and cease to question. Like soldiers on a route march who can't see the point of climbing up and down a mountain when there's a straightforward path round it, so are men and women when they question God's handiwork; and just as the soldiers would be silenced if they knew that the straightforward path was in fact infested with plague, so would men and women be silenced if they could glimpse God's overall plan.

This argument seems to me to be a cop-out: I can judge only by what I experience and if what I experience offers me no evidence of a master designer, much less a loving one, then I must speak accordingly. As David Hume remarked in his *Dialogues Concerning Natural Religion*, anyone who accepts the argument from design can conclude only 'that the universe, sometime, arose from something like design: but beyond this position he cannot ascertain one single circumstance, and is left afterwards to fix every point of his theology, by the utmost licence of fancy and hypothesis'. It seems reasonable, and fair, to say that if there were a God with all the characteristics attributed to Him by theists, we are left in a blind alley. Either God *could* improve matters but *will* not, or He *wills* to improve things but *cannot*. If the former hypothesis were true, this God would be a monster; if the latter, impotent. God's omnipotence and His benevolence cannot, so far as human understanding and experience are concerned, coexist in His nature. (That many theists recognize and are deeply worried by the force of this argument is illustrated in the thinking of Bishop John Robinson, of *Honest to God* fame (see Chapter 6). In a later book, *Explorations into God*, he suggested that theism was inadequate as a theory of the Godhead, and must be replaced with 'panentheism', or 'all in God' – a kind of mixture of theism and pantheism: but more of this later.)

## THE MORAL ARGUMENT

Immanuel Kant rejected (respectfully) all these philosophical arguments for the existence of God, for reasons similar to (but more comprehensively argued, of course) those presented here. In their place he proposed an argument based on the moral law. 'The only theology of reason which is possible,' he wrote in *The Critique of Pure Reason*, 'is that which is based on moral laws or seeks guidance from them.' Reason may cause us to form an idea of God, but cannot give any proof that there is any connection between this idea and reality. For this we need to fall back on our experience of right and wrong, which Kant believed to be based on an absolute which needed no defending, since it was universal: the sense of duty. 'Act only on that maxim,' he said in his famous so-called categorical imperative, 'that thou shouldst at the same time will it to be universal law.' This moral sense, he argued, is not relative to people, places, or situations. It stands alone, unchallengeable; and it is, so Kant suggested, God's presence in our midst, and all who are honest in describing their experience when making a moral decision will testify both to the fact and the strength of its existence. He concluded his *Critique of Practical Reason* with these often-quoted words:

> Two things fill the mind with ever-increasing wonder and awe, the more often and the more intensely the mind of thought is drawn to them: the starry heavens above me and the moral law within me.

He maintained that the strength of the moral law could be explained only as the presence of God, who is a moral God (or, we might even say, who *is* morality) in our midst.

It is the spirit of God, which gives the moral law its prevailing strength, by which I mean an inner moral life which is not possible purely on the basis of natural law. All moral good within us is the effect of the Spirit of God.

We need not question the validity of the evidence presented by Kant in this argument. Many people, perhaps all people except psychopaths and others suffering from mental sickness, at some time experience the sense of a moral imperative, and find it hard to explain why they feel as they do. But the strength of their conviction does not, I submit, require any kind of supernatural explanation. If the theory of evolution is, in its fundamentals, sound, then the strength of moral conviction can be viewed as relating, like everything else we do, according to the theory, to *survivability*. On this basis it could be said that certain forms of behaviour such as consideration for others, treating people fairly, self-control, compassion and so on (in Darwin's word, co-operation) are desirable forms of conduct because, on the whole, they are less likely to bring about the demise of the human race than are their opposites – malevolence, inequality, injustice, unrestricted violence and so on. If these qualities had been consciously allowed to become the dominant features in human behaviour, would any community have ever been able to survive, or two communities coexist equably? Would any two people have ever dared to sleep together? Murders and wars happen, of course, but are universally condemned except by those such as arms manufacturers who have a vested interest in their continuation. It could be argued that the same reason why I interrupted an earlier part of this chapter to visit a friend in distress was that I was doing my God-given duty, whatever I may personally feel on the matter. It could be said with equal validity that I acted as I did because, if ever I were in his predicament, I would hope that someone would do the same for me.

## THEISM AND THE VIEW OF MAN

It seems axiomatic that any kind of belief in a God who has all the attributes outlined earlier must influence the believer's views on the central issues of this book. For a start, if God created us, then we are His creatures; and if we are creatures of God, it follows that He is likely to have views about how we should be conducting ourselves, and of what our future prospects are. This is in fact the core of the sacred writings of the three theistic religions that I've mentioned, and I'll illustrate this with reference to all three of them.

The central theme of the Jewish sacred writings, the Old Testament, is that the Children of Israel, the Jews, are called to be the chosen people of God. He has revealed Himself to them as to no other people: to the fathers, Abraham, Isaac and Jacob; to Moses as he led them to the Promised

Land; and through the prophets, such as Amos, Isaiah and Jeremiah, who prepared them for the coming of the Messiah, the anointed One of God. With his advent, the Kingdom of God would be established on earth, and the Jewish people would be revealed as God's elect, a nation serving as 'a light to lighten the gentiles' (meaning everyone except the Jews). The central message of the Old Testament is 'They shall be my people, and I will be their God' (Jeremiah 32.38). Among modern Jews there are differences of opinion about the advent of the Messiah, but strict Jews still put their trust in the promises of old, and await his coming.

The whole image is epitomized in the idea of a *covenant* between God (Jehovah or, more strictly, Jahweh: the Hebrew means 'I am' or 'I am that I am': a fascinating ontological reference to which I shall later return) and His people ('testament' means 'covenant'). He on His part promises them His guidance, His protection, and, ultimately, their being crowned with glory; in return, they covenant themselves to remain faithful to Him: to observe His Commandments, keep His laws and worship Him alone. This belief in their own uniqueness has sustained the Jews through three millenniums of assaults by other nations and races; it has also separated them from other people with a greater finality than is to be found between any two other nations.

The idea of the covenant was carried forward into the religion which, though rooted in Judaism, soon spread around the Mediterranean and beyond, and became a catholic religion in the basic sense of that word (*kata holos*, 'through all'): Christianity. In the writings of the New Testament (New Covenant) the belief is expressed that the promised Messiah has come in the form of Jesus of Nazareth. Because the Jews as a nation failed to acknowledge his Messiahship, they have forfeited the right to be God's chosen people. This right has now been given to the followers of Jesus, and can be appropriated by all, of whatever nation, who accept his Messiahship: the accident of birth is no longer relevant. Thus the Christian Church (the Greek word is *ekklesia*, meaning 'called out') is the New Israel, and its basic creed is summarized acrostically in the Greek word *ichthus*, meaning 'fish'. (Visitors to the catacombs in Rome, where early Christians took refuge during Nero's persecutions, will have seen the sign of a fish scratched on the walls.) The Greek letters of *ichthus* when spelt out are: iota, chi, theta, upsilon and sigma, the first letters of *iesus, christos, theos, uios* and *soter*, meaning Jesus, Christ (Greek for Messiah), God, Son, and Saviour. The symbol of the fish was thus remarkably effective, serving not only as a distinctive sign (like a swastika, or the CND symbol) but also as a basic expression of belief, like the Chinese T'ai Chi-T'u, the diagram of the supreme ultimate, illustrating the Yang and the Yin (see Chapter 7). Thus Jesus is central to Christianity in a way not shared by any of the Old Testament figures. He is even described in John's Gospel as the *logos*, a word taken from Greek philosophy, akin to the Platonic idea of the Form of man; Jesus is 'the word made flesh', the Ideal incarnate (John 1.1–14).

This centrality of one person is also to be found in the last of the theistic religions to appear on the world scene, Islam. Its popular name in the West is Muhammadanism; Muslims object to this, but it reflects the unique role of the Prophet in Islamic consciousness. It does not go so far as to deify Muhammad as Christians have deified Jesus, but devotion to him is at least as firm as the Christian devotion to Jesus. The basic affirmation of Islamic faith is 'There is no God but Allah, and Muhammad is His Prophet'. As with both Judaism and Christianity, Islam teaches obedience to the will of God as the essential and basic feature of life among the faithful (Islam means 'surrender'). They must keep Allah's laws as revealed by the Prophet (who is alleged to have written the whole of the Koran, the Islamic sacred book); and they in their turn will inherit their reward. The Koran is more explicit about the reward for fidelity than either the Old or New Testaments. There is an earthiness about the Koran's description of paradise which give it an appeal south, as well as north, of the navel (see case study 9).

THEISM AND DUALISM

Where, then, in respect to the doctrine of the soul, does theism differ from dualism? Surely, it may be argued, the theistic view of existence is along Platonic lines. Don't they both teach that this life is a preparation for another, better, life in heaven, or paradise, or the ideal world – call it what you will? Are they not both united in affirming that the corporeal part of us – the body – is temporal, while the spiritual part of us – the soul – is immortal, indestructible? Should we not have therefore saved ourselves a chapter and dealt with dualism and theism under one heading, even if two subsections may have been needed?

The answer to these last three questions is no, no and no, respectively: certainly so far as Judaism is concerned, probably so far as Christianity is concerned, and to a certain extent so far as Islam is concerned. I must stress here that I'm basing what I have to say on the classical scriptures of these three religions, not on their developments over the centuries, which have often expressed fundamental departures from the ideas expressed originally. There is no question, for instance, that most Christians today, if asked their view, as Christians, on the soul, would express a belief in its immortality; and if we search carefully enough through the scriptures we shall no doubt find occasional texts which justify this assumption. The question, however, is whether this is the main emphasis of the whole Bible, and this is manifestly not the case. The Old Testament speaks of the realities of this world, not those of heaven. The Kingdom of God under the rule of the Messiah is to be

*here*: the Promised Land is tangible, its latitudes and longitudes known.
So far as life after death is concerned, all that can be looked forward to
– if that is the right phrase: it is never mentioned in the Old Testament
except with a sense of gloom – is *Sheol*, a grey, shadowy state which
may, just, be described as existence, but certainly not as life. The only
hope for immortality in classical Judaism is through one's offspring –
'through your seed and their seed for ever'. Hence the Jewish emphasis
on the importance of the family; and hence the commandment not to
commit adultery: the male had to be sure that the children his wife bore
him were his, not just because of the strength of the pair bond (there is
nothing distinctively Jewish about that) but because they represented his
hopes for the future after his death.

What then of the New Testament? It certainly expresses a stronger hope
about 'the life everlasting' than is to be found in the Old Testament. Just
before his death, Jesus spoke of 'going to prepare a place' for his disciples;
his resurrection is a (some would say *the*) central theme of the Gospels and
Epistles; and the last book of all, the Revelation of St John, speaks of 'a
new heaven and a new earth'. The point at issue here, however, is not
whether a belief in the life beyond is expressed in the New Testament –
of course it is – but whether, as the Platonic doctrine of the immortality
of the soul affirms, it is *available to all*, and whether it is experienced
*immediately after the death of the body*.

If the soul is immortal, then clearly the resolution of both these questions
is brought about affirmatively. If it is part of our human nature that we
possess an indestructible element, then logically this must be the case
for all human beings; equally logically, it cannot be subject to periods
of non-existence. Yet the emphasis throughout the whole of the New
Testament is that heaven will be available only to those who, through
faith in Jesus, have won for themselves a share in the triumph of his
resurrection; and even for these the joys will not be experienced until
'the end of the world', or 'consummation of the age', as the Greek can
also be translated. This concept is expressed definitively in Paul's first
letter to the Corinthians (15. 51f):

Behold, I shew you a mystery; we shall not all sleep, but we shall all
be changed, in a moment, in the twinkling of an eye, at the last trump:
for the trumpet shall sound, and *the dead shall be raised* incorruptible.
(italics added)

This sounds like a long wait, but for those who first read those words this
was far from the case. Like all the New Testament writers, they believed
that the end of the world and the winding-up of the present order were
imminent – that it would in fact happen in their lifetime. (Only when
we appreciate that this was a basic consideration and perspective of these

writings can we begin to understand either Christian theology, Christian ethics, or early Church history. See **Albert Schweitzer** *The Quest of the Historical Jesus*.)

The idea may be expressed at funerals today that the dead person is already in heaven, but that is a Platonic rather than a theistic view (at least as this is expressed in the religions under consideration). The Christian message was that after death there follows an indeterminate period of 'sleep' – unconsciousness, non-existence. Some will be 'woken' from that sleep (and as after any period of sleep, the waking moment will seem like the next moment after falling asleep); others, it seems, are never to be wakened. There is absolutely no clear line in theistic teaching about what happens to non-believers, or to those who disobey the will of God. For some there will be salvation after a period in purgatory; for others, perpetual torment; for others, the cessation of existence. The main point to note is that this new resurrected life is not for all. And the moment you affirm that even just one soul, or person, has been destroyed for ever, you have denied the doctrine of the immortality of the soul. (If, on the other hand, your belief in God's omnipotence leads you to affirm that in the end *all* souls will be saved, you risk removing the need to do something about obeying God's will *now*.)

A further difference between theism and Platonic dualism is to be found in their different views of the significance of the body. As we have seen, Plato held this to be of little importance, and his view is aptly summed up in his phrase *soma sema* (p. 20). The Bible, in contrast, has an infinitely more optimistic view of the body. In the Old Testament it is viewed as the container and focal point of all the emotions, noble or otherwise. The heart is the source of love, there is fire in the bones and passion in the blood (all our Western metaphors here are taken from this Semitic connection). We even have the bowels as an expression of outpouring, as in the phrase 'God's bowels of mercy'. Only familiarity with these images blinds us to their incredible vividness (see case study 7). In the New Testament the body is described as 'the temple of the Holy Spirit'; the Church is 'the Body of Christ'; and St Paul even uses the phrase 'spiritual bodies', which would have been as meaningless to Plato as it is to modern linguistic analysts. Mortification of the flesh has never been a central feature of theistic beliefs as it has been in some extreme expressions of Eastern philosophy such as Jainism (see Chapter 7). There have been Christian ascetics, such as Simeon Stylites and the so-called 'pillar saints' who spent their last months or even years meditating on top of a pole: but while these men had followers, they did not have many imitators, and their view of the total insignificance of the body has always been peripheral to the main emphases of theism. In fact, whenever the Christian Creed is recited, what is affirmed is a belief in 'the resurrection of the *body*': only after this, and not because of an immortal soul, does one proceed to enjoy 'the life everlasting'.

The New Testament makes a distinction between body (*soma*) and flesh (*sarx*). This latter word is always used disparagingly, that part of man and woman through which evil-doing is expressed. Vices such as greed, hatred and lust may have their roots in the mind but express themselves through the physical parts, by theft or exploitation, by acts of violence, by drunkenness, gluttony, or rape. The New Testament abounds with warnings not to let the body become prey to the desires of the flesh (see case study 19).

## ASSESSMENT OF THE THEISTIC VIEW OF HUMAN NATURE

Although, then, there are certain connecting links between dualism as expressed by Plato and theism as expressed in at least two of the major theistic religions, there are significant differences. For Plato, the immortality of the soul was central, and the idea of God peripheral. In theism, the reverse is the case. One could declare oneself a dualist on Plato's terms without in fact believing in God – not, at any rate, the God whose attributes have been outlined here (though the implications of that concession are important, and will be pursued in Chapter 6). Equally, it is possible, as in classical Judaism and a good deal of classical Christianity, to believe in God without believing in the immortality of the soul.

In fact, belief in God is more likely to occur when there is no belief in the immortality of the soul. Reflect on this for a moment. If you believe that your soul is immortal, so that, no matter what you do or believe in this life, it will make no difference to the certainty of your survival beyond the grave, is there not considerably less motivation or inducement to believe in God, whose main function is seen as that of creating the opportunity for survival for some of His creatures, on certain terms? That function is superfluous if the reward is automatically available for all. So, while many people have combined the two beliefs, the end product of Platonic dualism is to make God redundant, in logic if not in everybody's experience. (See case study 16 for an analysis of why people have maintained a belief in some kind of God.) Let us be quite clear on this matter: the dominant doctrine of theism, as expressed in the Bible and the Koran, is the sovereignty of God. He alone has the power and the authority to ensure that our destinies extend beyond the grave. This is no natural right, as in Platonic dualism (though 'process' would be an apter word than 'right' in this context): what is to become of us lies in God's hands; immortality is His gift to bestow.

It is here, I think, that the ontological inadequacies of theism are exposed and, with these, the unfortunate (some would say disastrous) consequences for many of those who have followed in the direction it leads. As we have seen, it establishes two modes of being: one is independent, uncaused, its essence involving its existence; the other consists of finite beings which do not necessarily exist of themselves, but must be caused to exist, and to continue to exist after first being brought into existence. The consequence of this has been that where theism has been the dominant doctrine of a community, people have lived more as servants than as autonomous beings. Their behaviour has been expressed as obedience to God's will as stated in their sacred writings; and these in turn have, generally speaking, been interpreted for them by their religious leaders – the elders and priests, not all of whom have held altruistic feelings towards their followers. In the hands of many of them, the scriptures have become special constables' handbooks, treated as an end in themselves rather than as guides along the way, often used by the unscrupulous few to control the gullible or impotent many (see case study 8).

Not all the consequences of this have been *bad*, of course: millions of theists have lived 'godfearing' lives in equanimity and with benevolence towards others. Nietzsche's words in *The Antichrist* – 'I call Christianity the one great curse, the one enormous and innermost perversion . . . the one immortal blemish of mankind' – will seem to even the most ardent critic of theism an overstatement, if only for its singling-out of Christianity uniquely for this castigation. But the pure fear induced in many worshippers through a sense of guilt, brought about by the suspicion that somewhere along the line, by their ideas, their words, or their actions, they have incurred God's wrath and so have lost the chance of gaining a heavenly reward, is too frequently found in religious writings (and in psychiatrists' surgeries) to be ignored. And alongside this fear the phenomenon of religious intolerance *has* found expression for three thousand years, an intolerance born of the determination to bring to nothing those whose claim to absolute truth rivals one's own. It is difficult to avoid the conclusion that over the centuries the minuses of theism outnumber the pluses.


*Case study 7*
*Biblical use of physical organs to express emotion*

It was suggested in the text that the Semites made no distinction between physiology and psychology and that the Bible often vividly illustrates this. Below are texts quoted from the Old Testament (in the Authorized Version) which illustrate this. Having perused them, ask yourself (yourselves) the following questions:

1   Do any of the connections between the physical and the emotional seem out of place, inapposite, or tasteless?

2   How far do you think the reference to the physical organ gives added piquancy to the point of view being expressed?

3 To what extent do you think our own language has been pervaded by this type of metaphor? (An example is 'the mouth of a river'; but is not that an example of coyness in not naming the part of the body from which excretion occurs?) See if you can come up with other examples of such euphemisms.

4 Does the connection made by the Semites seem to you in any way linked with our modern understanding of psychosomatic disorders? Can you think up any examples of how people change psychologically because of physical change, and vice versa?

5 Assuming your knowledge of the Old Testament is up to it, see if you can find examples of other organs which are given a similar treatment.

6 How do you think people with this view of psychology are likely to be influenced in their view of human nature?

(1) The bowels
  (a) 'My heart is like wax; it is melted in the midst of my bowels.' (Psalm 22.14)
  (b) 'Mine eyes do fail with tears, my bowels are troubled.' (Lamentations 2.11)
  (c) 'They shall not satisfy their souls, neither fill their bowels.' (Ezekiel 7.19)

(2) The belly
  (a) 'Mine eye is consumed with grief, yea, my soul and my belly.' (Psalm 31.9)
  (b) 'God shall cast them out of his belly.' (Job 20.15)
  (c) 'When I heard, my belly trembled.' (Habakkuk 3.16)

(3) The bones
  (a) 'Rottenness entered into my bones.' (Habakkuk 3.16)
  (b) 'His word was in mine heart as a burning fire shut up in my bones.' (Jeremiah 20.9)
  (c) 'A soft tongue breaketh the bone.' (Proverbs 25.15)

(4) The blood
  (a) 'Precious shall their blood be in his sight.' (Psalm 72.14)
  (b) 'Thy mother is like a vine in thy blood.' (Ezekiel 19.10)
  (c) 'I will take away his blood out of his mouth.' (Zechariah 9.7)

(5) The womb
  (a) 'The womb shall forget him; the worm shall feed sweetly on him.' (Job 24.20)

    (b)  'Ephraim is smitten . . . yet will I slay even the beloved fruit of their womb.' (Hosea 9.16)

    (c)  'Blessings of the breasts, and of the womb.' (Genesis 49.25)

(6)  The heart

    (a)  'His heart was merry, he went to lie down.' (Ruth 3.7)

    (b)  'God gave Solomon . . . largeness of heart.' (I Kings 4.29)

    (c)  'Where is he, that durst presume in his heart to do so?' (Esther 7.5)

(7)  The eye

    (a)  'Thine eye shall have no pity upon them.' (Deuteronomy 7.16)

    (b)  'My soul was precious in thine eyes.' (I Samuel 26.21)

    (c)  'Do ye to them as is good in your eyes.' (Genesis 19.8)

(8)  The ear

    (a)  'He openeth also their ear to discipline.' (Job 36.10)

    (b)  'Mine ears hast thou opened.' (Psalm 40.6)

    (c)  'Behold, their ear is uncircumcised, and they cannot hearken.' (Jeremiah 6.10)

(9)  The nose, the nostrils

    (a)  'The spirit of God is in my nostrils.' (Job 27.3)

    (b)  'Therefore will I put my hook in thy nose, and my bridle in thy lips.' (Isaiah 37.29)

    (c)  'They shall take away thy nose and thine ears.' (Ezekiel 23.25)

(10)  The bosom

    (a)  'My prayer returned into mine own bosom.' (Psalm 35.13)

    (b)  'Anger resteth in the bosom of fools.' (Ecclesiastes 7.9)

    (c)  'I . . . will recompense . . . into their bosom your iniquities.' (Isaiah 65.6)

(11)  The breasts

    (a)  'Thou shalt . . . pluck off thine own breasts . . . saith the Lord God.' (Ezekiel 23.34)

    (b)  'Thou . . . shalt suck the breast of kings.' (Isaiah 60.16)

    (c)  'His breasts are full of milk.' (Job 21.24)

(12)  The tongue

    (a)  'Every tongue that shall rise against thee.' (Isaiah 54.17)

    (b)  'I am slow of speech, and of a slow tongue.' (Exodus 4.10)

    (c)  'Destroy, O Lord, and divide their tongues.' (Psalm 55.9)

(13)  The teeth

    (a)  'I am escaped with the skin of my teeth.' (Job 19.20)

(b) 'They hiss and gnash the teeth.' (Lamentations 2.16)

(c) 'I also have given you cleanness of teeth.' (Amos 4.6)

(14) The lips

(a) 'How then shall Pharaoh hear me, who am of uncircumcised lips?' (Exodus 6.12)

(b) 'The lips of the righteous feed many.' (Proverbs 10.21)

(c) 'I am a man of unclean lips.' (Isaiah 6.5)

(15) The feet

(a) 'How beautiful . . . are the feet of him that bringeth good tidings.' (Isaiah 52.7)

(b) 'I . . . turned my feet unto thy testimonies.' (Psalm 119.59)

(c) 'He speaketh with his feet.' (Proverbs 6.13)

(16) The thighs

(a) 'He halted upon his thigh.' (Genesis 32.31)

(b) 'He smote them hip and thigh.' (Judges 15.8)

(c) 'I smote upon my thigh: I was ashamed.' (Jeremiah 31.19)

(17) The loins

(a) 'Lo now, his strength is in his loins.' (Job 40.16)

(b) 'She girdeth her loins with strength.' (Proverbs 31.17)

(c) 'I will loose the loins of kings.' (Isaiah 45.1)

(18) Various

(a) 'He taketh not pleasure in the legs of a man.' (Psalm 147.10)

(b) 'Their throat is an open sepulchre.' (Psalm 5.9)

(c) 'My liver is poured upon the earth.' (Lamentations 2.11)

(d) 'The iniquity of my heels shall compass me about.' (Psalm 49.5)

(e) 'The knees smite together.' (Nahum 2.10)

(f) 'It shall be health to thy navel.' (Proverbs 3.8)

*Case study 8*
*Religious education (RE) in schools*

The following letter was written by a parent to the governors of a high school in Bristol, England, concerning her child, who was a pupil at the school. Under the 1944 Education Act, which was still in force at that time, RE was a compulsory subject in the syllabus of state schools (this compulsory element remained in the Bill which replaced it). The theme of the letter is self-explanatory; read it and debate the questions that follow.

Dear Sirs – It is after a great deal of thought and consideration that, under the 1944 Education Act, I choose to exercise my parental right to withdraw my child from Religious Indoctrination. This will remain my choice until such time as Religious Indoctrination is replaced with philosophy and ethics.

It is not a decision I have taken lightly or in ignorance, but is one that is based on what I see my child is being taught on the subject. Instead of encouraging her to think, to investigate, and to use her reason, as she is in subjects such as science and mathematics, she is being taught to BELIEVE. Superstitions, beliefs, and theories should not be taught like demonstrated facts, and in any case alternative theories and beliefs should be offered, which they are not.

When you teach my child the Biblical account of Creation, will you also teach her that it is only one of many Creation myths?

In teaching her to believe the Biblical myth of Creation, how will you teach her to equate such a myth with geological findings and astronomical discoveries that conclusively prove the world and humanity to be far, far older than the writers of the Bible could ever have dreamed? How will she equate the marginal dates in the Bible, that give the date of Creation as being 4004 BC, with modern knowledge? Will you tell her that in making his calendrical calculations, Archbishop Ussher made some mistakes, and that these mistakes, along with thousands of others in the Good Book, have not yet been eradicated?

When you teach my child the Biblical account of Creation that says God made the world in five days, that on the sixth day He made man, and on the seventh day He rested, will you also tell her that this order of events is flatly contradicted in the second version as written in Genesis chapter 2?

Will you tell her that, according to the second version, God first made Heaven and Earth. Then He made man. In third place came the Garden of Eden complete with the tree of knowledge of good and evil, which He then instructed man to avoid? Fourth came the forming of the beasts and fowl (which man is requested to name) and the fifth and apparently final act is the forming of woman from one of man's ribs, since it was 'not good that he should be alone'?

Will you teach her that, according to the second version, woman, by allegedly eating an apple, condemned the human race? Will you teach her that woman has been designated second place in society as a direct result of this appalling untruth?

Will you tell her that St Paul, that great Christian and founder of the Church, held women in such low esteem that he insisted (among other things) 'Let the woman learn in silence with all subjection. But I suffer not a woman to teach, nor to usurp authority over the man, but to be in silence. For Adam was first formed, then Eve. And Adam was not deceived, but the woman being deceived was in the transgression.

Notwithstanding she shall be saved in child-bearing, (x) if they continue in faith and charity and holiness with sobriety.'

Will you tell her that the early church fathers held the same misogynist views against women? Tertullian said, 'Thou art the devil's gate, the betrayer of the tree, the first deserter of the divine law!' St Jerome simplified by saying, 'Women is the root of all evil'. St Augustine wanted to know, 'Why was woman created at all?' And dear St Ambrose described woman as being 'more fitted for bodily work . . . Remember that God took a rib out of Adam's body, not part of his soul (y) to make her. She was not made to the image of God, like man.'

Will you tell my child that this atrocious attitude was endorsed by later church authorities? Anselm of Canterbury (c.1033–1109) shows his contemptuous loathing of women in his poem 'De Contemptu Mundi' ('Concerning Contempt for the World'). In it he wrote, 'Woman has a clear face and a lovely form, she pleases you not a little, this milk-white creature! But ah! if her bowels were opened and all the other regions of her flesh, what foul tissues would this white skin be shown to contain.'

Odun of Cluny went even further in his description; he asked who could wish to embrace 'ipsum stercoris saccum' which, loosely translated, means a stinking bag of manure.

This disgraceful attitude to women can quite clearly be traced back to an imaginary woman who ate an imaginary apple, and I can no longer sit back and accept such superstitious nonsense being taught to my child under the guise of Humanities when there is nothing remotely 'humanitarian' in the teaching at all.

(x) Are you aware, Sirs, that because of the passage in Genesis that states 'in sorrow thou shalt bring forth children' women, until quite recent times, were denied any form of pain relief in childbirth?

(y) For your interest, women were considered unworthy even of possessing souls until a vote was passed by a majority of three at the Council of Trent (1545–64).

May I know, Sirs, what you propose to offer my child in place of Religious Indoctrination?

Yours etc.

1 Assuming that the writer is correct in her facts, how would you react to this letter if you were:
   (a) her daughter's RE teacher;
   (b) a member of the teaching staff at the school;
   (c) the head teacher;
   (d) a member of the governing body of the school;
   (e) a parent of another child at the school;
   (f) an MP or congressman facing a new education bill which

proposes to maintain RE as a compulsory subject in state schools?

2    Should indoctrination – that is, the presentation of one set of religious beliefs as at least *primus inter pares* (first among equals) if not superior to all others – be disallowed in schools?

3    If so, should RE be abolished altogether? If you agree to this, where would you slot in the school curriculum the discussion of philosophical and ethical issues such as we are engaged on in this book? Must this go too?

4    Should children be taught all religious beliefs? If so, how can the teacher avoid confusing the children (especially the younger children) with the enormous range of contrasting perspectives?

5    Is worship of God, however imagined or described, as in British schools, at least healthier than the fervent nationalism instilled in American schools by the worship of the flag? Or is this a red herring?

*Case study 9*
*The Koran*

The holy book of the Muslims, the Koran, is, like the Bible, impossible to paraphrase. The best that can be done is to select a number of texts to reflect the teaching as a whole, bearing in mind that this teaching is based on the five basic Islamic edicts or tenets: the sovereignty of Allah, prayer (five times daily), almsgiving on an organized basis, fasting (one month in the year) and pilgrimage (once, at least, in a lifetime). The first thirteen quotations below reflect one or other of these emphases. As you read them see if you can come up with a text from the Bible (Old or New Testaments) which conveys a similar message. What does this tell you about these three theistic religions? Quotations 14 and 15 reflect a distinctive element in Islam: the virtue of Holy War. Do you think there is a parallel to these in any part of the Bible? Numbers 17–22 express the Islamic attitude to women, and will be the subject of a separate comment with questions at the end. All quotations are from Pickthall's translation.

(1)    'Mankind were once one nation. Then Allah sent forth prophets to give them good news and to warn them, and with these He sent down the Book and the Truth, that it might judge the disputes of man.' (2.213)

(2)    'This your religion is one religion and I am your Lord, so keep your duty unto me. But they have broken their religion among them into sects.' (23.52–3)

(3) 'Be ye staunch in justice, even though it be against yourselves or your parents or your kindred.' (4.135)

(4) 'Allah loveth the equitable. The believers are nought else than brothers. Therefore make peace with your brethren.' (49.9–10)

(5) 'Man is rebellious that he thinketh himself independent.' (96.6–7)

(6) 'Woe unto worshippers who are heedless of their prayer; who would be seen at worship yet refuse small kindnesses.' (107.4)

(7) 'Be charitable; Allah loves the charitable.' (2.195)

(8) 'Feed with food the needy wretch, the orphan and the prisoner, for love of Him, saying, "We feed you for the sake of Allah only. We wish for no reward or thanks from you."' (76.8–9)

(9) 'They ask you about what they should give in alms. Say, "What you can spare".' (2.215)

(10) 'If ye publish your alms-giving, it is well; but if ye hide it and give it to the poor, it will be better for you, and will atone for some of your ill-deeds.' (2.217)

(11) 'If ye lend unto Allah a goodly loan, He will double it for you and forgive you.' (64.17)

(12) 'None punisheth as He will punish on that day.' (89.25)

(13) 'Tell those who believe to forgive those who hope not for the days of Allah.' (45.14)

(14) 'Retaliation is prescribed for you in the matter of the murdered; the freeman for the freeman, and the slave for the slave, and the female for the female.' (2.178)

(15) 'Fight in the way of Allah against those who fight against you, but begin not hostilities. Lo! Allah Loveth not aggressors. And slay them wherever ye find them, and drive them out of the places whence they drove you, for persecution is worse than slaughter. And fight them until persecution is no more. But if they desist, then let there be no hostility, except against wrongdoers.' (2.190–1, 193)

(16) 'They ask you about drinking and gambling. Say, "There is great harm in both, although they may have some benefit for men; but their harm is greater than their benefit".' (2.214)

(17) 'Women are your fields: go then into your fields as you please.' (2.223)

(18) 'Men are the managers of the affairs of women . . . Righteous women are therefore obedient . . . And those you fear may be rebellious admonish; banish them to their couches, and beat them.' (438)

(19) 'Divorce must be pronounced twice and then a woman must be retained in honour or released in kindness . . . And if he hath divorced her the third time, then she is not lawful unto him thereafter until she hath wedded another husband.' (2.228–9)

(20) 'The adulterer and the adulteress, scourge ye each of them with 100 stripes. And let not pity for the twain withhold you from obedience to Allah. And let a party of believers witness this punishment. The adulterer shall not marry save an adulteress or an idolatress . . . And those who accuse honourable women but bring not four witnesses, scourge with 80 stripes and never accept their testimony. They indeed are evil-doers – save those who afterwards repent and make amends.' (24.2–5)

(21) 'My Lord forbiddeth indecencies.' (7.133)

(22) 'Tell the believing women to lower their gaze and be modest, and to draw their veils over their bosoms, and not to reveal their adornment save to their own husbands and fathers . . . or their women or their slaves or male attendants who lack vigour or children who know naught of women's nakedness. And let them not stamp their feet so as to reveal what they hide of their adornment.' (24.31)

The last six quotations reflect an attitude to women to and with which Western countries are increasingly unsympathetic if not actually repelled. It reflects, as we saw, a male-dominated society which in extremes treats women like cattle (in fact the Mujahideen in Afghanistan still tattoo their women like sheep, according to one reporter in a reputable British Sunday newspaper). But you may feel that there is more to it than this: the final quotation above seems frankly prurient, and suggests that those who pay attention to such detail are uncertain about their own powers of self-control. Further, if you read ahead into Chapter 4 (pp. 82–3), you will see the reference to the changing role of women in Western society which, it is suggested, could presage the next major evolutionary change in the human species. How far do you think that the Islamic tendency represents, therefore, a refusal to evolve (if that is not a contradiction in terms)?

# 4 Determinism: man in chains

The word 'determined' is one of many which have a connotation in philosophy different from that of common speech. When we describe a person as determined, we normally mean that he or she is strong-willed, obstinate, or pig-headed (which are all, of course, the same quality viewed from different perspectives). When we use the word in philosophy, we are referring not so much to the firmness or fixedness of a person's behaviour as to the fact that this is because of forces over which he or she has little or no control. These forces may operate from within or from outside but the effect, either way, is the same: the sense of freedom of choice, which many people claim to have concerning various decisions that they make, is a delusion: none of us is free to behave other than the way we do and, on a wider scale, all that takes place in the universe occurs because, and only because, of what took place antecedently. We exist in a fixed universe.

The diagram indicates the kind of syndrome I mean:

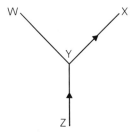

A person has, say, travelled along the path ZY and reaches the junction at Y. Among the possible next steps are the paths YX and YW (to which we could have added YT, YS and so on, according to the circumstances, but it will be valid to stick with just two alternatives). Assuming that the person follows the path YX, the determinist would argue that this was inevitable, granted that the route along ZY has already been followed. A choice other than YX could have been made if, and only if, ZY had been different. (It may be suggested that I have omitted the option of remaining put at Y. Leaving until the next chapter the question of whether, ontologically speaking, this is possible – that is, whether you can have being without also becoming – I would suggest that not to make a decision where options present themselves in this way is itself a decision, and should therefore be referred to as choice YP, or whatever.)

The opposite point of view is the belief in humanity's freedom of choice, whether in relation to moral behaviour, political opinion, sexual partner, or any other field where options seem to present themselves. This view is known in philosophy as *libertarianism*, and is another example of the difference between philosophical and common parlance. In common speech, a libertarian is one who does not seem to others to be strictly rule-governed, one who is anarchistic in his or her behaviour and, presumably, thinking. The word frequently refers to a person's sexual behaviour, but it can refer to the whole gamut of human behaviour. In philosophy, a libertarian is, quite simply, one who believes in the freedom of the will.

Over the centuries, the determinist position has been outlined in relation to a number of different areas of living, and with different degrees of comprehensiveness. In the subdivisions which follow, it will be seen that while some schools limit the determined factor in life to certain circumscribed areas, others spread the net much wider and in one case include even human thought processes. The libertarian view has also been expressed with varying degrees of absoluteness, but its general assertion is that, while there are certainly a number of mechanical forces which may be challenged but not overcome (to defy is not to defeat), there are areas where choice is possible, particularly in the moral field. In fact, so the libertarian argument goes, human beings are much more capable of making choices in a whole range of fields than many of them persuade themselves to be possible.

This last point is important. Both determinists and libertarians agree that there is a difference between the situation in the world as it actually obtains, and the situation as people conceive it to be. I may think that I am, on the whole, free to make whatever choices I do make: the determinist argument is that thereby I deceive myself. On the other hand, I may argue that 'I couldn't help' doing what I did because of factors over which I had no control; but the libertarian will describe such excuses as explaining away rather than explaining: personal responsibility for one's behaviour cannot be shed with a glib phrase.

A word here about the distinction between determinism and *fatalism*: this latter doctrine is the belief that the whole of the universe, together with every expression of life (which includes your life, and mine), is following a pre-set plan, rather as a computer is programmed to behave in a particular way. At no point can *anything* be changed: *que sera sera*. Actually, if we (for once) use logic on the matter, it is difficult to distinguish between this view and determinism *so far as the final outcome is concerned*. After all, to refer back to the diagram, if my choice YX is determined by ZY, then ZY was itself determined by the previous path (say CZ) and that one in turn by, say, EC, and so on *ad infinitum*. If we could return to the starting-point and then look forward in time, the outcome, while different in *emphasis* from that made by thoroughgoing fatalists (who view humanity as walking along an inescapable groove for the whole of life, on to its pre-ordained destiny) seems remarkably similar in *effect*. (See case study 11.)

In what follows, then, we study a variety of schools, in some of which the chains are looser (less determined) than in others, thus allowing individuals certain freedom to manoeuvre. But no determinist believes that these chains can all be broken.

## RELIGIOUS DETERMINISM: PREDESTINATION

Although it has never been more than a belief of a minority in the theistic religions (though Islam may be an exception), the concept of predestination has never been wholly unrepresented in any of them. The doctrine is based on the idea of God's sovereignty which, as we saw in the last chapter, is central in all theistic writings. Because this sovereignty is absolute, it follows that God must have chosen in advance those who are to gain the heavenly rewards already discussed. These favoured ones are known to Him, and nothing can alter their status (as nothing can change the fate of those doomed to damnation). One biblical passage which spells out this belief unambiguously is in Paul's letter to the Romans (8. 29f):

> For those whom he did foreknow, he also did predestinate to be conformed to the image of his Son . . . [And those] whom he did predestinate, them he also called; and whom he called, them he also justified; and whom he justified, them he also glorified. ['Justified' here means saved, or forgave.]

This theme was expressed with great clarity and directness by St Augustine, of Hippo in North Africa (354–430), probably the most famous of the early Church Fathers. He had become a bishop after having lived a 'worldly' kind of existence in his youth (he was the author of the famous prayer, beloved of theological students, 'Lord, make me pure: but not yet', for which much can be forgiven). About predestination he was adamant: only by God's initiative could anyone grow in moral or spiritual maturity; he himself believed that God had personally intervened in his life, and that He did so in the lives of others. When this happened, he averred, it was impossible for the recipient to hold out againstt him. God's 'grace', in a memorable phrase, was 'irresistible'. No human being had either the freedom or the power to *choose* what his response should be: the decision was final.

This idea is not unlike the fatalism expressed in the twelfth/thirteenth-century Persian poem, *The Rubaiyat of Omar Khayyam*:

> The Moving Finger writes; and having writ
> Moves on: nor all thy Piety nor Wit
> Shall lure it back to cancel half a Line,
> Nor all thy Tears wash out a Word of it.

The doctrine of predestination was given further clear and scholarly expression by the French Protestant reformer, John Calvin (1509–64). Like Augustine, his main concern was to preserve the sovereignty of God (which, in his case, was viewed as being threatened by the sovereignty of the Church of Rome). Accepting, as we must, he argued, that God is both omniscient and omnipotent: then, for a start, His perfect knowledge cannot logically exclude knowledge of events which lie ahead: past, present and future must all be included in His infinite wisdom. Hence He must know those who are to be 'saved' (and therefore, in terms of our theme, whose destiny is one of hope for the future life); and He must know this from the moment of their births or even, in fact, from the beginning of time. He must also know those who are to be damned eternally. Following from this, His omnipotence requires that the salvation or damnation of any individual happens in accordance with God's will. To say that He might *will* the damned to be saved but could not bring this about would be to deny His omnipotence.

The idea of God's creating people with the intention that they shall be damned eternally may seem harsh, even incomprehensible, to us, but since He is by definition the Author of what is right (whatever connotation we mortals may put on that word) it is not for us to question either His ways or His judgements. We may not understand, but that is quite beside the point: the decision in this, as in all things, is God's and God's alone; and, simply because it is *God's* decision, it is, by definition again, just. (An interesting question for discussion in the early hours – when verdicts are not heavy with significance – is whether it is better to have been created in order to be damned than never to have existed at all.)

Granted the premises, there is, it must be acknowledged, an awesome logic behind Calvin's teaching. The Church has been generally hostile to the idea, however, because it has recognized that to remove the idea of the freedom of the human will makes God – again using logic – directly responsible for all the evil in the world. From the philosophical point of view, the whole argument is *per se* a further reason for rejecting theism. (Historically, the contribution to human happiness made by predestinarians has been, in my view, in short supply: But that is another matter.)

## MECHANISTIC DETERMINISM: THE HUMAN RACE AS A SCIENTIFIC EXPERIMENT

This variation of determinism is the most comprehensive of all in its application. It is based on observation of the world around us, and proposes that what is true in the material world is also true of humanity. We know that matter breaks down into its constituent elements, the atoms, which are either inert or in motion. Inertia comes to an end, and motion in a particular direction changes, only as a result of energy exerted by other forms of matter in motion, which were themselves caused by antecedent physical factors, and so on *ad infinitum*. This may seem to the beginner to represent a relatively modern physical perspective, but in fact it is an ancient one, stretching back at least as far as the so-called atomists of fifth-century BC Greece. The most famous of these was Democritus (460–362), and his interpretation of the world was remarkably similar to that of modern physicists. Atoms, he declared, are in constant motion in the space between them and other atoms (a space which is, in proportion to the size of atoms, enormous); sometimes an atom collides with another atom, or a number of atoms collide, thus causing all concerned to change direction and form a different overall structure. In this scene, Democritus argued, there is no room for chance; all is determined, all has always been determined, and will remain so for ever.

Thus it is that the universe may be described as an enormous clockwork machine, behaving according to a set and unalterable process in which the word 'chance' reflects not the real state of affairs but only our limited appreciation of the infinite ramifications of the machine's components. If we had infinite knowledge we should know everything that would ever happen throughout the entire universe.

This image of a fixed universe was, not surprisingly, rejected by the Catholic philosophers. The idea of matter going its inexorable way towards it knows not what hardly conformed with the theistic image of a universe moving toward a goal appointed by the Deity; and the consequence was that until the time of the Renaissance a teleological interpretation was imposed over the atomistic theory. There is purpose in the universe, it was affirmed, and anyone denying this risked being charged with heresy. Thus the possibility of divine intervention was kept open: the stars might change in their courses, the sun might cease to give out light. But logically this seemed absurd, even to many in the Catholic fold, since it suggested that the Almighty might change His mind, which seems an odd way for an omniscient Being to behave. However, to be fair to the schoolmen, as these medieval philosophers are called, their main concern was to preserve a view of the universe as expressive of a benign plan, rather than one driven blindly forward by impersonal forces.

The final step of mechanistic determination was to include humanity and the workings of the human mind in the process. Following the scientific revolution of the Age of Enlightenment, numerous philosophers followed up the mechanistic emphasis to what seemed to be its logical conclusion. The English philosopher Thomas Hobbes (1588–1679) perhaps expressed this most directly. His most famous work, *Leviathan*, is basically a treatise on government, but it starts with a discussion on human nature. Hobbes suggested that man is in fact part of the universal mechanical process of cause and effect; this includes, he argued, not only bodily processes but also human psychology. Our thoughts, like our physical responses, are derived from sensations caused by external bodies on our sense organs ('stimuli'), which in their turn set up further reactions in us. Imagination and memory are two of the end products of these motions. 'All fancies are motions within us,' he wrote, 'relics of those made in the sense.'

Thus, Hobbes argued, human thought is derived from sense experience, and is part of the mechanical process. 'Whatsoever we conceive has been perceived first by sense . . . A man can have no thought representing anything not subject to sense.' Thinking, the formulation of ideas, is, then, not a process of *initiation* but of *reaction*. And the same, according to Hobbes, is true of our feelings and our imagination. He argued that there is in each person what he called 'endeavour' – a drive either towards or away from an imagined object or event. The drive *towards* he called 'appetite' or 'desire'; the drive *away from*, 'aversion'; and indifference either way he called 'contempt'. All moral judgements, he affirmed, are based on these three types of endeavour; consequently, any moral decision of any moral agent must be seen as simply that person's response to these drives or stimuli (an ethical theory known as nihilistic relativism).

> As in sense that which is really within us is . . . only motion, caused by the action of external objects but in appearance; to the sight, light and colour; to the ear, sound; to the nostril, odour, etc: so, when the action of the same object is continued from the eyes, ears, and other organs to the heart, the real effect there is nothing but motion, or endeavour; which consisteth in appetite or aversion to or from the object moving. But the appearance of sense of that motion is that we either call *delight* or *trouble of mind*.
>
> (*Leviathan*, Book I, Chapter 6)

The image of humanity which emerges from this, even though Hobbes still maintained that we have free will, is of beings who are part of a universal, mechanical process in which all our unique qualities, of mind, of vision, of feeling, or of imagination, are viewed not as creative or critical faculties but as responses to antecedent stimuli.

There is no logical or scientific procedure for disproving this theory (though case study 10 invites you to explore some of the practical consequences of accepting it). Investigations in the sphere of the neuro-sciences seem to give greater credence to its main emphases; but it remains difficult to see oneself as the kind of automaton that emerges from mechanistic determinism. In fact, if we were to take into account every discovery about *homo sapiens* and how (s)he functions, in the fields of (for instance) physiology, neurology, biochemistry, pharmacology and so on – not to mention psychology which I shall discuss in the next section – we could be forgiven for concluding that an octogenarian's biography could have been written from the moment of his or her birth! It may well be the case that if we had the history of every molecule in the universe we should be able to forecast the future of the universe – all its molecules included – with total accuracy. But since the universe itself would not be large enough to contain the number of books that this exercise would require, this is idle speculation.

I suspect that even scientists who pay lip-service to the mechanistic theory while in their laboratories behave differently when they appear in the world outside – the world of the arts, of human relationships and moral decisions: in a word, the world of *experience*. From, this perspective it seems that the mechanistic view of humanity discounts the vital fact of our *autonomy*, which is central to one's self-consciousness. By autonomy I mean qualities like personal awareness, individual responsibility, *self*-determination (note that). Whether or not I am deceiving myself in thinking that I possess these qualities, I live my life as though they are real. A surgeon's knife may well be able to change my personality with a single cut: but who is to say that my freedom of choice would not be operating in that new state, even though within narrower limits. After all, it would need only one further cut in the right spot to end all my choices for ever.

## PSYCHOLOGICAL DETERMINISM

Sigmund Freud (1856–1939) is not normally included among the determinists. He was not a religious man, nor did he hold a mechanistic view of human behaviour, such as we have seen in Hobbes. None the less, his research into the effects of the so-called subconscious on our observable behaviour produced from him theories which are in many respects deterministic in their emphasis. They imply that much of what we do is controlled by forces which are beyond any degree of self-determined control because, by definition, we are unconscious of them. To be fair to Freud, his view was that if we could become aware of what lies in our subconscious, we should be in a stronger position to change our behaviour, assuming (as was the case with most of his patients), that this behaviour were causing distress either to ourselves or to those immediately around us.

His theory of the workings of the human mind can be studied in any basic textbook on psychology, but may be briefly summarized here. He conceived of three aspects, or levels, of the psyche, and coined new words to describe them (and if you are already familiar with them it will indicate how enormous is the impact Freud has made). First, the 'id' is the fundamental reservoir of energy which provides us with our basic drives – the life and death instincts which control our appetites, impulses, loves and hates. Part of the id is the 'ego', which works towards the preservation and survival of the individual, and helps to suppress those impulses of the id which, being judged antisocial, are unacceptable in civilized society. (The male urge to procreate freely is an example of this.) This leaves open the question of how the ego decides what is acceptable and what is not. Freud proposed the theory that this happens through use of what he termed the 'supergo' (what we may loosely term the conscience), which, he said, develops in a child as (s)he matures. (Some children don't achieve this maturation, and so tend to be antisocial, or even psychopathic, in their adult lives.)

The trick is for the ego to keep some kind of harmony between the id and the supergo. If the latter is allowed to dominate a person excessively, (s)he will develop a morbid sense of guilt which may bring fear and misery into their life. If the urges of the unconscious id are not kept in control, powerful disturbances will develop in the individual, resulting in neurotic symptoms – or worse. The drive for the reproduction of the species was that to which Freud here gave most attention. He called this sexual longing the 'libido', and much of his research was concerned with interpreting irrational activity, such as dreaming, forgetting, unconscious acts and slips of the tongue (now often termed 'Freudian slips') in terms of sexual desires repressed because of social taboos. In particular, Freud believed that the sex drive began not at adolescence (or even later), as had been the general view of his contemporaries, but in early childhood (a belief which shocked many of these fastidious contemporaries with their image of 'innocent' striplings) and that, in Western societies at any rate, it was repressed into the unconscious. From there it proceeded, years later, to exert its influence, causing mental disorders in adults – hysteria, phobias and so on: all eidola, or phantoms. These eidola (my word, not Freud's) took over a person's behaviour, so that it is not too strong a term to state that, according to Freud, they determined it. He uses this word in fact when describing one of his colleague's patients, Anna O, who had hydrophobia (fear of water). Almost all her symptoms, he wrote, originated . . . as remnants, as precipitates, if you like, of affectively toned experiences, which for that reason we called *psychic traumata*. The nature of the symptoms became clear through their relation to the scene which caused them: they were, to use the technical term, *determined* . . . by the scene whose memory traces they embodied, and so could no longer be described as arbitrary or enigmatical functions of the neurosis.

(*The Origin and Development of Psycho-Analysis*,
1st lecture; italics in original.)

The way back to sanity, or to normality, or to socially acceptable behaviour, lay, according to Freud, through psychoanalysis, a lengthy process in which the patient is encouraged to return in his or her mind to earlier, forgotten periods of life, so that (if the analysis is sound) having discovered the *cause* of the phobia or whatever (that is to say, the singular events which brought about the initial process of repression) the patient may be in a position to cope with it and take steps towards recovery.

It is not my purpose to enter into a lengthy debate about the validity of Freud's analysis. Other equally eminent psychologists such as Adler and Jung expressed disagreement with Freud, particularly over the role of the sex drive, which, as we have noted, he had claimed to be a major factor in many mental disorders. The question at issue, so far as our central theme is concerned, is whether (accepting Freud's terminology, which is, of course, a question-begging procedure) the ego and superego are totally determined by forces outside and beyond the individual concerned. Are we, so to speak, *given* our egos and, normally, our superegos once and for all, or can we do something to change them? Can we, to put the matter at its starkest, autonomously decide not to feel conscience-stricken about certain forms of behaviour, or to develop a conscience on other matters? Granted that other people's attitudes constantly bombard us, influencing us unconsciously if not consciously, both immediately and in subsequent years, are we never free to throw off the pressures they exert and tread our own chosen path?

The experience of many people is that these steps are possible; they testify to the fact that the state of being well adjusted, which in Freudian terms means keeping the balance between the id, the ego and the superego, is one that can be achieved through conscious deliberation and honesty with oneself. If may be acknowledged that some people have got themselves so entangled with phantoms from the past that their present happiness is affected, and that for these the unwrapping process adopted and advocated by Freud may be valuable. But, if I as a strict amateur in this field may venture an opinion, too much can be and has been made of these alleged early influences, the eidola. Clearly, since our being is a unity and a continuity, what happened in the past of any one of us has significance for today: we build on it, and may learn from it. But the suggestion that everything in everyone's past, tucked away in the subconscious, is redolent of significance for the present seems, frankly, absurd. Much of most people's pasts (and maybe all of some people's!) is too trivial to be worth examining, except for the same kind of nostalgic pleasure derived from looking at old photographs. Occasionally something significant may turn up but normally the process is, I feel, one of self-indulgence, probably harmless but not very instructive. The main cause of visits to analysts in the Western world – and here I do some analysis of my own – is more the early death which is boredom than the deadly influence of eidola from the past. The people in the Western world today who might benefit most from analysis (simply because this means being listened to by *somebody*, even if you have to pay the listener to do it) are not the types Freud treated in Vienna – wealthy, middle-class women with too much time on their hands (as, today, with millions of women in the United States) – but unemployed teenagers who, because they have not yet been allowed to make a positive contribution to society, feel they have no hope of being accepted as mature adults. As the British comedian, Ken Dodd, astutely remarked: 'The trouble with Freud was that he never played the Glasgow Empire Saturday night.' The underlying determinism of Freud seems to me to be a counsel of despair, despite the hope that he has undoubtedly implanted in the minds of certain individuals. I prefer to believe that whatever lies in the subconscious is not static but rather is in a process of constant modification as new experiences, to which we all make our own autonomous contributions, are imposed upon the old. The verdict of Sartre, 'There is no such thing as psychological. Let us say that one can improve the biography of the person', may be too stark but, as I shall be affirming at greater length in the next chapter, seems to me to be pointing in the right direction. Freudianism may have some value in the treatment of abnormal behaviour, but in terms of our inquiry its contribution seems slight.

Freud's chief merit may well be his once-and-for-all removal of 'God' from the subconscious. By achieving this, be becomes part of a great triumvirate. Newton's discoveries in the world of physics made Him redundant, whether Newton recognized this or not, in the mechanical universe; Darwin achieved the same in the world of living species; and Freud removed the Almighty from the human mind and conscience. That is no mean feat.

## ETHOLOGICAL DETERMINISM: THE LAW OF THE JUNGLE

The word ethology has changed its meaning radically over the past quarter-century. It literally means the study of customs, or behaviour, and until relatively recently this was taken to mean human customs. One of my dictionaries (Collins) published in 1956 defines the word as 'the systematic study of human behaviour, intellect, and character'. By 1983, in Chambers, the word had become defined as 'the scientific study of the function and evolution of animal behaviour patterns'. This is a noteworthy change of emphasis, and reflects the pioneering work in the field undertaken by such men as Konrad Lorenz and Desmond Morris. Their books, *King Solomon's Ring* (Lorenz) and *The Naked Ape* (Morris), have popularized research in this field in a way that must make ethology the envy of many other academic disciplines (not least philosophy). So far as this brief discussion is concerned, 'ethology' will be taken to mean the study of both animal and human behaviour, and of the relationship between the two.

The fact that any connection between animal and human nature can be discussed dispassionately is an indication of how far the concept of evolution has entered into our thought processes. It isn't possible for people raised in the post-Darwin era (or, to be more precise, the post-acceptance-of-Darwin era) to understand how great a shock to the general public were his *Origin of Species* (1859) and *The Descent of Man* (1871). The shaking of the foundations which seemed then to have occurred was not dissimilar to that of two centuries or so earlier, when Galileo and other astronomers destroyed with one flash of a telescope the cosy image of a flat earth at the centre of a universe created to serve it. Through the work of Darwin and others, the long-enduring image of a world created in six days by an omnipotent God in the not-too-distant past (4004 BC, according to one scholarly estimate) with man as His crowning glory ('made in His image') was replaced with one of a world not created but evolving, its varied species coming into existence through modifications of earlier species, themselves developing and changing over millions of years, and ceasing to exist if they did not adapt to their surroundings, or environment – which is what Herbert Spencer meant in his memorable phrase 'the survival of the fittest', coined in his monumental *First Principles* (1860 ff).

From this extended process, so the new teaching proclaimed, the ultimate species emerged, relatively late on the biological time-scale (about 11.45p.m. on December 31, if we compress the 4.5 billion years of the earth's existence into the span of one year, though the period of recorded history occupies only the last few seconds before midnight): *homo sapiens*. And its ancestry was not the angels in heaven but the apes on earth, and before them lesser animals and reptiles, the fowl of the air and the fish of the sea, back to the molluscs, the jellyfish and sea anemones. No wonder Darwin was viewed by many as the devil incarnate; and no wonder *Punch* could publish a cartoon depicting an ape leaving London Zoo, a copy of the Bible under one arm and the *Origin of Species* under the other, and asking, 'Am I my keeper's brother?' Even today in some states of the USA, allegedly the most advanced nation on earth, it remains illegal for the theory of evolution to be taught in schools; and in the nation which first put a man on the moon the Flat Earth Society, if not flourishing, still has sincere and articulate members. Perhaps they have pondered too long over these words of Bertrand Russell:

> Organic life, we are told, has developed gradually from the protozoon to the philosopher, and this development, we are assured, is indubitably an advance. Unfortunately, it is the philosopher, not the protozoon, who gives us this assurance.
>
> (*Mysticism and Logic*, Chapter 6)

The basic tenet of ethology follows from this biological history: we cannot hope to understand human nature unless we begin with a study of animal nature and behaviour, since that is where human origins are to be found. What has emerged from ethological research is the recognition that the survival of species in relation to their environment has been possible only because of certain instincts that they possess. In describing these instincts, ethologists refer to basic drives which are not dissimilar to those of the id as defined by Freud. Most prominent among these drives, and possessed to a greater or lesser extent by all creatures, are the *herd instinct*, the *sense of territory, aggression* and *reproduction*. Only, it is suggested by ethologists, when we recognize that *homo sapiens* has inherited these instincts, and that they remain dominant factors in our behaviour, will we be able to understand and cope with the social and moral problems that we encounter; more to the point, we will remain a mystery to ourselves unless we make this connection.

Let us look at these four instincts in turn. The *herd instinct* can be seen occurring among animals as they congregate kind to its kind, ignoring, or rejecting, or, in extreme instances, destroying any creature that appears different from the group. Among the human species, one of the greatest afflictions is racialism, the belief that members of another race are by nature inferior to one's own, with the ensuing assumption that these others should keep themselves to themselves, and not automatically be granted the same rights and privileges that are assumed for one's own people. Sometimes in history this affliction has become an epidemic, as when Nazi Germany in the 1930s and 1940s adopted a policy of deliberate genocide towards the Jews; but in a wide range of societies there have been those who have expressed contempt for races other than their own, a contempt which has often led to interracial violence. We see it expressed by the Ku Klux Klan and the Black Muslims in America, by the National Front and the Rastafarians in Britain, and by the white nationalists in South Africa. Ethologists would argue that this disease is an (unfortunate) outcome of the herd instinct: the innate desire, inherited from our animal past, to mix only with our own kind, coupled with suspicion towards strangers which at times amounts to fear. Whenever we reject others simply because of physical, cultural, or behavioural differences we are, ethologically speaking, responding to this instinct.

It is often associated with that of *territory*. Species of various kinds establish a patch for themselves and guard it against intruders. Your household dog will view with suspicion, if not open hostility, another of his kind who accompanies any visitor you may have. By so doing, he is simply responding to the innate sense, passed on over millions of years, that a certain amount of the space around him is his, to be guarded jealously against any intruder who may pose a threat. Human beings share this instinct. In a communal building, where all space and pieces of property allegedly belong to all, individuals will stake out a personal claim for part of it. I recall once, as a new teacher in a school, being warned by colleagues not to sit in a particular chair in the staff room because that was 'Mr X's chair'. Try the experiment of encroaching on the space of the person sitting next to you in a train or restaurant. Look over his shoulder at what he is reading, finger his cutlery, put your matches down in front of him, and see how quickly he becomes nervous or angry. I have a theory that many broken marriages or partnerships would have survived if each partner had had some space that was recognized by the other as his or her own, such as the shed at the bottom of the garden in which I'm writing this book. Even the contents of someone else's briefcase or handbag should be secret, if this deep territorial instinct is to be preserved. It's no wonder that the biggest problem facing St Bernard with his monks of the **Cistercian** Order was that of destroying the sense of, and desire for, personal property.

Ethologists link this territorial sense with that of *aggression*, which sometimes leads to violence, and which seems to be an irremovable element in Western society (to look no further). In experiments on rats in a cage, it has been demonstrated that the creatures may coexist quite equably until their numbers are unnaturally increased beyond a certain optimum. Then they become increasingly aggressive and vicious towards one another (though some take an alternative escape route and become withdrawn, the equivalent, I suppose, of a rat nervous breakdown). Because human beings too need a certain amount of space, a place of retreat, in their lives, the implication here is that there should be a correlation of sorts between the numbers involved in any coherent group of people, and the amount of space available. A group of people of a certain number living within certain confines may feel themselves to be reasonably well knit together; but if too many people occupy too small a space, problems like those expressed by rats in the cage will begin to emerge. There can be few lonelier places on earth than in the middle of a rush-hour crowd in London or New York; and even the mildest of people can become aggressive in a traffic jam. Ethologists argue that a, if not *the*, major cause of escalating violence in our time is the threat to territory brought about by the numbers of people multiplying in our cities, where other people are increasingly perceived not as persons but as threatening objects, so that even a touch from one of them provokes an instantaneous recoil.

This aggressive instinct expresses itself in the mating habits of most species. The male will generally have no hesitation in seeing off any rival for the female of his choice; and this instinct for *reproduction* is as dominant in human beings as it is in other species and, generally speaking, continuously so. In fact men and women have been described as the only animals who eat when they're not hungry, drink when they're not thirsty, and make love all the year round. Relating to this, and the theme of much ethological writing, is the question of male and female roles. Among species generally, the male is the protector and provider, often the aggressor, while the female is the home builder and provider of comfort to the young. In some species, such as polar bears and elephants, the male and female meet only to mate, after which the one disappears while the other assumes all parental responsibilities. The question which ethologists raise is whether this role structure is not innate in human beings, and whether we are not being unnatural in suggesting that, apart from certain physiological differences, there is no essential difference between males and females: that roles can therefore be shared, if not reversed.

Here, I think, ethologists are following dogma rather than common sense. While I don't accept as sound all the emphases of feminism (assuming that there is a composite body of beliefs to be subsumed under that one word), it seems to me axiomatic on one central issue: the new situation brought about by the discovery of contraception, whereby the female can control her own sexuality. This has brought about a change in the human species so revolutionary that any comparison with other species on this matter is irrelevant. The revolution has in fact caused an evolutionary change, making redundant not only all inherited, or received, views on sexual morality but also all concepts of male dominance. If there must be a dominant member of any partnership then it can as easily and as naturally be the female.

The implication of this, it seems, is that instincts are not as lasting or as total in their effects as ethologists are prone to suggest. If this is true – as manifestly it is – of the instincts relating to the pair bond, it may well be so of the other instincts we've reviewed.

The outcome of ethological research has caused many people to look at themselves in ways unknown in earlier centuries. We have learned, for instance, that we can't treat our environment and its multitudinous forms of life as though it exists only for our personal gratification. The question which concerns us, however, is whether ethologists are right when they assert that human behaviour is innate and that human nature is inherited from species lower down the evolutionary ladder. Have we explained everything by acknowledging the existence and consequent pressures of these primeval instincts? This would surely be to deny the evidence of experience which suggests that, while we may never be able wholly to cast off these instincts, they can be recognized, modified and controlled – with the possibility that in time and if necessary they may be discarded. The discernible effect of feminist ideas on society, limited though devotees may consider them to be, suggests that this not only *can* happen but is happening already, as, I guess, it has always been happening.

My view is that ethological determinism, like the other varieties, does not take adequately into account the basic feature of the self, which is personal autonomy. Weaving its way through all the grooves and graves that we've been discussing is this basic, self-conscious *me*, whom I can modify if I so desire. But this will be viewed as a pathetic fallacy by adherents of the next school to be considered.

## BEHAVIOURISM: DETERMINISM THROUGH THE ENVIRONMENT

Are we born the way we are, or do our surroundings make us what we are to be? Do I choose to do X because I have inherited certain tendencies in that direction, or do I so choose because this is what others expect of me? This is the nub of the so-called nature/nurture debate. One school of thought which presents the case for the determining role of *nurture* is behaviourism.

In its origins, this is a school of thought which belongs in the field of psychology rather than philosophy, but philosophers in recent years have analysed its assumptions as they do in other discipline areas (this is part of a philosopher's job). Granted that psychology may be defined as study or observation of human behaviour, what then, it may be asked, is being observed? The individual person may claim that his or her behaviour springs from an internal consciousness, but behaviourists affirm this to be irrelevant. All that can be assessed, they suggest, is what is empirically observable: that is, what is tangible and scientifically verifiable. Subjective feelings, which are not open to such empirical observation, must therefore be discounted. (Much debate has occurred in behaviourist circles as to whether a *thought* is an empirical event, or action, and therefore a possible exception to the rule of observability. If you are interested in pursuing this line of argument, you might read J. B. Watson's *Behaviourism* or B. F. Skinner's *Beyond Freedom and Dignity*.) Philosophers of psychology, of whom Gilbert Ryle is one of the most eminent, have on the whole identified mental activity, that is, assumptions about the inner self-consciousness of the subject, with what are termed *dispositions* to behave in a certain way. Thus for a person to be reflective is to be disposed to avoid company, or to be disposed not to be hasty in making decisions. Using the analogy of a material object, a knife, in order to be able to cut, must have a disposition to be sharp. The basic problem with inner feelings and consciousness, the behaviourists claim, is that there can never be any reliable verification of a description of them. The words used by the describer may simply deceive the hearer, but the latter will never be sure of this one way or another. Even the depth analysis advocated by Freud is viewed by behaviourists as unreliable; assuming that there is a 'true' state of affairs to be discovered, there can be no guarantee that this has emerged during psychoanalysis. All that one can do, behaviourists argue, is to infer from behaviour what is really taking place in a person's mind. 'Inner processes,' wrote Wittgenstein, 'stand in need of outward criteria.' Body language, on this test, is more reliable than the spoken word.

The most eminent living behaviourist is probably **B. F. Skinner**. He has openly countered every theory of human nature so far presented. Dualism he has declared to be false; a spiritual relationship with the Almighty a meaningless notion; the idea of different strata of the mind irrelevant. The observable patterns of behaviour are, he believes, all that can count when trying to assess what a human being is; and observations along these lines he has carried out with scientific rigour. He believes that it is not by theorizing (or wishful thinking, as he would characterize many of the ideas thrown up) that we shall discover the truth about human nature, but by the disciplined process of presenting a hypothesis, testing it by observation and experiment, and so either verifying or falsifying it. Whether our findings then please us or not, they are what we must hold to if we are to be honest with and about ourselves. We must be empirical, not metaphysical.

Skinner may be described as an environmental determinist. He believes that it is our surroundings, the external factors in our lives, which make us what we are, not our so-called inner consciousness. Everything we do is conditioned: not, as Freud maintained, from within ourselves, but from without. Freud might have described a person as having an inferiority complex; Skinner would simply state that the person was (or was not) inferior (in the area under discussion). He views the moral sense as simply the sign that we have learned to be prudential amid conflicting interests: when we say 'I ought to do X' we mean no more than 'It would be in my interest to do X'. But unlike Hobbes, who viewed self-interest as innate in everyone, Skinner takes a line not dissimilar to that of Rousseau two centuries ago and views self-interest as the product of the human environment. And to be fair to Skinner, he has supported his theory by attempting, in his planned communities, to create practical expressions of the kind of environment in which co-operation may become natural and unselfishness flourish.

It would be absurd to deny that there is much of worth in what Skinner has said and done. It is clear that many of our moods and much of our behaviour is brought about by our environment – by, for example, atmospheric conditions and by what we eat. Any child knows that the time to ask a favour of a parent is after, not before, a meal; and most people experience a sense of general depression on a heavy (weather-wise) day. It is also the case that people tend to 'live up' to their environment: put them in dingy surroundings and they are apt to behave dingily; give them light, and space, and colour, and the difference will probably be reflected in their more enlightened behaviour.

The problem with Skinner, as with Freud, is not whether there is any truth in what he says but whether it is the whole truth. By arguing that all our actions are environmentally determined he leaves no room for the human will, which can triumph over the worst of conditions and conditioning. Furthermore, he leaves no room for human free choice. His argument is that, while we may think ourselves to be free, we are not. What credit are we to give him, then, for his experiments with the social environment? According to his own theory, the idea of these was introduced to his mind *by an environment which he proposed to change,* which is like people supporting a campaign to make themselves unhappy.

## SUMMARY

So is man in chains or is he totally free of them? Clearly, the whole business of living, from the moment of birth, if not of conception, is one in which we are, willy-nilly, being influenced by one factor or another. The baby is totally dependent on its parents; and their influence, for better or for worse, continues to impose itself on the growing child and probably remains, to some extent, throughout its life. As years pass, other influential factors exert themselves – friends, peer groups, community, place of work, interest groups and so on. We all read books or journals which express other people's ideas, and these may affect the decisions we take and the directions we choose to go. It seems too that we inherit in our genes certain characteristics that help to shape us, whether we are conscious of this or not; and everything that happens to us, or is said to us, is stored away in some recess of the mind, from which it may, to varying extents and with differing emphases, affect our subsequent behaviour as things forgotten, but never lost. All this implies that both nature and nurture help to form us in ways that it would be absurd to discount.

All this seems true as far as it goes: but if this *is* as far as it goes, then I as an individual person would then be compelled to view myself as entirely the product of forces and factors over which I could never have control; I would be, in Aristotle's simile, like the oak that was programmed in the acorn and grew according to the soil in which it was planted, and the climate which surrounded it. I would not have chosen to be *me*. Others might wish to show me off with pride, or hide me away in shame, but to them, not to me, must go any accolades or commiserations that are due.

Speaking for myself (and I am, after all, the only person I can speak for) this philosophy is inadequate because it overlooks a vital part of me: the *will* to freedom (cf. A. Schopenhauer, *On the Freedom of the Will*). I am free to reject all that I was brought up to do and believe, to turn against the mores of every community or group with which I may from time to time be identified; I am free to triumph over phobias and to conquer irrational fears. I am, in short, responsible for who I am and what I do: I cannot hold others responsible for either of these, convenient though it would sometimes be if I could. I may have been nudged, perhaps sometimes pushed, in certain directions, but in the end it is I who have chosen the way I have taken. I may have been raised to feel guilty about certain forms of behaviour, and to value highly certain features of life: but whether or not I continue to carry this guilt or these values throughout my life is up to me. I may require the assistance of friends here and there, and perhaps some chains will never be entirely removed: but I know that in certain vital respects I am at least sometimes free; and I would continue to affirm this even if the whole of the rest of the human race were to adopt a deterministic stance. I may be deluding myself, but I view as the important factor in the study of human nature – which includes *my* nature as well as that of others – my own individual approach to and experience of the mystery. To accept the determinist line seems to me an act of surrender of one's personal sovereignty or autonomy. To do this is to begin to die.

I am not suggesting however, that we may blandly accept the extreme libertarian view of man. Nor would I *want* this to be the situation; if there were no guidelines, no restrictions on human behaviour, then no patterns could be created, no habits formed, and nothing could ever be anticipated about anyone with the least degree of confidence. Forward planning would be pointless, timetables works of fiction, and diaries the records of individual fantasies. All would be chaos if there were nothing determined.

What seems clear is that my physical make-up imposes limits – maybe many limits – on my mental and emotional capacities. Even if I am free to choose between doing what I like and doing what I dislike – between, say, watching the 49ers and cleaning the oven (or between *anything* and cleaning the oven), I am not free to decide *that* I like the one and dislike the other. This may put me, according to some assessors, in the camp of the so-called 'soft' determinists but, if anything, I prefer to describe myself as an indeterminist. I accept, in other words, that the freedom I know myself to enjoy is expressed in (and in many ways is modified by) that which is 'given' to me – or imposed upon me willy-nilly. But it seems to me irrational – to pursue an argument of William James's – that I should, say, feel remorse about various actions taken and decisions made over the years if those actions and those decisions were totally predetermined. Logic may suggest that I am deluding myself; but logic, as I have maintained concerning several issues already, is only one of many tools for coping with the complexities of this problem.

Perhaps Pandit Nehru's picture aptly sums up what I am trying to say (it certainly reflects much of Eastern thought and that of existentialism in the West): 'Life is like a game of cards. The hand that is dealt you represents determinism; the way you play it is free will.'

*Case study 10*
*Fate*

> And that inverted Bowl we call The Sky,
> Whereunder crawling coop'd we live and die,
> Life not thy hands to *It* for help – for It
> Rolls impotently on as thou or I.
> > (*The Rubaiyat of Omar Khayyam*, LII)

These words by the eleventh/twelfth-century Persian poet reflect the classical view of Fate, as the antagonist of freedom in the drama of human life and history. In many of the Greek tragedies of antiquity, fate overshadows the action on the stage: there is an impending sense of doom, often relating to a curse that must be fulfilled (a fundamental thesis of many of the great fairy tales). Sophocles tells of Oedipus, doomed to kill his father and marry his mother; Aeschylus tells of the curse on the house of Atreus, and how Agamemnon brings Cassandra back to Troy; and in *Prometheus Bound*, Zeus sends Hermes to wrest from Prometheus the secret of what has been ordained for him by 'all-consummating Fate' or 'Fate's resistless law'. All this seems to confirm the sense of total impotence on the part of human actors in the drama, as expressed in Omar's poem. But Aeschylus leaves unanswered the question of whether Zeus could escape his doom if he could foresee what Fate holds in store for him. The suggestion seems to be that not even with omnipotence, but only with omniscience – knowing the past, the present *and* the future – can the chains of Fate be broken. Thomas Hardy's novels share the pessimism, the sense of unthwartable doom, of early Greek tragedy, and in his *Tess of the d'Urbervilles* he ends the story of Tess's tragic fate with a specific classical reference:

> 'Justice' was done, and the President of the Immortals, in Aeschylean phrase, had ended his sport with Tess. And the d'Urberville knights and dames slept on in their tombs unknowing.

Fate is sometimes personalized, sometimes abstractly conceived. Its Latin root means an *oracle*, and so connotes what is divinely ordained. What happens by fate is *fated* – destined and decreed in the councils of the gods on Olympus; or, maybe, by the decision of Zeus, the supreme ruler among the gods. But fate may be a supernatural destiny which not even Zeus can set aside. This, too, is reflected in Omar's poem:

> The Ball no question makes of Ayes and Noes,
> But Right or Left as strikes the Player goes;
> And He that toss'd Thee down into the Field,
> *He* knows about it all – HE knows – *HE* knows!

In the text we discussed the Augustinian doctrine of predestination. In defending this doctrine, Augustine attacked the views of Lucretius, for whom 'nature free at once and rid of her haughty lords is seen to do all things spontaneously of herself without the meddling of the gods'. Lucretius's view was that everything happens according to the laws of nature, *other than which there is no fate*. Augustine argued that Lucretius was simply a fatalist who happened to disbelieve in divine providence, *other than which there is no fate*. How far providence and fatalism are different is a matter for debate; certainly many who have accepted the former have spoken and acted as though they were fatalistically resigned, such as Troilus in Chaucer's poem:

> I am, he said, but done for, so to say;
> For all that comes, comes by necessity,
> Thus to be done for is my destiny.

> I must believe and cannot other choose,
> That Providence, in its divine foresight,
> Hath known that Cressida I once must lose,
> Since God sees everything from heaven's height
> And plans things as he thinks both best and right,
> According to their merits in rotation,
> As was arranged for by predestination.

The questions and quotations that follow are to allow you to explore this mystery a little.

1    How far is 'fate' a shorthand term for 'what is yet unknown' (because the events which lead to our 'fate' have not yet taken place)?

    Horace: 'Drop the question what tomorrow may bring, and count as profit every day that Fate allows you.' (Odes)

    T. E. Lawrence: 'Many men would take the death-sentence with a whimper to escape the life-sentence which fate carries in her other hand.' (*The Mint*)

2    Is it possible to equate fate with divine providence? If you accept this, does this imply that even God could not change the force of destiny? If you deny this, how do you tackle this dilemma expressed by David Hume:

> If voluntary action be subjected to the same laws of necessity with the operations of matter, there is a continued chain of necessary causes, pre-ordained and pre-determined, reaching from the original cause of all to every single volition of every single creature. No contingency anywhere in the universe; no indifference; no liberty . . . It then becomes impossible to explain distinctly how the Deity can be the mediate cause of all the actions of men, without being the author of sin and moral turpitude . . . To defend absolute decrees, and yet free the Deity from being the author of sin, has been found hitherto to exceed all the power of philosophy.

3    How do you react to these words by Karl Marx (*Das Kapital*)?

> I deal with individuals only insofar as they are the personifications of economic categories, embodiments of particular class-relations and class-interests . . . My stand-point is one from which the evolution of the economic formation of society is viewed as a process of natural history within which the individual cannot be responsible for relations whose creature he socially remains, however much he may subjectively raise himself above them. It is a question only of these laws themselves, of these tendencies working with iron necessity towards inevitable results. (slightly paraphrased)

Has Marx here replaced fate simply with the concept of historical inevitability? Are men only playing the part, described by Marx, already written for them in 'the scroll of history'? Should Marx have been included as a leading figure in a school of determinism? (See further, pp. 251–3.)

4    Do you find the idea of fortune more congenial than fate (fortune is to fate as contingency is to necessity)? Is there contingency in nature? Or are chance or the fortuitous in the order of nature, and freedom in human life, mere illusions cherished by human beings only through ignorance of the inevitable? Do you see fortune as the ally of freedom in the struggle against fate (fortune aiding and abetting human desires, misfortune signifying the element of chance)?

5   As you look on the way your own life has gone so far, do you
see any 'golden thread' along the road? Do you think things could
have gone otherwise than they did? If so, can you pinpoint particular
occasions when a conscious decision took you in a direction away
from a path you could have followed had the decision been different?
Even if you don't read a daily horoscope, do you ever, consciously
or unconsciously, think in terms of what 'fate has in store'?

6   Do you think, with Appius Caesar, that 'each man is the architect
of his own fate'? If so, do you agree with these words of **Karl
Popper**:

> We may become the makers of our fate when we have ceased
> to pose as its prophets.

What do you think he meant by this?

*Case study 11*
*Free will and freedom*

Here are a number of quotations about this complex issue. Read and
reflect on them, then tackle the questions that follow.

(1) 'The action of the soul consists entirely in this, that, simply by
willing, it makes the small gland to which it is closely united
move in the way requisite for producing the effect aimed at in
the volition.'
(René Descartes, *Passion of the Soul*, 41)
Does belief in the soul imply that we are free (because the soul
is not constrained, and so can liberate the body, perhaps)? How
does this religious view link up with the theory of predestination
(pp. 71–3)?

(2) 'I make not only the *effect* but also the *election* of that particular
effect necessary, inasmuch as the will itself and each propension of
a man during his deliberation is as much necessitated as anything
else whatsoever . . . It be not in his will to choose his fancy, or
choose his election and will.'
(Thomas Hobbes, *Of Liberty and Necessity*)
How far do you think this expression of determinism is one of
common sense? Do you agree with the statement in the text
(p. 86) that likes and dislikes are among the things that are
'given' – that is, we have no choice about them? Where, in
that case, does an 'acquired taste' slot into the argument? Are

there any (other) features of life that you would include among the 'given'?

(3)  'God determines our will to the choice of that which appears best, but without necessitating it in the least. It has the power of acting differently, or even suspending its action entirely, both choices being and remaining possible. Nevertheless it is true, and even assured from all eternity, that certain souls will not make use of this power in such and such situations. And since from the time when I began to exist it was possible to say of me truly that this or that would happen to me, it must be acknowledged that these predicates were laws included in the complete notion of me which makes that which is called I, which is the foundation of the interconnexion of all my different states, and which was perfectly known to God from all eternity.'

(G. W. Leibniz, *Discourse on Metaphysics*, 30)

How does Leibniz's conclusion stand up to the claim of the existentialist Bertold Brecht: '[I am] what [I] have done'?

(4)  'The river-bed of thoughts may shift. But I distinguish between the movement of the waters on the river-bed and the shift of the bed itself; though there is not a sharp division of the one from the other. . . And the bank of the river consists partly of hard rock, subject to no alteration or only to an imperceptible one, partly of sand, which now in one place now in another gets washed away, or deposited.'

(Ludwig Wittgenstein, *On Certainty*, 99)

Is this the view expressed in the second quotation above, but in different words?

(5)  'Which brings me to my conclusion upon Free Will and Predestination, namely – let the reader mark it – that they are identical.'

(Winston Churchill, *My Early Life*, Chapter 26)

Does this and the preceding quotation from Wittgenstein, suggest that the real distinction in this field is not between determinism and libertarianism but between determinism and indeterminism? In other words, that our freedom can be expressed only in a situation where much is determined, otherwise there is chaos, and the word 'free' is meaningless? Is the whole debate about free will and determinism ultimately a matter of minor variations in emphasis, or does the issue, in your view, divide people more deeply than that view suggests? If you think this is so, can you give examples of how such divisions might come about, and how they might express themselves?

(6)  'Man is condemned to be free.'

(J.-P. Sartre, *Existentialism and Humanism*)

Why 'condemned'? Is it because most people need a routine, a pattern into which they can safely fit, which provides their sense of security? How would you react to having (say) a year with nothing specific to do? Could you spend that amount of time without building up some kind of daily pattern? Or does Sartre speak of being condemned because, being free, we would have to accept responsibility for our choices? How far do *you* carry your own can? How much buck-passing do you engage in? Is yours the voice that remains silent or the one that speaks up when an awkward, embarrassing, or risky statement needs to be made?

(7)  'It's often safer to be in chains than to be free.'

(Franz Kafka, *The Trial*)

Do you think this follows from quotation 6? How highly do *you* rank safety?

(8)                 'Me this unchartered freedom tires . . .
           I long for a repose that ever is the same.'

(William Wordsworth, 'Ode to duty')

Are we involved here in a change in attitude with advancing years? Would Wordsworth have written this, do you think, at the time when he was enthusing about the French Revolution? Or is Wordsworth simply recognizing that total freedom means chaos, as discussed under the fifth quotation? Do you find the attitude expressed in the 'Ode to duty' more or less congenial/commendable than, say, that of Goethe during his *Sturm und Drang* ('storm and stress') period:

           'Es schlug mein Herz! Geschwind zum Pferde!
           Es war getan eh' es gedacht.'

('My heart beat: quick! to horse! Before thinking about it, it was done.')

(9)  'Remember that to change your mind and follow him who sets you right is to be none the less free than you were before.'

(Marcus Aurelius, *Meditations*)

Do you see a parallel between this view and that of Sartre: that there is nothing that belittles our freedom by seeking advice, since it is still *our* decision whether to accept and follow it or not?

(10)  'We have to believe in free will. We've got no choice.'

(Isaac Singer, 1982)

Discuss!

Some final questions for general discussion.

1   In what respects, if any, am I unquestionably free?

2   Are there any areas where I've often thought myself able to choose freely, but am probably not?

3   Are there areas where I've often excused my (bad) behaviour on the grounds that I could not have done otherwise, when I probably could have done?

4   Do people vary on the range of their 'freedom field'? If so, is any generalization about the question at all possible?

5   'Habits need not be kept out of force of habit' (R. S. Peters). Do you agree?

6   In what areas am I not free to choose (what areas of decision-making, or which aspects of *me* are beyond my powers to do other than I actually do)?

*Case study 12*
*Spot the instinct*

Below are a number of examples of human activity. If the ethologists are right, every one of them is dominated by at least one of four basic instincts, or drives: territory, aggression, herd and sex. See if you can identify which one (or more than one) is at work in these situations, with the following questions in mind:

1   Generally speaking, how conscious do you think the people concerned are that an instinct actually is expressing itself?
2   Do you find the expression of any one of them (somewhat) regrettable?
3   Should any restriction be made on the blatant expression of any one of them?
4   If you think that no instinct can really be said to be operating in some of the activities, what do you think causes people to engage themselves in these?

Be careful that you don't just jump to a glib conclusion. People of both sexes, for instance, often engage in sexual activity because of needs/drives other than sexual.

(1)   Choosing a holiday job as a beach boy rather than (the more lucrative) washing up in a restaurant

(2)    Sitting at the back in a conference

(3)    Returning to the same seat every time in the communal room of a hotel

(4)    Ignoring a stranger on his own in a bar

(5)    Wearing the colours of the local football team

(6)    Buying a hundred loaves of bread on hearing the rumour of a possible bread shortage

(7)    Attending a disco/party

(8)    Saying, 'Do you know who I *am*?' (emphasis on last word)

(9)    Wearing dark glasses in dull weather

(10)    Feeling afraid to open one's mouth in a group discussion/dominating a group discussion

(11)    A man beating up another who has seduced/gone off with his wife/girlfriend

(12)    Organizing a protest meeting in one's locality, against a proposed new development in your town

(13)    Dumping rubbish in the garden of the empty house next door/the occupied house next door/a local piece of waste ground

(14)    Refusing to accept congratulations on being runner-up rather than winner in a major sporting event

(15)    A girl strips at a party after having had one too many, but refuses all sexual advances which follow

(16)    Deliberately using long words among people you know won't understand them

(17)    Opponents on the abortion issue becoming physically violent with each other

(18)    Blowing one's car horn frequently and at great length

(19)    Having a personalized number plate on one's car (costing a month's wages)

(20)    Putting dozens of stickers on the rear window, indicating places you've visited

(21)    Parking next to the sole car in an otherwise empty car park

(22)    Wearing long fingernails/'loud' lipstick

(23)  Apologizing when accidentally touching a stranger

(24)  Not speaking to people next to you in a crowded train com-
      partment

(25)  Losing your anonymity in a doctor's waiting-room when the
      assistant loudly calls out your name

Does any instinct emerge from your reflections as more dominant than
the others? Or as more insidious?

    To what extent do you think survivability influences these situations?

# 5 Existentialism: being and becoming

In what has so far been discussed, I am conscious of having laid aside teachings which in the past were valuable to me – to some of which, in fact, I had for lengthy periods been totally committed. I now view these as characteristic of, for example, the lower reaches of a mountain and inferior to what lies ahead. In this central section of the book (Chapters 5–7) I shall therefore outline what seem to me to be the most rewarding contributions to the theme of the nature of humanity and the purpose of its existence, gleaned from many parts of the world and over many centuries. We shall be moving in an easterly direction: the first peak represents the best (as I see it) that Western philosophers have produced in answer to these eternal questions; thereafter, we shall leave the West behind and attempt to discover what insights may be gained from a far different culture, one which remains largely mysterious (in the sense of waiting to be revealed) to Westerners. Meanwhile the Western vantage-point from which I propose to make a survey, so to speak, is existentialism.

Readers who count their years of maturity (whatever that question-begging word may mean) as the 1970s at the earliest may not feel themselves deeply stirred by this word. It is, after all, long; it's ugly; and it's not very inspiring. Yet we need to go back only a few student generations earlier than the 1970s – to the 1950s and, particularly in the English-speaking world, the 1960s – to find an intellectual and social scene where the word was commonplace. There were existentialist views on art, an existentialist approach to religion, existentialist novels, plays, poetry and films: some people were described as existentialist even by the way they dressed or groomed themselves. However, not all those who used the word knew what they meant by it, such is the danger of being in vogue; and long before the death of the most famous (though not the deepest thinker) of the existentialists, Jean-Paul Sartre (1905–80), other fashions had overtaken it and it disappeared from public gaze. This was no great cause for sorrow from the philosophical point of view; but the sad fact was that it also faded into relative obscurity in the philosophical curricula of numerous universities and colleges and the gold (as I view it) was thrown out with the grit.

Part of the problem for anyone wishing to find out what existentialists had to say is that most of their books have been couched in, to put it mildly, difficult prose, often with newly concocted words and phrases whose exoticism bewilders the average reader, demanding such intense mental concentration that few besides those already committed to the existentialist perspective have been willing to make the effort involved in reading them. If you are among those who have held in their hands, for instance, Heidegger's *Being and Time*, or Sartre's *Being and Nothingness*, you will know that they lend themselves more naturally to weight-lifting exercises than to easy comprehension. What I hope to achieve here is to give an indication of the riches you have missed if you returned these books to the shelves unread.

My *modus operandi* here is different from that adopted in my previous book, *Living Philosophy*. There I outlined the views of several major existentialist writers in turn; here I shall deal with the subject thematically, referring specifically here and there to certain philosophers of the school. Not all of this will be a glowing testimonial, since not everything in existentialism do I find of equal value. We all wear blinkers of some kind – even the most enlightened of us.

## EXISTENCE AND ESSENCE

Perhaps the most famous sentence in existentialist vocabulary is Sartre's 'Existence precedes essence'. What does it mean? The distinction between existing and having being has already been described (pp. 8–9); as there are unicorns (unicorns have being) even though they don't exist – because they can be imagined – so, before I began to exist, I could be said to have had being as a twinkle in my parents' eyes (a twinkle soon to be removed by the actuality, I fear). It is with this actuality that we are here primarily concerned, after which we shall turn to the problems involved in our existence.

To begin with, we must lay aside any idea that we arrive in this world 'trailing clouds of glory'. The existentialist makes no claims to a previous existence, so does not speculate about the heaven from which we came or 'which is our home' (Wordsworth). Our home is here where we were brought into being. We may not like where we were born, to whom we were born, or when we were born; we may be surrounded (both literally and figuratively) by ugliness and squalor: but that is where, in Heidegger's phrase, we have been 'thrown'. By this word ('geworfen') he meant that we had absolutely no choice over where we began. To read anything but chance into the time, the place and the circumstances of our birth is therefore a **pathetic fallacy**, ascribing the human concept of purposiveness to a blind, unplanning process.

Let me apply this generalization to my own specific circumstances. I was born the eldest of four in the home of a Methodist minister. My father and mother met because he was sent by the Church to take up his first appointment in Lanarkshire, Scotland. If, as could have been just as likely, he had been sent elsewhere they would never have met and neither I nor my brothers and sister would have been born (and you would not have been reading this book). Similarly, it was pure chance that brought about my own marriage and subsequent birth of our three sons: the chance was the death in a road accident of my mother-in-law-to-be's cat. She (my mother-in-law, not the cat) developed a migraine because of this and sent her daughter to represent her at a meeting that evening where I was due to speak. A day later and she (my wife, as she was to become) was due to leave the area and take up permanent residence with a new job in another part of the country. One dead cat, three human beings.

With this blunt, some might say frugal, approach to our origins, existentialism removes *in toto* the idea either that we are destined in some way to be where we appear, or that any two people are 'meant' for each other. There is no golden thread, no overall plan, in this philosophy. We may look back on our lives and persuade ourselves that we can discern such a thread or a plan, but that is to assess life retrospectively, not prospectively. Anyone can read interpretations into the past; interpreting the future is an entirely different matter. We may of course *learn* from the past (and any sensible person will do so): but any kind of teleological interpretation – that is, one that looks forward to the end of the road – must be discarded. In the words of the music-hall song, 'We don't know where we're going until we're there.'

What then is this essence which existence is supposed to precede? Sartre sets off from the perspective of 'thrownness' (Heidegger's '*Geworfenheit*'): that we do not *choose* to exist but simply find ourselves existing. Our present existence is all; the rest lies in the 'not-yet' of the future. It is a mystery waiting to be revealed; and it will be revealed only gradually as we take step by single step, freely choosing to go one way rather than another. With these steps we express our choices about the ways whereby we shall exist; and so we create our own selves, our own essences. We are, or we become, what we make ourselves to be. Sartre expressed this perspective directly through one of his characters in *No Exit*:

> One always dies too soon – or too late. And yet one's whole life is complete at that moment, with a line drawn neatly under it, ready for the summing up. You are – your life, and nothing else.

Let us be quite clear at this stage not only as to what is being affirmed, but also about what is being denied, using Plato's perspective as a contrast to Sartre's. For Plato, as we have seen, everything in this life is a poor representation of the Ideal. This world is a pale reflection of heaven, human skills a feeble copy of the perfection to be found there, human creativity a shadow of the Ideal (or Forms) from which it takes its inspiration. In Plato's republic, the unseen Absolute is the only real and ultimate value; everything else is peripheral, transient, due to decay.

Existentialism rejects this perspective. It ignores the Platonic Ideals, allegedly experienced in an earlier existence in heaven, in favour of the reality of the here-and-now. Against the eternal, all-inclusive Absolute, it presents each individual as a separate being, having distinctive experiences which make him or her the person he or she is. There is no master-plan of a human being: we are made in nobody's image but our own. And nobody else can enter into our existence: it is ours, irretrievably ours, and no spirit or God can take possession of it. For each person, existence is his or her own individual universe, and neither stone walls nor iron bars (literally or metaphorically) can prevent them from experiencing it. Not that such restrictions are placidly accepted by existentialists (Sartre, for example, was active in social reform of the most radical kind): but the view prevails that, whatever the outward circumstances, the pure flame of existence can be experienced here and now within one's individual universe. Those whose perceptions of existence depend on external stimuli, such as drugs, or a pleasant environment, or a large income, are viewed as being like the prisoners in Plato's cave, except that here the reality to be found outside the cave is not that of the perfect Absolute but of personal freedom. (It is the freedom I observed one morning when a young house martin was forced to take its first flight because its parents no longer returned to the nest: I sensed from its squawks just before taking off the agony of facing the unknown; and experienced vicariously in its first glorious swoop the ecstasy of self-reliance.) This idea of freedom is central to existentialism, and we shall return specifically to it later.

BEING

The statement 'existence precedes essence' is, as we saw, Sartre's, and during the course of my comments on it I referred back to the distinction made in Chapter 3 between existence and being. It is now necessary to look more closely at this latter word, chiefly through the eyes of the greatest scholar among the existentialists (though he always preferred to be called an ontologist). **Martin Heidegger** (1889–1960).

Central to Heidegger's perspective is the fact of *Being*, a state which every human *being* experiences. Note that I have distinguished between 'Being' and 'being' in that sentence. With the lower case it is simply the designation of a particular species, so that we might describe any creature as a living being – including, as above, a human being. Our concern is with Being: the capital letter is purely an artificial device to avoid confusion (it is hoped). Being is the to-be of each one of us, the **sine qua non** of the words 'me' or 'you' having any meaning or content: without Being there is no me and no you. 'Essence' would be the wrong word to use here, for, as we have seen, we create our essences by the choices we make once we discover that we have Being. But we do not choose Being: we just *are*.

'Being' is thus both greater and less than 'essence'. It is the universe as any one of us experiences it. For me it is my universe, comprising not only my physical parts but also my world of thinking, imagining, remembering, hoping, planning, aspiring; all the ideas which formulate themselves in my mind, all the people I recall, all my memories from the past, all my intentions for the future, all the issues which, occasionally or frequently, slightly or overwhelmingly, weigh upon me; all my sense of confidence and all my anxieties, my sense of happiness and my regrets. All these are included in Being, in this case *my* Being, what Heidegger called '*Dasein*' or 'Being there'. Together they constitute my *field*, and I find this image totally rewarding, a true reflection of my response to the question of who and what I am. The phrase 'field of Being' will crop up (no pun intended) quite frequently from now on.

My Being (or, if you like, the Being of R B) is both what I am and what I am becoming: it is constantly changing, constantly adapting itself to new situations. It changes (or takes part in the *becoming* process) through the notions I may have of how I might alter (enlarge, modify, improve) my field: I may engage myself in new relationships, expose myself to new ideas, abandon old habits, read different books, travel to undiscovered places, or spend more time in contemplation or meditation. Any of these contributes to the *becoming* aspect of Being. At any point in my life a 'snapshot', so to speak, could be taken of the outward, physical form of my Being: but that snapshot, like an opinion poll, would be out of date before it could be revealed to others. Like the nucleus of an atom according to the quantum theory of physics, one cannot observe its mass and its velocity at the same time. Because Being is in a constant process of becoming, any 'still' has as much relation to the actuality as a still outside a cinema has to the motion picture to be viewed inside. The French film director, Jean-Luc Godard, tried to get round this one with his witty remark: 'Photography is truth. And cinema is truth twenty-four times a second.' But of course, with more sophisticated equipment, those twenty-four could be multiplied ten-, a hundred-, or a millionfold until, as in living reality, we reach infinity, when no split second, however infinitesimal, can be pinpointed as an identifiable event. Even as I gaze at students joining me in a philosophy seminar (which I do, of course, with a suitable sense of awe) I see them as they were a split second earlier, not as they 'are'.

The discernible extent of change, or 'becoming', in a person will vary from one to another. For some maybe the change will not appear very startling. Their likes and dislikes, their attitudes and opinions, their interests and prejudices become fixed or static: their field seems to alter very little. Of such a person it may be said 'He's always the same' or 'She never changes'. According to the perspective of the observer, this feature will be viewed as either a positive or a negative quality. From the point of view of the existentialists, it is tantamount to death. Unless Being is accompanied with becoming there is, so to speak, mass without velocity, a state of unconsciousness, Sartre described such a state as '*être-en-soi*', 'Being-in-itself', the unchanging condition of material objects – the way things are in the world. It includes not only the state of being at rest but also that of continuing forever in the same fixed direction. We shall return to this when discussing the concept of eternity (pp. 111–14). *Etre-en-soi* is inertia and is contrasted by Sartre with '*être-pour-soi*' or 'Being-for-itself' which is Being/becoming. I find Sartre's phrases odd, but underlying them is the ontological perspective that just as there can be no becoming without Being (that is obvious) so there can be no Being without becoming (that is less obvious but, from the vantage-point gained when we follow the existentialists, of central significance in our understanding of the issues we are reflecting on). Once the reality of this point has been perceived nothing, quite literally, can ever be the same again. As Aldous Huxley remarked:

> Consistency is contrary to nature, contrary to life. The only completely consistent people are the dead.

The existentialist answer to the question of what human nature is, then, that there is no such thing. The question is itself misplaced, since it implies that an unblurred snapshot of human nature can be produced. This snapshot, as we have acknowledged, can certainly be taken: but since what it portrays is immediately out of date, non-existent, the process of stopping the film (which is what is done when you state what human nature is) has value only as a means of seeing what we are not. Once this is realized, then we can appreciate how artificial are the explanations of human nature already considered: artificial because they all present a snapshot of what no longer exists as though it were an immutable reality. So we can confine to the sphere of discarded theories Freud's phantoms, Democritus's atoms, Lorenz's monkeys, Skinner's behaviourist observations, Aquinas's Master Architect and the saved soul of Augustine or Calvin. When describing Being we may use words like 'awareness', 'consciousness', 'openness' and so on: but in the end the only thing that can be done with Being is not to describe it but to be and to become. If we could grasp this then we should have come to see the enormous contribution which existentialism has made: a large part of Western ontology becomes redundant. We should be able to recognize that our Being-and-becoming are within our own scope and that we are free to choose what we are to be.

With this conception, another gain has been established in this elusive area: we have solved the problem of 'me' in such phrases as 'my body', 'my mind', 'my existence' and so on. This 'ghost in the machine', in Ryle's phrase already noted, is simply the field which is Being/becoming as I experience existence: the 'I' is just the shorthand term for that – potentially infinitely wide, but in reality somewhat circumscribed – arena of awareness. The 'I' is the whole of me; and the proof that I am, if proof I need, arises not just through the deployment of my rational faculties as Descartes averred but through every facet of my personality. Existentialism speaks of *homo sapiens* not just in terms of human reason but also in terms of the feelings, instincts, emotions, imagination and all the other qualities without which no one could be described as being 'whole'.

However, to state that the rational is not sufficient as a description of the to-be of us is not to say that it is not necessary, and I wish now to make some kind of rational account of ontological perspectives through existentialist eyes, beginning with their view of the *process* by which Being becomes – a process which they view as the eternally changing reality of the person. It is the process of *choosing*.

## CHOICE AND COMMITMENT

This is the most dynamic area of any field of Being. It is by the decisions we make when more than one form of behaviour seems open to us in a particular set of circumstances that we grow; and it is by refusing to take a decision (by letting someone else decide for us, perhaps) that we shrink. Even leaving matters in the 'pending' tray until it is too late for any meaningful decision to be made is a decision. As Sartre said, 'We are not free not to be free'; we cannot *not* choose. (Remember, Being and becoming are coexistent, co-essential, co-original and co-terminal.)

I don't want to give the impression here that *every* decision we make is laden with destiny. Some are clearly less fateful than others. It will normally, for instance, be no great earth-shattering matter what I choose to wear as I stand bleary-eyed before the wardrobe in the morning (though it might be – for example, if I were wishing to make some kind of statement via my clothes). The same goes for most of the day-to-day and year-by-year decisions I am called upon to make: the choice of birthday or Christmas presents, or of a new car; the acceptance or rejection of an invitation to speak at a particular function; whether or not to let my name go forward as candidate for a particular committee, or to retire from my college's table-tennis team. On the whole, while there could be exceptional circumstances which could make such decisions fateful, they are not such as to make me feel that I stand at a major crossroad in life from which there can be no turning back.

It's in the making of *moral* decisions that the *becoming* process is most telling, and it can bring the deepest anxiety to those involved. Should a family uproot itself in order to further the career prospects of one of the parents? Who, out of a number of potential recipients, should have prior claim on a hospital's limited resources? Does loyalty to one's group (a trade union, say) outweigh a strong conscientious objection to action proposed by that group (going on strike, say)? Sartre faced an even starker dilemma: when your country is occupied by an enemy power, do you risk your life (and almost certainly, whether they approve of your action or not, the lives of some of your fellow-citizens) by engaging yourself in direct subversive action against the enemy? Some of these more agonizing dilemmas may not come most people's way (perhaps because they avoid them rather than face them head-on) but most people are likely to encounter the need to make some kind of moral choice at some stage in their lives, even if it's only the question of how to coexist with a neighbour holding political views diametrically opposing their own.

From the existentialist point of view, the important point here is that, having made any decision, the person involved can never be the same again. Furthermore, all subsequent decisions, with this one behind them, will be affected by it. To refer again to our diagram (p. 69), every decision we make changes the line ZY into (say) YX rather than YW; which in turn means that the next decision will be made from the vantage-point X rather than W (which may mean – though you will never be certain about this – that you will face a decision which could never have confronted you at W; or vice versa).

## SØREN KIERKEGAARD

Among the existentialists, the process of choice has been discussed most comprehensively by the Dane Søren Kierkegaard (1813–55), often referred to as 'the father of modern existentialism'. In one of his books entitled, significantly, *Either-Or* he argues that it is as we stand at the divide (point Y in our diagram) that we most certainly face the opportunity for growth. The most agonizing choice that Kierkegaard had himself to make in his life was whether to marry his fiancée, Regine Olsen, or end his engagement to her and live a celibate life. His decision to follow the latter path was influenced by his sense that the pain that followed would allow him to feel the cutting edge of life more directly than could be possible in a state of connubial bliss. He has, of course, been criticized for his decision: psychologists have written obliquely about his masochism, feminists less obliquely about Regine's feelings. But these objections are beside the point: what matters is that it was through the agony of that decision and the consequent feeling of abandonment that

Kierkegaard was able to discover and express the insights which have commanded increasing attention over the years and have broadened and enriched the lives of many. The fact that he knew that Regine would also suffer because of his decision simply intensified his own sufferings, part of which, at least, was caused by the uncertainty which remained with him for the rest of his life as to whether or not he had made the right decision. It is certainly the case that if he had made this sacrifice for some patriotic reason (say) in time of war he would have received general acclaim. To make the sacrifice in order to experience life with more of its protective wrappers removed than most people experience, voluntarily or otherwise, and then to recount these experiences in the hope of enriching others along the way: this may be odd behaviour, but if it is to be condemned, so too must that of Buddha, or Socrates, or Jesus, or almost any martyr to a cause. (And next-of-kin also suffer when a martyr dies.)

Kierkegaard suggested that in the area of moral decision-making there are three categories of reaction. First, there is the attitude of what he called the *aesthete*. The word has come to mean a person with artistic gifts, or with a highly sensitive nature, but it is derived from the Greek word meaning to perceive or observe. For Kierkegaard, the aesthete is the person who sits on the sidelines and comments on moral problems without becoming in any way involved in them. Such a person will judge, say, the problem of racialism, or of inner city violence, from a variety of perspectives – psychological, sociological, historical and so on – without becoming in any way committed to the practical outworkings of the judgement (assuming the aesthete makes one at all: such a person is more likely to produce a statement along the lines of 'if this – then that . . . on the other hand . . . '. Kierkegaard reserved his strongest invective for such intellectuals who comprehensively analyse problems from their ethereal heights but otherwise contribute nothing to their resolution. (This is not to say that all analytical philosophers have been failures on this matter: many have been, and are, involved in conflicts at the coal-face as well as cogitations in the closet.)

The second reaction to moral dilemmas, according to Kierkegaard, is to take what he terms an *ethical* stance. This, it should be noted, he sees as an addition, not an alternative, to the aesthetic stance; he is not denying the value of analysis, but is suggesting that this is only the first step towards a more positive position (from scales to tunes again). To be ethical, in his phraseology, means not only to discuss the pros and cons of moral problems, but also to follow a particular ethical code. It means, for example, observing the principle of duty, as Kant proposed, or the Ten Commandments, the Communist Party Manifesto, or the Code of the Brownies: whichever it is, one commits oneself to living 'by the book'.

Kierkegaard accepts that this stance is a step forward from the purely aesthetic: the ethicist is at least doing something about moral issues besides merely observing and analysing them; but he remains critical of this new stance because of its highly impersonal, generalized approach to the problems. It is as if the moral agent has handed his or her individual powers of decision-making to a higher power, to whom or to which he or she defers at every point. The ethicist is as a judge administering a law with which he or she may privately disagree but which every judge is in duty bound to administer; or like a weak member of a family who shelters behind a stronger ('You touch me and I'll fetch my big brother'). Like a soldier who finds security in obeying Queen's Regulations (and maybe for soldiers this is the wisest procedure) he avoids the fear and anguish which might be involved if he had to decide issues for himself. It is infinitely less exacting for anyone to hold and put into effect the view that, for example, lying, stealing, committing adultery and killing are *never* to be condoned than to agonize over the question of if – and, if so, in what circumstances – exceptions might be justifiable. The ethical stance exemplifies what is termed absolutism in morals and there is no doubt that, at least on the face of it, it can give the upholder the appearance of authority, as many a timid congregation will testify after hearing a fire-and-brimstone sermon ('one man plus God is a majority').

The third and final reaction, Kierkegaard suggested, is one whereby the agent thinks his or her way into the heart of a moral dilemma, takes into account how various moral codes have pronounced on it, but then, so to speak, enters into the problem, so that it becomes part of him or her. The resolution of the problem may still be that of a particular received code, but it may not be so: and whether it is or not, it will still be a *personal* decision, arising not just from analysis of the problem, though this would of course be necessary; not just from knowledge of the 'law', though to be ignorant about this would of course be absurd; but from the crucible of individual experience, with the involvement of the whole Being. Kierkegaard called this the *religious* stance: one by which, rather than choosing between rival sets of rules or values, we so choose that, in Barrett's words, 'we summon good and bad into existence for ourselves' (*Irrational Man*, p. 147). Without this, Barrett adds, 'an abstract system of ethics is just so much paper currency with nothing to back it up'.

I am personally, as I indicated in Chapter 3, very cautious about using the word 'religious' except where it relates primarily to belief in God. Kierkegaard himself, as an ordained minister of the Presbyterian Church, would have been expected to believe and preach this, but the God of the Christian creeds was not, in fact, the God of his writings. Effectively his God was a God of faith and of hope: he believed that there was no divine master-plan, no revelation from on high, no certainty that the steps he took in faith would be proved right. Consequently his interpretation of the word 'religious' was different from that of common usage, and so long as we bear this proviso in mind, we can begin to appreciate the philosophy underlying the word's use. This is the thoroughly existentialistic *anguish* of the either-or situation, a situation to be embraced whole-heartedly since anguish is viewed as a positive state of mind. But it is more than that: it is the process by which one moves from the spectators' benches to the field of play. On that field, by being willing in the first place to *make* choices, and then by taking upon oneself the *responsibility* for any decision one may make (not letting others carry the can), one enters a state of readiness to move from adolescence into maturity. In a phrase which became popular in the 1960s, one comes of age. In Kierkegaard's own famous phrase, one makes the supreme 'leap of faith'.

Perhaps for Kierkegaard's words to describe the three responses – aesthetic, ethical and religious – I should wish to substitute derivations of three different words – observer, follower and initiator: but so long as we are quite clear of how he was using his chosen words, this seems of minor importance. What is important is that Kierkegaard has described with haunting clarity what truly moral Being is – or what it is to be truly moral. By the process he describes, the area of moral decision-making becomes, to return to Heidegger's word, part of one's field: in fact, a major part. *To be*, in Kierkegaard's sense of that phrase, includes to be moral: but it is a morality far beyond that of any written code. In terms of the 'Thou shalt nots' of, for instance, the Ten Commandments Søren Kierkegaard points to a state beyond good and evil. (See case study 21.)

## FREEDOM

If we are to accept Kierkegaard's account of the moral decision-making process, an essential requirement is that these decisions be judged to have been made freely. To describe as valid all that he and, later, Heidegger had to say, and then to fall back on any kind of deterministic stance, would be totally to undermine the perspective they had so painstakingly created. The idea and practice of freedom are thus central to existentialist thought, and we need to be clear about what this implies.

Freedom is both freedom *for* and freedom *from*; and the former can be appreciated only after we have clarified our minds about the latter. What is it, then, from which we are free? I've used a variety of terms in earlier chapters to indicate the range of forces from which, if we are to accept Being in all its potential fullness, we need to be both liberated and, more importantly, to *know* ourselves to be liberated. I shall epitomize these forces under the one term *phantoms*.

We are free, first of all, from the phantoms of the past. Countless events have occurred in years gone by which have become part of our field of Being. Some of these events – words cruelly spoken, deeds done uncaringly, relationships damaged by offence or neglect – we may now bitterly regret: and if we're not careful they will continue through the years to exert a disproportionate influence on our field – stunting it here, warping it there, always haunting us. The healthiest approach to this situation, I feel, is to recognize and truly accept that other events have occurred to change the field so that it is no longer what it was; and that by the choices we make from here on, the rebuilding process can continue. (The problem of finding that other people don't always realize that this process has actually occurred, so that they still relate to us as to our past selves, will be discussed later.)

I will not be so adamant as to affirm that no good ever came from raking over the past, but, ontologically speaking, the past is dead, and we are concerned only with the present as it eternally glides into the future: Being/becoming. As Aristotle remarked in his 'Nichomachean Ethics', quoting the Greek poet Agathon, 'Not even God can change the past.' Even if we substitute the more euphonious term psychoanalysis for my rather vulgar 'raking over the past' I think this approach holds true. The rebuilding process is not likely to be easy, and will probably involve considerable anguish on the part of the rebuilders; but the anguish will be positive because it will be a by-product of facing choice. As Heidegger said, time, or the process of becoming, is in any case linked with anxiety ('*Zeit*' and '*Sorge*' are one); the question is whether this anxiety is to be life-enhancing or life-denying.

If, for example, one partner in a marriage has done a grave wrong to the other, which he or she acknowledges, and they agree to make a fresh start and rebuild together, then, existentially speaking, they are in the process of creating for themselves vastly different fields which will increasingly blot out old offences. There seems nothing to gain, and much to lose, by disinterring what both partners agree was a wrong, undesirable set of choices. In other words, while it is impossible to return to point Y in the diagram once the decision to follow YX, or whatever, has been made, it is possible, by subsequent decisions, to move away from the direction taken in YX. Nothing can undo the earlier (wrong) choice; but as a new pattern in a Persian carpet is created from mistakes, so may a new field of Being. As it is, many people, apparently by choice, create for themselves a role not unlike that of released prisoners who – in their case, not at all by choice – find that though they may have paid their debt to society, a stigma from their past remains with them, causing doors to be shut, both literally and figuratively, in their faces. Stigmas need to be wiped out, or at least obliterated, not deliberately exposed.

If we are free from the phantoms of the past, according to existentialist thought, we are also free from those of the present. These haunt people in a variety of ways, but I will single out just one, because it has a wide range of ramifications: the concept of a comprehensive, overriding moral law or code to which human beings are called to render obedience. Sometimes this has been epitomized under the principle of duty, and for some people 'doing one's duty' is an acceptable rule of life. But the imprecision of that word has revealed its inadequacy as a guide: it is not always clear where one's duty lies (dealing with a school thief, for example – think about it), and sometimes one may be confronted with a clash of duties (home versus motherland, for example).

A more common basis than duty from which any demand for obedience is likely to spring is some form of written code of conduct. In suggesting that we can free ourselves from the tyranny of such a code, I don't wish to imply that we shall thereby find greater peace of mind, or sense of comfort: probably the reverse. Social life would be impossible without some sharing of values. But the problem is that the strength of any received code lies in its power to give a – what I believe to be bastard – sense of security to those who obey it, because it removes the need both to reflect on and to accept responsibility for one's behaviour. Any individual who speaks out against, or behaves contrarily to, an accepted code may become a social outcast, and will certainly have to defend the chosen stance right down the line. On the other hand, an individual who goes along with 'the book', even if this leads to behaviour that is cruel, cowardly, absurd, or quite irrelevant to the needs of the situation, is likely to meet little challenge or reproach.

Faithful obedience to a written code respected by others can, then, comfort the fearful and strengthen the weak; but it can also lead to a dependence that is akin to any other kind of crutch. Given a new twist to a situation, in which the ability to think, and assess, and act for oneself is essential, such a person would be likely to panic, or run away. Any received code can also set a person in a straitjacket so rigid as to effectively make that person inhuman, giving, perhaps, an easy conscience even as one wreaks havoc on those around. Dependence on 'the book', in whatever form it may have been compiled, has been more destructive of the process of Being than any other malady in the history of human travail. It has stunted initiative, destroyed independence and anaesthetized autonomy. To be released from such a prison-house is freedom indeed.

The entire concept of the received code is epitomized in the theistic view of God, the all-seeing eye which may create for some a sense of security, but in others induces fear or a sense of guilt. This is the image of One who knows all our dubious deeds or errant thoughts: 'the unseen Guest at every meal, the silent listener to every conversation'. From such omniscience there is no hiding-place; from such omnipresence there is no exit; surrounded by such omnipotence, there can be no personal authenticity. In such a condition no one is free, nor ever will be: Prometheus will be for ever impaled, and the field of Being reduced to a single furrow.

## DISCARDING LABELS

One significant act of freedom, which is in fact a basic symbol *of* our freedom, is the discarding of any kind of label or badge which classifies or categorizes us in one limiting form or another. To accept being classified is to accept bondage, because the act of classifying is one which by its sufficiency is exclusive and by its exclusivity is limiting. Labels are the hallmark of *être-en-soi*, not of *être-pour-soi*; they relate not to Being but to objects; they are the unreal snapshots referred to earlier. A person with a label (and of course I'm not here referring just to tangible objects they may wear, though these are candidates for inclusion under the category of 'unnecessary accretions to the person') diminishes him- or herself; the label overshadows the person and puts shackles on the total freedom of Being. Those who begin a statement with such words as 'speaking as a Catholic', or 'as a member of the hard left', or 'looking at this from the feminist point of view, I', have thereby clouded over the reality of who they are; and those who attempt to communicate with them will be contacting only an object, unchanged and unchanging. The contributions normally made by such people in public discussion or debate would, as a rule, be better made by carefully programmed computers.

Of course, the existentialist has to face the challenge: 'Well what about yourself? You're wearing the existentialist label.' Sartre's answer on numerous occasions was to deny that he was an existentialist: but his very need to do this reflects the determination of those around us to force all others into the straitjacket which the wearing of a label brings to pass. If to call oneself an existentialist is to adopt a label, then anyone who adopts the word for him- or herself may be accused of inconsistency. But since a central aspect of this philosophy is that one cannot be delimited in this way, this seems no more culpable than the act of a candidate for political office who describes him- or herself as 'independent'. (Normally one would be asked 'Independent what? Independent Democrat? Independent Conservative? A Jewish friend of mine when visiting Northern Ireland was asked by some colleagues whether he was Catholic or Protestant. When he told them he was a Jew they replied, 'But are you a Catholic Jew or a Protestant Jew?' I have found that the best answer to anyone who asks me how I designate myself is to follow Heidegger and declare myself an ontologist. Nobody knows what this means, and when I start to tell them they soon change the subject.)

## FREEDOM FOR

If existentialist Being is freedom *from* phantoms, it is also freedom *for* personal choice and growth. (It is also freedom to go to the dogs, commit suicide, or be a murderer, depending on the values we choose.) Sartre stressed that the greatest freedom is the freedom to say no. In the context of his own life, which included his activities with the French Resistance and his opposition to the French presence in Algeria, this was a totally positive statement, though of course a person who chose to be different just for the sake of being different would, ironically, then be in danger of assuming the label 'rebel', and so diminish him- or herself. Sometimes it may be right to be the violin soloist and lead, or go along with, the orchestra rather than the piano concertist and fight it. To be is not always to confront, though it is probably through acts of confrontation that the field of Being broadens and enriches itself most dramatically.

Being free *for* implies primarily the rejection of full-blooded determinism. Faced with a choice of directions, the existentialist believes that nothing that has gone before makes any of the options impossible too pursue. If this were not the case, the word 'option' would lose its meaning (you can choose any colour you like so long as it's green'). In the words of Immanuel Kant, whom Sartre greatly admired: 'Ought implies can.'

Any careful thought must indicate that this statement is axiomatic. To say, for instance, 'I ought (I have a moral obligation) to visit my sick, elderly mother, but I cannot (because I have broken my leg, or whatever)' is in fact ungrammatical. The 'ought' implies that there is a *preesent* obligation, which cannot possibly be the case if I am bedridden. The sentence should read, 'I ought to have visited my mother (it is the case that if I had been fit this would have confronted me as an obligation) but I cannot (therefore no moral obligation confronts me, therefore it is not the case that I ought to).' The person, on the other hand, who attends a cricket match or a ball game rather than visit a sick mother could well say at the end of the game, 'I had a moral obligation to visit her, and I could have done so.'

Whichever way they go, choices will create opportunities for subsequent choices. It is no more than a common-sense commentary on the human condition (and existentialists can make such comments as well as anybody else) to acknowledge that paths become patterns and actions become habits. What is done cannot be undone; the past cannot be changed. But – and this is the heart of the indeterminist argument – by the direction taken at decision-points or crossroads, the ill effects of any earlier (unsound) decisions, rather than being inexorably reinforced, can, if the agent so decides, gradually be compensated for, modified, or even annulled.

Thus the criticism of indeterminism that it is nonsense because of its claim that anyone can become whatever he or she wants to become is a – sometimes, I think, deliberate – misrepresentation of the position. The existentialist emphasis on this matter is simple and straightforward: the field of Being is not static, but changes with changing decisions. The *pattern* of the field is not forced on it by any external factor, though on many matters factors arising from *within* the field (the results of earlier decisions) will give an impetus in one direction or another whenever a decision is made. But there is all the difference in the world between an impetus and a compulsion. The existentialist doesn't suggest that there are *no* restrictions on moral choice (this would be to suggest that every field of Being returns to a fallow state with every decision that is made): what the existentialist argues is that any restrictions that manifest themselves are tendencies arising from within the field, not forces imposed on it from without.

Sartre's phrase 'free to do, free to be' often has deterministic scorn heaped on it, for the reason just mentioned; but in effect what Sartre is saying is that, because we are free to make the moral decisions we do when standing at some crossroad, and *since* that decision will change the field, whether in a small or large way, then our freedom is ultimately the freedom to be what we, by our freely made choices, have decided to make ourselves be. Thus we are free to be what we are not: in Sartre's words, 'My freedom consists in what I am not.'

One further thought may be added here. I am what I have made myself, not what I have made *of* myself. The latter phrase implies that I was presented at birth with some kind of basic essence and invited to proceed through life chiselling away at it. The implication of this, it seems, is that whatever modifications to the original essence I may make throughout life, the essentials of the finished product were there from the beginning, as the oak is contained within the acorn. It seems a more accurate description of my experience to say that throughout my life I have been responsible for the whole of my field – its size, its dimensions, its rich and its barren parts. By the decisions I have made, the priorities I have established, the values I have formed, the ideas I have developed, the relationships I have entered into, my field has become what it uniquely is: my creation, for which I alone am open to praise or blame. Like Sartre, I am always ready to listen to advice from others about the finished product as it is at present (and some of these others have more than their share of readiness to offer it): but it is up (or, in modern parlance, down) to me whether I choose or refuse to take this advice into my field.

## DEATH

The cessation of existence, or death, faces every living being, and its apparent finality has been the cause of greater anxiety among those who are aware of it than probably any other feature of our existence. In order to try to cope with this anxiety people – not just philosophers, but 'ordinary' people – have, as we have seen, propounded a wide range of theories to ameliorate if not totally overcome the starkness of the situation. Some have posited the concept of an immortal soul unaffected by the finitude of the body; others have looked to a new creation in which elements of the old are reborn, recreated, or reincarnated in a different (preferably improved) form; others have looked for some kind of survival through their seed (which seems hard on the celibate or childless). All of them have in common at least one feature: the desire to obliterate, if at all possible, the *fact* of death from their consciousness; to pretend that it is neither as final nor as absolute as it seems. So, in popular terminology, people do not die or cease to exist: they depart this life, or pass away, or fall asleep. These phrases, together with the thought-processes which foster them, reflect a natural dread born of a deep-seated reality: the inability of Being to conceive of non-Being, or nothingness. So belief in some form of existence after the death of the body becomes a cushion against the confrontation with the cessation of Being – a state which, when you think about it, is the ultimate in illogicality. Belief in immortality is a safety-net over the abyss of oblivion, a shield against the blinding realization of our impermanence. In this way, against all the evidence (for we all know *about* death, even though we shall never *know* it, death being by definition the cessation of, among other things, consciousness), it becomes possible for a person to avoid the anxiety of non-Being.

In settling for this protection, however, there is a risk to be taken, which not all believers in immortality have successfully avoided: the risk of losing touch with reality. It is possible to be like people in a lift when the cable breaks: being unaware of the appalling nature of the situation, they continue to feel secure, if not positively happy. The gain is that there is no panic, or sense of *need* to panic ('Crisis? What crisis?'); their loss is their false perception of the situation – a perception which will never be rectified since when reality hits them – literally – they will cease to be. To deny the reality of non-Being may indeed prevent the anxiety, to which the awareness of the fact of death leads, from entering their Being: but without this anxiety the danger is that their field of Being fails to become a real field but an hallucination, a dream, an imaginary universe created from self-deception and delusion.

In the real field of Being we come to terms with our finitude rather than deceive ourselves into believing it isn't there. This means not just that we acknowledge the limitations in the field – that there are certain sections which are never likely to be developed, some plans for it that will never be carried through, some parts that will never be fruitful, some no-go areas – though this is in itself a sobering thought: coming to terms with one's finitude is to know, not just as a cognitive experience but at the very core, or ground, of our Being, that Being itself is pervaded by non-Being. This may seem to some a pessimistic idea, but for the existentialist – or, at any rate, for one who is in tune with Heidegger's *Being and Time* – it is the only realistic ontological perspective. The stark fact is that, without the realization of non-Being (in the literal sense of making it real, or accepting it as real, in one's own field), Being is not real. Believing in one's own *immortality* risks – to put it no stronger – destroying the reality of Being and replacing it with the hallucination already mentioned. It is to risk trying to exist in a universe of make-believe, and so never truly *existing* at all.

This probably sounds a morbid (figuratively as well as literally), even paradoxical statement, but a few moments' reflection should indicate that it is the only positive way to find both reality and purposiveness (Being/becoming). Bereft of non-Being or, put another way, without the realization of the certainty of the cessation of existence which lies ahead of me, and to which I am inexorably moving, my field would be 'without form, and void' (Genesis 1). Remove the fact of non-Being and replace it with the concept of immortality and there is no place for change, or development, or growth, or by whatever other word we may describe the process of becoming, which, as we have seen, is inseparable from Being. If Being is eternal, it does not need to change, or grow: infinite Being, at least as contemplated by many believers in immortality, is *unbecoming*; it suggests that the snapshot mentioned earlier is eternally real, yet we know in our constant experience and as an ever-present reality that because to be is to be in a continuous state of flux, such a snapshot cannot be real. It is an attempt to portray mass without velocity, and neither of these can be independent of the other. In short, if there is Being there is also becoming – the two concepts are interdependent; infinite Being is immutable (unbecoming): therefore infinity, or immortality, the refusal to acknowledge the reality of non-Being, cannot coexist with Being. That, at any rate, is the existentialist conclusion, in reaction to specifically Western views of immortality as expressed in Plato's theory of Forms, or the theistic views of heaven, or paradise. We shall see in Chapter 7 that Eastern philosophy approaches the question from a different perspective, from which the West may have much to learn.

It may be argued that I am here referring to Being only as we mortals experience it, and that the whole argument is circumscribed by the limitations of human thought-processes which are inevitably restrained and blinkered, like prisoners in a cell. Acknowledge that there may be a different, infinitely wider dimension, it might be argued, and the whole issue would be transformed. As it is, we are mere human beings attempting to discuss the impossible, like debating variations of colour in a totally black universe. The reply to this is that *my* field of Being, the Being that I experience, is all that I can describe. To believe in personal survival after death is to add a new ontological dimension to existence. As an act of religious faith on the lines of Kierkegaard's blind step into the dark, this is fine; but as a philosophical commitment it is as unrealistic (and absurd) as teaching art as though there were an extra colour in the rainbow, or discussing human relationships as though there were a third sex. In this context, the concept of immortality is an alien form of thought. (See case study 14.)

Evidence for this bald affirmation is provided by the universal experience of *time*. Time is the union of the now and the not-yet into one continuously changing reality of experience. Immortality can have no part in this reality, since immortality implies immutability, a state of non-change. And to achieve *that* state we should have to enter into a different dimension from that of universal experience. In that dimension, the word 'now' would be meaningless, since the meaning of 'now' arises only from our awareness of the not-yet, with which it is contrasted. To be is to be in this process of time, and we cannot conceive of Being outside it. For the full significance and application of this difficult idea we shall need to study Taoism and the philosophy of Yin and Yang (see Chapter 7).

Without death, then, there is no life: death emanates from life and life from death. Nothingness, in Heidegger's words, 'is a presence within our own Being'. And only when Being is interpenetrated with non-Being does Being consist of anything at all. Everything of significance in life – our relationships, our abilities, our work, our skills, and so on – is made significant by the ever-present fact of death. All these features are given their poignancy by their transitoriness (would you be reading this book *now* if you knew that you were to live for ever?). This may sound, as I remarked earlier, a pessimistic philosophy (and many have so described it) but it is in fact the most positive ontological affirmation that could be made. Trying to avoid this truth because of the anxiety it brings with it is like trying to escape into the nursery world of timeless childhood. It is like an alcoholic man refusing to acknowledge that he has a mortal disease; like a doting mother who will not *see*, let alone acknowledge, the faults in her child; like Sigmund Freud in old age, refusing to face up to the cancer on his lip. In all these circumstances, recognition of reality in the situation will bring enhanced anxiety: but only by coming to terms with that anxiety can one truly be. We may wish it otherwise, but this is what Being is: permeated at every point by non-Being. This is one existentialist view of death, and Barrett (*Irrational Man*, p. 202) summarizes it in these words:

> Our finitude is such that positive and negative interpenetrate our whole existence. That man is finite is not merely a psychological characteristic of him personally or of his species. Nor is he finite because his number of allotted years on this earth is limited. He is finite because the 'not' – negation – penetrates the very core of his existence. And whence is this 'not' derived? From Being itself. *Man is finite because he lives and moves within a finite understanding of Being.*

## AUTHENTICITY

I have been conscious in recent pages of grasping (sometimes with difficulty) after the right words to express what is, I think, the heart of existentialism. We turn now to an emphasis in this philosophy which is perhaps more easily described. Existentialist writers have not always agreed about every idea they have expressed, but on one issue there is a common affirmation, though with differing extensions: *the essential characteristic of existentialist Being is authenticity*.

The basic component of authenticity is *autonomy*. This word means literally a law unto oneself, which has an undesirable connotation in the English-speaking world – that of a person who disregards, when they don't happen to suit him or her, both convention in general and accepted codes of moral conduct in particular. It is because of this that existentialism gathered unto itself the image of 'doing one's own thing', being different for the sake of being different, affronting any kind of accepted taste, dropping out, even, perhaps, seeking to create an alternative society. Against these criticisms I should want to stress that to be autonomous does not mean – or let us be precise and say it does not *necessarily* mean – laying aside the norms, the standards, the values with which one is surrounded, even though one may not be greatly enamoured of these. There is a universe of difference between rejecting for rejection's sake and accepting only after independently testing what is on offer.

To be authentic means in the first place, then, not to go along with any gusts that blow just because they're blowing. The existentialist's field is his or her own, not that prescribed by the local co-operative. Nor is it in some world of make-believe, and this leads to the second feature of authenticity: the person who possesses this quality shows a real face to the world – to friends and colleagues, neighbours and relatives: *and does not hide behind a persona, or mask*. We have already indicated the kind of tendency this represents when discussing the use of labels as a means whereby an individual shelters behind a group: this means surrendering part, at least, of one's authenticity, and is invariably divisive. Wearing a mask is another means of taking refuge in this way – hiding behind a smokescreen, sheltering behind status, or rank, or profession: never to stand bare-faced and be oneself.

Sartre uses the example of a waiter who, by showing excessive obsequiousness, pretends to be that which he is not. Maybe this was an extreme example; not every waiter can behave like Basil Fawlty in the British T.V. series *Fawlty Towers*: but the fact that people remember Sartre's waiter suggests that his choice of example illustrates clearly what to him was probably the gravest sin a person could commit: *mauvaise foi* – bad faith. By this he meant not being true to oneself, pretending to be other than what one is. Case study 15 will allow you to follow through this idea in a number of hypothetical situations.

In delineating his idea of authenticity, Sartre writes at some length about the *responsibility* of personal choice. His argument here has often been criticized and even more often misunderstood, so it would be well to read his precise words:

Of all the actions a man may take in order to create himself as he wills to be, there is not one which is not creative, at the same time, of an image of man such as he believes he ought to be.

It has seemed to some that he is here abandoning existentialist views and falling back on a view not far removed from Kant's categorical imperative (quoted on p. 53). To others it has seemed to be pure self-centredness ('What's good enough for me/General Motors/Yorkshire is good enough for everyone'). It may be that the words he chose here were somewhat infelicitous, carrying with them the risk of being misinterpreted, but what he was trying to say seems to me fair, unconceited and an unambiguous expression of the existentialist view of choice. It must be understood in the light of Sartre's teaching elsewhere, which included (1) choice is made freely: there is no external compulsion; (2) it is made with full knowledge of the circumstances, and the awareness that it will have import for future choices; if this is the case then (3) the choice stands every chance of being made without bigotry or prejudice: other people's interests will be considered besides the agent's own interests.

This may be criticized as an idealized picture of actual decision-making, since not *all* the facts of a situation can ever be known for certain. But that is quite beside the point: the individual moral agent making a choice may well at the time have every reason to believe that it is the best one possible granted the available information. Kierkegaard's anguish arose from being totally uncertain about the consequences of his choice, and in particular about whether a different choice would have yielded a more desirable outcome: he was quite certain about the circumstances surrounding the choice. Similarly, for Sartre, those with heightened awareness of situations are in a position to make more mature decisions, and others may well benefit from this circumstance.

This very maturity, however, brings with it the anguish born of awareness, of being an adult rather than a child. The adult has nobody else to blame for the choices made; cannot shelter behind social environment, psychological past, evolutionary history, God, or ancestry: carries the can. And it follows from this that, more than those who feel free to pass the buck, if an adult should prove to have been wrong in a choice, that man or woman is likely to have to face stern rebukes from their peers. But this is a small price to pay compared with the reward gained by each individual who turns away from the safety of conventional codes or absolutist ideals in favour of the creative anguish of unfettered choice. As D. H. Lawrence wrote in *The Phoenix*:

Away with all ideals. Let each individual act spontaneously from the for ever incalculable prompting of the creative wellhead within him. There is no universal law.

It's worth noting that in one respect, at least, this emphasis of Sartre's falls on the profit side of any existentialist balance sheet: it gives the lie to those who view this philosophy as expressive merely of self-centred egotism – something like Ayn Rand's objectivism with a kinder face (see p. 239). It means that categorizing existentialism as simply 'doing one's own thing' is proved to be diametrically wrong – a misinterpretation born partly of too glib an appraisal of the phrases used. It is a philosophy which explains the emergence of the pioneer or reformer in any community since, while the expression of authenticity may allow one to accept the surrounding mores, it may lead to the rejection of these. The risk for such a person has been pungently expressed by **Julian Huxley** in his book *Evolution and Ethics*:

> One of the unpardonable sins, in the eyes of most people, is for a man to go about unlabelled. The world regards such a person as the police do an unmuzzled dog, not under proper control.

The reward to be gained by positively embracing one's autonomy more than compensates, I think, for the sense that many people feel uneasy in the presence of anyone whom they cannot neatly slot into a convenient pigeon-hole.

The existentialist response to the question 'What is human nature?' is, then, that there is no point in attempting an answer because the question is itself question-begging. The questioner assumes, as Western philosophy generally has assumed, that 'human nature' is a definable entity, and that if we can just manage to agree about what it is, the whole problem will be neatly solved. Not so, is the existentialist response. Existence precedes essence and makes nature redundant. We begin to exist and from that point onwards we make ourselves as we will through our freely made choices. To state that there is such an identifiable thing as human nature is therefore to deny the validity of the whole existentialist approach.

The implications of this will be considered later in the book as we descend, so to speak, from the mountain peaks and try to take stock of what has been gained there, and how it may affect our understanding of Being. Meanwhile, let the last word be with Heidegger, the greatest of the existentialists, and with his expositor, William Barrett (*Irrational Man*, p. 221):

> Sartre has advanced as the fundamental thesis of his Existentialism the proposition that existence precedes essence. This thesis is true for Heidegger as well, in the historical, social, and biographical sense that man comes into existence and makes himself to be what he is. But for Heidegger another proposition is even more basic than this: namely, Being precedes existence. For without the open clearing of Being into which man can transcend himself, he could not ex-sist, ie stand out

beyond himself. Man can make himself be what he is only because all his projects are revealed to him as taking place within the open field or region of Being.

*Case study 13*
*Faith*

Kierkegaard's existentialist philosophy was centred on his view of faith as the only means of being sustained amid the uncertainties of life – faith rather than knowledge, for this, as we saw in the text, we could not possess. But what is faith?

It has been cynically described as 'believing what you know isn't true', which is absurd; but 'believing even when you can't understand' would be true for some people – like accepting the literal truth of the biblical account of creation because of the belief that these words were written at the dictation of God, who cannot lie, even though reason, as presented by the scientific evidence, seems to refute this; or, on the other hand, believing that there must be a logical explanation for some incident, such as phenomena allegedly caused by the activity of a poltergeist. Both these examples suggest that faith is, in the words of Tennyson's *In Memoriam*, 'believing where we cannot prove': and that might well be in line with Kierkegaard's experience. It is certainly more realistic (that is, an understandable and acceptable stance to take) than faith as described by Mencken: 'an illogical belief in the improbable'; and Kierkegaard's views seem to confirm the assertion of Chesterton that 'reason is itself a matter of faith'.

The questions that follow are intended to allow you to explore the phenomenon of faith a little further, chiefly by comparing and contrasting it with other (equally undefinable!) qualities.

1   *Faith and hope* Can you state how these differ (in their effects on behaviour, their spheres of relevance, etc.)? Is faith stronger than hope? – was Kierkegaard doing more than hope for the best? Would you rather belong to a 'land of hope and glory' than to one of 'faith and glory' and what would the difference be? If I write to someone, 'I hope to see you next week', am I saying more, less, or something different from what I'd mean if I wrote, 'I have faith that I'll see you next week'? Or I hope my soul will survive my death' and 'I have faith that it will survive my death'?

2   *Faith and belief* Are these cognate ideas, or can you extrapolate a distinction between them? Comment on this statement: 'I believe in the promise of fidelity made by my partner because I have faith

in him/her.' Has Voltaire offered a perceptive distinction with his words, 'Faith consists in believing when it is beyond the power of reason to believe'?

Discuss the differences of nuance in the following:

(a)  I believe in God. I don't believe in God. I believe there is no God.

(b)  I believe he'll arrive in twenty minutes.

(c)  'I believe in the ultimate goodness of things.'

(R. L. Stevenson)

(d)  I believe Beethoven is a greater composer than Paul McCartney.

(e)  I believe in fairies. I don't believe in fairies.

(f)  I believe in General Motors.

(g)  I believe my spouse loves me.

(h)  I believe I can win.

How different in meaning would the questions be if for 'I believe' you substituted 'I have faith'?

3  *Belief and knowledge* Is the difference between these simply based on the degree of certainty involved? Try substituting 'I know', or a cognate phrase, for the 'I believe' statements above. (You may conclude that we are too casual in our use of the words 'I believe'.) Should we keep the words 'I believe' just for statements whose truth cannot be verified? Could we then accurately and truthfully make the statements given in case study 29 (p. 286)?

Faith has been described as 'betting your life there's a God'. Leaving aside the religious reference, do you think that, on the whole, faith relates to those things in life on which we set greatest value, simply because they *cannot* be proved as a mathematical theorem can be proved? St Paul said, 'We walk by faith, not by sight': he was referring, of course, to the Christian faith, but could this not also apply to an atheist, or an existentialist? Reflect on your own values, those things which are the most rewarding features in your life, and ask yourself how far it would be possible, if you were challenged to do so, to *prove* the validity of what you hold to be important. (See also case study 24, esp. p. 232, qu. 4.)

*Case study 14*
*Death*

The state of death, or non-being, inevitably features prominently in any ontological discussion, and this book has been no exception. The range of attitudes to death is, as we have seen, enormous, and in this study we have put together a number of well-known (or quite well-known) statements expressing a variety of attitudes. Discuss them with the following questions in mind.

**1**  Is this statement saying any more than that death remains the 'great unknown'?

**2**  Does this affirmation do any more than clutch at straws?

**3**  Could I live as though this statement were true, and still be true to myself?

**4**  If this statement could be proved to be true, would it affect my priorities in life in any way?

(1)  'I was not. I was miserable. I am not.'
>                                    (inscription on an Indian gravestone)

(2)  'The dead shall be raised incorruptible.' (I Corinthians 15. 52)

(3)  'After your death you will be what you were before your birth.'
>                      (Arthur Schopenhauer, *Parerga and Paralipomena*)

(4)  'Christianity has made of death a terror which was unknown to the gay calmness of the Pagan.'
>                                    (Ouida, *The Failure of Christianity*)

(5)  'Ideal mankind would abolish death, multiply itself million upon million . . . until the accumulation of mere existence is swollen to a horror.'
>                                          (D. H. Lawrence, *St Mawr*)

(6)        'Sleep after toil, port after stormy seas,
>          Ease after war, death after life does greatly please.'
>                                    (Edmund Spenser, *The Faerie Queene*)

(7)  'A useless life is an early death.'
>                                       (J. W. von Goethe, *Iphigenie*)

(8)  'Any man's death diminishes me, because I am involved in Mankind; And therefore never send to know for whom the bell tolls; it tolls for thee.'
>                                          (John Donne, *Devotions*)

(9)  'I do really think that death will be marvellous . . . If there wasn't death, I think you couldn't go on.'
>                                    (Stevie Smith, *London Observer*, 1969)

(10)  'This is the end – for me, the beginning.'
>                          (Dietrich Bonhoeffer; before his execution)

(11)  'Men fear death as children fear to go in the dark; and as that natural fear in children is increased with tales, so is the other . . . It is natural

to die as to be born; and to a little infant, perhaps, the one is as painful as the other.'

(Francis Bacon, 'Of death')

(12)   'Sickness, sin and death, being inharmonious, do not originate in God, nor belong to His government.'

(Mary Baker Eddy, *Science and Health*)

(13)                'He is made one with Nature: there is heard
                    His voice in all her music, from the moan
                    Of thunder, to the song of night's sweet bird;
                    He is a presence to be felt and known
                    In darkness and in light, from herb and stone,
                    Spreading itself where'er that Power may move
                    Which has withdrawn his being to its own . . .
                    He is a portion of the loveliness
                    Which once he made more lovely.'

(P. B. Shelley, 'Adonais'; on the death of John Keats)

(14)   'He sought his former accustomed fear of death and did not find it. "Where is it? What death?" There was no fear because there was no death.

In place of death there was light.

"So that's what it is!" he suddenly exclaimed aloud. "What joy!"

To him all this happened in a single instant, and the meaning of that instant did not change. For those present his agony continued for another two hours. Something rattled in his throat, his emaciated body twitched, then the gasping and rattle became less and less frequent.

"It is finished!" said someone near him.

He heard these words and repeated them in his soul.

"Death is finished," he said to himself. "It is no more!"

He drew in a breath, stopped in the midst of a sigh, stretched out, and died.'

(Leo Tolstoy, *The Death of Ivan Ilych*)

What value, if any, do you think there is to be gained in reflecting on death? Should we simply view it, with Hobbes, as the 'great unknown', and leave it at that?

*Case study 15*
*Bad faith and authenticity*

Being true to oneself, and refusing to wear a mask or a label, or to play the role expected of you (unless this is an expression of the basic 'you' as you perceive yourself to be, in which case it will presumably not be playing a role) are all ways, according to Sartre, of avoiding bad faith. But sometimes (1) such ruses are more justifiable, and (2) they are harder to avoid, than at other times.

This case study is divided into various categories, each presenting a number of hypothetical situations. Reflect on these with the following questions in mind:

**1**  Is the person concerned
   (a)  greatly responsible for what takes place?
   (b)  only partially responsible?
   (c)  a victim of circumstances rather than a culprit?

**2**  If you find that bad faith is in fact being shown, or is likely to be shown, in any of the situations, do you think this to be
   (a)  very unfortunate;
   (b)  somewhat unfortunate;
   (c)  quite unimportant?
   Do you feel, in any of the situations, that the manner described is preferable to one of total openness? Do you think there is ever a case to be made for inauthenticity?

(1)  Overheard:
   (a)  'My name is Doctor Roberts. You have a table booked for four.' (a restaurant)
   (b)  'Professor Jones.' (answering the phone at the university)
   (c)  'Professor Jones.' (ditto, but at home)
   (d)  'Professor Jones's house.' (the spouse answering the phone)
   (e)  'As a sabbatarian, I cannot support the sailing of ferries to this island on Sundays.'

(2)  Grooming and dress: how do you react to
   (a)  a person who wears dark glasses in cloudy weather
   (b)  a beard on a man whom you know to have no facial deformities or scars
   (c)  a woman who always wears the latest fashions
   (d)  a person who clearly wears whatever first comes to hand
   (e)  a group of besuited men at a sports event, invitees to a company's 'hospitality tent'

(3)  Seen on office/study doors
   (a)  Dr Smith (lecturer at a college)
   (b)  Managing Director
   (c)  Chief Engineer
   (d)  Private (Head of Department at a technical college)

 (e) Joe (Manager of Wells Fargo Bank in a town in northern California)

(4) Hypotheticals: what would you do if
 (a) you are with a drinking companion who makes a racist remark or tells a crudely racist joke
 (b) ditto, but after dinner at your companion's home
 (c) ditto, but this companion could be financially useful to you
 (d) you are a smoker with devoutly anti-smoking parents. The time has come to make your annual visit to them. They don't know you smoke.
 (e) you are an atheist, but your father is a retired clergyman. When he comes to visit you, he asks you to join him in Sunday Communion at church.
 (f) you and your fiancé are due to be married. No member of either family is a church-goer, but both sets of parents want the ceremony to take place in church.
 (g) ditto about your beliefs, but the parents are church-goers
 (h) you and your spouse are both keen left-wingers, strong supporters of comprehensive, or state, education. All your child's friends attend a local fee-paying school – and you could afford for your child to do to same. Your child requests that s/he be sent there.

(5) Which of the following remarks can you most/least easily tolerate?
 (a) 'I'm older than you, therefore. . .'
 (b) 'I've been here longer than you, therefore. . .'
 (c) 'I'm senior to you in this firm (etc.), therefore. . .'
 (d) 'I've travelled around more than you, therefore. . .'
 (e) 'I've suffered more than you, therefore. . .'
 (f) 'I'm more qualified than you, therefore. . .'
 (g) 'When you've got a husband/wife/home/responsibilities (etc.) of your own. . .'

Do you think that to compromise on your principles in order to avoid a confrontation, or not to hurt another person, is always a sign of inauthenticity?

# 6    *The encounter between existentialism and theism*

While many professional philosophers in the English-speaking world have been sceptical about existentialism, certain members of the theistic camp made a bold attempt to take it into their system. My doubts about theistic ontology have been, and will continue to be, a constant feature of these writings, but the encounter we are here considering produced (or was created by) a number of remarkable men and women; and this exploration would be less than comprehensive if I were to turn to Eastern philosophy without first taking account of their highly significant contributions to the debate.

## PAUL TILLICH (1886–1965)

Tillich was perhaps the most famous of the philosopher-theologians in the 1950s and 1960s who attempted to combine with their own religious beliefs a philosophy that had been expressed primarily (though not exclusively) in atheistic terms. He was a German Protestant who during the 1930s sought exile in the United States, and until his death lectured in Systematic Theology at Union Theological Seminary in New York. He wrote voluminously and it is difficult to summarize his views in a few paragraphs. They were, however, popularized in the United Kingdom (where, as in the United States, he had become something of a cult figure) in a book published in 1963 by the then Bishop of Woolwich, John Robinson, entitled *Honest to God*. This book became something rare for one of its genre: a best-seller, with millions of copies sold in a dozen languages. Few books are honoured by a publication to mark the twenty-fifth anniversary of their first appearance, but *Honest to God* is one of these (*God's Truth*, SCM, 1988). In every sense it was a seminal work, and I count myself privileged that, as a friend of the author, I was one of a select few who read the typescript of the book before publication: forewarned was forearmed, but that is another story, recounted in *The Honest to God Debate* (ed. D. Edwards, SCM, 1964).

Tillich had experienced the advent of Nazism while still in Germany and had encountered the degrading, dehumanizing effects of its influence on German society. One consequence was that many people who had believed in an almighty God, 'Creator and Preserver of all mankind', had abandoned their faith and adopted a nihilistic attitude of despair. How, they asked, could an omnipotent and benevolent Being allow such evil not only to rear its head but also, apparently, to prosper? We discussed this problem in Chapter 3, but Tillich's answer was to turn back, in effect, to the philosophy and idea of God which Kierkegaard had offered. For him, as we saw, there had been no blinding light on the Damascus Road such as had sustained St Paul amid his persecutions and travails, his doubts and fears. All we can do, Kierkegaard had suggested, is to walk forward in blind faith. The 'either/or' situations demanded choice (and Nazism presented to Tillich as to millions of others an extreme example of such situations): this choice could be made not out of knowledge, for this we do not possess, but out of hope – the hope that all will be revealed at the end of the road. In this endeavour, God emerges, not as the One who shows us the way or provides all the answers, but as the *Ground of our Being*, the One who sustains us along the road.

This italicized phrase and its cognates, and the ontological position which it reflects, will increasingly occupy the high ground in this book. Tillich seized on it from his studies in Eastern philosophy and argued that this Ground of Being must be our basic motivation, a power that drives us from within rather than, as in traditional God-talk, 'out there'. By employing this phrase, Tillich was substituting the traditional image of a **transcendent** God with all the divine characteristics discussed in Chapter 3 with that of an **immanent** God – the inner light rather than the Lord of Creation.

Effectively, though the phraseology used by both men differed enormously, of course, Tillich here reached a position not dissimilar to Sartre's: when confronting either/or situations we can rely only on what strength we have within ourselves. Sartre described this strength solely in human terms while Tillich gave it a more divine dimension but in practice both reached the conclusion that, facing situations of conflict, we either find this inner motivation, or not at all. For Sartre this meant pursuing being-for-itself, choosing freely, acting authentically, and in the process accepting the responsibility of representing the human race. He stopped short of acknowledging the all-embracing Ground of Being, since he viewed essence as that to which each individual existence was moving, even though it could never be achieved; and this essence therefore remained a constantly unfolding mystery (unfolded as successive choices were made). For Tillich the inner motivation was the invisible God who can be apprehended only by faith. This God had often been proclaimed to be the ultimate motivation of people's lives, the core of their existence, their basic drive. Tillich, significantly, expressed this the other way round: these fundamental features of our lives, of which we are all aware, should be identified as God, the Ground of Being.

Why then introduce the word 'mystery' into this context? Surely, it might be protested, we know about drives and motivation; without them we should hardly be able to get out of bed in the morning, or face the problems of the day. Most of those who reflect on the matter for a moment or two are, however, likely to realize that the issue is more complex than is suggested by the simple, everyday words employed. Human motivation is hard to analyse and difficult to pinpoint. Motives are mixed and operate at different levels – primary, secondary, tertiary and so on. Tillich's argument is that underlying all these more ephemeral motives is the ultimate motivation, the Ground of Being. We may never know what exactly *is* our ultimate motivation, but the fact that we exist at all reveals that it is there. And the same, suggests Tillich, is true for the Ground of Being: the very fact that we *are* demonstrates this. Strengthened by the certainty of this, Tillich argued, humanity could aspire to more than was possible without this perception; in Heidegger's terms, the field was potentially richer. The tragedy of human existence, Tillich averred, is that we have lost touch with the Ground of our Being; or, in Sartrian terms, we have lost sight of the way towards our essence, settling for Being-in-itself rather than Being-for-itself. Tillich expressed the foreboding in his book of essays, *The Shaking of the Foundations* (pp. 161f.):

> The state of our whole life is estrangement from others and ourselves, because we are estranged from the Ground of our Being, because we are estranged from the origin and aim of our life. And we do not know where we have come from [Heidegger's '*Geworfenheit*', or 'thrownness', perhaps] or where we are going. We are separated from the mystery, the depth, and the greatness of our existence. . .
>
> We cannot escape, however. If that something is the Ground of our Being, we are bound to it for all eternity, just as we are bound to ourselves and to all other life. . . Despair means that there is no escape. Despair is the 'sickness unto death'. But the terrible thing about the sickness of despair is that we cannot be released, not even through open or hidden suicide. For we all know that we are bound eternally and inescapably to the Ground of our Being. [This] has become more visible to our generation than to preceding generations, because of our feeling of meaninglessness, emptiness, doubt, and cynicism – all expressions of despair, of our separation from the roots and meaning of life. Sin in its most profound sense, sin as despair, abounds amongst us.

Thus Tillich is affirming that because we have lost sight of the Ground of our Being, our existence has become estranged from our essence. Sartre had used different language to describe what essence meant in relation to existence, saying that it was the 'becoming' part of humanity, the being-for-itself; but he would have agreed with Tillich that, in ceasing to become, humanity had lost touch with its essence.

If Tillich had continued in that vein, it would have been possible to have been more than lukewarm in responding to his ontological discourse, and to have numbered him among the true existentialists. Unfortunately he did not continue in that vein (or, at any rate, not exclusively so). Rather, he fell back on the mythology of Judaism and Christianity, and so removed himself – or so it seems to me – from the central stage of this ontological discussion. I have suggested (p. 113) that Being without becoming (in-itself without for-itself) is equivalent to death. Tillich uses the word sin in preference to death in this context (though he no doubt had in mind that 'the wages of sin is death'), but his discussion of the matter is thus far, from certain perspectives, a valid one. But this validity is weakened if not totally nullified by his development of the argument. The estrangement between existence and essence, between man and the Ground of his Being, is symbolized, he suggests, by the Fall – the myth of Adam and Eve and the serpent in the Garden of Eden, the primordial event in which the first act of disobedience led to human corruption, which is alienation from God, the Ground of Being.

Tillich affirmed that this state of alienation could not be removed by humanity itself; the initiative had to be taken by the Ground of Being, and this He (for we must now move away from the neuter pronoun) achieved through Jesus Christ. In words which any student of Christian theology will find familiar, Tillich described Jesus as the bearer of the new Being, the creative power capable of overcoming the estrangement between humanity and God, which would enable us to recapture the Ground of our Being, thus bringing about the desired reconciliation between existence and essence. He wrote:

> When the apostles say that Jesus is the Christ, they mean that in Him the new eon which cannot become old is present. Christianity lives through the faith that within it there is the new which is not just another new thing but rather the principle and representation of all the really new in man and history. But it can affirm this only because the Christ deprived Himself of everything which can become old, of all individual and social standing and greatness, experience and power. He surrendered all these in His death and showed in His self-surrender the only new thing which is eternally new: love.
>
> (*The Shaking of the Foundations*, p. 186)

(All this had been expressed infinitely more briefly and less prosaically two centuries earlier in Charles Wesley's hymn on the Incarnation:

He deigns in flesh to appear,
Widest extremes to join;
To bring our vileness near,
And make us all divine:
And we the life of God shall know,
For God is manifest below.)

It is tempting at this point simply to join other critics of Tillich's professed existentialism and state that his expression of it, while perhaps helpful for those approaching the discussion from a similar background to his, was alien to the philosophy as outlined by its secular advocates – which was self-evidently the case. But since I am not assuming that any reader of this book has necessarily explored anywhere else in this field of inquiry, I prefer to be more pointed than this and state quite simply why I find Tillich's approach to be, in the end, fatally flawed.

The clue is given by Tillich's emphasis just mentioned: the uniqueness of Jesus. This emphasis, whether Tillich desired it or not, immediately divides those who find the Christ-myth valuable from those to whom it is offensive (including other theists, such as some Jews and Muslims). Even more important, it separates followers of Jesus from the Sartrian existentialists who are ignorant of or indifferent to the myth, and others, like myself, who are not attracted by the image of Jesus, and want nothing more than to obliterate this image from the consciousness. As a simple matter of fact, those parts of the New Testament which are of widest appeal (such as its emphasis on **agape**, or love) are expressions of values which have nothing whatsoever to do with the divine – values which have been expressed, in various forms, by virtually all schools of moral thought, religious or otherwise, since thinking began.

They – and we – are involved in the age-old quest for an ontological and moral perspective (perhaps a moral perspective based on the ontological), and the suggestion that we cannot undertake this on our own initiative, but rather can only respond to an initiative taken by some 'wholly Other', means, I suggest, the surrender of the existentialist values pinpointed in the last chapter. Where labels are being discarded, it provides one more eye-catching (at least as worn by most of its adherents) than the rest; where a universal expression of human nature and destiny is sought, it provides one which confines its adherents to their own separate cells; and where authenticity is called for – the ability, among other things, to work out one's own perspectives – it presents an image of alleged perfection to which its followers are supposed to conform. Furthermore (and of considerably more significance for the theme of this book) by presenting the Ground of Being as an entity distinct from individual Being, it creates a kind of dual ontology which is philosophically unreal, experientially suspect and historically disastrous. To equate the Ground of Being with the God revealed in and expressed by Jesus is to destroy the basic ontological perspective arrived at – one which, as we shall see in the next chapter, can produce a philosophy of harmony and unity, rather than one which sets men and women against their fellows, destroying the very Being of which it is supposed to be the Ground.

It doesn't of course need stating that, despite the inherent weakness in the system, many people over the centuries who have accepted the label of Christianity have yet found a broad ontological perspective. The mystics, such as Eckhart, are one example of these, and it would be surprising if there had not been many others. My point is that their perceptions have come about despite, not because of, the Christian umbrella under which they have sheltered (though I wonder, in some cases, whether this was not simply **faute de mieux**, so that they, at any rate in the early stages of their explorations, just followed the way that was there: *that*, like Mallory's reason for climbing Everest – 'because it's there' – would certainly have been an existentialist approach to the journey).

Tillich had studied widely enough in both existentialism and Eastern thought to enable him to write authoritatively in this field. The title of a new book about him (*East and West: A Mirror of Divine Duality*, T. Thomas) suggests that he was striving after the kind of harmony between the two which is my present purpose. My view is that, far from achieving this unity, Tillich (and with him Robinson, and other theists of the 1960s who took him as their mentor) achieved only a rare form of schizophrenia – a disease from which at the time I also suffered. The cure, with all the sense of liberation and ontological awakening that followed, began only after the long fight to expunge theism from my system. My book *The Christian Outsider* (1971) describes this struggle.

The story behind this book (rather than the book itself!) is, I think, unique in the annals of publishing. It was published by the Methodist Publishing House, the Epworth Press, as a sequel to *Honest to God*, asking, in effect, where do we go from here? The publishers obviously had misgivings, since they printed their own warning (or escape clause) opposite the title page:

> The Epworth Press is happy to publish what follows as a vivid contribution to the debate about the future of 'the Christian presence' in human society. It by no means endorses all the author's opinions.

(A somewhat superfluous disclaimer for any publishing house to make, one feels.) Within two months of the book's appearance, charges of heresy were levelled at certain sections of it. At the Conference of 1971, in secret session, the Methodist Church expelled me from the ranks of its ministry (adding another clause forbidding me to enter any pulpit as a lay preacher) on the grounds of 'false doctrine'. Apart from my own personal situation, Epworth were in a quandary with the book. Their response was to withdraw it. I shall therefore quote from it here, since what I said then still seems to me relevant to this present discussion.

I had, in the third section, entitled 'Non-theology', argued, with Robinson, that, on the whole, the word 'God' had historically been used to fill a gap in human knowledge, or people's ability to control their lives. I quoted such areas as the fertility of the soil, disease, birth, moral values and death, and suggested that in all these areas humanity was at the mercy of powers and factors beyond its control. Some deep-seated desire to leave nothing to 'chance' caused it to create the image of God who, while His ways may not always be understood, is in control, possessing a kind of overall plan of which human beings are granted only rare glimpses. I suggested that this 'God of the gaps' image (Robinson's phrase) must go (see case study 16 for a more extensive study).

> For some this will be painful, but, in Plato's words, they must be dragged screaming from their caves to take upon themselves the responsibilities which their ancestors had so lightly (albeit understandably) handed over to 'God'. . .

Is there then no area of life where God is not related to man at his weakest? Has not God stood in for man at his most dedicated and his most compassionate levels? An answer to this was offered a century ago by Ludwig **Feuerbach**. His aim in *Das Wesen des Christentums* was to humanise theology, and much of it has a strangely contemporary ring. He argued that man is to himself his own object of thought. Religion is the consciousness of the infinite which man experiences in his deepest moments – the infinitude of knowledge, of the number and intensity of personal relationships, of creativity and work, and so on. To none of these can there ever be a limit; and this situation is tidied up by projecting the inner awareness of the infinity of personal consciousness to the image of a personal God, all-knowing, all-powerful, all-present, all-loving. So God is the outward projection of man's inner nature, and religion 'nothing else than the consciousness of the infinity of the consciousness; or in the consciousness of the infinite, the conscious subject has for his object the infinity of his own nature'. [In Heidegger's terms, there are no limits to the field of Being.]

Thus God the great law-giver, God as love, God the all-wise, all correspond to some need in human nature. The danger, Feuerbach asserted, arose when man personalised this image to the extent of granting God a nature separate from his own. This resulted in what he termed 'a false and theological essence of religion' – 'religious masochism', with a belief in revelation and associated themes such as episcopacy, ordination, and the sacraments. Through these man was, so to speak, hoist on his own petard, controlled by the image he had created. Men have consequently lived in fear at the thought of the Judgment Day, when this God would assess the worth of their brief lives, and determine whether they should 'enter into their joy' or join the worthless in some kind of 'outer darkness'. Others have spent their lives in self-immolation before this image, overwhelmed by a sense of their own worthlessness, weighed down with feelings of guilt. Even when men have acted lovingly, wisely, self-sacrificially, Christian theology, at least, has encouraged some kind of induced humility, whereby the agent attributes his worthwhileness to the 'grace' of God. The result is that, ironically, the image of God representing man-at-his-best has been just as deadly for man's achieving to the full the depth and riches of his own humanity as was that of man-at-his-weakest. . .

It was something along these lines that Tillich was trying to present with his teaching of God as the 'ground of our being', and which John Robinson was presenting in *Honest to God*. Yet Robinson states that we are put 'on very dangerous ground' by Bultmann's answer to a challenge from Karl Barth (two further Protestants who tried to link their religion with the Existentialist philosophy): 'I. . . am trying to substitute anthropology for theology for I am interpreting theological affirmations as assertions about human life.' He proceeds to criticise Feuerbach:

> 'For, to Feuerbach, to say that "theology is nothing else than anthropology" means that "the knowledge of God is nothing else than the knowledge of man". And his system runs into the deification of man, taken to its logical conclusion in the Superman of Nietzsche and Auguste Comte's Religion of Humanity. . .
>
> The question inevitably arises, if theology is translated into anthropology, why do we any longer need the category of God? Is it not "semantically superfluous"?'

My own view is that the term is almost entirely 'semantically superfluous' though, as we have seen, it is often used as a shorthand expression for qualities which are difficult to express, and certainly cannot be expressed briefly; but it *is* a barrier to communication for the reason I have indicated: it lays itself open to a wide variety of interpretations. It is possible for one man to state 'I believe in God' (meaning a term summarising ideal human values, but rejecting any kind of personalisation); and for another to state 'I don't believe in God' (meaning a personalised being), so that, despite the apparent total contradiction in the two statements, they may express roughly the same beliefs. It is absurd that such a possibility should exist, and in any other sphere of life clarification would, rightly, be demanded. If, for instance, one man's interpretation of love was compassion, while another's was simply desire for possession, how could they without further clarification discuss what 'loving one's neighbour' means?. . . John Robinson says of his book: 'The beginning is to try to be honest – and to go on from there'. I suggest that one step further along the way is to drop altogether the word 'God' unless we are committed to an acceptance of the personal being 'in whom we live, and move, and have our being,' from whom we come and to whom we go. It seems hardly necessary to point out that if we continue to maintain *this* fiction, we remain in the dubious situation of having to explain how, in a world created by an omnipotent being, who is allegedly at the same time all-loving, so many thousands of millions of lives are stunted by malnutrition, disease, and illiteracy. We may understand and applaud the dedication of many who believe in him, and as a consequence of this belief work self-sacrificially to alleviate the evils of the world; but we shall be no nearer understanding why the diseases and other evils exist in the first place. To attribute them to man is an affront to human intelligence: how did *man* create leprosy? To see them as a challenge to man is an evasion: so was Hitler's menace in Europe.

The only escape route is the creation of yet another myth, epitomised in the self-sacrifice of Jesus: the God who shares the suffering of his own world. . .

(*The Christian Outsider*, pp. 86–9)

We are thus at the impasse described in our discussion of Tillich, which I believe to be inevitable whenever the attempt is made to produce theology alongside ontology. As I shall suggest in the next chapter, the phrase 'in whom we live and move and have our being' has now, since my studies in Taoism, come to have a broader and more valid significance than in my earlier theological days.

THE DEATH OF GOD

There emerged in the 1960s a school of theology (if, in this case, this is not self-contradictory) based on **Nietzsche**'s concept of the death of God, outlined in *Thus Spake Zarathustra*. In this book, he tells of the madman who cried out in the market-place:

Where is God gone? I mean to tell you! We have killed Him – you and I! We are all His murderers!. . . God is dead! God remains dead! And we have killed Him!. . . Is not the magnitude of this deed too great for us? Shall we not ourselves have to become Gods, merely to seem worthy of it? There never was a greater event – and on account of it, all who are born after us belong to a higher history than any history hitherto!

The thinking behind this startling phrase is perhaps epitomized in these words of Lewis Mumford:

We must change our fellow men from being contented animals to suffering Gods, conscious of a suffering world.

The theme was taken up at the time by such American writers as Tom Altizer (*The Gospel of Christian Atheism*) and William Hamilton, whose article, 'The death of God', in *Playboy* magazine at least ensured him a wider audience than that granted to most practitioners of philosophical discourse. After being briefly pursued in the United States and Britain the concept has died a good deal more quickly than its subject ('"God is dead": Nietzsche. "Nietzsche is dead": God', as the famous example of graffiti puts it).

Even at the time, among those who sympathized with the underlying philosophy behind this phrase – that the traditional presentation of the idea of God was ontologically unsound – it seemed a gimmicky way of expressing the idea. It was also open to gross misinterpretation among the non-initiated: 'God' is hardly a subject of which death can be logically predicated. If God did exist then, ontologically speaking, He must be eternal, undying; if He were deemed to be now dead, He could not ever have existed. The whole argument constitutes a dead end. (When Tom Altizer and I shared a platform on the subject at California State University in 1984, he informed me that he had turned to teaching English literature, which seemed to me a sounder *modus vivendi*. The audience, most of them new-generation students, found the concept of the death of God alien to their thinking, even where this was atheistic in its emphasis.) Even Nietzsche himself had to admit, 'God is dead: but considering the state the species Man is in, there will perhaps be caves, for ages yet, in which his shadow will be shown' (*The Gay Science*). Whether or not the dead can cast shadows is a matter more for science fiction than for ontological inquiry.

## MARTIN BUBER 1878–1965

We turn now to another existentialist/ontologist who wrote from a theistic background, in this case from the context of Judaism. One major aspect of Being is the encounter with other beings, the relationship between one field of Being and another. There is not only an *I* in my life but also a *thou*, or a series of thous: those to whom I can relate in a variety of ways, as they to me. The question we must ask is whether the I and the thou can, as seems to be implied in some of the *non-dualistic* philosophy which we shall explore in the next chapter, be made one. Many Eastern philosophies suggest that ultimately all distinctions between 'I' and 'thou' will evaporate as they are united in the Ground of Being. A major contribution to this form of thought was made in the West by Martin Buber.

Like Tillich, he fled from Nazi-dominated Europe in the 1930s. From 1938 he taught in Palestine, becoming Professor of Social Philosophy at Jerusalem. His most famous book was *Ich und Du – I and Thou*, published in 1923. It is brief – a mere thirty thousand or so words – but profound, not a word being wasted (Tillich would have made a dozen volumes of it, one feels). In it, he expounds the thesis that the essence of life – that to which, in Sartrian terms, existence leads – is the kind of relationship just mentioned; only these give life meaning and purpose. By relationship is meant the breaking down of the barriers between individual fields of Being (or, perhaps better expressed, finding common nourishment between individual fields). In relationship, each so encroaches on the other's terrain, so to speak, that it becomes impossible to state with certainty which part of the field belongs to 'me' and which to 'thee'. It should be emphasized (in case the word 'encroaching' implies any element of undesired intrusion by one on another) that we are referring here only to those relationships which are mutually undertaken. Many relationships involve a kind of smothering process rather than a sharing, but the partnership Buber describes is not any form of take-over bid.

He contrasts this I-thou with the universal experience of I-it. In this kind of encounter, the two fields of Being remain separate and apart, developing alongside each other but never overlapping. In these circumstances, it can, and often does, happen that each holds a totally distorted image of the other. This is not so much ignorance of the other's existence as misapprehension of what that existence entails. All of us have associates (neighbours, colleagues and so on) who know us a little (part of their field adjoins ours) but not enough to know comprehensively what our fields consist of. Nevertheless, they form an impression (hold an image) of the nature of this field, and in their dealings with us behave according to this image. Because of the limited nature of their comprehension, only sheer fluke will prevent this image from being a distortion, coloured by a fair number of presuppositions and prejudices based on experiences in their own fields.

A personal example may help to clarify this point. Most of my neighbours have a fixed belief that I am lazy. This is because, whenever any of them has tried to contact me before 9.00 a.m. I have almost invariably been either still in bed or quite evidently only just out of it. What most of them don't realize is that I never go to bed before 2.00 a.m., so that the actual number of hours I sleep is no more than average. (Those who return home late at night from an occasional party and see my light still on simply conclude that, at that late hour, I can't be up to any good, so I lose out, in terms of my neighbours' image of me, on both counts.) After twenty years of experiencing the results of their – in my view – distorted image of me, during which nothing I have been able to say or do has altered their conviction that the seemly times for sleeping are between 10.00 p.m. and 7.00 a.m. (a little leeway is granted), I have resigned myself to living with this burden (see case study 17). This is a simple example, and the distortion is of no great significance. But distortions can be more erosive of relationships than this, and this is especially the case when one person puts a label – political, social, religious, or whatever – on another and in every encounter between them confronts them in terms of that label. The result is that the assessment of the other is inevitably out of balance. Since the second party is likely to be holding an equally distorted image of the first, the result is the absurd situation in which each is relating, or attempting to relate, to a non-existent other. (There *is* the other, of course, because an image of him or her is held in the subject's mind, but this other does not *exist* because the image does not mirror the reality – another example of the difference between being and existing.) So we have Jews and Arabs in the Middle East, Catholics and Protestants in Northern Ireland, each seeing themselves as enlightened holders of the truth and their opposite numbers as benighted monsters, dominated by alien beliefs. Each side therefore remains an object, an *être-en-soi* to the other, producing, in these cases, situations that are quite literally deadly.

Buber contrasts this I-it relationship (if that is not a misnomer) with the I-thou where, as we have seen, it is impossible for the I to define him- or herself except by reference to the thou: the fields overlap, which is to say that there is something of the I in the thou and of the thou in the I. In this state, the I becomes familiar with the thou to the extent that each is, so to speak, at home in the other's field: there need be no pretence, no false or artificial display on either side. Each is to the other an authentic person, 'naked and unashamed'. This is not to say that in these relationships *every* part of the field of the I is exposed to that of the thou, or vice versa. The proportion will vary from relationship to relationship, and I guess that no one person will ever be familiar with every part of another's field. The basic requirement is that each is able to expose to the other what is needed within that relationship, even if this means only one part of each person's field, and only for a moment. Buber describes this as a 'reverential relationship', and gives an example of one brief encounter:

> In the deadly crush of an air-raid shelter the glances of two strangers suddenly meet for a second in astonishing and unrelated mutuality; when the All Clear sounds it is forgotten; and yet it did happen, in a realm which existed only for that moment.

We could all probably give examples of similar moments in our own lives: the look that two people give each other when they both perceive in a flash, by whatever labyrinthine twists of the mind, the ultimate, and possibly awful, significance of a piece of news; the electric charge of a male's eyes meeting a female's across a crowded room; a secret shared and communicated by no more than a glance between two people as a chance remark by another recalls an ancient memory. Such moments of intimacy we all know, and all give expression to the I-thou; without them, our fields would be barren indeed. In fact Schopenhauer expressed his sense of the grave significance of relationships in *Parerga and Paralipomena* in these powerful terms:

> Every parting gives a foretaste of death; every coming together again a foretaste of the resurrection.

There are obvious sociological comments that could be made to indicate the relevance of the I-thou concept to community life, and some examples are suggested in case study 17. In his book *Between Man and Man*, Buber shows that he is aware of this possible link, but is looking for an understanding of the human condition which goes beyond sociology:

> This condition is characterised by the union of cosmic and social homelessness, dread of the universe and dread of life, resulting in an existential constitution of solitude such as has probably never existed before to the same extent. The human person feels himself to be a man exposed by nature – as an unwanted child is exposed – and at the same time a person isolated in the midst of the tumultuous human world. The first reaction of the spirit to the awareness of this new and uncanny position is modern individualism, the second is modern collectivism. . . Individualism sees man only in relation to himself, but collectivism does not see *man* at all, it sees only 'society'. With the former man's face is distorted, with the latter it is masked.

With this emphasis, Buber moves from the sociological to the ontological. In *I and Thou* he had suggested that 'each of us is encased in an armour which we soon, out of familiarity, no longer notice'. The implication he drew from this was that only by the removal of this casing could any person discover his or her true identity; and since the removal of the casing (or exposure of the field, in the earlier metaphor) meant the admission of the thou into the I, it follows that each can find its identity only in the other.

This has obvious wide implications for the understanding of self. It is popularly suggested that the 'real' self is that which is to be found when no one else is around, when no thou is imposing him- or herself on the I. This, according to Buber, is false. Without the thou the I is barren; only in relationship with another do I discover who I am. The field of Being, left alone, will become sterile. So when asking the question, which is the real me, I must answer in terms of the variety of I-thou relationships which are fundamental to my existence. For most people (there may be exceptions) no one relationship will provide the answer, but they may find and express their Being in terms of a handful of people to whom, taken together, most, if not all, of their field may be exposed.

This leads to Buber's central theme: how far does I-thou relate to the Ground of Being? Buber's answer is akin to the opening words of the Tao

Te Ching, which we shall explore later: if there is an ultimate Thou of our lives, we cannot express this in words. The Tao Te Ching states:

> The Tao that can be told is not the eternal Tao.
> The name that can be named is not the eternal name.

Buber's approach reflects this: he suggested that all talk *about* God (discussion of His attributes, His nature, His will and so on – the kind of talk in which we have in fact engaged ourselves in earlier chapters) was at an I-it level, making God into an entity, a thing, an object for discussion, not the Ground of Being, which is beyond all discussion and analysis. As Ruth Robinson, wife of the author of *Honest to God*, wrote in her short book *Seventeen Come Sunday*: 'When you get to the Thou, God is no more.' This, as we shall see, is very close to the position of Buddha, who viewed Nirvana as a state beyond the Gods, of Advaita Vedanta, viewing the idea of gods as of a lower order than that of Brahman, and of Taoism, where there is no god-talk at all. It is the expression of Kierkegaard, stepping forward solely in faith, and, in a different but related way, of both Heidegger and Sartre, both professed atheists, but the one deeply involved in ontological exploration relating to the Ground of Being, the other in the pursuit of essence, to which every individual existence moves. Just as Cordelia, simply because she loved Lear, her father, could not 'heave her heart into her mouth' (because the very attempt to describe how much she loved her father would have denied the validity of her words) so it is ultimately impossible to speak of the Thou of one's life. (How trite, after all, the words 'I love you' usually are on people's *lips*.)

This emphasis of Buber's provides a link, then, between the ontological views of the existentialists and those of the particular Eastern schools of philosophy which we shall be considering. He seems to have been moving away – at any rate, in some of his writings – from the theistic position of his Jewish faith to a more universalistic perspective. In tackling the question of whether the I-thou relationships with which we are all familiar point to a fundamental Thou, in whom all individual I's and thou's are made one, he points the way – uniquely, I feel, for one of the Western tradition – beyond the I-it of so much Western theistic ontology towards the unity of the Ground of all Being.

That Buber is a signpost rather than the goal is a consequence only of the particular field into which, in Heidegger's terms, he was 'thrown'. He wrote from his Jewish context, and applied his I-thou teaching particularly in that field. Much of what he wrote is profoundly valuable, of course, outside this context: the concept of I-thou has no barriers, and Buber's practical application of it to the socialist kibbutzim in Israel is acceptable as one example of its political implications. Equally valid is his attack on analytic philosophy as an example of I-it in its non-involvement and aloofness (as with Kierkegaard's aesthete).

It must be viewed as unfortunate that in his later books – *The Prophetic Faith* and *Moses* – he applied the I-thou concept to that of the biblical covenant between God and His chosen people – a concept which, as we saw earlier, is central to Jewish belief. He himself was a good deal more liberal in his delineation of the chosen people than were many of his fellow-Jews (and he still remains the *bête noir* of the conservative Zionists) but it seems that he could not remove entirely from his thinking the sense that *some* are specially called to find the Ground of their Being, the ultimate Thou of their lives. Yet the direction of his thinking is towards the universalism of much non-theistic ontology, and he is, I believe, a superbly positive link between West and East. It is interesting to speculate what he might have written if he had moved further East than Israel after leaving Europe.

The same cautious judgement must also be made on Robinson, whose 'thrownness' was the Church. I believe this commitment limited the insights which he might otherwise have been free to offer. One paragraph in his *Honest to God* hints at what might have been in store. Referring to Buber, he criticizes the anthropological approach of Feuerbach, Marx's precursor, that the ultimate 'Thou' of one's life is just the sum total of the individual thou's. This, Robinson argues, is sound as far as it goes, but leaves much unexplored and unexpressed:

> To assert that 'God is love' is . . . to say, with Buber, that 'every particular *thou* is a glimpse through to the eternal *Thou*', that it is 'between man and man' that we meet God, not, with Feuerbach, that 'man with man – the unity of *I* and *thou* – is God'. Nevertheless, as Bonhoeffer insists, 'God is the "beyond" in the *midst*'; 'the transcendent is not infinitely remote but close at hand'. *Thou* is met only *in, with and under* the finite *thou*, whether in encounter with other persons or in the response to the natural order. (op. cit., p. 53)

We are here bordering on an Eastern perspective, and we must now turn our explorations in that direction.

*Case study 16*
*The God of the gaps*

> God is the immemorial refuge of the incompetent, the helpless, the miserable. They find not only sanctuary in His arms, but also a kind of superiority, soothing to their macerated egos; He will set them above their betters.
>
> **(H. L. Mencken)**

These rather brutal words reflect an acceptance of God's existence based on a perspective totally different from that presented in the text of Chapter 3. The arguments rehearsed there were all deductive, following through an argument logically, or looking rationally at empirical evidence. From these general principles a specific conclusion has been drawn by theologians: God exists. The point that Mencken is making, however, is that for many people – perhaps for most people – belief in God is based not so much on these deductive methods, as on the inductive. That is to say, people begin with their personal experience or experiences and reach a particular conclusion which validates those experiences (in the same way that a certain 'tick' in the orbit of the planet Uranus led astronomers to conclude, long before Pluto was discovered, that another planet must exist).

The inductive argument for God's existence, expressed in general terms, goes as follows. Throughout the centuries and across the five continents, there has been expressed by *homo sapiens* a particular recurring feature: the need for God. Not every representative of the species has felt or expressed this need, but enough have done so to make, for instance, the study of a tribe's religious beliefs a compulsory element in the *modus operandi* of any social anthropologist. It would seem, so the argument proceeds, extremely illogical if, in the presence of this near-universal need, God does not exist. It would then mean that nature had brought about a need that could not be satisfied, which would be a unique happening. All other human needs – for food, drink, warmth, shelter, sex, company and so on – are capable of being met (even though not all people actually have them met, of course): with the need for God, however, people would for ever be totally frustrated. And this seems, on the face of it, absurd and – more to the point – unnatural. Therefore God must exist.

Mencken's argument is not to deny this widespread need, but to question the ground on which it is formed. His basic argument – expressed more delicately by John Robinson in *Honest to God* – is that we have made of God a stopgap. He has been introduced into human thinking in order to take over when human frailty or igno-rance can achieve or understand no more. In a situation fraught with impotence, the idea of an omnipotent God has taken over; in one of folly and inadequate knowledge, the all-knowing, omniscient Deity; in the loneliness of isolation, the omnipresent One with whom one need never be lonely again. In other words, God has been introduced as a compensation for human weakness and inadequacy: He is the God of the Gaps, whose name is on every insurance policy as the Author of those geological and geographical events which are totally beyond human control: the flood, or famine, or earthquake and so on: the so-called 'Act of God'.

It may be instructive to reflect on the areas where human inadequacy so expresses itself. The following are examples; you may have others to suggest.

(1)  *Seasonal weather*: early agricultural communities were totally dependent on this, and starvation in many areas was always a real possibility for whole tribes. Fickleness of climatic conditions in many parts of the world led to the belief that this was controlled by a superior being or beings (god(s)), and that (s)he must be approached and placated in certain ways before (s)he would grant what people needed. Hence (a) the growth of ritual associated with the bringing of seasonal weather (Rogation, Harvest, etc.); and (b) the development of the idea of sacrifice to please the deity: ('the first fruits', or the killing of an animal, or, **in extremis**, human executions).

Note: the person who emerged as a central figure (if not the all-important person) in such communities was the one who claimed to be able to communicate to the deity what the people required, and to interpret to the people what the deity required of them: the witch doctor, or *high priest*.

(2)  *Health*: there has seemed no guaranteed way of ensuring this. Disease seems to strike blindly, and no consistent pattern can be regularly discerned. Hence, again, in primitive communities the link between disease and the deity – both as a sign that illness means being 'touched' by God, and that only God knows how to cure. The witch doctor or his (her) equivalent again is given prominence.

(3)  *Birth*: fruitfulness, fecundity, are signs of God's blessing: 'Go forth and multiply' (Genesis). The number of offspring is seen as the indication of God's will for the parents. How else to explain a huge family for one couple, barrenness for another?

(4)  *Death*: is the area **par excellence** where *homo sapiens* is out of control. God represents the sole hope for eternity of existence: human beings, granted the right conditions, may hope to partake of His eternity.

(5)  *Morality*: God is seen as the sanction for this, so that a particular moral code can be given a divine status, thus lifting it above the level of expediency to one of eternal truth.

The 'God of the gaps' argument suggests that one reason for the decline in belief in God is that in these areas of inadequacy, people have increasingly learned how to cope.

(1)  While people still pray for clement weather, particularly in times of drought, increased communication and trade between different

parts of the world have meant that what is lost in one area may be compensated for elsewhere.

(2) The discoveries in the field of medicine and surgery have made many religious activities on behalf of the sick to be redundant. (Though note that there still exist faith healers, people who believe that disease is a spiritual rather than physical problem; and many of those who believe in doctors still pray regularly for the sick.)

(3) The discovery of birth control has made God redundant in this area (hence, perhaps, the Roman Catholic opposition to artificial forms of birth control?).

(4) While death is inevitable for all, early death, or death of infants, is far less widespread, at least in the 'developed' world, than it was, say, a century ago. The 'hold' of God in this area is therefore reduced (though never to be finally eliminated).

(5) The discoveries of evolution and the study of social anthropology have immensely broadened out our understanding of the so-called moral sense, though many people still retain the belief that God is the source of this.

Some basic questions:

1 Are there any other areas where you think God has been introduced as a filler of gaps? (You may wish to include, for instance, mental disorders and demon-possession.)

2 All the above are areas of human weakness. Are there areas of human strength in which men have introduced the idea of God? Have Tillich and Buber anything to contribute here?

3 If people were immortal, do you think the idea of God would survive? How far is number 4, above, the key to continuing belief in Him?

4 Why do people feel uneasy in situations with which they cannot cope, or faced with problems to which they don't know the answers? Is there an underlying sense of purposiveness in most people which causes them to feel that, while they cannot cope, somebody (God) can, that while they don't understand, somebody (God) does, so that they can leave these situations and these problems to Him? If you think this is the case, do you see it as a sign of maturity or immaturity? And how fairly do you think Mencken expresses the motivation behind all this?

5 Is the God of the gaps dead?

*Case study 17*
*I and Thou*

In the examples that follow, some kind of communication will occur between you and another person or persons. Some of these may be of the I-thou type; others may be no more than I-it; some (perhaps most) somewhere in between (I-you).

Reflect on them in order

**1**   to determine in your own mind which category occurs so far as you personally are concerned;

**2**   to check whether a category could be improved (from I-it to I-you, or from I-you to I-thou);

**3**   to decide what you should say or do in order to bring about this change;

**4**   to resolve whether any such change is actually possible, or even desirable.

(1)   What kind of relationship do you have with the following:
   (a)   your regular postman/milkman/garbage collectors (dustbin men)
   (b)   the porter in any establishment you visit regularly
   (c)   the people who live opposite you
   (d)   the driver on your regular bus
   (e)   your boss, or immediate superior
   (f)   the mechanic at you local garage
   (g)   the handyman who does odd jobs at your home
   (h)   the other members of a group/political party to which you belong
   (i)   your colleagues?

(2)   How much would you tell about yourself to the following:
   (a)   the people you meet in connection with a particular cause or charity
   (b)   your friends' parents
   (c)   people you meet on holiday
   (d)   your doctor
   (e)   (if you are a nurse) your patients
   (f)   regular fellow commuters
   (g)   your next-door neighbours
   (h)   your postman, milkman, etc.

    (i)    a regular visiting door-to-door salesperson

    (j)    the local shopkeepers

    (k)    the local vicar/policeman

    (l)    the attractive unattached male/female down the road?

(3)   Categorizing: how destructive of I-thou are the following statements?

    (a)   I can sum up anyone straight after meeting them.

    (b)   (Of a neighbour) We've nothing in common: we never talk.

    (c)   My name is Mr Brown.

    (d)   You're a lecturer? Well, what do you know about real life?

    (e)   He's a snooty bastard: he never talks to anyone.

    (f)   (By a teenager) I had to spend my holiday with a load of old fogeys.

    (g)   (By a middle-aged person) Don't go to that resort: it's full of yobs.

    (h)   I've nothing in common with my parents so I seldom visit them.

    (i)   (By an Easterner) Californians are all crazy.

    (j)   (Of Vice-President Dan Quayle) You can tell he's insincere: look at his eyes.

    (k)   (Of Vice-President Dan Quayle) You can tell he's sincere: look at his eyes.

    (l)   I don't like the look of him, so I shan't vote for him.

(4)   Drawing conclusions: how would you react to the following?

    (a)   A policeman visits the house next door.

    (b)   Your neighbours shout at each other regularly.

    (c)   You see a crowd of people coming from a bingo hall/dog track/Catholic church.

    (d)   A fellow guest at a party speaks to nobody.

    (e)   A fellow guest at a party talks incessantly about his/her work.

(5)   How far is your relationship with a person influenced by these characteristics?

    (a)   (S)He lets her/his garden go to ruin.

    (b)   (S)He stammers/is deaf/has a physical deformity/is prematurely bald/is lame.

    (c)   (S)He is a freemason/a Jew/black/a Marxist/an animal rights activist/a member of the National Front.

    (d)   (S)He is a heavy drinker/is a notorious philanderer/though middle-aged, wears jeans/speaks in clichés/is much less bright than you/uses the latest Americanism.

(6) How much of a deterrent to a close relationship do you find the following?
   (a) When you ask how (s)he is getting on, (s)he always replies, 'Not so well as you.'
   (b) (S)He never misses a chance to stress that (s)he is a born-again Christian.
   (c) (S)He brings every conversation round to the need to restore capital punishment.
   (d) (For females) (S)He is blatantly more attentive to you than to any male.
   (e) He talks interminably about his pet dog/cat/pigeons.
   (f) He calls his wife 'the wife'.
   (g) (S)He reads the *Daily Telegraph* / *Sun* / *Guardian* / *L.A. Times* / *Washington Post*.

(7) National characteristics: what image of a person do the following conjure up in your mind?
   (a) an American
   (b) an East European
   (c) an Englishman
   (d) an Italian
   (e) a Frenchman
   (f) a German
   (g) a Russian
   (h) a Scotsman
   (i) an Irishman
   (j) a Spaniard

   Is the approach to such people any different if thought of in the following terms?
   (k) a Yank
   (l) a Pole
   (m) a Pom
   (n) an Iti
   (o) a Frog
   (p) a Hun
   (q) a Red
   (r) a Jock
   (s) a Mick
   (t) a Dago

How do you think I-thou relationships become established? By choice? Chemistry? Design?

Is an I-it relationship ever inevitable – or always regrettable?
How far does *choice* establish any depth of relationship?

# 7　Eastern ontology

The initial reaction of any Western intruder on the Eastern philosophical
terrain will inevitably be one of confusion and disorientation (no pun
intended). Right from the start, the initiate will find the style of expression
totally at variance with its Western counterpart. It is colourful, dramatic,
full of imagery; pictures are created in words, verbal paintings which
appeal to the eye and the imagination as much as to the powers of reason
and logic.

The strength of Eastern (as with Middle Eastern) languages is the paucity
of adjectives, which are the bane of colourful prose. With these in short
supply, the effective way to describe anything – whether a scene, a person,
or an idea – is to express it by means of a metaphor or, if the description is
extended, through an extended story. Any reader of, for instance, the Bible
will be able to confirm this. In the Four Gospels, the Christian message
is put across largely by parables; and the Old Testament, judged solely
as literature, is among the world's greatest works of art, simply because
of the vividness of the imagery and colourfulness of language, together
with the cadence of its style. A king is not 'the greatest' but the 'king of
kings'; people are not numerous, or plentiful, or massed, or crowded, or
thronged, or populous, or multiferous, or inexhaustible (as is my supply
of adjectives from the *Thesaurus*): they are 'as the sand upon the sea-shore';
and so on. The same is true for the countries whose philosophies we shall
be exploring; the prose style of their languages assumes a vitality which
adjectives, on the whole, make impossible. To encounter for the first
time expressions of philosophies of life which have influenced millions
of people for thousands of years is itself quite an adventure; but to find
these expressions couched in prose which immediately brings into play
the inner eye of the imagination can be a considerable culture shock
for anyone raised on the prosaic literalness of our Western style of
writing.

Brief examples of Western and Eastern philosophical prose should suffice
to emphasize this point. Both are from mainstream works in both the
cultures. The first is from Kant's *Critique of Pure Reason* – a seminal work

in the West – and the second from the Tao Te Ching, which has the same status in the East.

> A *priori* synthetical judgments are possible when we apply the formal conditions of the *a priori* intuition, the synthesis of the imagination, and the necessary unity of that synthesis in a transcendental apperception, to a possible cognition of experience, and say, 'The conditions of the *possibility of experience* in general are at the same time conditions of the *possibility* of the *objects* of *experience*, and have, for that reason, objective validity in an *a priori* synthetical judgment.'

> Once the whole is divided, the parts need names.
> There are already enough names.
> One must know when to stop.
> Knowing when to stop averts trouble.
> Tao in the world is like a river flowing home to the sea.

The exotic *manner* of Eastern philosophical writings is only the first of the mysteries confronting any Western explorer in the field; having become accustomed to this, he or she is likely to be staggered by the variety and disparity of the ideas themselves. For every viewpoint on the issues under discussion – the nature of Being, the existence of God, immortality, teleology and so on – there are many alternatives, some of them totally alien to each other. To summarize this panoramic range of expressions under the generic term 'Eastern' must therefore be recognized as simplistic. Even the term 'Hinduism' is confusing, since under that umbrella are subsumed countless forms of belief, some of them having in common only their source in the Indian subcontinent (as the word 'Hindu' implies).

When you reflect on this, it is not surprising. After all, if an Asian friend were to ask me what are the chief ideas contained in Western philosophy, my response could only be to offer directions to a library. At the very least, my friend would have to read something like Russell's *History of Western Philosophy*, which would give its reader some of the flavour of the subject: but that contains 789 pages, plus an index of 52 pages (double columns): in this chapter I have about a tenth of this. What is required, then, is to be scrupulously selective, and this I propose to be. In the first place, I shall limit myself to those themes in Eastern thought which relate to our central field of exploration – who or what we are, and why we're here – so that we shall look at Eastern metaphysics rather than, for instance, Eastern epistemology, or Eastern views on ethics and moral behaviour. This will still leave an enormously broad terrain, so I shall select those emphases which I have personally found to be most rewarding, by which I mean those which I've found most fruitful in *my* field of Being, which is not to say that the same is, or will be, true for other initiates. Furthermore, I shall be outlining these Eastern ontological perceptions through the crucible of my own experience. The aim of this book is not to provide some kind of dictionary of ontology, but to express the issues raised as I perceive them and as they affect me.

Most Eastern philosophers are likely to be highly critical of this approach, of course. For example, His Divine Grace A. C. Bhaktivedanta Swami Prabhupada, in his introduction to a book on the **Bhagavad-gita**, *Bhagavad-gita As It Is*, states emphatically that these ancient writings must be taken as they stand if they are to be fully appreciated, not just commented on or modified from outside the fold of commitment. 'It is like this,' he writes: 'if we want to take a particular medicine, then we have to follow the directions written on the label of the bottle. We cannot take the medicine according to our own directions or the directions of a friend not in knowledge of the medicine.' I accept this rebuke and suggest that those wishing to approach the oracle more closely than is possible here should prepare themselves to take appropriate action by booking a passage to India. The fact is that from where I stand not all aspects of Eastern thought seem equally valid, or valuable. If I had been 'thrown' elsewhere, no doubt the aspect would have been different. But I wasn't, and it isn't.

There is one further problem which makes any kind of generalization about particular Eastern schools impossible to make (though I shall be attempting to do so). Changes in approach to certain issues have occurred within particular schools of Eastern thought over the centuries: the dispersion of Buddhism into the **Mahayana** and **Hinayana** (or **Theravada**, as modern Buddhist prefer) – the 'greater' and 'lesser' vehicles (roughly speaking, the more liberal and more conservative schools) – is one example of this. While being aware of such developments, it is impossible to introduce them comprehensively into this brief introduction, bearing in mind that the main purpose behind the discussion of them in the first place is not to provide an authoritative outline of their teachings – this has been done much more comprehensively elsewhere (see pp. 308–9) – but to suggest how, in conjunction with (particularly) existentialism in the West, a new ontological perspective may perhaps begin to take place. This perspective is explored in the final chapters of the book, and it is by their insights (if any) that what I am about to discuss should be judged.


## India: Buddhism

Buddhism is one of the three Indian philosophical tendencies classified by traditional Hindu scholars as *nastika* or heterodox (that is, a mixture of ideas). The other two tendencies are diametrically opposed to each other. First, there is **carvaka**, which teaches a kind of materialism such as was seen in the Western world during the Age of Enlightenment. Carvaka denies the existence of the soul, or spirit, or whatever other name we may give to the non-material self. Opposed to this is **Jainism**, which was flourishing in Buddha's time (and still has some half a million followers) and to which his teaching was in part a reaction. Jainism teaches that the material world, including the human body, is transient and totally of no importance: the aim of every human being is to free the spirit from the world of matter; and, so far as Jainites were concerned, this meant adopting a life of extreme asceticism. Self-denial for its own sake was central in their teaching, and it was (and still is) not unusual for a Jainite monk or nun to starve him– or herself to death, since death from the wilful withholding of sustenance to the body was seen as a sure step to sainthood.

Buddha's heterodoxy meant that he took a middle way between these two extremes, and his philosophy is often described as 'the Middle Way'. He began life as Gautama Sakyamuni, an aristocrat brought up in luxury, and his father did all in his power to prevent the young Gautama from setting eyes on the darker aspects of life. It was only after he had married and had a son that he was to come face to face with these, and the experience was to cause him to abandon the luxury into which he had been born. What changed him were the Four Signs (written in capitals because they have become part of Buddhist lore): he encountered a sick man, an old man, a dead man and a wandering recluse. All these revealed to him (what millions of others learn virtually from the cradle, of course) that life isn't one unending round of happy harmony, but is pervaded throughout by **duhkha**. This word is normally translated as suffering, but the meaning of the original, while it may be hinted at in this translation, is not fully revealed by it. Duhkha includes pain, sorrow, dissatisfaction and so on – all the sensations we experience which may be described as suffering. But it is more basic than that. It means the sense of unfulfilment that overtakes a person who realizes – early or late in life – that he or she will never achieve all they had hoped and planned for in earlier years; that there are areas of their life (parts of their field, in Heideggerian terms) which will never be fertile; that certain relationships will never be developed, certain skills for ever denied to them. It was what Sartre described as the realization of one's own limitation, causing another existentialist to advise her students, 'Set out to face the long littleness of life.' Some would describe this as a pessimistic philosophy; others would reply that it is realistic and honest, a recognition that life is in some respects a second-, or even third-best experience, and that it is self-deluding to believe otherwise. Duhkha epitomizes this state of discontent.

Buddha's response to his newly-found experiences was to leave his home and family and life of luxury for ever (the kind of step to be taken, as we have seen, by Kierkegaard). He spent some time at the feet of religious leaders of the Jainite tradition but discovered that self-mortification for its own sake took him no further in his quest for a satisfying philosophy of human nature and destiny. Eventually, through a trance at a place called Bodh Gaya, he gained 'enlightenment' or awakening ('Buddha' means 'the awakened one'). We cannot know what exactly happened to him during this period of trance, but it was to change his life and, with it, that of millions of followers.

After achieving insight, Gautama taught throughout India, founding a mendicant (begging) order, the **Sangha**, a community which soon spread throughout southern Asia and, some centuries later, to the Far East. Buddhism has over the centuries developed a proliferation of schools, some of great subtlety and complexity, but our purpose is to pinpoint those central features which have impressed themselves on successive generations down to the present day. (Buddha wrote no books, so we are dependent, for an understanding of his philosophy, on the records of his disciples written during the decades after his death.)

BUDDHISM

The general philosophy of Buddhism may be briefly summarized, before we turn to specific issues. We discussed earlier (pp. 8–9) what we mean by 'Being' – the 'to-be' of us. Buddha taught that there are three important 'signs of Being'. The first of these is duhkha, already mentioned, with which normal experience is inextricably enmeshed; its emphasis, as we have seen, is that suffering, sorrow, disappointment and so on, are inevitably linked with our world, which is essentially one of time and change. The purpose of philosophy, according to Buddha, is to show the nature and origin of duhkha and to reach the way to end it.

The second sign of Being is **anicca**, or impermanence. This concept is not dissimilar to the existentialist emphasis on *becoming* as the reverse side of Being, but Buddha gave this a unique twist. The whole world, he said, as far as we have experience of it, is an ever-changing process, a whirling storm of discontinuous points. Each point exists only for an instant, coming into being only to disappear at once. Consequently there is no such thing as permanence, for even what seems to be the most solid of objects, like a mountain, is subject to the remorseless law of change and decay. Buddha knew nothing of bodily cells, of course, but if he had, this knowledge would have served to strengthen his theory. The cells I have now are not the same as those with which I began writing this page; and, if I should survive that long, in seven years every cell presently in my body will have been replaced.

The third sign of Being is the application of the idea of anicca to the human person, which is expressed in the concept of **anatta**, or non-self. What we call personality, according to Buddha, is not a continuing entity (as most of us probably believe) but a series of consecutive states, each one causally linked to both its predecessor and successor, but each enduring only for a moment before it is replaced. One moment of consciousness leads to the next, as the flame of one candle lights another: the flames look the same, but the candles are different. The concept of immortality is therefore at best a wistful dream, at worst an irrational denial of a fundamental fact of nature. It is this thirst for permanence, with all its corollaries and ramifications, that causes duhkha, since this thirst can never be satisfied in the dimension of Being-in-time, the dimension we all experience. Duhkha ceases only with the attainment of what Buddha termed '**Nirvana**', when the flame of separate personality is blown out (Nirvana means, literally, 'blowing-out'), a state beyond existence and non-existence as we know them. Buddha believed that by meditation a person could progress towards, if not actually achieve, this state. (His rather conservative views about the possibilities of this were later modified by some of the more liberally minded of his successors.)

Buddha summarized this philosophy in his 'Four Noble Truths':

(1)    To live means to experience duhkha. In this world, a certain amount of dissatisfaction is inevitable.

(2)    The origin of duhkha lies in craving or grasping after such things as wealth and power, the fulfilment of one's physical (and, sometimes, mental) wants.

(3)    The cessation of duhkha is possible through the discarding of selfish goals: in effect, by ceasing to be concerned only about 'my' status, 'my' satisfaction and so on. (This gives the lie to those who accuse Buddhism of preaching a philosophy of 'save-yourself-and-be-damned-to-the-rest'. In one sense, of course, I can never escape from my own field of Being; but this need not mean that I close my eyes to others' fields. Buddha is arguing that when we express such awareness and concern, the 'becoming' aspect of Being is strong; or, in his terminology, we move closer towards Nirvana.)

(4)    The way to the cessation of dissatisfaction, which can lead to enlightenment, is what is known as the Noble Eightfold Path, or, simply, the *middle way*.

This eightfold path is often misinterpreted in the West as being like a ladder with eight steps, each of which has to be climbed before proceeding to the next. A better image would be a door with eight apertures of increasing size, the final one being able to contain the others, and so on down the row. (In fact, such is the nature of the eight steps, three apertures would suffice for this analogy, since steps 1–3, 4–6, and 7–8, belong together in similar categories: the first three relate to attitudes of mind, the next three to moral behaviour, and the last two to inward awareness, or contemplation.)

The eight steps are:

(1) *right views*: one must be open-minded, in accordance with Buddha's own philosophy

(2) *right aims*: one must desire what is of real value, and can be shared with others

(3) *right speech*: everything one says should be true and kind

(4) *right behaviour*: self-control is the key element if inner peace is to be achieved; consequently, such behaviour as taking drugs, stealing, fornication and so on, must be viewed critically, since they are likely to reduce the control over one's mind and body.

(5) *right livelihood*: one should not do any work which may harm another person, or an animal; for instance, one cannot follow the path and be a butcher, or a soldier

(6) *right effort*: the body's selfish drives must be rejected; if, as many affirm (like the English philosopher, Hobbes, two millenniums later), we are basically selfish, then this selfishness must be replaced by altruism

(7) *right mindfulness*: one must learn to meditate and to strengthen one's vigilance so as to avoid committing an evil deed through thoughtlessness

(8) *right concentration* (or contemplation): the road to Nirvana necessitates withdrawal from the material world; this can be achieved only through long hours of quiet contemplation and introspection, which will lead to the state of total peace and joy.

The path has been called the middle way because it lies between the two extremes of self-indulgence and self-denial. It offers few precise moral injunctions (there are some, but these are put forward more as good advice than commandments): basically, Buddha is suggesting that any behaviour that fuels the fire of egoism will be ultimately harmful in the quest for Nirvana. But in the end each person must work out the implications of this in terms of his or her own ways of living and behaving. A person can, after all, only live *his* or *her* life, and we must all follow the path we are on as long as we are able to. As **George Fox**, the Quaker and pacifist, said to a soldier: 'Wear thy sword as long as thou canst.' Just as no traveller can reach a chosen destination by travelling in the wrong direction, so no one who wants to end duhkha can succeed if he or she adopts the wrong life-style.

Buddha's approach was, as a matter of fact, entirely practical and prudential; it was strongly criticized by many of India's holy men because it left out all reference to ritual, or belief in a deity. Buddha's view was that, since no one can possibly know the Hindu deities (assuming they exist at all, and he was ambivalent about this) it was pointless either to invoke their aid or worship at their shrines. His argument was quite simple: we are independent of the gods, and by our own decisions, our own deeds and thoughts, each of us can reach the blissful state of Nirvana. It was not his wish to found a religion, and he would have disapproved of those followers who, after his death, attempted so to transform his philosophy (and giving later commentators the problem of sorting out the primary from the secondary in Buddhist thought). He would have approved of Sartre's reply to a student who affirmed that he would follow the philosopher to the end of the world: 'Be a man and do not follow me, but yourself.'

## BUDDHIST ONTOLOGY

What I have presented so far is, I hope, a reasonably accurate summary of the basic 'bones' of Buddhism. To make these bones live in the context of Western thought (the context within which I write) it will be necessary to express the ideas in terms of a culture which is alien to that which gave them birth. This is, of course, to misheed the admonition quoted on p. 147, but short of suggesting that we all move into a Buddhist country and practise the Buddhist way for some years, there seems no alternative. The questions which spring to mind, so far as ontological considerations are concerned, are: what does Buddhism teach about the doctrine of the immortality of the soul? Does it teach reincarnation? Where *is* Nirvana? In short, is there any real link between Being and becoming as expressed in Western ontology, and as Buddha perceived them?

The popular answer in the West would probably reflect the image of Buddhism with which I for one was raised. It is of an ascetic whose aim in life was to overcome all physical desires in order to save his soul; who believed that only by achieving release from this desire could he avoid being reincarnated in the world – and that any reincarnation might take him further forward or backward in his quest than an earlier one; the final goal being to attain Nirvana, a holy state of perpetual bliss experienced in heaven in harmony with the Creator of the universe.

It is true that if we were to study every variation or modification in Buddhist ideas over the centuries and throughout the world we should probably come across one passage or another to justify our holding this view of Buddhism. (The Bible, or the Koran, may similarly be used.) But careful study of the earliest expressions of the philosophy shows that this image is an almost total distortion of the reality. The reality, for a start, is that *Buddhism and the doctrine of the immortality of the soul are incompatible.* We discussed this issue in the context of existentialism (p. 111–14), and there I suggested that immortality and immutability (or unchangingness) were two sides of the one coin. This seems to be the case by logical inference.

For anything to be immortal, eternal, it must have reached or be capable of reaching a point beyond which no improvement can be made. (With eternity at one's disposal, it would seem logical that any being would, sooner or later, achieve this state.) Having attained perfection, there is no longer anything to strive for, or move towards: the now and the not-yet (to refer back to my earlier definition of time) are one and the same, and time is no more. We shall see, when looking at the teaching of **Advaita Vedanta**, that this non-dualistic concept (meaning, in this context, that there is no longer I and thou, or now and then) did find expression in India: but not in Buddhism.

Buddha, in contrast (and he was criticized by many of his contemporaries because of this contrast), may be viewed as more of a pioneer of the existentialist expressions of Being and becoming. His teaching about anicca, impermanence, indicates that in his view nobody is the same from one moment to the next. The person I am now, while linked existentially with the person I was a moment ago, and the one I shall be in the next and successive moments, is not the same person. If we accept this view of existence, the concept of immortality is out of place, and the question of whether or not our souls are immortal does not, or should not, arise.

To many of Buddha's contemporaries, this view seemed not dissimilar to that of the adherents of the philosophy of carvaka, or materialism, mentioned earlier. Was not 'Buddhism' just a way of saying that a person is no more than the sum of his or her chemical parts, subject to the laws of matter like all other objects in the universe? If the essence of a human being is change, what difference, other than in degree, is there between a person and a dog, a flower, or even a stone? If anicca is the basic reality of the universe, then surely, all are in the same boat?

In one sense this is fair comment, and Buddha would not have denied it: everything and everybody that exists is subject to the truth that nothing endures – and we shall see later how the Taoist philosophy tackled this stark reality. But to say that a person possesses nothing that endures is not to say that a man or woman can be summed up solely in terms of physical characteristics or components. It is to ignore, for a start, all the psychical and aesthetic features of a person – mind, imagination, aspirations and so on. The doctrine of carvaka, Buddha held, has no satisfactory answer to the ontological problems raised by the possession of these qualities. It also ignores the reality of personal self-consciousness, the unifying factor which persists amid the process of continuous change – the factor which enables me to speak of *my* body, *my* mind, *my* imagination, and so on. Buddhism speaks of *selfless persons*, not of matter in motion.

This phrase is the title of a dissertation to which I refer the reader (*Selfless Persons* by Steven Collins, CUP, 1982). It is, like so much vocabulary used in ontological discourse, probably new to you and needs some definition. We are selfless because we have no immortal essence. The word 'self' is thus used as in a debate on dualism centred round the concept of the immortal soul. Buddha is among those who reject this concept, which may, from our Western perspective, place him in the camp of the *monists*: those who believe that reality consists of a single substance or entity. Since we have seen that Buddha was certainly not a materialist, and since he could hardly be termed a spiritualist, it is beginning (I hope) to emerge that it is impossible to approach Buddhism – and we shall see that the same is true for the other Eastern schools we shall discuss – with convenient ready-made Western labels or badges. We are in a world of different thought–patterns, and we would be wise to approach them divested of all Western presuppositions.

Having established the significance of the word 'selfless', what are we to make of Buddha's idea of the person? This word describes the reality which we all share: the continuity of *awareness* which links each change and each moment. The field, in Heidegger's terms, is in a constant state of flux; but it remains identifiably *my* field; amid all the change, my Being, the to-be of me, endures. If I were to try to describe this to-be of me, I should probably have to discuss the nature of my field, the components of my Being, so to speak. But Being is itself more than its components, otherwise we should simply be affirming that a person is just the sum of his or her parts. If this were a correct diagnosis, it would follow that, say, a dog would no longer be the same dog if it had lost its tail, its snout, its hind legs, or whatever. Yet you could remove all these parts and more, and still be able to say, this is the same dog (grossly mutilated, certainly, but still the dog). The same is true of a human being. Ask yourself how much of *you* would have to be removed before you ceased to be you. It may be a viable exercise to speak of machines or manufactured implements in this way: a cricketer may admittedly boast of having used the *same* bat for donkeys' years while conceding that 'it's had three new handles and four new blades', but generally speaking there is a moment when a piece of engineering or a work of art, or anything put together by human ingenuity, ceases to be what it had once been: it loses its essence, its *pour-soi* in Sartrian terms. This is not the case with a human being (even though, as Sartre drily remarked, some people come close to it by getting themselves stuck in a groove). Only at death does the person cease to be a person (and *maybe* – without pursuing this issue – we can equate intensive brain damage with death if awareness of Being ceases at that point): and at death the change is not just one of removing parts but of transforming the nature of the whole. A corpse may, ironically, look more *like* a human being than a living person who has been horribly mutilated or deformed.

What, then, according to Buddha, happens at death? Are we to assume that, as Ulysses asserted in Tennyson's poem, it 'closes all'? Granted the premiss that there is no permanent self, this seems to be a logical inference to make: after all, if there is no permanence of self between one moment and the next during life, how much more must this be the case between life and death. Can we not therefore simply take it that Buddha's concern was for this life only, that the intention behind following the Noble Eightfold Path is to alleviate duhkha here and now, and that the kingdom of heaven – to use a phrase cribbed from the New Testament – is not 'beyond' but here, present in our midst? (See reference to Bonhoeffer, p. 138.)

Buddha's answer to this basic query is an unambiguous 'yes and no'; but in order to make sense of this we must introduce two words which are central to Buddha's teaching, the one gleaned from Hindu thought, the other, one of Buddha's own creations. The first we have already met, *karma*; the second is *rebirth*.

## KARMA

Death may be described as the end of the present chain of experiences (it needs no great insight to perceive that – a child will be conscious of some such idea as it holds a dead bird in its hands). But during this present cycle, according to much Indian thought, a series of good and bad effects have accumulated – decisions made which have caused happiness or suffering to others, insights gained or opportunities neglected, bringing about either the enrichment or the defertilization of the individual field of Being. Any person's style of life, and the sum total of that person's deeds and misdeeds, has, according to this philosophy, built up karma. The word literally means 'actions', and the traditional Hindu view was that the karma accumulated by the end of the present cycle of experiences would determine the starting-off point in the next cycle. Thus the doctrine of karma was closely linked with that of reincarnation, a central theme of much Hindu thought. The conditions of the next incarnation – the so-called 'accident' of birth was no accident, according to this belief – resulted inexorably from the karma accumulated during the present incarnation, as this one resulted from the last, and so on.

Westerners often misinterpret the word as suggesting a fatalistic view of existence, akin to our use of the words doom, or destiny, implying that whatever happens happens as part of a predetermined programme from which nobody can deviate – along the lines of Omar Khayyam's fatalism, quoted earlier (see case study 10). Admittedly, some who pay lip-service to the idea use it sometimes as an excuse for unacceptable behaviour: it is not unknown, for instance, for an Indian found guilty of a crime to plead karma as a mitigating circumstance (totally mitigating, if it is valid); but this is to distort the notion, which affirms that though our starting-point in life has been fixed by karma accumulated previously – in the cycle before this one – the decisions we make thereafter are the result of our own free choices. (See case study 20.)

Buddha accepted the basic philosophy behind the concept, but gave it a new emphasis. In the first place, he had his own suggestions to make as to how a person should proceed in life in order to build up good karma. He was, for instance, as we have seen, convinced that the extreme asceticism preached by the Jainites was a less sure channel than they supposed; and he saw less value in ritual, and even less in the worship of 'the gods', than was assumed by most of his Hindu contemporaries. These modifications were important, and will be discussed again as we try to express a comprehensively West/East ontological perspective in the final stages of this book: but Buddha's supreme contributions in this field were, first, to link the concept of karma not with reincarnation, but with rebirth; and secondly – and central to all Buddhist teaching – to express both of these concepts, as was true of everything he said, in relation to the experience which alone gave meaning to any of his, or his contemporaries', ideas: Nirvana.

REBIRTH

The theory of reincarnation is familiar enough to Westerners, even though it is held by relatively few. It implies that human beings possess an indestructible element, the soul, which passes through various incarnations in different bodies. I've already suggested that the basic test of this theory can only be its effects on the believer, since there is no method of verification open to us (see pp. 30–1). The main problem, as I perceive it, is that it *ought* to lend itself to one's being able to recall one's previous incarnations: this seems not unreasonable if there is continuity of consciousness through incarnations, which the doctrine of the soul's immortality makes feasible. From the ontological perspective of this book (that is, discussing the nature of Being only as I *am*, affirming only from my own experience) there seems little, therefore, to be said in favour of the doctrine.

Buddha's theory of rebirth was quite different, and relates to his idea of selfless persons. He accepted from the doctrine of karma that at the moment of death each individual has with him or her the sum total of their deeds and misdeeds (in Sartre's words already quoted: 'You are – your life, and nothing else'; or, in Brecht's words, 'Man is what he has done'). Buddha's view was that this accumulation, this karma, is always, at the end of a person's life, in one of two states: either it has led to the enlightened state of Nirvana, or it has not. If it has not (and, for Buddha, if not for his successors, this would be the case with nearly everybody), then that person must undergo a further cycle of experience, and probably many more thereafter. Each new cycle will begin with exactly the karma achieved in the previous cycle, which means that the circumstances of the new life (material, mental, spiritual) may be radically different from those in which the previous cycle began: it may sometimes involve even a descent from a human being to one of a lower species. The difference between this idea and reincarnation is that, because Buddha did not accept the notion of the continuity of self, the link between the person who dies and the reborn being is, as it were, the *handing on of the karma*. This means, to use the terminology employed in earlier chapters, that after a person's death 'another' inherits that person's Being, which then continues to become – to develop, one way or another – throughout the remainder of that cycle; and so on.

Perhaps this difficult notion may be clarified somewhat if I apply its implications to myself. Because of the karma I have accumulated in this life, I am unlikely to have brought about the conditions for my entering the enlightened state of Nirvana (not even my greatest admirers would deny that). My karma has therefore created the conditions for a rebirth, and it is this fact that establishes the continuity between 'my' present life and 'my' future life. There is to be no continuity of consciousness in this rebirth, for that would suggest a reincarnational philosophy and would imply a permanence of self which doesn't exist from one moment to the next in this life, let alone through and over the great divide between one cycle of experience and another. The new Being will, however, take over my karma; this will determine what his/her/its initial circumstances are to be – whether these are to be felicitous or handicapped, with strong or weak features, laden with opportunity for growth in his/her/its field of Being or weighted down by frustration. Thus my eyes in this life should be set not just on the goal of, say, personal fulfilment, important though this is, but of building up karma which will be pregnant with potentiality for the next cycle.

I should point out that one of the issues about which latter-day Buddhists debate is that of whether, in the rebirth, there is continuation of self as well as of Being. Had Buddha written as voluminously as his near-contemporary, Aristotle, a definitive answer might have been possible. As it is, we can only pursue the idea of rebirth on the lines that Buddha seemed to be suggesting; and what I have outlined seems – to me, at any rate – to accord with those lines. And if the value of the theory is to be tested by its practical consequences – the **pragmatic** approach of William James – it seems to score high marks, for its emphasis is not on speculating about the future, but on preparing here and now that which would be worthy to be handed over in the future. Thus we achieve a motivation to live a mature existence – that is, looking beyond the immediate gratification of the senses, and maintaining a long-term, even eternal perspective (though – an important corollary – without the imposition of a God before whom all will stand on the Day of Judgement). My sole aim in life, then, is to build up karma which *I* need not be ashamed to hand over. No two parents, looking at their newborn babe, could have a greater responsibility than that. *And its unverifiability is irrelevant.*

## NIRVANA

All this is, however, secondary to Buddha's central teaching, which is about the attaining of enlightenment, or Nirvana. This is – or should be, according to Buddha – the ultimate aim of every person: rebirth occurs only when that aim has not been realized during a specific life cycle. With the attainment of Nirvana, we pass beyond that cycle of birth and rebirth. In Nirvana we have reached perfection, which means that no further change can occur; the process of rebirth is neither necessary nor logically possible, since being reborn implies that perfection has not yet been attained.

What then is Nirvana? We have seen that it literally means 'blowing out', but what exactly is blown out? It cannot mean the extinguishing of any self, or soul, or essence, or whatever other word is used to describe an immortal element in us: as we have seen, there is, according to Buddha, no permanent self, only anicca. What Nirvana extinguishes is not self, but selfish desires. It is the pursuit of these which builds up 'bad' karma, the elimination of these which builds up 'good' karma; and the state in which these desires are totally eliminated is one of release and enlightenment. This is Nirvana, the state which Buddha claimed to have attained. In existentialist terms it is the release from all forms of acquisitiveness, of the desire to *have* rather than to *be*. It is the realization that one's field of Being is self-generating, that it needs no stimulation from outside itself in order to be fulfilled. All the resources one needs *to be* are found within Being itself. It is not, then, a case of learning to 'do without' *per se*, but of reaching a point where *one is not conscious of doing without anything*. Self-denial – such as Buddha observed among the Jainites – undertaken for its own sake may not in fact eliminate pride in achievement, as weightwatchers gloat over reduced pounds. More to the point, deliberate self-denial does not necessarily eliminate the *yearning* for that pleasure, or luxury, which one is denying oneself. What Buddha was speaking of was release from these deeper yearnings, after which nothing will seem like self-denial. The enlightened state is one in which it is realized that the material, tangible things on which many set such great store as a means of giving their lives a tang – wealth, possessions, ambition and so on – are of a lower order than Nirvana because they are artificially induced means of creating a field of Being. Take *them* away and the field is derelict; in Nirvana, Buddha affirmed from experience, the field requires no artificial input.

It is difficult to develop this part of Buddha's discourse further without resorting to analogies, which are notoriously double-edged if they are extended too far. It may be not unhelpful, however, to describe the state of Nirvana as like that of an alcoholic who has lost, or overcome, the craving for the source of addiction. With the addiction, the craving for the next means of assuaging the thirst (in the broad sense of that term, of course) will dominate virtually everything the alcoholic does, clouding vision, establishing life's priorities, controlling use of time, money and abilities. Released from this fever, the alcoholic feels a sense of profound liberation: he or she is freed *from* dependency on an external source of satisfaction, and freed *to* use their time and energies according to their own volition. The 'dry' alcoholic can look with compassion on those still controlled by their drug and know that the artificial pleasure derived from it cannot compare with the natural joy derived from no longer wanting it (though I suspect that no alcoholic will ever totally arrive at that point).

Perhaps a more helpful analogy is one taken from the near-universal experience of sex. I hesitate before using this analogy, because we in the Western world are so ambivalent on this matter that many readers may consider it a taboo subject – at any rate, in the context of a discussion on human nature and destiny. Among those where Buddhism was born, however, there would be no such reluctance to introduce this unique human experience into the discussion: in fact, as we shall see, many expressions of Hinduism openly proclaim the orgasmic experience as analogous to the Fourth State, beyond that of 'normal' existence (see case study 25). The analogy I wish to pursue is between Nirvana and the post-coital state, the state in which the lust and, sometimes, pathological obsessiveness of arousal has been assuaged, and replaced by a state of clarity and serenity (not always to the same extent, of course). The most rewarding conversations between a man and a woman (and, for all I know, between two people of the same sex) occur just after intercourse; and, to coin an old joke, the sleep of the just cannot compare with the sleep of the just after.

There are obvious dangers in this analogy. It may be suggested, truly, that this blissful state is achieved precisely by indulging in that for which there was an earlier craving, whereas Nirvana, according to Buddha, is to be found only when this, or any other, craving ceases to impose itself on the mind or feelings, the imagination or the will. This is a fair point, and to that extent the analogy is misleading. But within its own terms of reference it is surely valid. The post-coital state will, of course, not last for ever: within a matter of days, or even hours, the urges that had been assuaged will return. But would anyone enjoying the post-coital state exchange that state, at the moment of enjoyment, for one of renewed sexual desire? Isn't this state the goal of sexual activity? And if it were possible to remain in this state, would anyone opt for the continuing renewal of desire? Maybe the best sex is like Wordsworth's definition of poetry, emotion recollected in tranquillity; if so, those couples who are 'past it' may, paradoxically, be enjoying richer sex lives than the young! You may or may not find this analogy helpful, but one aspect of it leads to an important consideration. *Is the state of Nirvana not only the quenching of selfish desire, but also the quenching of self?*

If this seems an unappealing notion, think of it in relation to the above analogy. I have just referred, rather whimsically I suppose, to 'the sleep of the just after' – the sleep which follows the attaining of a deep feeling of tranquillity and contentment. This sleep means slipping peacefully into unconsciousness, from which the subsequent awakening is likely to be reluctant. Would it therefore be too dreadful a consideration that this is a foretaste of Nirvana?

It may be that some readers object to the idea that we wake up reluctantly: perhaps for many people the birth of a new day brings with it the possibility of new voyages of discovery, from which there is no desire to escape through the oblivion of sleep. But this has not been the experience of most people world-wide over the centuries. Those whom Buddha was addressing would be among the vast majority for whom the birth of a new day meant the start of another round of travail and drudgery, of frustration and disaffection. Even in the world of the twentieth century, this is the norm for billions of people. In Buddha's time it was rare to experience things otherwise. With this in mind, who would not want to escape from what was in effect the tyranny of existence? Given the choice, would not most people have opted to sleep on rather than awaken to the travail? And so, on the wider scale, given the choice between slipping peacefully into annihilation, or being reborn on the treadmill, would there be any question as to the outcome, so far as the vast majority were concerned?

All this is of course highly speculative, but this is the case with all the concepts which we are currently tackling. What we can state for certain is that Nirvana, whatever the blowing-out implied, was for Buddha the goal of existence. And because he believed that this state of enlightenment could be realized only after a long preparation through many rebirths, he was more concerned to teach his followers how to tread the path towards it than to describe what it was like to achieve it. To follow this Eightfold Path in all its fullness would, in any case, mean joining the *Sangha*, the order of mendicant monks founded by Buddha. No one engaged in normal full-time employment would be able to spend the hours of daily meditation and reflection required in steps 7 and 8. Thus the desire to join the order could be taken as a sign that the individual concerned was close to Nirvana, which for most people must remain a distant prospect.

In the centuries after Buddha's death, this conservative emphasis on Buddha's part was considerably modified, particularly among adherents of the Mahayana or 'Greater Vehicle' school of Buddhism. It would be not unfair to characterize this modification as in some respects the return of traditional Hinduism into the Buddhist field – teaching which Buddha had discarded, and for which he had been held by many Hindus to be a heretic. One of the most important changes was the development of the cult of **Bodhisattvas** or 'Buddhas-to-be'. Followers of this cult argued that the process of enlightenment (or attainment of Buddhahood) would reveal that there is a **Dharmakaya**, or 'Body of Being' which underlies Being as we experience it. They suggested that this Dharmakaya, by whatever name it may be called (such as the Absolute, or Ground of Being) may be identified with Nirvana. It must, however, be doubted whether this is consistent with Buddha's own teaching. The idea of the extinguishing of a flame, however this be interpreted, seems quite different from that of the Absolute. The concept of an underlying essence with which all Being is ultimately to be at one (if it is not so already) is certainly worth exploring, but it must mean leaving Buddhism proper (that is, in its originals) and proceeding through other Eastern fields, which we shall shortly be doing. The man whose last words were 'Work out your own salvation with diligence' would hardly have responded positively to the concept of Bodhisattvas.

An essential element in Buddhism, as in a good deal of Eastern philosophy, is meditation. This is not the place to make any kind of analysis of this procedure, even if this were within my capabilities. In terms of our own explorations in ontology, the important feature to bear in mind is that this practice should not be thought of as a form of communication with another spiritual Being, such as God, as prayer might be described. Meditation should rather be recognized as a process of concentration on Being as a reality in itself, a means of exploring one's own field. Methods whereby the whole personality may be enabled to concentrate for lengthy periods may vary from school to school (see, for example, case study 28), but the end of all Buddhist contemplation is the same: the discovery of the riches within one's own field of Being, the turning of the mind away from an ethos which is reliant only on external stimulation, and thus to move closer towards the state of enlightenment, Nirvana, where Being is all, and the yearning for possession is eliminated. The inner resources which are realized by this process have been discovered by many people over the centuries; but by their very nature, they can be communicated from one person to another only by example.

Buddhism thus emerges as a thoroughly humanistic philosophy. More, I think, than any other Eastern philosophy, it teaches that all the resources we need for fulfilling lives are to be found within our own fields of Being. Buddha has been worshipped by many of his successors, but it was alien to his teaching that this should occur. He dispensed with all traces of theism, arguing that karma operates as a natural fact of existence; it no more depends on an omnipotent God for its operation than does Nirvana. In fact, the two forms of thought, theism and Buddhism, belong to different worlds. There are no favourites in Buddhism, no chosen few: karma is totally indiscriminate in its operation, as unbendable as the law of gravity. It solves the problems raised for theists by the existence of 'natural injustice' (or, to use a thoroughgoing Western word, evil) and shows how eventually, if through countless rebirths, these injustices will be ironed out. We may criticize this philosophy as leading to overcomplacency about, say, social conditions in the world (and we shall return to this later) but one glorious consequence is that Buddhism refuses either to claim unique inspiration for itself or to divide followers and non-followers into segregated camps. In Buddhism there is no equivalent to the Muslim 'There is no God but Allah and Muhammad is his prophet', or to the Christian 'I am the way, the truth, and the life: no man comes to the father but by me'. Such exclusivity is alien to the Buddhist field.

Thus Buddhism is probably the most accessible of all Eastern schools to our Western way of thinking – perhaps because Buddha had at least one feature in common with our linguistic analysts: he did not speculate on matters that he had not personally verified (even though, in behaviourist terms, nothing in his own inner experience *could* be verified). He might even be described as an agnostic on many issues about which other Eastern thinkers claimed to speak authoritatively. It is all the more surprising, therefore, that the expression of Buddhism which has been most in vogue in the West is probably its most extreme 'anti-Western' form, which became popular in Japan: Zen Buddhism. In this school, the inadequacy of Western-style logic to explain what the enlightened person has perceived is illustrated by the use of the – effectively – unanswerable question, known as a **koan**. Some people may well consider these questions to be insane, if not inane, and will refuse to reflect on such forms of interrogation as 'What is the sound of one hand clapping?' or 'How do you get a cat out of a bottle?' The purpose of these questions, however, is simply to reinforce the emphasis, made with varying degrees of force throughout most schools of Eastern philosophy, that truth is channelled not merely by the reason, but through every aspect of the person, including the instinct, the imagination and the feelings. In fact, Zen argues, logic is likely to be quite inadequate as a means of perceiving truth – hence the koan (see p. 286).

Zen also takes a firm stand against reliance on any form of written word, or Scripture, as authority for truth. Truth must be found by direct apprehension within one's own Being, not by subservience to words on a page. The imposition of any book of rules, serving the same purpose as a special constable's handbook, is therefore ruled out in the quest for Nirvana: there is no Zen equivalent of the Bible or the Koran. Anything written may serve as a guide, or indicator, in this quest, but in the end, only the goal is a fitting subject of reverence. To revere the guides rather than the goal – as millions do with the Bible and the Koran – is as if a man were to point at the moon and ask you what you see and you reply, 'A finger.' (If that makes you laugh, as it did me when I first heard it, then you are instinctively acknowledging the inanity of sanctifying the dead word rather than the living reality.)

There are certain criticisms of Buddhist ontology which must be made, but I shall reserve these until after considering another product of India.

*Case study 18*
*Death and the Self*

The following piece was first published in shortened form in the *Guardian* newspaper in October 1987. You may feel that, strictly speaking, it belongs with the material presented in Chapter 2, but it should also serve a purpose

in the context of Eastern thought, particularly that of Buddhism. Read it
and discuss the questions that follow (5 and 9 are somewhat specialist).

When Gautama the Buddha, 'who found salvation in psychology,' sat
down under the sacred Bodhi-tree he made a discovery so stupendous it
marked a decisive break with Hinduism and brought a major new religion into the world. He discovered (or decided) he hadn't got a soul.

The central affirmation of Hinduism is Tat tvam asi, 'That art thou':
our atman, soul, the divine spark in each of us, is Brahman, God or
the Absolute, the divine fire, to which each spark is destined finally
to return, to find there in the dancing flame a joyful end to its painful
separation.

Life for the majority was hard; hence this essentially pessimistic view
in which the human soul, tied to the inexorable wheel of fate, has
to endure a seemingly endless cycle of birth, death, bodiless state,
and reincarnation, until moral perfection (or perfect understanding) is
achieved and the soul is freed from the treadmill.

Buddha, a rigorous ascetic who had been born to luxury, now,
under the tree of Enlightenment, found the Middle Way. Peering
within himself he found no self, no enduring core, only a changing
bundle of desires. Selfish desiring bound him to the Wheel. Cease
desiring, the bundle would dissolve, he would find peace, the lasting
peace of annihilation. Practising non-attachment, he preached by word
and example the eightfold path to blissful extinction. No soul, no God
either. Here suffering, there silence and the Void.

Later, Buddhism divided into two major traditions, one preserving
the Founder's atheism, the other reaching back to the original Hinduism,
retaining belief in God and the soul (the final state, Nirvana, being
paradise, not extinction) while grafting on the Four Noble Truths of
suffering, its cause and cure. All Buddhists therefore follow together
the eight-fold path, whatever their differences about the soul and its
ultimate destiny.

In the Judaeo-Christian tradition, too, there have been problems
with the soul. In the earliest Hebrew thought, man did not possess
an immortal soul within his temporal body. He *was* a body-soul and,
when the breath of life departed, dust returned to dust. There was, it
is true, in keeping with Middle Eastern thought generally, a shadowy
underworld from which (to give advice) Samuel might be recalled by
witchcraft, but it was no full life, still less paradise. Earth's labours,
griefs and joys had been exchanged for silence, thirst, and perpetual
gloom, yet in that realm there were no rewards and punishments for
what had gone before. Rulers or slaves, there men and women kept
their earthly rankings and were beyond the reach of the gods, of whom
Yahweh was but one, with limited territorial powers.

Early Christianity soon took on gnostic overtones but, as it made its way in the hellenistic world, the notion of mortals entering the eternal life here and now through union with their Saviour-God and being given resurrection bodies after death tended to be overlaid by the Greek concept of an eternal soul freed by death from its earthy prison.

What survived might be the whole personality, recognizably the same inner being as had given character and direction to the body here, or it might be some pure essence. Plato, for instance, whose thinking encompassed several possibilities including the transmigration of souls as in Eastern thought, put forward the view, unsurprisingly for an elitist philosopher, that only our reasoning faculty would survive. Therefore those few who were capable of rising to the heights of pure cerebral activity could, in their practice of philosophy, anticipate the separation of soul from body and, dwelling in the world of Forms, savour death's privileges: release from cloudy emotion and bodily distractions, the untrammelled freedom of the mind to find and follow Truth.

His pupil, Aristotle, took an opposing view, and the Western tradition since has been marked by their difference. For Plato, value implied permanence and this was assured by the survival of god-like reason in the world of unchanging Forms. For Aristotle, there was nothing to survive bodily death. When the lamp shattered, the light went out, not off to somewhere else. Nor did the transience of all things earthly deprive them of value. Rather, it added to their poignancy, lending point to our proper use of each fleeting moment.

Descartes, the father of modern philosophy, started a lively hare with his contribution to the mind-body problem. He took the realm of the intangible very seriously but, paradoxically, his Cartesian dualism came close to banishing it for many. For him, the world was made up of two incompatible substances: incorporeal mind (or consciousness) and physical matter, which included the body and brain. So radically did he separate these two substances, treating man as a mechanism mysteriously linked with his mind through the pineal gland, that he unintentionally gave powerful impetus to the reductionist view of the world as a giant machine (for him it was a machine *plus*) with every living organism just another smaller machine. From such a standpoint the mind is what the brain generates, the soul a ghost no longer believed in.

Philosophy in this area today is heavily pregnant with new sciences coming to birth. Freud and Jung have lined up on opposite sides, neurologists probe the mysteries of the brain, and computer research foreshadows living self-conscious beings initiated by but increasingly taking over their own development and transcending humans in the next phase of evolution. If this happens, the distinction between machine and organism will become blurred to vanishing point. 'Robot' will seem then an absurdly out-dated work for a living creature coming to birth in a laboratory, receiving multiple sensory inputs, gaining experience and growing mentally, subject to emotional development and the maturing process, in some ways much as hummans are, and all this possibly within the lifetime of many of us. Who then will believe that souls are grafted in at birth and depart at death?

'Soul' is today a term little used in psychology, suggesting as it does a supernatural entity expected to endure unscathed once its brief temporal home has perished. Controversy in professional circles focuses rather on the relation of 'mind' to brain: is the mind more than what the brain does, and, whatever be the nature of the personal centre that has evolved among the less primitive creatures, can it escape the decay and dissolution to which the natural world is subject?

In Whitehead's massive metaphysical system, a deliberate attempt by a modern Platonist to integrate the accumulated wisdom of experience with advances in the natural sciences, death is accepted as in one sense final. Nothing survives to enjoy new adventures in some other realm. Yet Whitehead held it reasonable to believe in 'objective immortality', that nothing of value is ever lost. What is past does not recur. There are no second chances. Each moment is thus invested with immeasurable importance for it is its *only* moment. No repetition robs it of its unique value. Yet once passed it is preserved forever in the memory of God, as fresh as in that brief instant when it flared into existence, one note to sound forever in the symphony of being.

If this were the full story, the Receptacle (Plato's word) would be a mere museum of the past, keeping untouched everything as it occurred, indifferent to quality, piling up the fair and the ugly, the virtuous and the vile. But temporal events do more than enter the memory of God; they are taken up, selected, sifted, woven together into the ever-richer harmony that is God's concrete actuality.

It would perpetuate a childish, magical notion of Deity to suppose that anything is achieved, even by God, effortlessly and without pain. To Love is inevitably to suffer; to enter sympathetically into all life is to suffer infinitely. By willing the creation, by 'othering' itself in creation, Love that is potential becomes actual, becomes vulnerable to experience, embraces struggle and defeat as well as victory, finds out by loving what loving entails, is wracked by misery and doubt, surprised by joy, learns wisdom in the only way it can be learnt, by suffering.

Certainly this is speculation on the grand scale, but it is teasing out the implications of the evolving universe as we experience it, extrapolating from human artistry to the Divine Artist, drawing our picture of the Divine Parent in process of development from what we know of every human parent in loving relationship with children. Moreover, in this proved view of reality, what we give to God is then given back to the world, as God, enriched by each contributing relationship, however painful, continues as the lure of persuasive love to interact with all that is coming to be.

If, however, we are God's children and we die, is a dead child more than a remembered child in God? Would not remembrance alone be a defeat for Love? Could it be that we wake from a seven year, or a seventy year, dream to find that in our larger Self we are ourselves the Dreamer? Of this 'subjective immortality' Whitehead was unconvinced, though he did not rule it out.

Many modern philosophers are sceptical about life after death, partly from negative considerations of what might survive the body's dissolution, partly because descriptions of the after-life are invariably so banal. An eternity spent doing anything less than co-creating the universe sounds like a recipe for hell. With objective immortality the problem does not arise. The curtain for each of us comes down. God will continue to draw on whatever there was of value in our joint performance. There is for us no Second Act. Yet the Play goes on. With subjective immortality we are, in our larger Self, the Dramatist, and the universe itself the unfolding of the One Life in which we all improvise our bit parts in a play that never ends.

Philosophical endeavour includes informed speculation and does not preclude the leap of faith – 'he thinks he was not made to die, and Thou hast made him, Thou art just' – but, strictly from the standpoint of reasoned enquiry, how much of this is so and whether we do or do not consciously survive our death remain matters on which, to paraphrase a recent philosopher, 'we shall just have to wait and see or, as the case may be, not see'.

The ultimate destination need not divide us. It is as if two travellers think they discern a road leading to the top of a range of hills on the horizon and agree to make their way there. Both could justify the journey in terms of what they can see on this side of the ridge, and for one of them this is enough. If the road should end at the top, neither would feel their effort had been wasted in arriving there, but the second traveller is fortified by the expectation that the road goes on, down into another valley and then up and over range upon further range, to end perhaps at some city or a distant sea, or to reach unexplored territory offering new challenges to the pioneer spirit. Meanwhile night is falling, there are tents to be pitched, a fire to be lit and a meal prepared. There will be time to talk of these things later by the fire, as the darkness expands their imagination and the stars come out overhead.

Patrick Lewin

1 How does the individual soul's union with the universal Soul (Atman uniting with Brahman) compare with traditional theistic

belief? Could you accept Atman/Brahman and still term yourself
an atheist?

2    If the soul is immortal, does this not ultimately (in terms of
     human experience and need) make God superfluous? How far is
     the theistic view based on the desire to survive death, and the
     conviction (or hope) that somehow an immortal God can make this
     possible?

3    The article described Buddha's discovery of 'the lasting peace of
     annihilation'. Do you find this preferable to, or harder to accept
     than, the concept of eternal life? In what way(s), if any, do you
     think the two concepts are synonymous?

4    Do you think that followers of 'Greater Vehicle' (Mahayana)
     Buddhism are justified in calling themselves Buddhists?

5    What is now the Jewish teaching about the soul? Granted that the Old
     Testament view is accurately described in the article – 'dust to dust'
     – how do you think Jewish morale (to put it at its most mundane)
     has been sustained amid centuries of persecution, culminating in the
     Holocaust?

6    Do you think that the idea of the soul has arisen primarily as a
     psychological device to cope with the enormous injustices of life
     in this cycle of experience, or is it rather an idea which has
     developed from centuries of personal experience on the part of
     billions of people? How natural to your experience is the idea of
     the soul?

7    Is there a distinctive Christian view on the soul? Is it possible to
     disentangle this view from the hellenistic overlays which have come
     upon it? Read the passage from Hospers in case study 4 and ask
     yourself the meaning of the phrase 'spiritual bodies'.

8    In what respects is it the case that 'Freud and Jung have lined up on
     opposite sides'?

9    Is the writer's vision of computers as 'self-conscious beings . . .
     increasingly transcending human beings' in your view any more
     than a science-fiction nightmare? If you reject this criticism, in what
     respects do you foresee that the vision will become a reality? What
     changes, if any, do you think should be happening now in individual
     attitudes and ideas? What are the implications of the idea so far as
     universal metaphysical beliefs are concerned?

10   'Is a dead child more than a remembered child in God?' What
     is the author eliciting through this question? How far do you

think it reveals the inadequacy or unacceptability of Whitehead's views? How close are Whitehead's views to those of Taoism?

11   Do you agree that the wisest attitude to take about this whole matter is to wait and (not) see? See case study 6 for some of the implications of commitment or non-commitment of oneself to a belief in the soul.

12   If it turns out that there is nothing on the other side of the mountain, does this mean that any road that we perceive on this side is in fact a mirage?

*Case study 19*
*Asceticism*

The word asceticism is derived from the Greek *askein*, meaning literally 'to exercise'. In the context in which we have been using the word, it refers to exercise of self-control, normally over physical desires: sex, food and so on. We have seen that followers of certain creeds took this practice to excess, believing that extreme asceticism was a virtue in its own right, a sure way to sainthood. Thomas More, for instance, even when he was Henry VIII's Chancellor, wore a hair shirt next to his skin as an expression of his service to the Almighty.

The exercise that follows is to let you reflect on this by no means uncommon assertion of certain values, and to explore it as a possible *modus vivendi*.

1   *Historical expressions of asceticism*
    (a)   the Jainites: no taking of life, starving oneself to death the supreme virtue
    (b)   the Pillar Saints of Christianity (early Middle Ages): men who spent their final years on top of a pillar (fed by followers from below) in order to contemplate God without distraction
    (c)   bans on free love, alcohol and so on in many key religious writings: Buddha, the Ten Commandments (adultery), the New Testament, the Koran (alcohol)
    (d)   bans on drugs of any kind, including tea and coffee (the Mormons)
    (e)   bans on the arts, such as the pictorial expression of religious beliefs, the enacting of plays in public, etc. (the Puritans)
    (f)   bans on the eating of meat: Buddhism, Judaism (certain meats), Islam (certain meats), Hinduism (certain meats)
    (g)   acceptance of celibacy (for monks and nuns of a wide range of religious beliefs and, in the Roman Catholic Church, also for parish priests who have to mingle with women as part of their daily routine)

**2**    *The purpose of asceticism*

    (a)    to control the incessant urgings of the flesh (sex, in the New Testament)

        But    (i)    since we are born with these urges, is it not unnatural to curb them?

               (ii)    certain societies (see Thor Heyerdahl, *Love in the South Seas*) have encouraged their peoples to glory in expressing and fulfilling themselves through the flesh: are they likely to be less happy/fulfilled because of this?

    (b)    to foster the spiritual side of life

        But is there any evidence that this is more likely to be achieved by rigorous self-denial than through living a 'natural' existence?

    (c)    to develop personal autonomy: not being prey at any or all times to the 'weaknesses' of the flesh

        But    (i)    doesn't the excessive pursuit of self-denial suggest a neurosis rather than autonomy?

               (ii)    isn't the strongest expression of autonomy that of knowing when to stop satisfying the body? Doesn't extreme asceticism suggest that the person concerned doesn't trust him- or herself to maintain self-control? Doesn't self-control mean temperance rather than total abstinence? (Greek *egkrateia*, self-control, means literally 'holding oneself in'.)

    (d)    to ensure a reward in heaven: 'If there's no heaven after all the sacrifices I've made here, then there really is no justice,' said a Trappist monk, given permission to speak to a TV interviewer (no doubt his last indulgence!).

        But    (i)    isn't this rather a selfish motive?

               (ii)    is the dichotomy between 'the world, the flesh, and the devil' and those seeking salvation by rejecting it a healthy one?

               (iii)    assuming that this way of preparing for the world beyond is based on an image of how that world operates, is it one to be looked forward to?


**3**    *The other extreme*

Not all admonitions in religious writings or communities have involved the extreme other-worldliness of the ascetics.

    (a)    Many expressions of Hinduism illustrate religious rapture in boldly sexual terms (see case study 25).

    (b)    The Koran includes in its description of paradise the presence

of nubile maidens who are there solely to please the men in
whatever way they desire.

(c)   In early Christianity a sect called the Antinomians (literally
'against the law', meaning the divine law) took as their central
theme: 'Let us sin that Grace may abound.' They believed
themselves to be saved come what may, so they wanted to
give the forgiving God much to forgive.

(d)   Most practices of asceticism have, in any case, been expressed
as a reaction to communities which have taken self-indulgence
to excess, illustrated in such songs as 'Enjoy yourself, it's later
than you think'.

4   *Some questions for reflection*

(a)   Is there not, generally speaking, a kind of pendulum in society,
bringing about extremes of expression in matters of personal
indulgence? For example, the rigours of the period of the First
World War and its aftermath, followed by the 'letting-go' of the
1920s followed by the further rigours of the Second World War
and the 1940s, then the 'swinging sixties', hippies and flower
power with, today, a swing back to greater self-discipline?

(b)   How far do you think *fear* causes many to abstain? Is this necessarily weaker than occasionally indulging, but not to excess?

(c)   Is it in any case healthy to 'let things go' occasionally? cf. Aldous
Huxley: 'Life is routine intermingled with orgies.' Or do you
think a constant middle way between indulgence and repression
is healthier?

(d)   Do you think there is any value in occasionally giving up
a personal indulgence, e.g. fasting once a week, abstaining
from stimulants (tea, coffee, alcohol) for a while, having an
occasional 'Lent' even if not in the official period for this? If
you have practised any of these, can you analyse the value, if
any, gained from it?

(e)   John Stuart Mill said that ascetism was of no value *per se*, but
only in so far as it increased the sum total of human happiness.
What do you think?

Many practitioners of the ascetic life have argued that the discovery of the
spiritual element in life, or what I earlier described as 'the numinous', was
enhanced by denial of the satisfaction of physical needs. If this were found
to be the case, would it help to modify in any way your view of either the
value of asceticism or the need for the numinous? Do you think there may
at least be something to be said for the advice: moderation in all things?

## India: Hinduism

When writing of Buddhism it is possible to be relatively succinct. This is not because there is little to be said about it but because, though there are variations of emphasis in different schools, there is a strong, central consistency in its view of human nature and destiny. Though expressions of Buddhism in, say, China, Japan, Tibet and Sri Lanka have marked differences from its expression in India, its source, they are still recognizably Buddhist. With Hinduism, however, we enter a more complex scene, as the name suggests: it is derived from the Urdu word for India, *Hind*, and with it we embark on a diversified range of experiences. Even though it is found almost exclusively in the Indian subcontinent (so that it cannot be claimed that, like Buddhism, modifications have arisen because of the adaptation of the original to widely differing cultures), its range of expressions is incredibly varied, reflecting a dispersion as broad as the compass in its three thousand years of history. In some forms, a central role is played by a god, or a number of gods. Students of Hinduism will know about, for instance, Shiva and Vishnu, two gods who, according to Hindu mythology, had many incarnations. Shiva is represented in Hindu sculpture by the lingam, the upright pillar in Hindu temples shaped like a phallus. He is the Lord of the Dance, dancing out the continuous creation of the world. His consort, Kali, has a necklace of skulls, symbolizing the inexorability of time. Vishnu, it was believed, had numerous incarnations (**avatars**) of whom, according to orthodox Hindus, Buddha was one. Otherwise his most famous avatars were believed to have been Rama and Krishna, the god who is described as the inspiration of the Bhagavad-gita (see p. 176).

Any visitor to India is likely to have seen temples which give evidence of the vividly visual Hindu tradition; and the emphases and expressions vary from village to village and from shrine to shrine. But there is a wholly different tendency in Hinduism, away from religious or social myth towards pure philosophy. In this philosophical approach, Hindu mythology is not so much cast aside or derided as seen as a crutch for those who may need it. But those who can, are invited to throw away their crutch and reflect through philosophy on the meaning and purpose of existence; and it is with this approach that we are concerned.

### THE SIX SYSTEMS OF INDIAN PHILOSOPHY

The knowledge covered by Indian philosophy is vast and provides the subject-matter for many thousands of volumes of texts, compiled over a period of at least three thousand years. The most ancient sacred literature of the Hindus is called the **Vedas**, dating back to an era before 1000 BC (about the time of the earliest writings of the Old Testament). At that time the major Indian civilization was centred round the Indus valley. The next period of Indian history (1000–600 BC) took place in the region between the Himalayas and the mouth of the Ganges river (Bay of Bengal); the **Upanishads** (meaning the secret doctrine, the essence, of the Vedas) were brought to light at this time. From approximately 600 BC (the post-Vedic period) the six orthodox systems of Indian philosophy, together with Jainism and, of course, Buddhism, evolved. All of these systems were inspired by the teachings of the Upanishads, regarded by **Shankara** (who will be a major figure in this present study) and other great philosophers of that time as 'revealed truth with absolute authority' (though, as we have seen, Buddha accepted no such absolute).

My purpose is to expound particularly on only one of the systems of Indian philosophy, Advaita Vedanta, because the ontological perspective of that school is particularly rewarding for students in this field; but a very brief consideration of the other five systems (*upangas*, literally 'high limbs') of Vedic philosophy should, by placing it in context, help to pinpoint its significance.

The first system is *Nyaya* (literally, 'going into a subject'). It is the science of logical proof and epistemology, and thereby represents the closest of all Hindu philosophy to the Western analytical approach to the subject (and shows how dangerous it is to generalize about 'Eastern Philosophy'). It was formulated by Gautama (560 BC), a contemporary of the Buddha. He compiled the accepted principles of his field into the *Nyaya-Sutras*. The opening verse of these **sutras** (literally 'threads') says that supreme felicity is attained by the knowledge of the true nature of sixteen categories, namely: means of right knowledge, object of right knowledge, doubt, purpose, familiar example, established tenet, members of a syllogism, confutation, ascertainment, discussion, controversy, cavil, fallacy, equivocation, futility, and disagreement in principle. The first nine deal more strictly with logic, while the others are used to prevent or overcome error: but all are used to discover truth as far as truth can be verified in the course of human pronouncements or expositions of points of view. Until recently the teachings of Nyaya were best preserved in Tibet. A student of the monastic university of Lhasa was expected to spend four years studying Nyaya before specializing in his chosen field.

Secondly, *Vaisesika* (or Vaisheshika) aimed at developing an intellectual insight into the true nature of reality by identifying objects by the characteristics which differentiated them from other objects. It was known as a doctrine of liberation (*Mokshashastra*), and in its chief text, the Vaisesika–Sutra, deals with the Supreme Spirit (though, it should be noted, without referring explicitly to God). This philosophy was founded by Kanada (literally 'Atom Eater') in the third century BC. Kanada was otherwise known as the Rishi Kasyapa, one of the seven great Vedic seers. His study dealt with the smallest possible properties of (or differences between) the nine 'eternal realities': fire, earth, air, water, ether, time, space, soul (Atman – see below) and mind. His name recalls the atomism of Democritus, and it would not be out of place to view Vaisesika as the Eastern parallel to Western atomism. Kanada concluded that the fundamental means of escaping from human bondage was to attain a direct vision of the reality of the self (which places him in a very different field from Buddha).

The third school of Hindu philosophy is the oldest: *Sankya* (or *Shankhya*: variations of transliteration are possible). It literally means 'pertaining to number', and is held by many to be the most notable attempt of all the schools in the realm of pure philosophy; the philosophical foundation of all oriental culture; and the key to all Eastern symbolism. It was developed in the sixth century BC by Kapila, who enumerated the various levels of any object from the grossest to the subtlest, putting them in twenty-five categories. He classified the mind as part of objective *prakriti* (nature and all its expressions) and stated that prakriti is external to the real self (*purusha*). Thus he concluded that there are two ultimate realities – spirit and matter – and that all misery is born of matter, the body, and is an illusion in a state of liberation. We are here not far removed from the dualism of Plato, with his insistence that the things of this world are but a shadow of reality and that the only true reality is the universe of Forms. According to Sankya, all the levels of existence and the 'reality' which underlies them can be directly experienced through *yoga* (literally 'yoking'). It thus provides the intellectual backing to the school of Hindu philosophy which is probably followed most widely in the West.

*Yoga* (from the Sanskrit word *Yuj*, 'to join' or unite) finds mention as long ago as 3000 BC in what is now Pakistan (the civilization of Mohenjodaro). It became known as a philosophical system during the third century BC as a result of the *Yoga Sutras* compiled by Patanjali. The Sanskrit language (the basic language of this, as of all, Vedic teachings) has remained virtually unchanged since the fourth century BC, and consequently these sutras are as understandable to us today as when they were first written (a rare phenomenon when dealing with ancient texts). The purpose of the sutras, however, is not to present a sequential argument on Western lines (or even according to the discipline of Nyaya) but to describe, so to speak, the stages of a journey that is unfamiliar to us. It does this by means of threads, or knots: each sutra is a knot to be unravelled by a **guru** (*gu*, 'from darkness', *ru*, 'to light'). Its aim, like that of most Eastern (and some Western) philosophy is to transform rather than inform. Yoga was an indispensable part of the philosopher's training in India, where the idea that 'reality' can be comprehended by the 'unenlightened' is like 'trying to catch the air with a pair of tongs' (*Maitri Upanishads*).

The eight elements, or 'limbs', of yoga are: yama (the principles of life), niyama (the qualities of living), asana (posture), pranayama (increasing life through breath), pratyahara (retirement of the senses), dharana (focusing, or concentration), dhyana (meditation) and samadhi (settled mind). These 'limbs' are described in the *Yoga Sutras* as the means of finding self-realization by stabilizing our 'unbounded consciousness' – thoughts disconnected, flying in all directions, so to speak – so that we may develop what is described as **Siddhis**, or supernormal (not, note, supernatural) powers which may transform us into a state of enlightenment. *Siddhi* literally means perfection, and is an archery term meaning to hit the centre of the target, as opposed to *sin*, which is also an archery term, meaning to miss the target.

The technique used to develop siddhis (with which yoga practitioners will be familiar) is *sanyama* (coherence), a state in which dharana, dhyana and samadhi are brought, or experienced, together at the threshold of consciousness (*ritambhara*). From this level of consciousness life becomes an expression of a field of all possibilities. Sanyama results in 'the state in which activity and silence are equally balanced in the mind', 'Effortless Being'. When this balance is permanent, there is enlightenment. The siddhis are useful only in that they nurture this enlightenment. (See case study 28 for a fuller outline of Yogic teaching and practice.)

The fifth system of Indian philosophy is *Mimansa*. As a system it is divided into two sections. The first, *Purva* (earlier), is usually known as *karma mimansa*, as it deals with action (karma); the second, *Uttara* (later), deals with knowledge (**jnana**) and is referred to as *Vedanta*: Vedanta has become the sixth system of Indian philosophy, and will be the main theme of this section. Karma Mimansa was the philosophy of Jaimini, a disciple of Badarayana, who lived in the 'Sutra' period of India (between 600 and 200 BC). Jaimini's system is usually regarded more as a work on practical ethics than pure philosophy, though in this age of 'applied philosophy' this distinction seems not too important. Jaimini's sutras accept the philosophical concepts of the other systems, but state that 'salvation' cannot be achieved by knowledge alone – deeds are also required. Jaimini inquired into the nature of 'right action' (dharma) and provided a general summary of the rules for the interpretation of Vedic texts. All Hindu ritual, ceremonies and laws depend on Mimansa.

These five systems, along with Vedanta, constitute what are classified by Hindu scholars as **astika**, or orthodoxy. There are many others not so classified, but even a limited awareness of these mainstream systems should suffice to indicate that the philosophical field from which Advaita Vedanta emerged was as wide and as deep as any similar field in the Western world.

## ADVAITA VEDANTA

This school has been popularized in the West through its advocacy by such well-known writers as **Aldous Huxley** (*The Perennial Philosophy*) and **Christopher Isherwood**. They outlined the philosophy in a contemporary format ('Neo-Vedanta'), taking as their mentors the

Indians Swami **Vivekananda** (1863–1902) and the more famous Sarvepalli **Radhakrishnan** (1888–1975). Many Hindu scholars feel that Westerners have paid a disproportionate amount of attention to the Advaita Vedanta school of Indian philosophy, thereby limiting the rewards that are theirs for the asking if they would search more comprehensively. Any rapid perusal of the first part of this section will indicate that there is considerable truth in this criticism, or caution. My path throughout this book is, however, one that I have trodden out for myself: and just as in the West one school, existentialism, seemed to offer a more direct route than most towards the goal set at the beginning, so in the East – or, at any rate, in India – Advaita Vedanta seems particularly propitious.

The word Vedanta means the end, or goal (that is, the truth to which they were leading), of the Vedas (the ancient Indian sacred texts mentioned earlier). Its teachings are based on three main sources: the *Upanishads*, which have contributed in some form to most schools of Hindu thought, and were written between the eighth and fifth centuries BC; the *Bhagavadgita*, written in the period following the Upanishads (probably around the second century BC – but see the cautionary word about Indian dates below) and containing some of the highest expressions of Hindu thought and devotion; commonly known as the Gita, it is the nearest the Hindus come to having a Bible (Mahatma Gandhi and his family read it through together once a month); and a collection of sayings – 'threads' – called the Brahma Sutras or *Vedanta Sutras*.

The best-known Vedanta scholar, who wrote a commentary on the Gita, was *Adi Shankara*. Historians feel that he lived around the eighth century AD, but Indian tradition places him some 1,200 years earlier. This would clearly place the date of the Gita much earlier than stated above. Fortunately, the issue does not affect the theme of this book, which is to extrapolate those elements of the teaching which seem valuable today in formulating a comprehensively satisfying ontological perspective. We can therefore safely leave aside the historical question and concentrate on the message. (As Shankara is a title, it may refer to more than one person.)

The word Advaita describes Shankara's system. Literally, it means 'non-dualistic' – a concept we have already met in Western thought, but its Indian meaning is idiosyncratic and must be allowed to emerge as we outline the general tendency of the philosophy. Like Buddhism, Advaita Vedanta expresses the view that the purpose of philosophy is not so much to discover 'the truth' for its own sake as to help people to find appropriate forms of action or behaviour. One central fact of life as we experience it is what I termed earlier the fact of limitation: that the world is characterized by sorrow, frustration and despair, and that, while some may not be hit by it as hard as others, all share in this. Buddhism proposed that the way out of the impasse which this creates is to build up good karma, so that, for example, the reborn 'me' will begin with fewer of these limitations, leading eventually, even if through many rebirths, to the state of Nirvana, the state beyond duhkha, from which no rebirth is needed. Advaita Vedanta also recognizes the fact of karma but proposes an even more immediate way of coping with it. This is to seek to be rid of its bonds and shackles, *in toto*, here and now.

How this is to be achieved involves us in studying the philosophical method proposed by Advaita Vedanta. This begins with an analysis of human consciousness and means looking unflinchingly at human experience until we see for ourselves the truth about it. The three signposts to truth are: direct experience, reasoning and trustworthy reports on other people's experiences. Advaita teaches – what we must all know from experience to be true – that there are three daily recurring states of consciousness. First, there is *deep sleep*, which is characterized by unity and unawareness (perhaps we should say unity *because of* unawareness); secondly, there is *dreaming sleep*, which is characterized by duality and partial awareness (duality in the sense that there is both the self-consciousness of the person in the dream and the existence of others outside that consciousness: even in dreams there are both things or people perceived and the dreamer's inner reflections on those perceptions); thirdly, there is the *waking experience* which I have as I write away here, and you presumably have as you read (and if you've dropped off, that comment, like this one, is superfluous); this state is characterized by duality and ordinary awareness – the duality of the perceiver and the perceived, and one's subjective awareness of this as a regular experience.

These three states are symbolized in Hindu writings (in reverse order to their mention above) as A, U and M, making the sound OM; and both reason and experience confirm their reality. But according to the Advaita philosophy – and here lies its distinctiveness – there is a fourth state of consciousness which brings about **moksa**, or liberation, characterized by both awareness and non-dualism. This state is called **samadhi**, and is described in the Mandukya Upanishad:

> What is known as the fourth portion – neither inward- nor outward-turned consciousness, nor the two together; not an undifferentiated mass of dormant omniscience; neither knowing nor unknowing – because invisible, ineffable, intangible, devoid of characteristics, inconceivable, undefinable, its sole essence being the assurance of its own Self (eka-atma-pratyaya-saram); the coming to peaceful rest of all differentiated, relative existence (prapanca-upasamam); utterly quiet (santam); peaceful-blissful (sivam); without-a-second (advaitam, non-dualistic): – this is Atman, the Self, which is to be realised.

The attainment of this state, so it is attested by those *rsis*, or seers, who have achieved it, removes one's sense of limitation (as described when discussing Buddhism) by revealing a universal dimension which is here for all to enter, independently of their social, mental, or physical handicaps or shortcomings; more important within the context of Hindu thought, it makes the whole syndrome of karma redundant because by entering the fourth state one is freed from its bonds and burdens. Thus Advaita Vedanta is closer in line with the later developments of Buddhism, which suggested that the state of Nirvana was available *now* for those with ears to hear and eyes to see. (The original concept of Nirvana is of course not at all the same as that of the Fourth State, or samadhi since the latter is testified to by those who have gained it as one of heightened awareness, rather than of 'blowing-out'.)

Before we proceed further in this highly complex field, referral should be made to the idea of 'trustworthy reports'. Who is making these reports and how trustworthy is 'trustworthy'? After all, it may be argued, many people testify to having seen flying saucers; others describe how they hold lengthy conversations with people long deceased; yet others assure us that they have experienced a variety of exotic manifestations of extra-sensory perception; we don't take their word as final, so why should we pay any more heed to these seers, or gurus, than we (or most of us) pay to those who testify on these other matters?

Whatever conclusions we may draw as to the worth of their affirmations, one test whereby we may assess the integrity of the seers is whether they have any financial or psychological axe to grind – are they acting for monetary gain, or in order to boost their egos? – or whether they are testifying to their experiences simply because they *have* experienced them, have found them rewarding and wish to share them with others. There may well be charlatans among those claiming to be seers (it would be a unique experience in human concourse if there weren't) but many of them seem to be describing a state that they have found to be blissful, and expressing the desire only that others should share this state. Of course the experience of the Fourth State is indescribable and, in analytical terms, unverifiable, lending itself to exploitation of the gullible by the cynical; but every experience of the numinous which I mentioned earlier (pp. 32–3) is equally unverifiable despite the millions who bear witness to it; it is the case every time one person says to another 'I love you.'

What one has to say, I think, is, look and see. Do these people seem to you to be more than attention-seekers, or money-makers, along the lines of many of the American TV evangelists? If so, their testimony may be freely rejected (unless, of course, despite these drawbacks, you feel there may be something of worth in what they affirm). Most of the seers are in any case not professional globe-trotters or engaged in permanent contemplation, but people who combine their insight with the fulfilling of a daily job like most other people. To enter the Fourth State doesn't involve the explorer in remaining in it permanently. This would mean abandoning everything included in what for most people is 'the daily round, the common task', which is quite contrary to what Advaita Vedanta is teaching. Its affirmation is that, with the enlightenment achieved through experiencing the Fourth State, one achieves moksa, as already described, amid the daily routine. Any Western reader who has practised yoga, for instance, will know about moksa, and that the mature yogic expert will have attained it. In his *The Philosophies of India*, Heinrich Zimmler states:

> The self-transforming change of emphasis becomes a well-known and controllable experience for the skilled practitioner of yoga. He can make the states come and go, their spheres appear and disappear, according to his will, which leads him . . . to a philosophy of phenomenalism. Through his sovereign yogic power the gross aspect of reality is, for him, devaluated; for he can produce the subtle, fluid forms of the inward state of vision whenever he likes, fix them and retain them as long as he requires, and after that, again according to his wish, come temporarily back into touch with the exterior world. Such a virtuoso is not subject and exposed helplessly to the waking state, but enters into it only when and as he wishes – his real abode or homestead, meanwhile, being the 'fourth' at the opposite end of the series. (p. 376)

Thus what to most people is the 'normal' state of awakening, the third state, becomes, for these seers, merely optional, re-evaluated and reinterpreted from the 'fourth' state. And those who broadcast this do so, generally speaking, not for personal or financial gain but from the desire that others might benefit from the experience.

## BRAHMAN AND ATMAN

In order to understand the ontological emphases of Advaita Vedanta, we must take into our fields two further words which are central in Hindu thought, and dominate the philosophical teaching of most of their schools. The word **Brahman** will be familiar to many readers, but it is a word difficult to express in Western terms without begging a large number of questions. 'Ultimate reality' is one such term, and 'holy power' another. The Vedanta uses the formula '**Sat–Chit–Ananda**' – 'being-consciousness-bliss', or the pantheistic soul of the world. I prefer the phrase already introduced (Chapter 6): Ground of Being.

What this phrase is meant to convey is, quite simply, the realization that the world is an expression of Being and that this is the only ultimate reality. A myriad things in the universe will come into Being and then pass away, but amid this transience, Being endures. Ignorance of this reality leads many people to overlook the fact that the material world, the world of 'things', of getting and spending, will not endure: that this world is, from the enlightened perspective of the fourth state, mere illusion (**maya**); and this ignorance causes not only suffering in the Buddhist sense (duhkha) but deprives us of the joy which enlightenment brings. In some Vedantic writings, including the Bhagavad-gita, Brahman, the Ground of Being, is identified with God in the theistic sense of one who is omnipotent Lord of All; in others (again including the Gita) it is related to God in the pantheistic sense of one who is expressed in all that has Being (or, simply, *is*). In others, the idea of *godness* is viewed as below that of Brahman: a step towards the final truth, perhaps, but not the final step.

> This that people say: 'Worship this god! Worship that God!' one after another – this is (Brahman's) creation indeed! And he himself is all the gods.
>
> (Upanishads 1.4.6)

Thus we unfold the unity, the non-dualism, of Advaita Vedanta: it is a form of non-dualism quite different from the normal use of this term in the West, where it is normally contrasted with dualism, as discussed in Chapter 2. In the teaching of Advaita this whole debate is irrelevant, because the non-dual experience is one that absorbs both body and soul (or mind, or whatever other connotation we may wish to introduce). Equally, the non-dualism of Advaita is based on the belief that there is no dichotomy of relationship between God and 'His people' as in theistic writings: instead, Advaita teaches that the realization of Brahman comes about through the realization of the Self. That is, we discover the Ground of Being when we find out what our Being is. In Hindu language, we experience **Atman**.

Again, this word is not easily expressed in Western terms. One could replace it with the word soul, but this would be inadequate because Atman can mean either body, mind, or soul according to the circumstances. Ninian Smart, in his *The Religious Experience of Mankind*, describes it as the 'still centre' from which an individual's thoughts, feelings, actions and so on, proceed. It may perhaps best be described as a person's individual living entity: my Atman is my basic Being, from which my field of Being extends. In the teaching of Advaita, it is, as already mentioned, identified in sound by the letters A, U and M, creating the sound OM. This indicates that the Atman combines the states of dreamless sleep, dreaming sleep and the awakened state in one Self.

But the Atman is more than this, since these three states leave out the fourth state, the state of enlightenment. This is a state of silence, so no sound needs to be added to the A, U and M: one can say, therefore, that OM represents (or may represent) all four states of consciousness and that together they describe the Atman. All four coexist in the same person and illustrate again that, having gained enlightenment, one does not throw off the three lesser states; in fact, the enlightened man or woman, according to this teaching, may not be distinguishable, on first encounter at any rate, from any other person on the street or in the office. (It is important to get across the fact that in talking about enlightened people we are not concerning ourselves with people who have rejected 'the world', adopted a life of hermitage, withdrawal and self-denial and look different from everyone else: that is the Jainite tradition, not that of Advaita.)

What then is the distinction between Atman and Brahman? The answer is, basically none at all. The Bhagavad-gita states, 'He who knows himself in everything and everything in himself will not injure himself by himself.' This reflects Shankara's statement that just as there is no essential difference between the space inside a jar and the space outside it, so there is no essential difference between the individual Atman and the universal Brahman. This is the claim made in what is arguably the central text of the Upanishads: **Tat tuam asi**: 'That thou art'. It is the claim that Atman and Brahman are one; that my Being permeates the Ground of all Being, which pervades and actuates the whole universe. As salt dissolved in water flavours all the water, so does Atman pervade Brahman. 'That which is the finest essence – this whole world has that as its soul. That is Reality. That is Atman. That art thou' (Upanishads 6.9.4.)

Advaita thus teaches that Brahman makes all things one, so creating a link between the '**Prakriti**' (nature) and '**Purusha**' (cosmic spirit) of the Sankya system, which as we have seen is more akin to the type of dualism encountered in Western philosophy. Advaita concludes that the only difference between humanity and the gods (assuming these exist) or between individual Being and the Ground of Being, is one of degree. The realization of this is the one supreme goal of Vedanta, as Nirvana is the goal of Buddhism. Brahman is, so to speak, the mountain peak towards which we are bound, whether we know it or not. We all *start* at different points according to our karma accumulated in the past (on this Buddhism and Vedanta are agreed) but the aim for each of us is enlightenment, the achieving of the fourth state. Each individual must work out for him- or herself how best to move towards this. One may listen to the counsel of those who have gained enlightenment, but it is impossible to generalize about the path to be taken, since no two seers have themselves followed the same path. Everyone, it is believed, will ultimately attain the goal, and nobody is in a position to judge whether he or she is managing better or worse than their neighbour along the road to the summit: thus nobody can dictate to, or show contempt for, others. All will be one with Brahman in the end, as finally the silence of the fourth state makes the other three states redundant, so that the sound of the OM can no longer be heard.

The fourth is soundless: unutterable, a quieting down of the differentiated manifestations, blissful-peaceful, nondual. Thus OM is Atman, verily.

He who knows thus merges his Self in the Self – yea, he who knows thus.

(Mandukya Upanishad)

Whether or not the deliverance from maya which this experience brings about means deliverance from the cycle of reincarnation can of course be a matter only of speculation; and Advaita Vedanta claims to speak not in speculative terms but of realities that have been experienced by many through the centuries, and can be experienced by all. None the less, from the ontological viewpoint, it seems not unreasonable to state that this deliverance may in fact occur. If Atman, individual Being, subject to non-Being, were one with Brahman, the Ground of all Being (which must be eternal since Being cannot, by definition, not be), might it not then be possible to affirm that Atman endures even when confronted with non-Being because it functions no longer as separate Being (separated, that is, from the Ground of Being) but rather as part of that which must endure eternally? Shankara's contribution in this field was to affirm not only that this is so, but that we can also *know* it to be so by awakening to the fourth state. Thus the philosophy of Advaita Vedanta adds a new element into our ontological explorations. With existentialism we studied the nature of Being particularly in association with non-Being, death, or nothingness, and followed the fruitful line of inquiry into the nature of Being and becoming. With Buddhism we saw how valuable might be the concept that one is responsible for the building up of good karma for the sake of the rebirth of a being or, if you like, Being in a new cycle of birth and death and, ultimately, Being in Nirvana. We have now, in Advaita Vedanta, reached the point where the sense of individual Being may be transcended by the Ground of all Being, so that all the joys of Nirvana (even though this state as spoken of by Buddha is not synonymous with the fourth state as described by the Upanishads and by Shankara), need not be contemplated as a future event but experienced here and now, with the implication that this experience will be eternal. (In the sense of eternity as it confronts *me*, described on pp. 210–11, the question of how long, objectively speaking, this will last is irrelevant: subjectively the experience will last for ever since, ontologically speaking, I shall never know non-Being.)

After a brief recap on Buddhism and Advaita I shall want to make some criticisms of this philosophy; but these will not in any way cloud the fact that it represents, to my mind, one of the highest peaks in Hindu ontological thought.

BUDDHISM AND VEDANTA: WHAT HAVE THEY IN COMMON?

Even a newcomer to Eastern studies must have recognized certain similarities between the two philosophical systems which have been considered. The common thread running between Buddhism and Vedanta includes the following features.

(1)   They both build their philosophy on experience, rather than deducing what reality is like by pure reason (as in Western rationalism) or analysing words (as in linguistic philosophy).

(2)   They both view the purpose of philosophy as trying to understand experience, not for its own sake, but in order to change it.

(3)   They are both teleological, regarding life as having an intelligible purpose.

(4)   They both evaluate the present state of man as one of suffering or unfulfilment, and claim that the function of philosophy is to teach men how to end this.

(5)   They are both eudaemonistic, that is, they both see the goal of life as the attainment of happiness.

(6)   The ethics of both are prudential: their teachings are concerned with working out the most effective ways of reaching a certain end in certain circumstances, not with the mechanical application of universal principles.

(7)   They both recognize and emphasize the freedom of men and women to choose what is good.

(8)   They both stress that the essence of morality is the destruction of egoism.

(9)   They both agree on some basic rules – the prohibition of homicide, theft, adultery and lying.

(10)  They share common ideals of conduct and attitude (see the quotation below).

(11)  They both rest on a view of human nature that sees members of the human race as more than clever animals.

(12)  They both place high value on individual consciousness, as opposed to conformity to social standards.

Many of these emphases are epitomized in the Buddhist concept of selfless persons, and the Advaita view of non-dual reality – the water-drop entering the sea. The consequence of both schools in terms of human behaviour is that the liberation from self, of which both speak, is seen to be incompatible with either the assertion of personality or the injury of others. The ideal human being, according to Vedantic morality, and with which Buddha would not have differed greatly, may be summed up in these words from the Bhagavad-gita (16: 1–3):

> Fearlessness, simplicity of heart, steadfastness in knowledge, almsgiving, control of the senses . . . austerity, straightforwardness, non-violence, truthfulness, absence of anger, renunciation, peacefulness, absence of deviousness, compassion to all beings, freedom from acquisitiveness, gentleness, modesty, perseverance, vigour, fortitude, forgiveness, purity, absence of hatred, and freedom from arrogance.

In one sense, this is simply a list of desirable human characteristics, which might be compared with other people's, or other schools', lists: but the basic emphasis on non-assertiveness emerges from this description, and this is one of the major contributions of Eastern thought to the – generally 'macho' – mores of the West.

## ADVAITA ONTOLOGY

It seems fair to state, therefore, that the philosophy of Advaita Vedanta has a good deal in common with some of the ontological perspectives which have been adumbrated in Western existentialism; and some of the implications of this commonality will be drawn out in the concluding chapters of this book. However, it would give a wrong impression if no cautionary word were to be added, since, like most readers, I guess, I have a major reservation. This concerns the extent to which Advaita, non-dualism, expresses the Being-becoming process which, I have suggested, is essential if the to-be of us is not to be nullified. Being and becoming are indivisible in that Being that is not at the same time becoming has, quite simply and logically, ceased to be. In other words, *immutability, or unchangingness, and nothingness are ontologically synonymous.* I have argued this case earlier (pp. 101–2) and have been, by implication, critical of the theistic view of eternal bliss: adoring eternally an immutable God in an immutable heaven. This could be, on the lips of some of Buddha's spiritual descendants, a partial description of Nirvana: but if Nirvana is a state of selflessness – as I have suggested it was for Buddha – then the eternal bliss can be only a state of non-awareness, or nothingness. So the inevitable outcome of both Buddhist and theistic ontology is that in the end is nothingness. And I find it difficult to see that the doctrine of Advaita removes this prospect from our perceptions. The idea of the Atman's absorption in the eternal Brahman implies, left to itself, a state of Being without becoming. In a word (a technical word in this context) it lacks **dynamism**, the constant confrontation with change, which is the 'other side' of Being.

I am aware of the need to be cautious when making a definitive criticism of this kind in regard to this or any other Hindu doctrine. For a start, anyone raised in the Western linguistic tradition will assume that, apart from when making puns, or other plays on words, words are taken at a constant level and assumed to mean what they say. (They don't always achieve this state of clarity of course, but that is generally the aim of the one who coins them.) In strong contrast to this approach, Sanskrit, the language in which Hindu philosophies have all been expressed, operates on different levels of meaning at the same time. This is a device known as **'Sandhya bhasya**; or 'twilight language', In the Upanishads, for instance, it is stated that 'knowledge is structured in consciousness' but 'knowledge is different in different states of consciousness'. Thus there may be several strata of meaning in any statement, and the newcomer must approach the terrain only with extreme tentativeness. Only by face-to-face discussion with an enlightened teacher is much headway likely to be made, and even then the conversation will be cryptic rather than direct.

For me to state, then, that non-duality is synonymous with death, or non-Being, is to invite criticism from those for whom 'twilight language' is the normal means of communicating ideas. K. Silvaraman, for instance, in a contribution to the Open University textbook *Man's Religious Quest* (p. 137) defends the dynamism of moksa, arguing that 'contrary to the belief that it cries halt to all dynamism [it] may be interpreted . . . as implying the eternal conquest of the negative'. The significant issue here is the process which Silvaraman proposes as a means to 'conquer the negative' or, in the phraseology of this study, come to terms with non-Being, the nothingness of the existentialists. This process is indicated (some might say the game is given away) by the words I've just omitted from that quotation: 'with the support of the authentic theistic tradition'. By that last phrase Silvaraman is implying the belief in a personal God to whom individual human beings can relate and respond.

This is of course one man's interpretation of Advaita, based on a particular choice of emphases in the Upanishads. We saw in the quotation on p. 180 that Brahman is described as being 'all the gods'; but there are other passages where 'the authentic theistic tradition' is more surely expressed. The question is, which of these the more accurately reflects the Advaita doctrine?

Whatever conclusion we may reach about this issue, the fact remains that we are left with an ontologically unsatisfactory perspective. Either we have the non-dualism of the Atman's absorption in the Brahman, which debars dynamism because there is no more *becoming*; or we fall back on an alternative Hindu tradition and create a becoming process – dynamism – by conjuring up the idea of a relationship which is two-way because of the 'I' which is the individual and the 'Thou' which is God: and being two-way (and as long as it stays two-way) possesses dynamism. But if this is the case, we are thus using God as Berkeley used Him to justify his theory of perception and as Kant used Him to straighten out his ideas on the moral law and universal justice: the *deus ex machina*, or God of the gaps. Such an ontological perspective seems as unreal as a process of perpetual motion based on the assumption that there is always someone around to give it a hand if things go wrong.

Voltaire suggested that if God does not exist, it will be necessary to invent Him. If that thesis were true, the central theme of this book would be nullified. That it is not true is indicated, I feel, in the final area of our exploration, where a comprehensive ontological position is established without recourse to gods outside the machine. But to discover this, we must leave India and proceed to the more rewarding peaks of China.

*Case study 20*
*Karma*

Westerners tend to view the concept of karma, outlined on pp. 155–6, as at best an unverifiable excuse for mistakes, at worst a total cop-out. The situations presented below are designed to allow you to reflect carefully on this assumption. The issues to bear particularly in mind are as follows.

1   Which of the situations (if any) are totally beyond human control, and which are capable of some form of modification or control given the application of an amount of human energy – physical or mental?

2   How far does the usefulness or otherwise of the doctrine of karma depend on the extent to which control is possible?

3   Do you find any worth in the concept of karma even in situations where control is possible?

4   Do you reject the idea of karma even in situations where no control is possible?

The situations are as follows.

(1)   One's child dies of meningitis.

(2)   A child raised in a family of thieves is found guilty of theft.

(3)   A beggar curses karma for his poverty and illiteracy.

(4)   A beggar finds peace of mind amid his poverty and illiteracy because he believes this state represents the just deserts of his previous incarnations.

(5)   A soldier finds inner tranquillity in the trenches because his commitment to the doctrine of karma brings him to a 'whatever will be, will be' philosophy of the situation.

(6)   The third world war begins after years of escalation of tension in the Middle East.

(7)   The third world war starts because computerized signals on American radar screens are misinterpreted.

(8)   The third world war starts because a megalomanic ruler seeks to rule the world.

(9)   In a family of teetotallers, one member is an alcoholic.

(10)  The daughter of alcoholic parents is an alcoholic.

(11)  You are one of five people shortlisted, from an original 100 applicants, for a particularly desirable job. You learn at the interview that there was nothing to choose on paper, between at least fifty of the applicants, and that you were selected at random.

(12)  A man accidentally dies of a heroin overdose.

(13)  A plague of locusts destroys a farmer's crop.

(14)  Seasonal weather fails to materialize and a community faces starvation.

(15)  Your town is on the direct route of a hurricane's path. At the last minute the hurricane changes direction and your town is saved.

(16)  You are the sole survivor of an air crash.

(17)  A couple who long for children are childless.

(18)  Despite taking careful precautions a couple become the reluctant parents of six children.

(19)  The country is run by a government whose policies you despise, but the majority of your fellows look forward enthusiastically to re-electing them.

(20)  You meet, marry and are totally contented to live for the rest of your life with a particular person.

(21)  A child is born with a severe mental handicap/physical malformation.

(22)  A person, after a life of ups and downs, contentedly reaches extreme old age.

(23)  An athletic young person is made paraplegic as a result of a road accident.

(24)  Despite hard work on your part, your business does not prosper.

(25)  You are a homosexual/lesbian.

(26)   Comment on your height/looks/health/sex/disposition

Finally, comment on the following true story. A Christian missionary in India was recounting the life of Jesus to a group of Hindus, who were hearing the story for the first time. They listened in respectful silence as his ministry, miracles and teaching were recounted; but when the narrative of the crucifixion was reached, the listeners broke into spontaneous raucous laughter. After the missionary recovered a little from the deep sense of shock into which this apparent example of inhuman and immature levity had thrown her, one of the listeners said, 'What an absolute villain he must have been in his previous life to suffer such a fate in this one after living so exemplarily.'

*Case study 21*
*'Beyond good and evil' in Advaita Vedanta*

The following outline begins in general with material relating to the text (pp. 175–85) and applies it to a concept which sounds strange in most Western ears. Study the points carefully, then discuss the questions at the end (intended only to get the discussion going: how it develops is up to you).

(1)   *Vedanta* ('the end of the Vedas') is one of the six orthodox systems of Hindu philosophy, based on the Upanishads, the Gita and the Brahma Sutras.

These texts are said to be authoritative, because they record the experiences of seers, but these experiences are in principle open to anyone.

(2)   *Advaita* ('non-dual') is the form of Vedanta which teaches that ultimate reality is one, and that this unity (Brahman) can be realized in peak experiences.

*Shankara* (date uncertain: see text) is the great philosopher of Advaita Vedanta.

(3)   *Epistemology* (theory of knowledge) in Advaita Vedanta: there are various levels of truth.

As perceptual errors are 'sublated' by social perception, so social perception is 'sublated' by knowledge of ultimate reality (truth as a spiral staircase).

(4)   *States of consciousness*: contrary to Western preoccupation with rational thought, Vedanta stresses the four states – dreamless sleep, dreaming, waking and the fourth state.

Reason is only one way of knowing, and is inferior to intuition because it is indirect.

(5)  *Aims of life*: everyone wants to be happy. At the level of social perception the aims are pleasure, ambition and justice, which bring relative happiness.

Liberation brings ultimate happiness.

(6)  *Justice* (dharma): there are no absolute prohibitions or imperatives. Appropriate behaviour varies with social role and stage of life. It is right for a student to be chaste and right for a householder not to be chaste. It is wrong for a teacher to be aggressive and right for a sportsman to be aggressive. The source of norms for behaviour are tradition (necessary for social stability) and interdependence (necessary for social cohesion). The sanctions are consequence, not guilt or retribution.

(7)  Those who try for *liberation* outgrow norms of justice. They practise bodily, mental and emotional self-control, working towards personal harmony and peace.

(8)  They leave behind the pairs of *opposites* (dualities) – heat and cold, light and dark, hatred and love, misery and pleasure.

(9)  By stabilizing the lower aspects of the person (body, mind, personality) they reach the *ground of being* (reality, consciousness, happiness), which is impersonal and one in all individuals (cf. Jung's collective unconscious).

(10)  The *liberated person* is bound by no rules or duties, but acts spontaneously from joy and for the welfare of others. This can lead to political action (Gandhi), teaching (Ramakrishna), celebration in music (Nanak), or poetry (Tagore), work for the poor (Vivekananda) or the mentally ill (Meher Baba), etc.

(11)  Liberation is awareness of *non-dual reality* (the water-drop enters the sea), so is incompatible with assertion of personality or injury of others.

This is the state beyond *good and evil*.

The questions are as follows.

1  Can you give examples of how perceptual errors are 'sublated by social perception'? Obvious examples are the psychopath who believes God is telling him or her to kill certain people (though – note – some religious leaders have encouraged such behaviour) and

the child or immature adult who creates a fantasy world in his or her mind. Can you think of more 'normal' examples?

2    Explore the idea of 'truth as a spiral staircase'. Do you find this a helpful image? If not (or in any case), what alternative image might you use?

3    Is it psychologically possible to seek unhappiness?

4    Do you agree that reason is inferior to intuition, because intuition is a more direct means of 'knowing'? How far are things you know based on reason, how far on other faculties? Think of this in relation to (for example):
knowing the alphabet
knowing your subject
knowing the person next door
knowing your partner loves you
knowing a certain philosophy/religion is true/false
knowing that God exists/does not exist
knowing that a person is telling the truth/lying
knowing a billiard ball is red and not blue
knowing a child is in danger
knowing that conflict is imminent in a certain part of the world
knowing that Richard III was a good king
knowing that you are alive/fit/healthy/happy

5    Give further examples of forms of behaviour which may vary according to one's social role and stage of life (para. 6). Do you think it in any way morally risky to suggest that there is no repository of morality in our midst (e.g. the Ten Commandments) and no absolutes to guide us? Is this relativistic view of right and wrong a licence to license? If you consider that human beings still need the concepts of good and evil, how far is this opinion based on a belief that the idea, beyond good and evil,
(a)   is demonstrably erroneous, or
(b)   is good, but people are not yet 'ready' for it?
May it be that the acceptance of the 'beyond good and evil' view of life is an approach which is suitable for some but not for others? Is it right for an enlightened person to pass beyond good and evil, but wrong for one who is not yet enlightened?

6    How far do you think it desirable to pursue the impersonal as described in 9 and 11? D. H. Lawrence argued that, in the end, each individual is one and alone, isolated from all others (see p. 275). Is this view more, or less, natural than the image of the drop of water entering the ocean? Is it a matter of temperament? Or do

you think both views express a part of the truth, and that the ideal is some kind of harmonization of the two?

7    Does/need the refusal to assert one's personality imply the refusal to be assertive? How does Gandhi's expression of non-violent resistance slot into this approach? Is the phrase 'a belligerent pacifist' a contradiction in terms – or another example of
   (a)  the inadequacies of Western-style logic, and
   (b)  the inability (assuming that the phrase is being used as a criticism) to come to terms with the whole idea of beyond good and evil?

8    Nietzsche argued that the 'overman' (*Übermensch*) had passed beyond good and evil because he had freed himself from the shackles of received religious beliefs (especially about the status of human beings *vis-à-vis* the deity) and moral codes imposed 'from above'. How far do you think Nietzsche and Advaita Vedanta are in accord about this state?

## China: Taoism

China was one of the countries into which Buddhism spread and where it received a sympathetic response. Its ethos of non-aggression encountered there a philosophical school with a similarly relaxed approach to life's vicissitudes – one of reflection, humility, intuition, with, perhaps, an element of what we in the West would call stoicism. These were the Taoists, or followers of the Way. This philosophy is associated with **Lao Tsu**, a teacher whose dates are generally given as 604–531 BC. His thoughts are contained in one of the most famous of all Eastern writings, the **Tao Te Ching**. Whether Lao Tsu was an actual person or not (the name means 'Great Teacher') and, if so, the actual author of the whole of the Tao Te Ching is uncertain and unimportant. The importance of Taoism lies in its message, not in its famous names. This message was further outlined in a larger book, the **Chuang-tsu**, compiled some two centuries later than the Tao Te Ching.

The meaning of this title is 'The Book of the Way and its Power', but it is the Tao (pronounced Dao), or Way, which is the central feature of the book's philosophy. The word is used in a mystical sense, relating to the unity and inner harmony of all life. This unity is not, as in theistic thought, between human beings and their Maker, but the contentment which a person achieves through awareness of being a part of the underlying principle of the universe, the Tao, the inexpressible source of living; we may in fact use an earlier phrase and describe it as the Ground of Being (though without, as we shall see, some of the implications associated with that phrase in other schools we have reviewed).

> The greatest Virtue is to follow Tao and Tao alone.
> The Tao is elusive and intangible.
> Oh, it is intangible and elusive, and yet within is image.
> Oh, it is elusive and intangible, and yet within is form.
> Oh, it is dim and dark, and yet within is essence.
> This essence is very real, and yet within lies faith.
> From the very beginning until now its name has never been forgotten.
> Thus I perceive the creation.
> How do I know the ways of creation?
> Because of this.*
>
> (Tao Te Ching, ch. 21)

The nearest that Western philosophy approaches to this concept is in the Greek expression of the *logos*, the underlying principle in all things. In Hindu thought we have seen the idea expressed through the doctrine of Brahman, and in Buddhism, the Dharmakaya. It may be reflected (though this would be a matter for considerable debate) in the Jungian concept of the 'collective unconscious' – the sense that, at the deepest level, all expressions of human consciousness are united in a common source: that ultimately we are all – in a deeper sense than is implied in common usage – 'of one mind'.

Taoism says more than this, however. The basis of its ontology – its theory of Being – is that in nature there is a fundamental unity which has a characteristic pattern. An individual who realizes this will recognize that he or she is part of the continuous stream of nature and has the choice of either fighting against this stream, and so creating disharmony both in his or her own life and in the lives of those around, or accepting being part of the stream and flowing with it, thus experiencing a life of harmony with that which is his or her source, sustainer and goal.

> Something mysteriously formed,
> Born before heaven and earth.
> In the silence and the void,
> Standing alone and unchanging,
> Ever present and in motion. . .
> I do not know its name,
> Call it Tao.
> For lack of a better word, I call it great.

---

* All quotations in this section are from the Tao Te Ching, translation by Gia-Fu Feng and Jane English, published by Wildwood House.

Being great, it flows.
It flows far away.
Having gone far, it returns.

(ch. 25)


Man follows the earth.
Earth follows heaven.
Heaven follows the Tao.
Tao follows what is natural. . .

Force is followed by loss of strength.
This is not the way of Tao.
That which goes against the Tao
   comes to an early end.

(ch. 30)


To lose touch with the Tao, therefore, brings about discordance to the individual; on the other hand, someone who lives his or her life in the knowledge of the Tao will find the kind of release from suffering (unfulfilment, frustration, dissatisfaction) which Buddha had described when pointing the way to Nirvana. Where Taoism is different – and is in fact closer to Advaita Vedanta – is in stating that those who perceive the Tao and follow the Way will achieve this state – or something akin to it – here and now. Mahayana Buddhism had of course modified the original conservatism of Buddha about the attaining of Nirvana, arguing that Buddha-hood was possible for all during the course of this life: but there is a major difference in emphasis between the (original) concept of Nirvana and of Tao. In Nirvana, each person's selflessness (and I discussed on p. 154 the problems associated with this word) remains at an individual level: Being, however this is defined, is peculiar to that person; everyone must work out his or her own salvation; and, when this has been achieved, there will be no more concern for the universe around us, the world we now know and experience.

The Taoist perspective is totally different from this. Where Buddhism speaks of the need to obliterate the world around us, Taoism speaks of oneness with it, the absorption of the individual into the whole. The doctrines of rebirth, or of reincarnation, have no place in Taoism: in contrast, it speaks of finding the Tao in this cycle of experience. Similarly, it knows nothing of the 'blowing out' of Nirvana, but of finding one's true Being in the Tao. Its philosophy is based not on the concept of 'selfless persons', but of persons fulfilled and completed by following the Way. In short, *it does not offer deliverance from this present cycle of experience but presents this cycle as*, for those with eyes to see, *the only true reality*. It proclaims 'the beyond in the midst', and so expresses unreservedly, two and a half millennia before Tillich and Buber were to struggle to express the same idea (but hampered and, I think, in the end defeated by their theistic blinkers), the vital principle of all ontological discourse.

In other words, Taoism suggests, our present experience of Being can provide a totally fulfilling ontological perspective. Rather than rising above nature, we become at one with it. Rather than acting against nature, we flow with it. Rather than trying to find ourselves by escaping from nature, we discover ourselves in it. And the goal of all existence is to find this Way, a Way that is truly 'beyond good and evil'.

> Empty yourself of everything.
> Let the mind rest at peace.
> The ten thousand things rise and fall while the Self watches their return.
> They grow and flourish and then return to the source.
> Returning to the source is stillness, which is the way of nature.
> The way of nature is unchanging.
> Knowing constancy is insight.
> Not knowing constancy is disaster.
> Knowing constancy, the mind is open.
> With an open mind, you will be open-hearted.
> Being open-hearted, you will act royally.
> Being royal, you will attain the divine.
> Being divine, you will be at one with the Tao.
> Being at one with the Tao is eternal.
> And though the body dies, the Tao will never pass away.
>
> (ch. 16)

Where, it may be asked, does this view differ, except in terminology, from that of Advaita Vedanta? Vedanta speaks of the underlying Brahman, the Ground of Being, which may appear not too different from the idea of Tao; and the Atman, the personal self, whose destiny is to be at one with Brahman, seems similar to the Taoist concept of individual absorption in the Way. Should the two not be seen, therefore, as differing expressions of essentially the same philosophies of Being?

There are, I think, two grounds for rejecting this view as over-simplistic. The first is quite straightforward: in Advaita Vedanta the individual is encouraged to awaken from present ('normal') reality into the non-dual experience of the fourth state. This, as we have seen, is a state beyond all present experience – a state which in fact indicates that present experience is not normal at all – if under 'normal' we include 'the ultimate'; and the aim in life is to come to realize this. Oneness with Brahman thus involves us in a process of rising above the state of Being that we presently experience. We must, so to speak, close our eyes to what we perceive with our senses, and seek to view things with an inward eye (some exponents of Advaita, as of other Hindu schools, even refer to a 'third eye'); and, it is suggested, what is thus encountered makes redundant what the other two eyes have hitherto presented to our consciousness. So Advaita expresses an element of *escape* from present 'reality' into a world of deeper, more durable significance.

Admittedly, Taosim also suggests that we must learn to look at the world around us, including the people in it, in a different way from that which is normally called for. But in following this Way (or by being called to see things in this way) we are not expected to rise above it all, but to view it in a deeper sense than most of us are used to. Thus, as I indicated earlier, we are not called to turn our backs on nature, much less to view it as unreal; rather, we are invited to commit ourselves more comprehensively to it, to embrace it, so as to more fully understand it. And this understanding will reveal to us, so Taoism suggests, that we do not need to go 'beyond' in order to find the Ground of Being: to state once again: the 'beyond' is already in the midst. Therefore, rather than seeking to close the eyes we have to what they present to our senses, in order to perceive with an 'inward eye' what is beyond the senses as we presently deploy them, Taoism invites us to open our two present eyes more widely, so that we may see what is already there to be seen if we will but look for it. Even this fairly bland description would cause many Taoists to raise their eyebrows, since it suggests that an element of searching is needed if the Tao is to be found. On the contrary, the process of 'seeing' is not that of the detective looking for clues, but of one who has been mystified by a situation and suddenly 'sees' the truth of it. How this happens, and why some people perceive and others don't, is, as Kierkegaard indicated, a great mystery. But having reached this point (and for the Taoist the word 'enlightenment' here would be inapposite because it begs too many questions) one can only quietly rejoice and hope that others will come to see things the same way.

So the Taoist makes no effort to persuade people to dispense with their existing fields of Being in order to experience one that is allegedly more satisfying and enduring; rather, the Taoist suggests that our present fields have infinitely more natural riches than most people, busy with the process of adding a new crop here, or finding a rich vein there, get round to realizing. In every field there is, if we did but realize it, treasure beyond price. In fact, Taoism suggests, all the riches of every field are ours to enjoy if we could just abandon the sense of sole ownership – the belief that this field is mine, and nobody else's, needing to be cosseted and guarded against intruders. To follow the Way is not, therefore, to take the individual path up the mountain in the Vedantic tradition, but to open one's field to the rewards at its peak. Mahomet, so to speak, does not go to the mountain: the mountain comes to Mahomet.

The second major distinction between Taoism and Advaita Vedanta relates to the issue discussed on pp. 184–5. There I suggested that the doctrine of Advaita leads to an ontological dilemma: either one interprets the union between Atman and Brahman non-theistically, in which case one reaches a position in which the final outcome is nothingness (or so it seems); or one avoids this by the artificial method of producing a God who, by creating a two-way relationship, enables dynamism, the becoming process, to occur. The artificiality of this God-of-the-gaps approach has been stated already in these pages: and I believe the Chinese have shown us how to avoid this.

## YIN AND YANG

Taoism offers an ontology of Being-and-becoming without recourse to artificial aids in its view of the nature of *change*. Simple observation of life must assure any observer that this is the central characteristic of all things: winter moves inexorably into summer, and summer just as implacably back into winter. The cycle of life runs its course and new life begins; the fruit dies, giving birth to new fruit, which grows by stages which cannot be observed at any one moment but reaches maturity and withers and perishes, and leaves the seed of a further new fruit, each in its season, showing forth strength and weakness, expansion and contraction, light and shade, all harmoniously interrelating and interacting in a totally fulfilling and fulfilled unending cycle of events. The whole of nature may thus be described, in existentialist terminology, as a process of Being and becoming: Being becomes Being *ad infinitum*.

> Returning is the motion of Tao.
> Yielding is the way of Tao.
> The ten thousand things are born of being.
> Being is born of not being.

Thus we see in Taoism a new and original approach to the problem of Being and nothingness, and it represents a (typically Chinese) middle way between the Western desire for action, for change for its own sake, for becoming without Being, and the traditional passivity of Indian thought where the ideal, which we have seen expressed in both Buddhism and Vedanta, is Being without becoming. In the West we have velocity without position; in India, position without velocity: this is a generalization, of course, but as a generalization is a fair reflection of our studies so far. Taoist ontology, however, brings the two together in a balanced and harmonious way, which is to be found elsewhere (with different emphases of course) only in existentialist thought. The potentialities of the linking-up of these two schools of thought will therefore be the guiding thread for the remainder of this book.

This balance, this harmony, which I have so far illustrated only from the world of nature, is given vivid expression in Taoism (and, in a

different way, in Confucianism too, as we shall see) by deploying the
typically Chinese concept of the Yin and the Yang. This is illustrated
by the ancient Chinese symbol called **T'ai Chi T'u**, or 'Diagram of the
Supreme Ultimate:

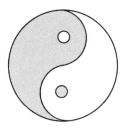

The areas of the two parts, it will be noted, are equal, and together they
make a complete circle. The dark side, the Yin, contains some light, Yang,
and the Yang some Yin. Draw a diameter anywhere across the circle and
each section will include some Yang and some Yin – thought there will
normally be more of one than the other. The Tao, so its followers suggest,
is manifested in the interplay of these two forces, completely different, yet
each constantly drawing the other to itself; each in fact containing within
itself the seeds of its opposite; neither capable on its own of completing
the circle of life. The T'ai Chi T'u thus symbolizes the eternal process of
Being and becoming.

> The Tao begot one.
> One begot two.
> Two begot three.
> And three begot the ten thousand things.
>
> The ten thousand things carry yin and embrace yang.
> They achieve harmony [*ch'i*] by combining these forces.

(ch. 42)

To the uninitiated, the first cryptic stanza here will, understandably,
appear meaningless. It represents the Taoist view of the cosmos, which
is illustrated below:

The Tao gives birth to the One: *T'ai Chi*, or primordial breath

The One gives birth to the two: *Yin and Yang*, which is our specific area
of concern and will be explored further

The Two give birth to the Three: these are the watery underworld,
earth and heaven – a representation of the cosmology not dissimilar
to the three-tiered picture which dominated Western thought until the
Enlightenment. This is the image on the macrocosmic level; on the

microcosmic level, the Tao gestates head, chest and belly – the intellect, love and intuition – a threefold division of the person reminiscent (though, of course, with differing emphases) of Plato and even, later, Freud. On the spiritual level the Tao is seen to be ever gestating, mediating and indwelling within us.

The Three give birth to ten thousand things: the myriad creatures that inhabit the universe. This cosmological structure may be epitomized in this diagram:

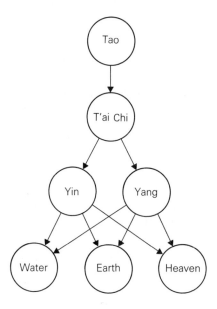

The Yin and Yang were words originally used to describe the dark side and the sunny side of a mountain, and this usage is enough to indicate the sense of completeness which comes about when there is a union of opposites. We traditionally interpret Yang and Yin in terms of masculinity and femininity; the Yang represents strength, as in a male: activity, movement, creative power, rational thought; the Yin corresponds to the more reflective qualities of the female: receptivity, stillness, complexity, intuitive wisdom rather than rational thought.

The Chinese applied this principle to virtually every area of life. For instance, the organs of the body are categorized as either Yang or Yin organs, and the remedies when they malfunction must be of the same category. The principles of homoeopathy, treating like with like, are Yang-Yin principles. Foods are similarly categorized (meat is Yang, for instance, and salads are Yin) and the healthiest diet, it is taught, is one which combines both elements. So far as our ontological quest is concerned, the

Yang and the Yin in harmony allow for both action and reflection, avoiding the extremes of the former, found in the materialism of the West, and of the latter, in the 'otherworldliness' of Buddhism and Vedanta with their ideals of Nirvana and Brahman. In the Tao both are harmoniously contained: the Yang moving and changing into the Yin, the Yin moving and changing into the Yang. 'The Yang having reached its climax retreats in favour of the Yin; the Yin having reached its climax retreats in favour of the Yang' (Wang Chung, AD 80, quoted in Joseph Needham, *Science and Civilisation in China*, Vol. IV, p. 7).

Thus the Tao does not represent a static (and therefore dead) state, but one that is dynamic and static at the same time. The Ground of Being, in Taoist thought, is not an immutable, eternal state of 'bliss' (or whatever cognate term may be used) but an eternal balance of opposite poles, forever changing, forever the same. In a word, and it is the key word, it indicates how we may achieve a state of *harmony*, or **ch'i**. This word can be applied, like the concepts of Yin and Yang individually, to many practical spheres. Buildings should be designed according to ch'i, and, more to the point, the direction they face should be determined by this consideration: otherwise they will be out of harmony with nature, and bring a state of unease to their occupants.* But fundamentally the harmony is one with nature – going with, rather than against, the stream. On this basis, a man is as old as his arteries, a woman as healthy as the food she eats, and both as vital as the soundness of their sleep.

> Do you think you can take over the universe and improve it?
> I do not believe it can be done.
>
> The universe is sacred.
> You cannot improve it.
> If you try to change it, you will ruin it.
> If you try to hold it, you will lose it.
>
> (ch. 29)

I mentioned earlier the distinction in Yang and Yin between rational thought and logical reasoning on the one hand and intuitive or reflective wisdom on the other. Here, as in other respects, Taoism is the Yin to the Western analytical Yang. It stresses, as we have seen that Zen Buddhism stresses (pp. 162–3), that by going all out for cogent and logical consistency the West generally has missed out on the insights available to people if they

---

* Even the direction of furniture in a room should accord with ch'i, as I may have discovered at a week-long summer school at which, on the first night, I could not sleep at all, but, having the following day turned my bed round ninety degrees, I slept deeply for the rest of the week.

use the Yin side of their personalities. We have seen that this stricture did
not apply to Kierkegaard: his attack on the 'aesthete' (see page 104) was that
of a person who has been awakened on those who remain asleep. In this
sense, Taoism represents a state of being fully awake: one recognizes the
value of the intellect but comes to appreciate that it is only one of several
channels of understanding and wisdom available in any field of Being.

> The five colours blind the eye.
> The five tones deafen the ear.
> The five flavours dull the sense.
> Racing and hunting madden the mind.
> Precious things lead one astray.
>
> Therefore the sage is guided by what he feels and not by what
> he sees.
> He lets go of that and chooses this.
>
> (ch. 12)

The supreme expression of the rejection of rationality as the sole guide to
life's labyrinthine ways is found in the **I Ching** – the 'Book of Changes',
This is the first of the six classics of Confucianism into which, it has been
said, 'the seasoned wisdom of thousands of years' has flown. This book,
which escaped destruction in the book-burning by the Ch'in monarchs in
213 BC, is a book of divinations to which, according to legend, Confucius
as editor added a commentary. It consists of sixty-four hexagrams made
of broken and unbroken lines, with accompanying text. The hexagrams
are made by combining any two of the following trigrams, each named
for a different natural phenomenon:

| Heaven | Thunder | Water | Mountain |
|--------|---------|-------|----------|
| ───── | ── ── | ── ── | ── ── |
| ───── | ── ── | ─── ── | ── ── |

| Earth | Wind | Fire | Lake |
|-------|------|------|------|
| ── ── | ───── | ───── | ── ── |
| ── ── | ───── | ── ── | ───── |

The choice of hexagrams is made by the chance throwing of coins or yarrow
stalks. It may be used, and its message interpreted, by an individual on his
or her own; more frequently a petitioner will approach an elder or seer in
order to have the message of the hexagram with its corresponding text
interpreted.

The I Ching can, of course, be used at a variety of levels. In popular usage
it may be a means of fortune-telling, not dissimilar to (though considerably
more sophisticated than) reading tea-leaves. At a higher level – and this

remains its normal use – it is used to guide a person when making difficult decisions, for which all the intellect in the world will not provide an answer. We must all be familiar with the kind of dilemma referred to here. Whom should we short-list out of these hundred applicants for a post, half of whom have similar qualifications? Shall we go to X or to Y for our holidays this year? Which of two equally attractive houses shall we buy? Shall I take on this new job offered to me, or not? In these situations, while reason may provide us with a list of points for and against each alternative, it will not help us decide; and, *faute de mieux*, the use of the I Ching may help to put our minds at ease, and so make the decision a more comforting one.

At the highest level, it may be used – as it was originally intended to be used – in applying the Yin-Yang philosophy in the sphere of moral or metaphysical dilemmas. Here the book is used to illustrate the basic harmony of nature, and how the individual (usually with the guidance of a person long experienced in this field) may best adapt him- or herself to it or, more basically, become at one with it. It is a form of meditation and reflection which may seem odd to the uninitiated, but has been found by those who use it continually to provide an insight into the great ontological issues which have been the focal point of this book. As some achieve this through yoga, others through the illogical koans of Zen Buddhism, others through meditating on a scriptural text, and others through transcendental meditation, so have many through use of the I Ching. The test must be not whether the practice is reasonable – whatever that may mean in this context – but whether people through this channel achieve their aim. It seems that many do so.

The philosophy of Taoism can, then, be briefly summarized. What is the purpose of life? To become aware of the Tao, and realize this in one's life. How is this to be achieved? By being natural. To be, for the Taoist, is not only infinitely more important than to have, but also more important than to do. We shall see in a moment how the most famous Chinaman of all applied the Taoist principles in a practical way; but the classical Taoist perspective is summed up in this terse statement:

Therefore the sage does nothing, teaching no-talking. (ibid., 2)

This may sound negative (and I shall be suggesting that the most comprehensive ontological perspective must harmonize this view with some of those from existentialism) but its positive aspect lies in what follows for those who are not frenetically consumed by the desire to be up and doing: recognizing the Tao makes one available for others.

## CONFUCIUS 551–479 BC

The Taoist perspective was given its own emphasis by one whose name is uniquely familiar beyond the continent of Asia: Confucius. This is the Latinized version of his Chinese family name – K'ung – and title (meaning 'master') Fu-tzu. He lived at a time of warring overlords and gross exploitation of the masses. His concern was therefore that whatever value there was in Taoism should not be the preserve solely of those who had turned their backs on worldly affairs, but should be applied in the heart of them. In this I believe his instinct was sound, and in following it through in his writings he established himself as a (very early) forerunner of the existentialists. His view was that, simply by existing, people had interests which were bound to clash. The purpose of government – whether nationally or, more importantly from Confucius's point of view, locally through the civil service – was to ensure that some semblance of fair play should be seen to be done. Otherwise – and this he believed, was the danger if the Taoist philosophy were left as a purely private preserve – matters could easily become anarchic. And in anarchy none of the populace benefits, since the spoils go to the strong: the bully, the barbarian, the butcher.

Confucius's teaching centred round his desire for moderation in all things: nothing in excess. His ideal was the negative of the golden rule: what you do not want doing to yourself, do not do to others. This ideal is, when carefully pondered over, an extension of the Tao into the sphere of human relationships. If we all belong ultimately to the same stream, then we must learn to empathize with others, since they and we share the same essence. I cannot achieve happiness if my brother is unhappy; and this reality is made more poignant if I know that I am directly responsible for that unhappiness.

Confucius's views on government are, I think, hauntingly relevant. In his day they were viewed as revolutionary (hence his failure to reach the pinnacles of success in his service of the state); in some countries they would still be treated so today.

(1) The purpose of government is to provide for the welfare and happiness of its people.

(2) The right to govern depends on the ability to make the governed happy and secure.

(3) All citizens are entitled to equal justice before the law.

(4) Excessive taxation and barbarous punishments should be abolished.

(5) The best government is that which governs least, and dedicates itself to the development of the character and culture of the people.

(6) Aggression by any state or nation should be outlawed.

(7) The state should be a co-operative enterprise, run for the economic, social and cultural benefit of *all* the people.

(8)   The right to govern does not come by heavenly decree.

(9)   Only people possessing integrity and ability are fit to govern. Wealth, breeding and influence must play no role in the selection of leaders.

(10)  Hereditary rulers may continue, but their actual power must be delegated to ethical and capable administrators.

(11)  Education can help to develop the virtue, the ability and the strength of character which the new leaders need.

(12)  No nation can be governed by restrictive rules and negative punishments. The leaders must set positive examples by their own moral behaviour.

(13)  The police state, built on fear and suspicion, must fail; the commonwealth which relies on mutual understanding, goodwill, moral integrity and alleviation of suffering, will prevail.

Some of these ideas relate, of course, more directly to a discussion on political theory – and in that field they vividly foreshadow the writings of Locke and Mill – but the majority touch directly on the issues with which we are preoccupied. In fact, Confucius has been viewed as one side of the Chinese coin, of which the other is Taoism: Confucius is the Yang to the Taoist Yin. As in both existentialism and Taoism, he is not arguing that all men are born equal, or that they can all contribute equally to a community's resources. He is arguing that the healthiest community is one that is not divided by the lust of the few to control the lives of the many. Any community should be united in compassion, which means that those called to rule should not hold the rest in contempt, and those called to serve should not envy their masters.

Confucius was an optimist, believing that people had a natural capacity for goodness and harmony – the Chinese word for this capacity is **jen**. He was wise enough, however (and in this he foreshadowed Aristotle's view of the role of the state to make men good), to suggest that this *jen* should be cultivated in a social way, rather than left to find its own expression as opportunities might arise. The implication of this is that society should be so organized that those who have reaped richly shall share the fruits of their good fortune with those who have failed to prosper. (We shall look at this issue more closely in Chapter 9.) Left to themselves, according to Confucius, the successful, because of this natural capacity for goodness, *may* be willing voluntarily to hand over a percentage of their rewards, as wealthy people have been known to patronize the arts. But just as the arts could founder if this were their only source of subsistence, so might the alleviation of poverty. The good in people *may* emerge voluntarily; state legislation can ensure that no oversight occurs.

Confucius's philosophy, which is comprehensively expressed in the **Analects** which appeared soon after his death, would today fall under the umbrella of 'applied philosophy' and therefore is not central to the ontological emphasis, *per se*, pursued in this book. Its importance, so far as we are concerned, lies in its attempt to express Taoism in the world of public affairs, and so indicate that, by concerning ourselves with ontological issues, we are in no way removing ourselves from the world of making and doing. In this world, Confucius's unique contribution is summed up in the word *li*. This can hardly be translated into a single word, since it is rich in connotations, and epitomizes what has become a whole way of life for millions of Chinese. It stands for propriety, a sense of personal dignity, good taste, emotional discipline (not wearing one's heart on one's sleeve), an awareness of ceremony, courtesy, a respect for nature and for all things. It is alien to the brashness of much of Western culture, but the person who possesses *li* believes that virtue is its own reward, and that all the riches for a fulfilling life, sought by many through external stimuli, are to be found within the individual. In other words, as I stated earlier in a different context, all we need for Being is to be found within our own field. As Confucius said:

> The higher type of man seeks all that he wants in himself; the inferior man seeks all that he wants from others.

We have thus in our study of some of the central features of Eastern thought reached the point at which we must attempt to find a *modus vivendi* between it and some of the insights from the West. The issue we face is whether, in particular, existentialism and the East can find mutual enrichment together. Having, so to speak, reached their climaxes, can each retreat into the other?

*Case study 22*
*Exploring Yin and Yang*

In the following situations – most of them belonging to an 'everyday' category – there is normally a choice of ways to cope; these may be divided into

(1)   a totally Yin approach;

(2)   a totally Yang approach; and

(3)   a mixture of both (somehow or other).

How does/might the Yin-Yang concept illuminate or help to resolve the problem?

The situations are:

(1)  the exploitation of one race by another: the blacks by the whites
     in South Africa, the native Indians in America and Aborigines in
     Australia by their (predominantly) white rulers, etc. (Is this simply an
     example of evolution – the survival, or dominance, of the fittest?)

(2)  the exploitation of females by males: lower rates for similar work,
     certain career structures unavailable, patronizing attitudes ('No,
     my dear, after you'), sexual harassment, etc. (How far do you
     consider it to be confusing to associate the Yang tendency, however
     slightly, with the male psyche and role, and the Yin with the
     female?)

(3)  dealing with awkward pupils: how should a teacher cope with an
     obstreperous member of his/her class who persistently interrupts the
     learning process, to the amusement of some, but to the annoyance
     of many in that class?

(4)  the raising of children: you may feel that the application of both Yin
     and Yang applies here more than in most other situations. What in
     practice do you think this implies?

(5)  A colleague (at work, school, or college, etc.) has made a statement
     which you know to be factually wrong and must be corrected
     before others act on his/her misinformation to their cost. The
     correction must be made publicly, and you know this could cause
     the person concerned (who was genuinely, but unusually, mistaken)
     great embarrassment. How do you proceed without causing him/her
     loss of face?

(6)  You disagree strongly with an opinion expressed by a colleague, but
     know that the opinion is sincerely held. How do you affirm your
     point of view without belittling his/hers? (Different from (4) because
     (4) concerned facts and this is about values.)

(7)  dismissing a person who is simply not up to the job/has been guilty
     of some malpractice

(8)  making an apology: how would you do this without demeaning
     yourself? Is there a different approach and form of words according
     to the nature of the issue for which an apology is necessary? For
     example:
     (a)  being proved factually wrong after hinting at the other person's
          ignorance;
     (b)  being proved wrong about another person's motives for a certain
          act of behaviour;

(c) having let someone down (broken a promise, forgotten to deliver a message, overslept and missed a crucial engagement, been proved to have lied on a certain matter, etc.).

How would you categorize the following forms of apology?

(a) 'I'll let you off' (after a dictionary had confirmed that your colleague was wrong about a certain spelling, and you right).

(b) 'I was wrong. What I said/did was unpardonable. I unreservedly withdraw my remarks.'

(c) 'I'm an absolute rat, a snivelling worm, a disgrace to the human race.'

(9) Your partner has admitted to having been unfaithful to you. You love him/her dearly, and all the indications are that he/she genuinely regrets this lapse and is determined to make amends.

(10) You wish to show your total disgust about a point of view expressed by an acquaintance (racist, sexist, etc.) which you find loathsome. Do you or do you not 'go over the top' in the expression of your anger?

(11) How do you draw the line between assertiveness and bullying? Is such a line necessary?

(12) How do you draw the line between directness, bluntness and rudeness? Are these all the same thing from different vantage-points, or could you make a distinction?

(13) How valid are flattery/white lies in any relationship?

(14) A friend/colleague has a deep inferiority complex. You don't view him/her as being among the world's geniuses, but don't think he/she is as dim as they seem to think. How do you set about boosting his/her ego?

(15) How do you cope with a person – friend or colleague – who has lost his/her temper with you? Granted that the soft answer turneth away wrath, is there a place for an eyeball-to-eyeball confrontation?

(16) Ending a love affair against your partner's wishes because you have found someone else whom you prefer: how would you/do you think you ought to proceed?

(17) How do you cope with a pompous/patronizing/conceited colleague?

Do you find Yin-Yang *very helpful/fairly helpful/no help at all* in these situations?

*Case study 23*
*The Tao and politics*

From an initial investigation of the philosophy of Tao, it may appear inapposite to mention it in the same sentence as politics: the two fields, it might be thought, are distinct and separated from each other, belonging to two opposite poles.

The extract which follows suggests otherwise. It was written as part of an article in the *Guardian* (March 1988) by a practising Buddhist and student of Tao, Mike Page. His argument is that politics is no more out of place for followers of the Tao than is the Yang to the Yin or the Yin to the Yang. Just as these two complement each other, so, Page suggests, may involvement in political decision-making spring from the 'laid-back' approach to practical affairs reflected in Taoism.

Read what Page has to say, and then pursue the suggested lines of inquiry.

It is an awareness of inevitable change that motivates politicians, sooner or later in the cycle of their power, to go for radical change. Taoists would say that if a person finds himself in a position of power, he should try to do as little as possible, leaving the balance to be achieved by the yin and the yang, those twin controllers of change. But, alas, the average politician, male or female, becomes, given half a chance, an exponent of the masculine, yang, rationalising drive for power at the expense of the gentler yin element.

It is interesting, however, to see that hidden in the yang is always the seed pearl of its opposite. . . One aspect of change is conflict: conflict between what is and that which is being born out of what is. Politicians are either good at managing change and conflict or they are not. Much of their energy goes into persuasion and resisting persuasion. There is conflict and much butting of heads against brick walls.

Taoists, by contrast, say that the best way of controlling change is to go with the flow. The wise politician is he or she who, in the words of Lao-tzu, governs a state like cooking a small fish: very, very carefully and lightly.

The ideal ruler, according to Lao-tzu, is one who shares with his fellows the understanding that change is inevitable, and that anything that he or she does is destined to have only a marginal effect on the world. Such a one would in any case, knowing this, be unwilling to seek office: such a one is more likely to find himself in power by virtue of the people's trust in him.

The Tao Te Ching is full of sound, if unwelcome, advice for the politician. As chapter 57 and 58 have it:

The more laws and restrictions there are
The poorer people become. . .
The more rules and regulations,
The more thieves and robbers.
When the country is ruled with a light hand
The people are simple.
When the country is ruled with severity,
The people are cunning.

. . . In all opposites is found the yin and yang. In all conflict is to be found the dynamic balance between the two. Hidden like a jewel in the centre of any conflict is its resolution.

Small comfort to people beset by the seemingly inexorable march of big business, agribusiness, nuclear energy and engines of war. Nevertheless, they may find comfort in the enigmatic Taoist belief that everything contains seeds of its own cyclic development.

Lao-tzu would advise politicians to roll with the punches. Like good martial artists, they should give way willingly and lovingly where there is pressure in order to be able to advance positively and lovingly in the new direction leading to their goal. In such a way a spring of discontent could bring forth a harvest of content.

A good soldier is not violent,
A good fighter is not angry.
A good winner is not vengeful,
A good employer is humble.
This is known as the virtue of not striving.
This is known as the ability to deal with people.

                                                              Mike Page

1    How realistic do you find this affirmation to be? Its general thrust
     is perhaps summed up in the beatitude, contained in the Sermon on
     the Mount: 'Blessed are the meek, for they shall inherit the earth.'
     How long do you think they would keep it after inheriting it? (Or
     is that being too cynical?)

2    If all potential politicians followed the philosophy of 'waiting for the
     call' how many do you think would be called?

3    Many people refuse to involve themselves in politics, not from a lack
     of interest but from a sense of frustration that nothing can be changed.
     Would you think it fair to describe this attitude as one of negative
     neutrality? And would you consider it too eulogistic to describe the
     Taoist approach as one of positive neutrality?

4    If the assumption made above is true, and events in fact move
     cyclically, is this a justifiable excuse for non-intervention in events

on the ground that one is waiting for the 'tide in the affairs of men' to flow in the right direction?

5   How far do you think the non-striving of Taoism must sometimes be balanced by existentialistic involvement of oneself in the strife? Or do you think that the real issue is that, on the whole, the Taoist approach has hardly ever been expressed in political affairs?

# 8  Recapitulation: an East-West synthesis

In the middle section of this book I have explored certain existentialist and Eastern ontological perspectives discretely: that is to say, there has been little attempt to compare findings in the two zones. In these final chapters I want to try to bring the two together into some kind of unified statement. I hope that whatever harmony is established between the two is not achieved artificially: there are clear differences of emphasis, if not quite wide divergences, on some of the issues, and these must be acknowledged. But the book has been written in the conviction that what the two have in common is more significant than where they differ; and even then I believe the conflicting forces can be held together to the enrichment of anyone, whether from the West or from the East, who wishes to achieve a comprehensive ontological perspective. This may seem a bold claim, but I hope to be able to give it some substance.

## THE EXISTENTIAL SITUATION

So far as the state of Being is concerned, there never was a time when I was not and there never will be a time when I shall not be. At first sight this statement must of course seem absurd. Obviously things happened before I came into being, and will go on happening after I cease to be. But that is to view the whole situation from an I-it perspective – not from within my own Being but as an external observer. In the context of Being as I perceive and experience it (and I can view matters *only* from this context) *time does not exist* outside or beyond my Being. If, like Rip Van Winkle, I were to sleep for twenty years, the waking moment would still, for me, be the one immediately following that of going to sleep. Others would no doubt relate to me events of the intervening decades, but these would be to me no more than diversionary tales, unrelated to me, because, not having experienced them, they could not be part of my Being. I would be able to read the accounts with the same degree of detachment with which

I read the newspapers – even when the reports are on areas I know and situations at which I was present (even, in fact, when they are describing *me*: one's reading of such a narrative never goes beyond the I-it experience because this is the me not as I perceive myself, but as someone else has perceived me).

CONDITIONS OF BEING

So, while there actually was a time when I was not, since I was not, that time is nothingness from the context of my Being. At a certain moment in time, however, I came into Being, or became aware of Being, or began to be: the nothingness was overtaken by Being. The problem that faces us now relates to the conditions of the individual being when he or she first begins the cycle of experience – when time comes into being for that person. The accident of birth – to use a phrase to which many Easterners and some Westerners would take exception – does not produce equality of conditions. We all have our own fields of Being, but there are enormous differences between them. Some fields contain fertile ground on which, it seems, almost anything can grow; others, the most barren of ground, in which fruitfulness seems a forlorn hope. Even two potentially fertile fields may vary radically in their scope for development. One may be set in an environment in which growth, extension, variation of crop, so to speak, are given every encouragement to take place; the other, amid tawdry surroundings where there is no inducement to do more than bring forth the meanest, most basic crops. Others still, whilst set amid potentially fruitful environments, may be landed with ground which, however strong the external encouragement to grow and be fruitful, seems limited in what it is capable of achieving. Heidegger's sense of *Geworfenheit* (thrownness) seems to be undeniably expressive of the reality of our arrival: while we may all be equal in that we all have Being, the word 'equal' is quite inapposite when discussing fields of Being. (A major problem is caused by those vociferous people who proclaim the equality of human beings, because they cannot or will not acknowledge this distinction.) The issue is not whether Jack's as good as his master but how to relate to people in a world in which no two fields of Being are the same. (This problem will be faced directly in the next chapter.)

The acceptance of *Geworfenheit*, or chance, in this context seems to bring us to a point where existentialism and Eastern philosophy diverge. After all, neither Buddhism nor Advaita Vedanta speaks of chance as the determining factor for the conditions of birth, but of karma, the consequences of actions and decisions belonging to previous cycles of experience. We have seen that, according to the doctrine of karma, where each of us is born, and the circumstances of our birth, do not come about by chance but as a direct consequence of past (mis)deeds, so that effectively we plant ourselves where we are born, reaping inexorably what we have sown, no more, no less. This being the case, how can we mention karma and *Geworfenheit* in the same breath?

The answer lies not in concentrating on how we began this cycle of experience, but in what we make of it. Clearly, while the believer in thrownness can offer no explanation for the gross inequalities of fields that people possess, so that the phrase 'no natural justice' can find easy expression on his or her lips, the believer in karma has a ready-made explanation to hand which, if so inclined, he or she can use for selfish purposes. The person born into luxury can justify his or her good fortune through this doctrine, while the one born among thieves can explain his or her unsociable behaviour likewise. (The sincere believer in karma would argue, of course, that the former should rejoice in these fruitful circumstances and use the opportunities so provided by being charitable to others, while the one brought up to thieve should turn away from this folly and prepare for the next cycle by ensuring that he or she has a better start than in the current one: see case study 20.) When viewing the scene prospectively, rather than retrospectively, however, there seems little to choose between the two. Effectively, what both are saying (and this is true of other theories, of course) is that there is absolutely nothing that can be done to change the initial conditions of Being; and the fact that for the existentialists this is, so to speak, the first (and, probably, only) round, while for the believer in karma this is probably one of a sequence of cycles which maybe began aeons ago, makes not a scrap of difference to the initial advice which both schools would give to those about to embark on life: if circumstances are bad, don't whine; if they are good, don't rest on your laurels; the key factor is not where you are but where you're going. Stop envying or jeering at other people's fields and get on cultivating your own.

## AIMS AND OBJECTIVES

What should anyone, at whatever stage of the cycle of existence, be aiming for? At one level one could answer this by affirming that, since the nature of Being is to be, the aim is survival. For many people, born into the most wretched of conditions, this is in fact all that can presently be sought after, and their existence poses a strong challenge to those whose basic needs have always been satisfied – who, in fact, may never have become conscious that they are not granted these automatically by right of birth (see Chapter 9). (The irony is that many of those who have found few restrictions in developing their fields can not only be blind to those whose fields are virtually non-existent, but also poison their own fields by allowing them to be overtaken by a single cancerous growth, so that they are reduced to dependence on the next shot, or the next drink.) The final aim of living is expressed differently in the different schools of philosophy which we've considered, but they can, I think, be reduced to one word: the achievement of *happiness*.

This word immediately begs a number of questions. It has found expression in the West in relation to a variety of philosophical schools, all of them equating it with pleasure, whether the aesthetic pleasures of the **Epicureans**, the 'lower' pleasures of the flesh, or the 'higher' pleasures advocated by Mill and his school of utilitarianism. The Eastern schools look to a state more permanent than any of these. For Buddha it is a state beyond desire, the achievement of an inner contentment that is independent of any kind of external stimuli – mental, physical, or emotional. It is the quest for fulfilment through the resources built up within a person's own field of Being. For Advaita Vedanta it is the awakening to the Fourth State, the step beyond the present normal range of experience to a stage of enlightenment, in which all the values of the present state are put into a perspective born of a different dimension. The awakening to this state is the discovery of Brahman, the Ground of Being: the realization that there is a basic essence which underlies and contains each individual Being, or Atman.

Thus happiness is viewed as both evolving from and extending beyond the present range of experience. This view is fortified by the Chinese perspective that all our separate paths are steps towards the universal Way, the Tao which subsumes every Being and all Being, not in the static state of Nirvana or Brahman, but through the dynamic of perpetual change, which is the essence of the universe. If it is the case that the universe is contained within my Being (and, as we've seen, from my perspective this is so) Tao provides the parallel to this: Being, including my Being, is contained in the universal Tao. And I can become aware of this if I, so to speak, break down the barriers which keep my field as a private plot, and make it available to all; or, more accurately, by removing my self-imposed barriers, my perception of the field will become more panoramic, no longer a separate entity but part of the total landscape which its barriers had kept hidden. Thus, through the Tao, will happiness be found.

Existentialists, it must be acknowledged, are less clear-cut in their expressions of overriding and long-term aims: their concern is rather with immediate objectives (to which we shall turn in a moment). The exception here is Buber, whose philosophy of I-thou implies the breaking-down of barriers between individual fields of Being. On this issue, in fact, he is more specific than any of the Eastern philosophies. While acknowledging, as we have seen, that not all I-thou relationships endure for long, he argues that, even with limits caused by impermanence, the experience hints at a happiness deeper than can be found solely in the privacy of self. To accept and be accepted by the 'thou' of one's life is, in Buber's thought, an ontological experience which looks naturally beyond the union of I and thou to union with the Ground of Being, or, in different terms, (not Buber's terms, of course) oneness with the Tao.

Even the atheist existentialists did not bar this perspective from their fields. Heidegger wrestled with the idea of the Ground of Being, and the natural direction of his ontological perspective is towards the realization of this. Sartre's view of essence is only roughly sketched, but the implication which underlies his advocacy of *pour-soi* rather than *en-soi* at least does not exclude (though he did not explore this idea) the consideration that 'movement towards' requires an object for the preposition: without this, the concept of *pour-soi* remains unnecessarily empty. To discover one's essence Sartre takes to mean the realization of the self one chooses and since he sees this as a non-ending process, the consideration at least remains open that the fulfilment connoted by *pour-soi* is to be found not in the isolation of individual Being but in the unity of all Being. Clearly I don't wish to put words into Sartre's mouth on this issue – he has enough of his own – but this seems a line not out of step with his basic perspective.

One existentialist philosopher whom we did not consider in Chapter 5, Nietzsche (1844–1900), expressed an aim which also takes us beyond the present range of experience. He expressed this as *Übermensch*. This word is often mistranslated (or, at least, misinterpreted) as 'Superman', but the German word means 'Overman', which may not convey much meaning in its English translation, but, as used by Nietzsche, was pregnant with significance. His vision was that of human beings who are no longer confined by the barriers which, in his view, cloud and shroud a person's field. These barriers include the theistic concept of a God to whom deference and obedience are due, the more neutral but none the less equally restrictive bonds of convention, and the view that only the rational is real. Nietzsche's *Übermensch* is unconfined by any of these restricting forces: he is beyond divine aid, freed from the tyranny of public opinion, unbound by the cold precision of logic. Russell, in his *History of Western Philosophy*, paints a contrasting picture of the egotistical, bullying Nietzsche and the unassuming, compassionate Buddha (pp. 738–9) but this picture reflects an exaggeration of some of the tendencies of Nietzsche's final, tormented years and, more to the point, a gross (and typically Western) misunderstanding of Buddha. Having passed beyond the outer trappings of their respective messages there is, in at least one respect, a surprising element of unity: both are suggesting that ultimate happiness is to be found not in the 'normal' state of Being as most of us have probably encountered it but by moving to another state – 'higher', 'freer', 'more mature': call it what you will – beside which all normal experience must be judged to be, at best, preparatory. The link between Nietzsche and Buddha may be no more than tenuous, but it's there.

By stating, then, that happiness is our ultimate aim, I am not advocating just an ephemeral sense of well-being, much less a momentary 'high' (at least, not as this is generally looked for) but a state, beyond the normal human condition, which can be described only in ontological terms. But this may well seem to many readers to be an aim so far removed from present experience that it hardly impinges on existence as we know it. Are there any steps towards even a suggestion of the kind of enlightenment earlier described which we could be taking *now*? Assuming we agree, however vaguely, about the ultimate aim (and maybe the issue is relevant even if we are, in that useful American phrase, taking a rain-check on that) what should I or you, the reader, be doing about it?

The answer is summed up in a phrase which has dominated these writings: by developing one's field of Being. Numerous indicators have been offered over the three previous chapters which it is hoped will help to clarify what this process might involve. In brief, it begins with the realization that existence is a process of Being and becoming: Being rather than having (or even, in some schools, doing – though this will shortly need consideration) and becoming rather than stagnating: *être-pour-soi* rather than *être-en-soi*. This is, if you like, the quantum approach to ontology: the realization that we are in a constant state of change, never the same from one instant to the next, as the electrons of an atom are in a constant state of motion around the nucleus. In human terms this means that we should be constantly looking from the now to the not-yet. This will certainly produce a state of anxiety because it will mean our surrendering the artificial security of the customary, a security nourished by the blinkered perception that change is unreal, as reflected in the proverb 'Plus ça change plus ça la même chose'. In one sense this is true – the sense provided by the philosophy of Yin and Yang, as we shall see: but in existentialist terms this is a glib diversion from reality, a means of avoiding anxiety. Nobody finds change comfortable, but those who hide their eyes from its reality are grasping at death or non-Being.

The question of how to live with change is answered variously by the different philosophical schools that we have explored, ranging from deep contemplation on the one hand to active involvement in politics on the other. The bringing together of these two extremes within a consistent ontological perspective is one of the paradoxes we shall be considering in the final chapter. Buber's philosophy of I-thou seems to me a natural *via media* between these two. He, more, I think, than any other writer in this field, indicates how we can grow through relationships, so that by the interflow between two fields of Being, leading sometimes to the union of two or more individual fields into one, the becoming aspect of Being may find sure expression. But while welcoming Buber's insight here, there is also the need for caution, especially among those who bandy the word 'relationship' around as though all human intercourse were on the I-thou level advocated and described by Buber. Where this happens, there is – indeed, by definition, can be – no attempt by one person to take over the field of the other, or others; rather, each is, so to speak, available to the other(s) and open to any new insights or perceptions which they may have to offer. It is, however, quite clear to anyone with just a modicum of sensitivity and perception that many relationships, including those between long-standing sexual partners, don't fit into this pattern, with its potential for mutual growth, but rather into one in which one person in the relationship denies the other the freedom to be. The wife who daren't speak out of turn (and if this were permitted would be lost for words); the member of a group who is driven into ever more self-destructive activities by other stronger members of the group; the child who cannot find himself in his parents' presence: all these and millions like them show how sometimes a person's field of Being can be poisoned by relationships. In coming to appreciate I-thou we have to be aware of Buber's strictures on I-it. Sartre was surely swinging to the other extreme to make a dramatic point when he put the words 'Hell is other people' into the mouth of one of his characters in *No Exit*: but there is enough truth in the statement to make us cautious in suggesting that relationships *per se* lead to happiness in that they are *automatically* creative.

With this proviso in mind, few people, granted the opportunity to study his writings, would find Buber's insight irrelevant to their condition. This is stated from the vantage-point of having experienced I-thou, which in Hindu terms would be described as having gained insight or enlightenment. From this perspective it seems incredible that our schools make no specific provision for such studies. The implication of this seems to be that philosophy, and specifically metaphysics, is only for those who may accidentally be 'touched' by the subject. My conviction is that if any subject is to be made compulsory in schools, philosophy is that subject; and, more specifically, ontology, West and East.

My earlier identification of happiness as the motivation for the process of becoming may seem to some readers at least surprising and perhaps quite wrong when we relate this to some of the other writers whom we have considered. In particular, Kierkegaard, far from pursuing happiness, seems, by his own conscious choice, to have deliberately turned his back on it. But this simply reminds us that happiness is not a quality which can be easily equated with an identifiable feeling like pleasure. The problems to which this confusion gives rise can be seen in the Utilitarian school of moral philosophy. Bentham's attempt to create a 'happiness quotient' through his felicific calculus, and Mill's qualification of happiness into higher and lower pleasures seem to me to miss the point that Kierkegaard realized and that, with greater catholicity of expression, has long been realized in the East. *Happiness is the state of being ontologically whole*, and all the issues and examples introduced by the Utilitarians, even when applied to the ideal of an egalitarian society, are basically at best incidental, largely irrelevant, and sometimes harmful to the fundamental significance of this state. As I shall shortly indicate, I am in fact deeply concerned about numerous injustices in society: but this concern arises from the ontological stance of Being and becoming, and the unhappiness caused when people, either by their own folly or by the blindness or wickedness of others, experience the diminution of their fields of Being. By their stress first on our freedom to choose and secondly on our using that freedom in the 'either-or' situations identified by Kierkegaard, all the schools of thought which we are reviewing lifted the idea of happiness beyond the mere 'usefulness' of the Utilitarians to the heart of Being itself. And this happiness can be found even amid situations of gross injustice and extreme deprivation.

This seems to be a convenient point at which to pause and consider specific examples of people whom I may be discussing; otherwise the discussion will be in danger of being as divorced from the 'real' world as that of some of the linguistic analysts who have come in for some criticism. The examples I'm offering are all people known to me (suitably disguised here, which may be an expression of bad faith on my part) and many people would say of them (as they, if asked, would certainly say of themselves) that they are happy. My argument is that they are not, ontologically speaking, whole.

(1) The first is one who exemplifies what I will term the *closed mind* type. He established his views on virtually everything at an early age, and has proceeded through life, so far as can be judged from his expressed opinions, without modifying any of them. No new experience seems to alter his perceptions and no new evidence on any issue is allowed to enter his consciousness if it contradicts his fixed beliefs. Anyone who knew him in his earlier years would be able to predict, with enough accuracy to put money on the outcome without taking any real risk, what he will say on any issue that arises and how he will react to anyone he meets.

This seems to me to be a person whose field has been totally neglected. It grew during the earliest years, but no attempt thereafter has been made to develop it. With the hardening of the arteries has gone the hardening of beliefs (or prejudices). May this state not be described as one of Being without (or with very little) becoming? It certainly seems to me to be a state as near to non-being as it is possible to be without actually ceasing to be altogether. My experience is that ten minutes in the presence of such a person, roughly every five years, is as much as the relationship, requires (or can take).

(2) The second is the opposite of this: one whose philosophy of life – notion of values, ontological perspectives, issues over which to enthuse, and so on – change with every ideological gust of wind that blows. She always has a ready answer to the question of the 'meaning of life', but the answer changes with the changing seasons. Even those who meet her regularly find it difficult to keep track of her convictions, and those who meet her only infrequently cannot equate the person they encounter at one stage with that of another. This person moves from fad to fad; her field extends further than that of the first person described, but is just as

neglected. Areas of the field that were in the past (if only briefly) lovingly tended are now left to decay. Only at the limits of the field is there any life at all.

Of such a person F. H. Bradley once remarked: 'His mind is open; yes, it is so open that nothing is retained; ideas simply pass through him.' The person I'm describing seems similarly to be one so comprehensively involved in *becoming* that she has no time to *be*; she has no essential consistency except that of changeability. Is she any further than the first person from the state of non-Being?

(3)   The third example is of a set of parents whose whole lives revolve around their children and grandchildren, so that they find, so far as can be judged, total happiness without leaving the family homestead. Many of the ontological perspectives and other issues presented in this book, even when expressed in terms of possibilities that they might apply to themselves if they so chose, seem to them unnecessary; their happiness has been presented to them on a plate (or in a cot) and while they may be sympathetic to those who wish to go out and extend their fields, they feel no urge to do the same.

These people present a challenge to many of the emphases of this book, but the conclusion to reach seems to be that adopted in Advaita Vedanta: no two people need follow the same path, and nobody on one path should criticize those who take a different one. Their becoming process may be slow, but it may be just as real for them as it is for others who move further, move faster and have a wider field.

The only danger for these people is that since their slice of field is comparatively small, it is more at risk of destruction than is the case for those who do not, so to speak, keep all their eggs in one basket. Deprivation and loss are part of the cycle of most people's existence. The loss of part of one's field will always therefore be a setback: but it does not terminate the *becoming* process. It may, however, be a different story if what was one person's *part* is the *whole* of another's field.

BEING-AND-BECOMING IN THE EAST

This advocacy of the becoming process may well be accepted as a fair depiction of Western existentialist views but as at best tangential, perhaps even irrelevant, to much of Eastern philosophy. Taoism, for example, seems to advocate non-involvement in human affairs, with the result that many of the areas which seem fruitful for the process of becoming – areas where the either-or dilemma occurs, even if not always agonizingly – are, following Taoist advice, to be left alone. The Taoist of old looked bemusedly at the Confucian with his concerns for the rectitude of civil administration; such concerns seemed to him trivial compared with the finding of the Tao and its philosophy of 'let things be'. Similarly, Buddhism seems to present the ideal of withdrawal from the normal activities of daily life rather than commitment to them – at any rate if one is to follow the Eightfold Path comprehensively: it was, after all, Buddha himself who indicated that one sure sign of being close to nirvana was the desire to join the *Sangha* (the order) and turn from worldly activities to the way of the monk.

The link here seems to be provided by the philosophy of Yin and Yang, and the insistence that each is incomplete without the other. To advocate a total commitment of oneself to the Yin tendency would be to suggest to any interested reader, male or female, that the only way to find happiness is to become a recluse and abandon the pursuit of worldly affairs such as politics or social justice in favour of a life of contemplation. I'm sure that if I wholeheartedly advocated this *modus vivendi* I should place the basic emphasis of this book beyond the possibilities and (though less certainly?) the desires of most readers, even those sympathetic to the basic proposal. On the other hand, to advocate the reader's total self-commitment to the Yang approach – a process of constant activity and involvement in external affairs, always changing one's field and developing new areas in the name of commitment or 'broader experience' – may well mean, as we saw with one of the examples mentioned above, that in the end the field is no richer than that of one who has spent an entire life tending one small plot. 'To be is to do', as existentialists have proclaimed, is only half the story; it must be complemented by 'to be is to reflect'.

The ideal state, it seems to me, is one in which these two approaches are harmoniously balanced. In the harmony of Yin and Yang one *is*, healthily and comprehensively, attaining a many-faceted process of Being which includes both opting in and opting out, commitment to civic life and all that that involves, and withdrawal from it in order to find refreshment in or at the fount, or Ground, of Being. If this is the case, one may make so bold as to affirm that Sartre would have made a more lasting contribution to the basic concerns of this book if he had practised regular meditation; and Buddha, if he had taken an active stance against the injustices which surrounded him.

FREEDOM

Whether the Yang or the Yin is the predominant emphasis in any person's life, there is total consistency among all our sources on one basic issue: the choice will be freely made. To be is to be autonomous,– that is the message. We may not be able to do other than seek happiness (it is a psychological impossibility to seek unhappiness) but each individual is free to choose the path towards this state. An individual may decide to follow a well-worn path, or to take advice as to which path to follow, but the decision to follow (or ignore) that advice is not determined by factors beyond his or her own autonomous will. **Marcus Aurelius** emphasized this when he wrote:

Remember that to change your mind and follow him who sets you right
is to be none the less free than you were before.

(*Meditations*, Book VIII, Chapter 27)

At any point, the follower of a well-worn path remains free to diverge
from it and beat out a new trail of his or he own. To be is not only to
be indivisible: it is also to be indetermined, independent of any take-over
bid by another; and this remains the case even though many, by their
pusillanimity, allow it to happen, and many others, motivated by personal
power, encourage them to allow it.

A corollary of this freedom, expressed in every ontological perspective
examined, is *personal responsibility*. This remains basic even if the ultimate
aims are differently expressed in the various schools. Whether we speak in
terms of essence, Ground of Being, Brahman, Nirvana, the Fourth State,
the Way, or the Tao, the decision to commit oneself to one of these is that
of the individual concerned, and the means that man or woman adopt in
order to pursue this aim (which may not necessarily lead them towards it)
are in their field of responsibility and no one else's. What they attain as a
result of their decisions (in Indian terms, the karma they build up) is the just
reward or punishment for the way or ways by which they have chosen to
use their time, their abilities and their possessions. Either may well not be
alone in the steps he or she takes; others will probably be sharing part of
the journey, and must therefore share the responsibility for the way that is
chosen. But a responsibility shared, unlike a burden shared, is not halved,
but doubled.

A significant parallel to this application of the belief in individual freedom
is summed up in the phrase which has been encountered in various schools
throughout this book; *beyond good and evil*. This obviously relates at one
level to certain issues which are the proper concern of the moral philosopher:
absolutism and relativism, ends and means, and so on; but these are not our
concern here. In ontological terms it expresses the view, outlined above,
that nobody has the right to claim that only his or her own path is the
right way, and that the path chosen by others is the wrong way. This
tolerance about variations in metaphysical emphases and perspectives must
be applauded, which implies that those who proclaim 'I'm right, you're
wrong' must be shunned. All schools or personal expressions of opinion
have a right to be heard, except where they affirm that they alone have
a right to be heard.

Those who go along with this ultra-liberal pronouncement should,
however, recognize what it is they're committing themselves to, and,
in particular, the risk they are running by making such a commitment.
The fact is that millions of people exist whose whole Being, as expressed
through their actions and opinions, runs counter to the Way, however this
is described by the different perspectives of this book. The world is not

full of Taoists peacefully and harmoniously sharing in the unity of Being. It has more than its share of mercenaries and psychopaths, exploiting and destroying those whom they confront. Are we, following the philosophy of 'let things be', to do nothing, either in criticism or restraint, about such people?

From the perspective we have reached, this problem is difficult but not insuperable (or at any rate no more insuperable than many other problems, not least the problem of Being itself). Either those who live in this way know, within themselves, that theirs is a barren path (in Taoist terms, that they are missing the Way), in which case, if there is any truth in the perspective, they will reap what they have sown and fail to find happiness; or they delude themselves into believing that they have found happiness, in which case we face the insuperable problem of bringing to a state of enlightenment those who steadfastly turn their faces against it. It may be necessary, on the ground of public safety, to restrict the freedom of some people (such as psychopaths), but the more important perspective was presented by Buddha: those who are not ready should be objects of sympathy rather than condemnation. I state this approvingly, while recognizing that it represents an ideal that few people seem able to achieve.

So far as what society loosely terms 'immorality' is concerned, the perspective 'beyond good and evil' is that no form of behaviour is wrong in itself, but only in the consequences it may cause to both the perpetrator and the recipients of that behaviour. Thus it must be desirable to kill a rabid dog, or a soldier dying in agony on the battlefield, or to steal a loaded gun from a homicidal maniac. From this perspective it would also be wrong to state that, for instance, adultery is 'wrong': rather, to state that if a person acts in this way, certain consequences will occur which may or may not be fruitful in his or her field, or in the fields of others; and whether they are fruitful or not will vary from person to person, couple to couple, and situation to situation. This is one aspect of the state beyond good and evil (there are others) and it requires a degree of tolerance and openness in people which few in fact attain. The Tao is not easily achieved (see case study 21).

## 'IRRATIONAL' MAN

I have stated that to be is to be indivisibly, and the implications of this (probably) cryptic remark point to a further area of unity between existentialism and Eastern thought: both are concerned with the whole of Being, not just certain facets, or a single facet, of it. In particular, both take as axiomatic the fact that a human being is more than just an intelligent animal. This does not mean that they view intelligence as unimportant, but that they place it alongside other aspects of Being which together make up the field. They take, on the whole, the middle way between the extreme of declaring the rational faculties to be worthless (though Zen Buddhism at its most extreme seems to imply this) and that of holding that only what can be rationally explained is worth discussing, or even capable of being discussed philosophically (as positivism and empiricism affirm – and, indeed, as most of Western philosophy tacitly assumes).

It is important to be aware of the implications of this particular middle way. *It does not write off reason.* Almost all the originals from which the ideas presented in these pages have been taken have been put together on a rational basis. The arguments of the existentialists, of Buddhism, even of Advaita Vedanta, represent a cogent account of an ontological perspective, which readers may discuss intelligently or otherwise. Taoism certainly goes further than other schools in affirming the inadequacy of reason, but even Taoism doesn't suggest that reason is irrelevant in finding and following the Way: only that it will not in itself be totally enabling in the process. So the main emphasis that emerges is that *reason is necessary* for the achieving of a sound ontological stance on matters, *but it is not in itself sufficient.* For instance, reason will be needed in order to understand the relationship of Advaita's Fourth State to the other three states, but it will not enable a person to enter this State. For most people, reason is a major commodity in the field of Being (even for those who are not over-endowed with it): but it would be a limited field that subsisted on reason alone. Man, the thinking animal, is not therefore enough if the totality of Being is to be expressed. That totality includes the instinct, the imagination, the feelings, the emotions, the will: only then can it be said that we are speaking of the whole person and not just a computer-like figure, a brain on legs. This is not being irrational, much less a-rational, but superrational (in German 'Der Überrationale' along the lines of Nietzsche's Übermensch).

Many Westerners find this idea difficult to take (though Kant expressed it with supreme authority in his *Critique of Pure Reason*) but, when you think about it (if that is not question-begging), a good deal of life is conducted on the basis of the overrational or superrational. Most of our moral decisions – probably all the moral decisions that really matter to us – are based on factors other than the rational. What does it *mean* to decide 'reasonably' how to behave in a set of circumstances? We may describe certain forms of behaviour as 'unreasonable', but in this context we normally mean something like 'socially unacceptable', or 'inconsistent with other expressions of behaviour'. Any sense of moral obligation that we have, if we reflect carefully on it, goes deeper than reason, even if we are able to 'give reasons' for our behaviour. Irrational behaviour is one thing (many a medal has been won after such behaviour in battle, if the truth were known); immoral behaviour lies in a totally different category, and is perhaps what most people mean when they describe someone else's behaviour as 'unreasonable'.

How far are any of our relationships either based on reason or capable of being accounted for by reason? I may state that I *know* that certain people love me, but this 'knowledge' has little, if anything, to do with reason. It is based on a deeper perception than intellectual awareness – one which recognizes the limitations of reason while not (to reiterate an important point) discarding this quality altogether. The concept of I-thou is one that any reader must know to be real; but it is simply not in the same world as that of rational thought.

We all accept as self-evidently true that works of art cannot be judged by reason alone; that political affiliation for most people springs from more than a careful analysis of the parties' programmes; and that most of the things we do to express our personalities – such as choosing the clothes we wear, or the decoration and furnishing of our homes – don't rely on the faculty of reasoning. So if all these facets of life (which is life as we all encounter it, not just the quirk of a few mystics or other oddities) take us beyond the rational, why should ontological perspectives be viewed as at least suspect and even totally unacceptable just because they are unverifiable at the court of reason? Most people, as a matter of fact, are deeply concerned about the issues raised in this book, even though they wouldn't necessarily wish to pursue them on the terms introduced here. But their concerns and their convictions enter far more deeply into their Being than simply an academic appreciation of the issues. To neglect, or reject, discussion of existentialist or Eastern ontology because there can be no 'bottom line' like that on a company's accounts seem to me as absurd as my refusing to make love with my wife unless she can demonstrate, with evidence that will hold up to scrutiny in a court of law, that she has never been unfaithful to me. (See case study 29 for further examples in this field.)

One example of ontological exploration which embraces, in its search for evidence, a good deal more than can be offered purely by reason is illustrated in the next consideration.

ETERNAL BEING (OR BEING ETERNAL)

I have suggested several times in these pages that from my perspective (the only perspective I can adopt with total confidence) I am eternal. What was before my coming into existence was not and is not, so far as I am concerned; and after me, likewise – not even the deluge. I have every reason to be certain that before I was there was life, and that there will continue to be life after I am. But that type of knowledge is of the I-it, not the I-thou variety: I may know *that* something is or is not the case, and I can know *about* something or someone: but to know something or someone from within my own Being is knowledge in a different dimension – one which for me is eternal. This knowledge, these perceptions, are part of the to-be of me; and if, by advancing senility or through brain damage, these things were to be removed, the to-be of me would not know this; by pure logical inference, I can never know that I have ceased to know what I once knew (and I am referring here, of course, to a state beyond forgetfulness: if I know that I no longer know – have forgotten – what I know I once knew, I am in a different state from that of not knowing that I ever knew it). The last day of my life is also the last day of the universe.

Amid the continuity of Being is the impermanence, or mutability, of my field of Being. As I reflect on this, I am aware that it is not the same field today as it was a year, a decade, or half a century ago. I have developed areas which were earlier ignored (an interest in ontology, for example) and neglected areas which were once well tended (things theological, for example). To others, who also perceive changes in me, it may follow that a changing field (say, one that looks older than when first encountered) means a changed Being. Yet within the context of my own Being I am not old, or even older, but just me – as, forty years ago, I wasn't 'young' but just me. The to be of me is constant amid all the inevitable becoming which I experience. My Being is the central core, the Hindu Atman, which, for me, has been eternally unchanged and unchanging. This, and not Buddha's discontinuous persons, is what I know from the ground (lower case) of my own Being, and it is from this that I must speak, rather than build theories in the air, so to speak, of what it is to be.

If Being is, then, continuous, what is to be the place, in our philosophy, of non-Being? Heidegger reminds us that unless we come to terms with this reality, we shall be living an artificial existence. I have indicated how the awareness of non-Being may affect everything we do consciously or unconsciously. But is the ultimate approach to Being the realization and acceptance of the fact that 'death closes all'? Must this I-it knowledge take precedence over the I-thou? Western philosophy has produced no satisfactory answer to this, except through theories, developed on an I-it basis, of the soul's immortality; and theism has produced similar doctrines on a similar basis. None of these is ontologically sound; and to find this soundness – or even something which only just begins to approach it – we must look East.

With Buddha we may so engage ourselves in the Being-becoming process that we see the end point, so far as this present experience is concerned, as the lead-off point for another person in another cycle. Perhaps the classical Jewish view, that immortality is gained only through one's offspring, is related to this doctrine, while not, of course, being totally identifiable with it. This viewpoint would, I think, provide an excellent basis for living (and therefore scores maximum points from the pragmatic point of view) but it is not a proposition that can be confidently expressed on the basis of experience. I have absolutely no knowledge of (I do not know) any cycle of experience except this present cycle, and am totally ignorant of the next cycle and the one who will inherit my karma, or whatever name is given to the sum total of my life. (In fact, if I did know for sure who that was to be I'd be making preliminary inquiries into his/her/its background *now*: as Humphrey Lyttelton said when asked where jazz would be in twenty years' time: 'If I knew that, I'd be there already.')

With the teaching of Advaita Vedanta about the Fourth State we seem to be moving away from the area of pure speculation into one about which there is certain declared evidence, even though this would not stand up in any analytical school. The awareness and experience of the state which this philosophy affirms to be a reality has been attested to by many men and women over the centuries, by no means all of them from a Hindu background. The testimony itself is not a matter of speculation but of fact: we can read it (or hear it described) for ourselves. Any speculation therefore must be as to the validity of the *evidence*. This may be a pack of lies, though there is no way of proving this; even if it represents the truth as the testifier sees it, it could still be a misinterpretation of the experience. Nevertheless, there remains enough evidence (including that of the Christian mystics) to suggest that, even if the awakened experience is unverifiable, it cannot be ignored in any ontological discussion which is trying to do justice to all expressions of Being and becoming that confront us. It is difficult not to conclude that many of the descriptions of the awakened state appear to be genuine, that is to say sincere, accounts written by genuine people, that is to say non-charlatans.

One of these descriptions has become famous in the West, not least because it was written by a Westerner and a scientist who is not, presumably, in the business of garnishing what he perceives with flights of fancy. Fritjof Kapra wrote *The Tao of Physics* in 1975, and since then it has been read by millions of people and in a dozen or more languages. Its famous opening paragraph (to which, as to the book as a whole, the reader is referred) ends with these words:

> As I sat on that beach my former experiences came to life; I 'saw' cascades of energy coming down from outer space, in which particles were created and destroyed in rhythmic pulses; I 'saw' the atoms of the elements and those of my body participating in this cosmic dance of energy; I felt its rhythm and I 'heard' its sound, and at that moment I *knew* that this was the Dance of Shiva, the Lord of Dancers worshipped by the Hindus.

It may be argued that few have experienced such an extraordinary happening (and that in any case we can manage without Shiva) but this does not invalidate what Kapra describes as having happened to him. If we include this experience alongside others which I earlier termed 'the numinous', experienced in a variety of contexts, to which millions can testify, there seems ample evidence to suggest that, whatever the explanation, these experiences happen. So far as our ontological quest is concerned, this in turn suggests that there is a world of experience beyond what we normally perceive with our everyday senses (if 'everyday' is quite the word for what are, after all, miraculous); that the field of Being may be enriched by these experiences; and that they may even constitute grounds for transforming the concept of Being commonly held among Westerners. I am acknowledging, therefore, that there may be a case for concluding that the enhanced state of awareness which is gained in these moments of awakening, or enlightenment, is in fact more real than the reality we daily experience when we awaken from a dream.

My grounds for not advocating this philosophy wholeheartedly are outlined on p. 185. In brief, my hesitation arises because its non-dualistic basis seems to me ontologically unsound, lacking dynamism: it offers (so it seems to me) Being without becoming, and since my experience has invariably included both, I cannot conceive of non-dualistic Being except in terms of death. Without change we have, quite literally, monotony which is a harbinger of death. The idea of 'perpetual bliss', apart from being inconceivable (like an orgasm lasting for ever) is, to me at any rate, undesirable. It is in the perpetual balance between activity and reflection, darkness and light, sorrow and joy, that the most complete ontological perspective is to be found. The idea of life as a perpetual orgy, so to speak, is no more appealing to me than one of permanent drudgery.

My criticisms of the philosophy of the Fourth State are made only apropos of the assertion that it gives a complete account of human destiny: about the fact that it describes one form by which the numinous is experienced in human life, I have no doubt, as I have no doubt that others experience the numinous through the arts, or nature, or relationships, or in chance, and briefly recalled, memories: 'the brave Music of a distant Drum'. Nor do I doubt that, for many people, various forms of meditation help to create a state of preparedness for such revelations, or (since that word implies a revealer) inspirations. It is only when I read the pages of the Tao Te Ching that I realize that, for me at any rate, Advaita Vedanta does not comprehensively reflect my ontological perceptions. I feel more at home, in the sense that this feels more natural, in the Taoist expression of the underlying unity of Being as found in the eternal dynamic of the Yin and the Yang. When I blot out, as far as is ever possible, the material world of making and doing and earning and spending, and get the 'feel' of the natural world, with its ever-changing but ever-returning seasons, the sense of the oneness and harmony of Being, including my Being, grows continually. It seems difficult to accept that these are merely erratic moments in an otherwise tranquil norm. Though more short-lived than that norm, the memory of them endures out of all proportion to the time they occupy. Just as most people's family albums are full mostly of holiday photos, representing perhaps 4 or 5 per cent of their actual time together as a family, so I seem to retain these times of insight with an intensity which puts other experiences in the shade. Is this because we are comparing the supernatural (in the ontological, not the theological, sense) with the natural? Do these moments hint that we must redefine what it is to be natural?

## TELEOLOGY

Related to that last question is the issue of whether there is a final goal to existence (as is implied in the question of what our destiny may be). The Buddhist doctrine of Nirvana and that of the Hindu Brahman not only suggest that there is a goal, but also speak with assurance about the nature of that goal. The existentialists made no commitment to this perspective, and in this they are joined by the Taoists. I feel this to be profoundly right. The teleological view of Being is, I think, anti-ontological (if I may coin a word): it suggests that Being happens for the sake of something else; that Being, or, at any rate, Being as I encounter it, is a means rather than an end, having an instrumental rather than an intrinsic status. The Tao Te Ching seems to speak with greater authority by its expression of the view that *Being is*; or, to put it more comprehensively, the Being-becoming process *is*. It is not contingent, not part of a wider plan or purpose, but is simply because it is. We're here because we're here (there was more truth in that war song than the lyricist probably realized). *Being/becoming cannot not be.* It is, by definition: and because it is, the question of what it is *for* is meaningless. To be is an end in itself.

The Taoist (or, to be more accurate, the Chinese) doctrine of Yin and Yang perfectly represents this perspective. We do not need to think of a goal of creation but rather to recognize that having met its goal in the one, the universal Tao returns to meet its goal in the other; and so eternally. So we have a continuous cycle of Being, timeless, yet experienced in time, encountering death, yet constantly new, a union of opposites and a harmony of dimensions, the Tao which cannot be named or described, limited or defined. In the words of Marcus Aurelius (the Lao Tsu of the West): 'All things from eternity are like forms and come round in a circle.' And time, which sweeps all things away, renews all things. So, to reiterate the point, the question of the purpose of Being is absurd: Being is, and cannot not be. To ask what it is *for* is as pointless as asking what people, or wasps, or roses are for.

I used the word 'eternally' in that paragraph, and thus laid myself open to the charge, often levelled by Western materialists against advocates of the Tao, and of other expressions of Eastern ontology, of being concerned only with my own personal survival after the end of this present cycle of experience. Such criticism is born of ontological ignorance. I hope it has become abundantly plain over these pages that I am not interested in the concept of the immortal soul, in heaven, or reincarnation, or any other theories which speak of survival after death. In purely logical terms, there can no more be survival after death than the square of two can be five, or than I can be in London and New York at the same time. The issue to which Taoism, in particular, directs us is to eternity as it is experienced within the context of Being. Spinoza, in his *Ethics*, said, 'We feel and know that we are eternal'; but this is an expression of an I-it experience, and, furthermore, one with which many people, including myself, would disagree. I don't *know that* I am eternal: *I know that* I shall die. What I *know* is eternity since my Being never was, and never can be, in a state of non-Being. Death can never be the thou of the I which is my Being, since death is not a state of which any kind of relationship can be predicated.

What this ontological perspective brings about is release from the fear of death, since death truly is, for me, no more. The mythology which creates an image of Death, 'the grim reaper', as a living Being who may communicate with one he is about to 'take' seems to me the most nightmarish of all our descriptions of death. It is also ontologically absurd. Either Death 'gains' by possessing those who die, which implies that, being in his power, they continue to be, therefore are not dead at all, therefore he has not gained anything; or they do in fact cease to be, in which case no gain is made. The fear of death – in this myth as in others – is not the fear of non-Being, since then there can be no feelings at all, whether of fear or otherwise; it is either the fear of the process of dying, represented by the diminishing of the field of Being, the loss of faculties, the cessation of I-thou relationships; or it is the fear, illustrated in, for instance, Dante's depiction of the Inferno, of 'a fate worse than death'. Those who have created such imagery – and few of these have written or spoken in these terrible terms other than from a theistic background – bear the most awesome of responsibilities: that of removing all chance of happiness from millions of people whose basic motivation was for just that: the attainment of happiness.

If it is the case – as my experience occasionally suggests that it might be – that individual Being finds its deepest fulfilment in union with other Being (I-thou, the awakened state, Brahman, Dharmakaya, the Ground of Being, the Tao), may this not be an indicator for our ontological perspective? The *concept* of the indivisibility of Being suggests that this is so, and this seems to be confirmed by what we all find that it actually *is* to be. In rare moments, if human testimony throughout the centuries is to be heeded, the sense of individual Being, separate and distinct from all other manifestations of Being, is lost, and is replaced with a sense of unity of Being *per se*. Similarly, while we know that individual beings will cease to be, Being itself continues. In the midst of death we are surrounded by life: there is Being as well as nothingness. And it is Being that is supreme, for we perceive that in its presence of death, life persists. It seems therefore a natural response to normal, non-fantasized, non-sentimentalized experience to suggest that awareness of the Tao (or whatever name we may choose to describe this experience) indicates the eternity of Being. All the evidence suggests that individual consciousness ceases with death; but the Tao of universal consciousness or Being seems manifestly to be stronger than death. *The nature of things is to be, not to not be*; the universal essence is Being, not non-Being. Existence, we could then continue to say, clearly precedes essence: but essence cannot be described except in terms of the Tao, the Ground of all Being. My essence is thus, quite simply, to be at one with the Tao, to belong to the unending cycle of Being-and-becoming in all that is.

This last point may, understandably, be accused of being speculative, even a case of whistling in the dark, but, if so, it is speculation arising not from some gigantic step of imagination or fantasy unrelated to any real facet of Being, but from those rare moments of insight which I, along – so far as I can tell – with many others, have experienced. We are not dealing with the unnatural or even the supernatural as the word is commonly used but with the natural as it is sometimes given to us to see it and perhaps as it really is all the time if our eyes were open long enough to recognize it. This is no advocacy along the lines of the psychological and ontological nonsense currently in vogue in the United States under the prominent leadership of Shirley MacLaine: talk of ESP, astral bodies, extra-terrestrial beings belongs to the philosophical kindergarten. What I have attempted to describe is Being as it actually is, and what, without any inconsistency with what it *is*, it might be becoming.

## Case study 24
## The Tao and theism

The following piece is an article written by the author for the *Guardian*. It was written in response to an article by a former vicar of the Church of England who had left the Church because of his changing beliefs. He explained how he found it more rewarding to follow Eastern paths, particularly that of Zen Buddhism, but that the theistic idea of a personal God, loving him and desiring union with him, remained strongly in his psyche. He found it preferable to think of this God in female terms, however; and he concluded with the words, 'I am still seeking my Beloved; and I do not know where to find Her.' See what you make of the issues raised by discussing the questions that follow.

## DOWN THE ROAD OF HEALTHY ANXIETY IN PURSUIT OF THE WAY

### (AUTHOR'S TITLE: WHERE THERE'S THE TAO THERE'S A WAY)

Those who reject Christian dualism as an unsatisfactory, even offensive myth need not feel forlorn. The moment of rejection should be viewed rather as a sign of having grown up. Adult reasoning confirms that either God *can* remove injustices of the world but doesn't *wish* to, or He wishes to but can't. In the first case He is a monster, and in the second He is impotent.

Since I refuse to worship any Being whom I hold in contempt, I therefore reject the theistic concept of God.

In 1971 the Methodist Church judged my book *The Christian Outsider* to have contained false doctrine, and expelled me from its ministerial ranks as a heretic. Thus is exemplified another aspect of the unholy dualism brought about by theistic philosophy: between 'true' and 'false' beliefs. I do not, however, feel abandoned: rather, liberated, released into a higher dimension.

For those who feel bereft at the loss of the father-figure of theism, there are two steps that can be taken, one represented primarily in Western philosophy, the other in the East. The first step, in the direction suggested by Nietzsche, is to accept that all the comfort, all the favours, all the forgiveness and, above all, all the moral strength sought for in this imaginary God must now be found in and through our own strength.

We shall almost certainly experience anxiety in this new state, but it will be a healthy anxiety. So, following Kierkegaard, we move forward in hope, but never (and this is crucial as an antidote to those Catholics, Protestants, Jews and Muslims who are convinced that they've got it right) able to prove that our choices are, or have been, the 'right' choices. In fact, the words 'right' and 'wrong' become increasingly threadbare as these existentialist steps take us beyond good and evil.

But we need to go further than existentialism if we are not to remain islands unto ourselves alone. As I contemplate the world I inhabit I am, in my darker moments, filled with despair because of its rapaciousness, its indifference to human suffering, its exaltation of transitory material values. But slowly I am growing to recognise that beyond all this is a universe of tranquillity of which I am a part.

I know that the numinous truly exists; that it does so without needing any God to sustain it; and that it enables me to cope with the frustrations and injustices of living. This idea was given expression centuries before theism made its life-destroying mark by numerous Eastern philosophers.

For me, the highest peak is in the teaching of Lao Tsu about the Tao, the Way. The pursuit of this Way assures me that there is a river into which my single stream of being must flow, along with many other expressions of being; and though attempts may be made to flow in contrary directions, ultimately there can be no being beyond the living waters of that river. And ultimately the river will find its way to the sea which is the ground of all being.

I don't know whether or not this implies immortality, nor do I care. From within my own being I am, after all, eternal. Ontologically speaking (that is to say, from the point of view of *being*) there never was a time when I was not and there never will be a time when I shall not be. Nor shall I ever know non-being, or death. I know *that* I shall die, of course, but to know *about* is different from knowing. The travails of death are the travails of the living, not of the dead. Being – my being – is eternal.

I do not care, either, that I cannot pray or talk to the Tao. It is enough (in fact it is everything) to be aware of it and at one with it, since by following the Tao one achieves the state beyond good and evil. This is what it means to find the Thou of one's life, and it is a lessening of its infinite worth to describe it as either 'He' or 'She'.

Here is wisdom. Beside it, the follies of theism seem like the stumblings of a child trying to walk; and the inanities of current materialistic values exposed as the acceptance of existence without essence.

Here are the questions:

1   Do you think the contrast between God as either a monster, or impotent, is too stark? Viewed solely from the perspective of human experience, is it possible to believe in a God who is both all-loving and all-powerful?

2   What is meant by a 'true' belief? Where belief, rather than knowledge, is concerned, is the distinction between 'true' and 'false' a valid one to make? Which of the following would *you* call a true, and which a false, belief:
    (a)   There are living creatures on other planets far distant in the universe.
    (b)   Animals have souls.
    (c)   The British, and their American descendants, are descended from the lost tribes of Israel.
    (d)   One's fate is foretold in the stars.
    (e)   Miraculous cures for disease come about by prayer and/or faith.
    (f)   Moral choices are, or can be, freely made.
    (g)   The earth is flat.
    (h)   Certain people have 'second sight'.
    (i)   It is unlucky to walk under a ladder.
    (j)   Ghosts haunt certain buildings.
    (k)   Reincarnation occurs.
    (l)   This life is a preparation for a 'better' life.
    (m)   Some races are born to serve others.
    (n)   Some people are born leaders.

(o)   The Pope, when speaking *ex cathedra*, is infallible.

(p)   The Bible/the Koran is infallible.

(q)   The state of being 'born again' is one beyond the normal state.

(r)   Every event is part of a divine purpose.

(s)   The rights of animals are as important as those of human beings.

(t)   I am composed solely of matter in motion, devoid of a soul.

3   Do you think that the majority of the human race is mature, or strong enough to 'do without' the comfort many people derive from believing in God? Is Nietzsche's picture of the 'overman' just an example of wishful thinking?

4   'Faith means betting your life that there is a God.' Is this an acceptable way to proceed, assuming that atheism is the same in reverse?

5   Is the author realistic in his understanding of the numinous? Wouldn't it be both simpler and more natural to state that certain experiences strike certain chords in us which produce the effects about which he eulogizes irrationally?

6   If we accept the Taoist belief that we are individual rivers flowing into a universal sea, where does this leave those with murder and mayhem on their minds? Are we all, however profoundly varied our values may be, to be united in this way?

7   How do you react to the ontological perspective on death outlined in the passage? How far do you feel that it makes irrelevant all considerations about an immortal soul?

8   Do you think the author would have written those words if he had been living his days out as a peasant working laboriously from dawn to dusk? Isn't such a peasant, like the negro slaves in the cotton fields, much more likely to dream of heaven and a happier experience after the grimness of the present reality?

9   Isn't it the case that most people need 'someone' to talk to – call this God or what you will? Isn't the author therefore again separating himself from most of his fellow human beings by dispensing with the idea of prayer?

10   Does it matter if the majority of human beings reject the perspective presented in this article? Granted that the views it criticizes have been props for the majority of the human race hitherto, isn't the basic issue about whether these same props will serve in the future?

11   Is it fair to suggest that people must be prepared to experience more anxiety in their lives than will be acceptable to those seeking a purely

comfortable existence? What need is there to keep nagging at these issues if ignorance is bliss?

12    'If God does not exist, then all things are possible.' The author meant this to be a criticism of atheism: do you think it could also be a commendation?

13    In the final paragraph, the author brings capitalism and theism together for criticism. Is this fair? How far have theistic beliefs and capitalistic enterprise been historically self-supporting?

14    How far should Taoism be viewed as a philosophy rather than a religion?

*Case study 25*
*Sex in Eastern religion and philosophy*

Many Westerners, particularly those raised in, if not adherents of, the theistic tradition, find themselves to be at least disturbed, often shocked, and sometimes disgusted by the relaxed and frank way in which the sexual union between a man and a woman is discussed in Eastern religious and philosophical writings. While in India a guide to sexual fulfilment and harmony such as the *Kama Sutra* is treated with the respect that Westerners accord only to the writings of such people as Jung or Freud, in the West it was banned for centuries, is treated by many as a 'dirty' book and has just been advertised at the time of writing (1989) by a well-known firm with the inscription: 'Warning: sexually explicit throughout'. (Such a caution in this instance seems as necessary as one accompanying sales of the Bible which states 'Warning: religiously explicit throughout'.)

If this were a manual on the theme 'A healthy person is a sexually fulfilled person' it would be relevant to continue in this vein; but the concern in this case study is to concentrate on one specific element in this Eastern attitude: that sexual bliss mirrors the most profound religious and philosophical beliefs. This could itself be the subject of a vast tome, so we'll concentrate on two examples, one from India and one from China. The quotations and illustrations are from two books which you may wish to peruse in their entirety: *Oriental Erotic Art* by Philip Rawson and *The Tao of Love and Sex* by Jolan Chang (Wildwood House). The latter is cheap enough to buy but the former is more expensive. It is, despite its unfortunate title, an academic study of sex in Eastern culture, philosophy and religion; perhaps because of its many 'totally unexpurgated' pictures, it is retained on the 'reserved' shelves of most public libraries, which means that you'll have to convince the librarian that you are a 'serious' student of the subject before you'll be able to borrow it.

*Hinduism*

The following extracts from Rawson, together with the illustrations, should give a hint of the emphasis found in certain elements of Hindu belief.

> Of all the [body] fluids, the most significant is the male semen. For it has the power of creating life, and must therefore in some special way transport the generative principle. . . There is great deal of evidence in the *Upanishads* and in modern research that the male semen was felt somehow to be the physical form of the ultimate Brahman. . .
>
> Semen is white, and masculine. The feminine analogue was red: not exactly the blood, but embodied in the menstrual discharge. The combination of these two energies in joyful sexual intercourse was felt to be the creative factor in pregnancy; and such sexual intercourse was a metaphor of the higher type of divine intercourse which constantly creates the world. But since the cosmic energies involved were somehow cognate with the bodily energies, the whole vast cosmic creation itself was ultimately a function of bodily energies which the human experiences in his or her own body. The two, human and cosmic-divine, were not separate. The human was a pattern of the divine.
>
> (*Oriental Erotic Art*, p. 28f)

Not only is human sexuality a mirror of divine creativity; representations of the divine, whether orally or in visual form, do not hesitate to depict this creativity in unmistakably sexual terms or imagery; and this is not by coy, blushing references, but in a blatant exultation in the exquisite

Celestial lovers. Stone carving at Khajuraho circa 1000 AD.
Reproduced by permission of The Hutchinson Library.

Multiple sexual intercourse among the Apsaras in the celestial bounds of a temple, Khajuraho circa 1000 AD. Reproduced by permission of Giraudon.

pleasure of male and female in spiritual harmony brought about through genital harmony. (Don't forget: the sculptings of which we show a few examples were not made to surround a house of 'ill repute', as at Pompeii, but as parts of shrines in temples of adoration and worship.) Rawson writes:

> Along with the named deities of the Hindu pantheon, we find the Apsaras. Thes celestial beauties posture alluringly on the fabric; they dance, make music, and, above all, embrace and pleasure their worthy lovers by a variety of erotic techniques. The temple itself thus demonstrates that sensual lure of perfect, and hence trans-human, sexual enjoyment. Furthermore, the presence of these celestial courtesans represents a major part of the glory of the deity whose home the temple is. Some Hindus assert that they also give pleasure to the deity so that he feels well disposed towards the people. . . In India, divine

presence is associated with the sense of deep sexual arousal. (ibid., pp. 57, 61)

Rawson later describes certain Tantric rites, whereby men and women, not married or even, necessarily, previously known to each other, seek to discover the bliss of divine ecstasy through prolonged, if possible non-orgasmic, sexual intercourse. He comments:

> This is perhaps the most powerful and uncompromising practical expression we know anywhere in the world of the implications of the idea of sexual polarity within Deity. It consummates completely the spiritual meaning of the act of sexual love, giving ordinary lovers a goal towards which they can aim. By making their acts divine, lifting them out of the mundane, the fading, the banal, it may lead them to experience the Great Duality within their own organisms. (ibid., p. 72f)

My guess is that in this material is enough to inspire argument and discussion without needing much prodding from me. It is likely that some people will consider the whole matter to be nothing but filth, and an act of self-indulgence on the author's part (and revealing not a little about the state of his mind). If you are one of those who reacts in this way, and recognizing that many people react quite differently, do you think this is

(a) because of your upbringing
(b) the result of parental attitudes
(c) a reflection of cultural attitudes in your society, or
(d) a genuine sense that these Hindus are or were, quite simply, lascivious: in other words, they have/had strayed from the path of purity? Which (to digress from the main issue for a moment) do you think is preferable: that children be encouraged to engage in sexual intercourse from the age of puberty or that they should spend that period taking sneak looks at forbidden magazines in the cloakrooms?

Other questions which you should be tackling are:

(a) In the light of the fact that in the West lust is regarded as one of the seven deadly sins, is it not expecting the impossible that people should be encouraged to reflect on the divine, or the numinous, in these terms?
(b) Even if the sinful element of the experience is got rid of, doesn't the whole of Western culture prevent anyone from experimenting along lines described in Rawson's book? Can one ever, for instance, imagine Western centres of worship appointing female courtesans as divine acolytes? Would *you* wish them to do so? If not, why not?
(c) Even though the parallel between sexual ecstasy and the

experience of the numinous has its obvious dangers, and lays itself open to exploitation, is it not worth pursuing in the light of the fact that at its best it is among the most sublime of human experiences? The New Testament doesn't hesitate to use the pleasures of food as a parallel to divine pleasures (cf. Jesus: 'I have meat to eat that ye know not of'). Would it really be too much to expect people to think similarly of sexual pleasure ('I have an orgasm to offer which will truly cause the earth to move')?

(d) Isn't is a wiser approach to sex to state, with the Hindus, that here is a power which, like nuclear power, if left uncontrolled can destroy a person, so we should experience the joys within careful control, rather than, with the New Testament (and like the anti-nuclear lobby), seek to ban it totally?

### Taoism

The Hindu approach is basically that of interpreting the divine in terms of human sexual experience; the approach of Taoism reverses this, and suggests that human sexuality can, when the principles of Yin and Yang are rightly understood, reflect the divine (though that word would not spring normally to Taoist lips). Jolan Chang (*The Tao of Love and Sex*, p. 35) quotes Wu Hsien, whom he describes as a Tao of Loving master during the Han Dynasty (206 BC–AD 219):

The male belongs to Yang.
Yang's peculiarity is that he is easily aroused
But also he easily retreats.
The female belongs to Yin.
Yin's peculiarity is that she is slow to be aroused
But also slow to be satiated.

Chang continues:

In the Taoist scheme of things, man is a Yang force, and he has all the attributes of maleness. He is more volatile, more active and quicker than a woman, who has the attributes of Yin, the female force. She is more placid, her movements calmer – but ultimately she is stronger. A common analogy used in ancient texts when comparing the relative strength of men and women was to liken them to fire and water. Fire belongs to Yang and, though quick to ignite, it is overwhelmed by water, a Yin force. Taoist thought suggests that all forces occur in conplementary pairs. Fire and water, heaven and earth, sun and moon, inhaling and exhaling, pushing and pulling, etc., and that each of these contrary forces belongs to a sexual power – either Yin or Yang. Yin and Yang, although separate forces, are really part of the same ultimate unity and therefore necessary to one another. (op. cit. p. 35)

*The Tao of Love and Sex* is an attempt to illustrate what the application of this principle may mean in the sexual relationship between a man and a woman. In one paragraph (p. 108) Chang writes:

The Tao suggests that a man develop his loving skills so that he can both satisfy and appreciate his love partner. 'Satisfaction' in this Taoist sense is not only the attainment of immediate pleasure but in a deeper more metaphysical sense involves the cultivation of a mutual tranquillity. When the Tao of loving talks about 'technique', it does not just mean your ability to thrust and ejaculate in a controlled way, but the development of all your senses so that you can arrive at a true harmony of Yin and Yang. Love-making then is not just a mechanical thing but a total experience. A pianist can develop a mastery of fingering technique but he is still nothing more than a technician. It is only when he brings his full senses and imagination to bear on his music that he becomes a true artist. Loving ecstatically is very much like that.

You will probably need to read more of this remarkable book in order to discuss the issues it raises with any degree of confidence (or authority), but certain basic questions arise from these passages, which typify the remainder of the book. I hope that female readers will forgive me if the questions seem very much those which occur to a male: perhaps your first exercise should be to prepare an alternative list!

1    In the light of the Yin-Yang expression of the *complementary* nature of the male-female roles – elsewhere, as well as in the sexual area – does it not suggest that the phrase 'the equality of the sexes' is meaningless? (Does the word 'equal' ever have any meaning when discussing human qualities?)

2    Granted that the Taoist view of sex suggests that the idea of 'giving her one' is a total distortion of what sex is all about (isn't it?), is there any place for the primeval male desire (see Chapter 4 on the primitive instincts) to cast his seed comprehensively and liberally?

3    How far do you agree with the Taoist perspective that one major ingredient of happiness is a fulfilled sex life?

4    What, then, do you say of those people who, whether by choice, by accident, or by misfortune experience a life of celibacy?

5    In the West, lust is listed under the seven deadly sins. Do you agree?

6    The viewpoint expressed in *The Tao of Love and Sex* has been described as 'a philosophy for beautiful people'. How do you react to the plea that a person may be too ugly to attract a member of the opposite sex? Do you think that 'there's someone for everyone'?

7    To the extent that there is some truth behind the last question, do you think our society would be more healthy if it condoned the existence of houses where men or women could pay for sex? At the *Lady Chatterley* trial in 1960, the then Bishop of Woolwich affirmed: 'Sex with a prostitute is better than no sex at all.' Do you agree? (Remember that in India the courtesan is highly regarded as a respected member of the community.)

8    Some societies initiate youngsters into sex by introducing them to older members of the opposite sex, on the grounds that it is natural for a beginner to learn from a more experienced person. Do you agree?

9    Should we be more open about sexual instruction in schools? How would you react if you heard that your local school were adopting *The Tao of Love and Sex* as a textbook? (Think very carefully about this one: haven't we created a society which remains prurient on sexual matters, but glories in the slaughters carried out by its nation's forefathers?)

10   How far do you think that what the book describes is possible between members of the same sex? What should be our attitude to these people?

11   How far do you think that pornographic magazines, strip joints and the like are the inevitable consequence of unnatural taboos about sex in Western society? Would the Taoist view of liberation put an end to these more effectively than by banning them?

12   In the phrase 'free love', what is meant by 'free' and what is meant by 'love'?

13   Is the phrase 'the battle of the sexes' a truer representation of the state of things than the Taoist view of their complementariness?

14   How far do you think that the Taoist perspective is one of 'letting nature take its course'? Granted that this view of nature is in any case central to the Taoist perspective, do you think that the book's advocacy of the need for serious attention to be given (particularly by males) to the ways of loving is a desirable supplement to this?

15   The basic aim of the book is that the longevity of the male's love-making should be increased, to the greater satisfaction of the

female. This will demand more patience on his part, and a greater degree of sensitivity towards his partner than – according to many females – is usually shown. How far does this represent the laid-back attitude of the East rather than the frenetic hyper-activity of the West? How might Westerners adapt themselves in their sexual behaviour? Is the idea of a day-long assignation between a husband and wife, as the book advocates, hopelessly unsuited to our life-style? Or might it be the key to the transformation of Western values – being rather than grabbing, finding wholeness in the duality of Yin and Yang rather than seeking it vainly in the eternal clash of Yang versus Yang?

**16** Is that last question too pretentious, and should we not in any case be pursuing our philosophical enquiries by more mentally demanding activity, such as discussing the meaning of meaning or the theory of knowledge? How would the final injunction in *The Tao of Love and Sex* affect philosophical discourse: 'Love a hundred times without emission'?

# 9   *The Tao in the world*

Any reader who has steadfastly followed the argument so far may well be in a mood to demur at this stage. Throughout the preceding pages I have been critical of the analytical approach to philosophy, the aesthetic in Kierkegaard's language, because it is no more than a commentary on, rather than a commitment to, the process of living.

But, it may be protested, much of what has been said in the name of both existentialism and Eastern philosophy also seems to belong to its own discrete segment of experience. We have explored the nature of Being to the point of becoming quite ruminative; we have made lateral leaps in our views on the Ground of Being; we have committed ourselves to the idea of the Tao: but have any of these, it may be asked, been any more than flights of fancy, satisfying, perhaps, to the author, but leaving the world unchanged, as linguistic analysts leave it unchanged? What is there in all this that is likely to impress itself on the world in which we live, and move, and have our Being? Has ontological discourse any relevance in this world, or is it condemned to be just as much the private concern of a select coterie as are Wittgenstein's *Tractatus* and the quantum theory of physics?

It would be odd indeed if ideas about the nature of *Being* – a state shared by everything and everyone – had no application in the world of *beings*, and I propose now to respond to this implied rebuke. Of course once one begins to direct ontological – or any kind of philosophical – discourse into the 'real' world, the ideas lose the mystic protection they enjoyed when in the preserve of a private coterie; in other words, they run the risk of being both understood and, more to the point, disagreed with. Realizing that this is the case, I shall now take that risk, armed with two concepts which have strongly asserted themselves in the foregoing pages: *from the West, I and thou; and from the East, Yang and Yin.* Many of the great human problems of our time – perhaps all of them – can, I think, be tackled, if not actually solved, with the insights derived from these two remarkable and surprisingly comprehensive philosophies of life. They are surprising because, when first encountered, they don't look like the kind of ideas with which to explore and perhaps transform the world; yet to live with these ideas for just a few months can change one's whole perception of the world as it confronts us daily, both through the media and at first hand. It is difficult to avoid the conclusion that if these two sets of insights were put into practice, many of the problems which confront and possess us would be no more.

## THE FOUR Ms

The world that I know is the Western world; its culture, for better or for worse, has been my culture until now, and looks like remaining so for the foreseeable future. It seems to me that it is dominated, and to a considerable extent torn and divided, by four dynamic Yang forces – forces, that is, motivated by aggression, the desire to possess, to control, to acquire, to mould, to change. These forces are materialism, Marxism, Muhammadanism and – to retain the alliterative 'M', though this is slightly artificial – Moses. By this last I mean the theistic tradition expressed in Judaeo-Christianity.

About the last two I have already written at some length, and my antipathy to both – on grounds explained in the relevant contexts – is, I think, unambiguous. I have briefly considered the merits of Marxism, and shall indicate later why I consider it to be irrelevant to our inquiry. Meanwhile, I shall concentrate on the first of the four Ms.

## MATERIALISM

The gravest challenge to the central emphases of this book is materialism in its commonplace, non-philosophical connotation. It is the belief that what you have is more important than what you are: indeed, what you are, from the materialistic perspective, depends on what you have. It is (still being alliterative) the worship of money, or Mammon, the belief that the worth of a human being, like the worth of a painting, is determined by price. It leads to the acceptance of monetarism, the belief in the supreme importance of market values. Not only are these values accepted as the controlling factor in human affairs, but every encouragement is given to keep things that way. The result is a situation in which every man or woman is seen as being in a state of rivalry with their neighbour: one of tacit, if not open, conflict. It is the acceptance, with the philosopher Hobbes, of the state of war as the basic reality of human intercourse. Each of us, according to this theory, is, whether we care to acknowledge it or not (and even if we're not conscious of it) continuously trying to do our neighbours down. Three centuries after Hobbes, **Ayn Rand** expressed this belief in her philosophy of **objectivism**, embracing with eagerness the view that the great and the strong should become greater and stronger, while the lesser representatives of the species should be driven to the wall or beneath the sod. A similar emphasis has been made by **social Darwinists**, with the added element that this warfare is viewed as an expression of not only human nature, but the whole of nature. Competition is the name of the game and altruistic deeds are simply diplomatic pawns in that game.

In the doctrine of materialism the Yang factor is given full range. In the world of making and doing and, above all, selling, the only reflection called for is on the price of a commodity; all other reflection is for dreamers. Nor is there any place for sentiment: if you start feeling sorry for people as you trample on them you're likely at least to remove your boots and so reduce your trampling power. This Yang factor is epitomized in the macho male at his worst: bullying his way through public and private affairs, viewing those around him – men and women alike – not as ends in themselves but as means to his own ends. People are there to be grabbed, with a business or a body to be acquired. If this seems exaggerated, think how many people in their millions have, over a decade or more, viewed and discussed and gloried in TV series like *Dallas* or *Dynasty*. It is difficult for many people not to be touched by the envy such programmes arouse, or to avoid the fantasies to which they are midwife. Some of these fantasies are a harmless form of escape from a life of unexciting routine – the element of orgy in the balance of life described by Aldous Huxley (p. 168): but some are a genuine expression of destructive urges inherited from our evolutionary past. The question is whether these urges should be continuously revived, or left to fade from our primeval memories. Granted that there was a time when the male needed these qualities in order, quite literally, to keep the wolf from the door, are they still to be encouraged when this has become no more than a metaphor?

## BROTHER'S KEEPER OR KEEPER'S BROTHER?

Lest this discussion become too discursive, I want to select one issue which puts materialism in the dock. Apart from any value inherent in such a cross-examination, it will illustrate what has been a constant refrain of this book: that analysis will take a person only to the point of knowing what any problem actually *is*; it will not provide the answer. This will arise not from an intellectual breakdown of the issues involved, but through some other aspect of the person which it is difficult to express in words. In the end, I feel, there is a numinous quality in the making of value judgements as important as the one I propose to discuss. By 'numinous' in this context I mean that there are no defined routes whereby it can be demonstrated either that those who choose one way are wrong, or that those who choose the other are right. Yet the two paths from the point of decision diverge so radically that it is difficult to contemplate how two people choosing differently can thereafter continue to have anything in common. Their fields of Being will – or so it seems – vary so comprehensively that it is hard to imagine how anything developed in the one will find any ground for fruitfulness in the other.

*Is altruism natural?* That is the issue (though not in such terms) which has received critical examination in recent years in the Western world, particularly in Britain and the United States. The central point of contention on which it focuses is the question of whether it is 'right' for the successful people in a country to give – not as a loan but as a non-returnable gift – a certain percentage of the fruits of their success to those who have been unsuccessful. The question is not whether this action could be deemed *reasonable*: that is another question altogether, and one, I think, to which the answer must be in the negative; by which I mean not that altruism is unreasonable, but that reason has no part to play in, is irrelevant to, this question. Reason may indicate what the options are, and may hint at the likely outcome of taking one path rather than the other; more than that it is not equipped to achieve. Our concern is quite different, though the term used may be question-begging. There is a firm body of opinion that it is in fact natural ('right-and-proper') that the strong should help the weak in this context. Very often, it is argued, it is only the accident of birth which enables one to succeed while others go to the wall. A person born into an advantaged home – whether this be defined in monetary or cultural terms – starts off with an enormous advantage over one born into deprived circumstances. We see, for instance, in Britain today children from the former group of families sent not to state schools for their education but to fee-paying schools where, as a direct result of the cash provided, they will be given more attention by their teachers than is possible for those attending schools where the staff-student ratio is higher. This gives those whose parents can afford the fees an advantage over those who are not so fortunate. A further factor in Britain (which may be unique to this land) is the incredible snobbery about public schools, which often means that job prospects for graduates of these schools are higher than for those in state schools, even when there is nothing to choose between the two sets of abilities. The old school tie mentality is not as strong as it was, say, a generation ago, but it remans a dominant feature of the community's ethos.

A further element of natural injustice is the unequal distribution of aptitudes. Some people, whether by chance or from their parents, seem to be born with a higher range of skills and abilities than others, whether intellectual skills or those associated with physical activity. Consequently tasks which to many are beyond consideration will be readily accessible to others. Sharpness of both brain and body can certainly be increased by practice, but some will always exceed others no matter how much practice the others put in. And those who exceed are normally more likely to succeed.

Granted these two factors of birth and of natural skills, so the argument proceeds (and only a person totally obtuse would deny the force of these factors in society), the difference between success and failure seems largely, even if not entirely, a matter of luck. The person born with more than average brain-power in a home with professional parents stands a considerably greater chance of developing his or her field than does one born into deprived social conditions, surrounded by others in the same mould, and not encouraged to sharpen what wits he or she has, because of the slow-wittedness of both parents and neighbours. It is quite understandable that such a person will be more likely than the first to become unemployed, because he or she won't have produced the skills which create openings for one's employment; more likely to get ill, because of both adverse environmental circumstances and parental lack of wisdom on such matters as food and hygiene; more likely to turn to crime because the rewards of living don't seem to be coming his or her way as he or she sees them going the way of those more fortunately placed; and more likely to be homeless because they are unable to afford a decent place to live. Throw him or her in with others similarly disadvantaged and you have the recipe for enormous social problems.

Thus we arrive at two cultures within a nation: the one prosperous, well-fed, well-housed, securely employed, generally fit and reasonably fulfilled, the other deprived, dissatisfied, with no present joy and little future hope. And it seems to be a matter mainly of chance whether one is in one group or the other. What is more natural, then, than that those who are lucky should recognize this state of affairs, and share their good fortune with those who through no fault of their own have been denied this; that they should willingly accept a taxation system whereby a percentage of their rewards is channelled to those without any reward; that homes should be provided for the homeless, tertiary education for even the slowest-witted, social services for even the most feckless, a living wage for the unemployed. Without this kind of co-operation, it is argued, society becomes a jungle, virtually a state of war (and perhaps increasingly threatened by actual internecine warfare). Just as the wise virgins in the parable should have given the foolish virgins a share of their oil (see Matthew 25) so the strong and able should help the weak and incapable. We are our brothers' keepers: we are responsible for one another and any society which rejects this basic assumption will destroy itself by greed and acquisitiveness. For this reason altruism is natural: we shall not survive otherwise.

Against this standpoint are arrayed those who believe precisely the reverse. They probably wouldn't recognize themselves by the phrase but they are effectually social Darwinists. They believe in the survival of the fittest, however that term be interpreted. They (or most of them) won't deny that there is an element of luck about a person's origins and initial motivations, but they argue that this is at best only part of the story, and for many who present it in defence of their shortcomings it is no more than an excuse. Nature has decreed, so they argue, that survival depends on self-determination; not in the existentialist sense of possessing free will, but in the general sense of establishing one's goals and dedicating oneself to achieving these. Some people may get to the top by graft or connection, but, if they are incompetent, they will be found out in the end and be pushed to the sidelines. Generally speaking, those who succeed do so because of their willingness to sacrifice leisure-time pursuits in order to concentrate on professional achievements. If their successs means that others fail, then this must be seen as a natural fact of life; just as there can be only one winner in a race, so the population at the pinnacle of success is, like the atmosphere, rarer than at the base.

It is the drive to succeed (even if this be interpreted at its most elementary level, as simply the urge to survive) which has motivated everything worthwhile in human history. This has been a story of achievers and non- or under-achievers. Sometimes luck may have played its part, but on the whole the achiever has been one who has made his or her own luck. The ingredients of successs, as will be attested by millions, have been unchanging since time began: application, dedication, industry; and plenty of people from less advantaged backgrounds have achieved it: the 'log cabin to White House' syndrome may be dead so far as creating American Presidents is concerned, but the 'slum tenant to company director' is a path which any may pursue even if few reach the ultimate goal.

If, however, (so the argument proceeds) you so order society that virtually half (or more) of what the successful ones earn is siphoned off for the benefit of those left behind, the whole point of the struggle has been removed. If everyone is to have prizes, what's the point of the race? The drive to succeed is effectively emasculated, with the result that those who *will* to succeed will go elsewhere where their talents may be more comprehensively rewarded. At the same time, because the losers know that they will share the spoils whether they make any dedicated and demanding effort or not, this policy encourages laziness, or, at any rate, less than complete effort on the part of any who prefer to take the way of least resistance in preference to one that is littered with challenges and calls for self-sacrifice. To reward indolence in this way encourages further indolence, until those at the receiving end of the share-outs begin to consider these their 'right', rather than what they are: an enforced extraction from the achievers of what they have honestly gained through the application of their time, talents and resources in the natural process of survival.

Of course one may feel sorry for those less fortunate: but this sorrow is not best expressed by what is, in effect, charity; that is, dealing only with the symptoms of the problem, not the cause. The achievers are in fact dealing with that cause, because, as a simple acknowledgement of reality, their achievements will have spin-offs for others. The person who makes a better mousetrap than his or her neighbour (who then goes to the wall) will find that the demand for those mousetraps will require him or her to employ others, not skilled in *designing* mousetraps, but able to produce them to a given design. Further back than this, you are helping to employ those involved in providing the wood for the wooden part of the mousetrap, and metal for the metal part. Further back still you are helping to employ those who tend the trees to be used for the wood, or mine the metal to be used in the trap. This in turn keeps in employment those who make the tools to cut the trees, and the machines to mine the metal. And so on almost *ad infinitum*. The number of people who are benefiting from one person's original idea for a mousetrap is inestimable. This being the case, why should a person be deprived of the incentive to continue putting a bright idea into practice? Altruism, given a free hand, will destroy the urge to be a pioneer, to break new ground, to create, or improve, or transform. It destroys initiative, removes motivation and puts a sodden blanket over basic human drives. Altruism makes eunuchs of us all.

We thus have a completely different image of society from that held by those who believe in the naturalness of altruism. There we had people divided into two camps by the luck of the draw: here we see the camps filled with, on the one hand, the forward-looking and forward-planning, hard-working, responsible, conscientious; and, on the other, the idle, the feckless, living only for the present and unwilling to make any sacrifice for the future, eating what they haven't worked for, spending what they haven't earned, enjoying the fruits of others' labours without even having the grace to feel grateful. The only way to shake people from their lethargy, so the proponents of this perspective believe, is to bring them to the realization that without achievement of some sort there can be no survival; that food is earned with the sweat of one's brow; that dollars don't grow on trees. It may mean a shock for many to have to come face to face with this reality, but it is a necessary shock if they are to confront nature as it always has been and, presumably, always will be. Those who don't pull their weight perish: the grasshopper will die as the ant survives.

For those who cannot pull their weight because of physical or mental misfortune (and these represent a small minority of those in receipt of public support) it may be possible to make special provision. But even this must be looked at with care: nature has no place for the infirm; at the very least we should be ensuring that we don't waste hard-earned resources in officiously keeping alive those who have played no part in the garnering of these resources. If this means an earlier drawing of the blinds for some than they might have hoped for, too bad. Just as the achieving of life on this planet was a chance in a trillion in the first place, so we must accept that, for every individual, life is a chancy business, full of flukes, and flops, and freaks. This is what nature is: to wish it otherwise is, as the word suggests, wishful thinking; to will it otherwise, and express this will in related action, is to express a death wish and the practice of genocide. Whenever the altruist's belief that he is his brother's keeper is put into practice, it leads to the mistaken belief, on the part of the one being altruized (to coin a word!) that he is his keeper's brother. This is no more true than it is for an ape in the zoo (it is social Darwinism, not Darwinism proper, that we are, after all, dealing with).

With these bald statements we are presented with two philosophies of life so diverging that any compromise between them is impossible. Most governments try first one approach, then the other, in the hope that in the long term some kind of balance will be achieved. Our perspective is not political but ontological, and from that perspective the basic point to make is that there is no way whereby one can demonstrate by the rational means of inquiry adopted generally in the Western world, that one of these approaches is 'right' and the other 'wrong'. Applying the analytical rules expressed by A. J. Ayer (quoted in Chapter 1) the whole issue must be acknowledged to be one that is not open to philosophical discussion, since no kind of verification is possible one way or the other.

EXISTENTIALISM

From the vantage-point of perspectives explored in the core of this book, there is, however, much to be said. For a start, following the emphases of existentialism, we can accept the fact that this is a real issue confronting us, one that is bound to affect the vast majority, if not all, of the citizens of any community, and therefore an issue about which we must be prepared to commit ourselves. For most of us, this commitment must be made from vantage-points which are well away from the mainstream of political decision-making, but each person can add a little weight to the pressure, in one direction or the other. Most people can find some outlet, even if it is only discussing the issue with friends and neighbours, for the view either that taxes should be lowered (and so provide less for the needy) or that they should be increased (with the intention of providing more). And at a general election the nation as a whole (as Britain did in 1987 when social Darwinism won hands down) can indicate its preference.

So, existentialism tells us that a decision must be made, and that any individual should be involved as far as possible in the process. It cannot say, any more than logical positivists can say, which of the two courses is the more 'reasonable'. But it can speak from the perspective of existence leading to the achievement of essence. We may here, I think, adapt Sartre's argument that any person's free choice, made on the basis of comprehensive knowledge of the facts of a situation, is likely to have implications not only for the chooser but for those around him or her. If my personal fulfilment, être-pour-soi, can be achieved only at the expense of the fulfilment of others (that is, if my pour-soi reduces others to en-soi) then I am deluding myself about my fulfilment. Consequently, from the existentialist perspective, the path seems to take me along the first of the two roads.

The same conclusion seems to follow if we view the problem from Buber's perspective and reflect on which approach makes for an I-thou as opposed to an I-it situation. It seems difficult to perceive how this can be at all possible under the umbrella of social Darwinism. Some may claim to have an I-thou affinity with their rivals as they transform them into their victims, but this appears to me to be possible only if you divorce your personal life from your operations in the community as a whole. Having made your rival bankrupt you could, I suppose, take on his mortgage for him, but this is as irrelevant to the central issue as are private donations to charity in a society which reduces overall its contributions to those in need. The second of the two social philosophies inevitably creates an 'us-them' society, which is nothing more than the plural of 'I-it'. The successful will have viewed the unsuccessful as subjects of exploitation, a means to their own personal ends, not as ends in themselves; if the successful had thought otherwise, the drive to succeed would have been at least modified and possibly destroyed altogether. Any other view would imply the abandonment of the entire underlying philosophy.

EASTERN PERSPECTIVES

Social Darwinism, whether under the name of monetarism, capitalism, market forces, or whatever euphemism may be introduced to replace any of these (though it is a sign of the times that people no longer feel the need to disguise these terms when outlining their values), is a wholehearted embrace of the Yang tendency. It is aggressive, assertive, exploitative; it is bold, creative and potent. Left unmodified or unbalanced it will bring civilization back inexorably to the jungle state from which, laboriously and over many millennia, the human species has been slowly dragging itself. The counter-balance to this Yang tendency is provided, according to the Chinese perspective, with the reflective, caring, compassionate Yin. The Yang tendency will make barons of the few, but will reduce the many to serfs. Under the Yin tendency, the fear of the many that they will always be mere pawns in the hands of the big operators will be removed. While they may never be successful (few pawns become queens) they can at least be sure that their lack of success will not lead to their being ignored or sacrificed in the name of some 'greater good'.

The ethos of a community brought about by this approach is one devoid of fear, or, at any rate, of fear that arises from the system itself. It is not an *equal* community in the sense that all share equally in its rewards: there will always be those whose share is above, or below, the mean of a community's resources: the Yang tendency which produces 'successful' people is being tempered, not destroyed, by the Yin. The result is the creation of a community which can at least begin to describe itself in terms of happiness, with the hands of the strong employed to lift up rather than beat down the weak. And this is no starry-eyed piece of idealism, as anti-liberals in the United States pretend: it is a description of communities which already exist, if not to the extent that some would wish. The idealism lies not in

contemplating the existence of *a few* communities who successfully balance
the Yin and the Yang, but in envisaging this on a world scale. Such a vision
reflects the greatest single development needed among human beings if the
unity of Being is to find expression in a world shared precariously by four
or five billion representatives. This must mean that the profit-making West
(and parts of the East too) must learn to share rather than to exploit. If it is
the case (and it is) that I cannot be happy if those in my immediate circle
are unhappy, then it needs only a broadening of the imagination to reflect
on this reality on a national, and finally on an international, scale.

All this is expressed in the Taoist philosophy, and in the Tao Te Ching.
'He who knows he has enough is rich' (Chapter 33) contrasts well with the
description of the West made by the economist J. K. Galbraith as having 'a
vested interest in euphoria'. To find the Tao is to realize one's unity with
all Being, and that includes all human beings. The divisiveness endemic in
social Darwinism is a consequence of ignoring the Way, and since the Tao
alone ultimately endures, is doomed to self-destruction. The hope which
the Tao presents lies in its way of harmony and co-operation, in which
the strong help the weak as a natural expression of their strength.

> Therefore the sage takes care of all men
> And abandons no one.
> He takes care of all things
> And abandons nothing.
>
> This is called 'following the light'.
>
> What is a good man?
> A teacher of a bad man.
> What is a bad man?
> A good man's charge.
> If the teacher is not respected,
> And the student not cared for,
> Confusion will arise, however clever one is.
> This is the crux of mystery.
>
> (op. cit., ch. 27)

This may be described as a philosophy of the middle way. It contrasts
starkly with Western materialism by its concern that those who can fend
for themselves should express concern for those who cannot (for we may
interpret 'good' and 'bad' as 'strong' and 'weak' in that passage). But it
also contrasts with the communist answer, which is simply, in the name
of the system, to replace the 'teacher' with 'the student' regardless of their
respective merits or demerits. The Taoist view (to quote from the New
Testament) is that 'unto whomsoever much is given, of him shall be much
required'. Taoism does not try to 'put down the mighty from their seats'

nor to send the rich 'empty away'. Rather, it views all, whether rich or poor, powerful or defenceless, as part of the same universal stream and therefore belonging together. By the Way of Tao, everybody is his brother's keeper and everybody's keeper is his brother, as these words suggest:

> Know the strength of a man,
> But keep a woman's care!
> Be the stream of the universe!
> Being the stream of the universe,
> Ever true and unswerving,
> Become as a little child once more.

> Know the white,
> But keep the black!
> Be an example to the world!
> Being an example to the world,
> Ever true and unwavering,
> Return to the infinite.

(Chapter 28)

The irony is that the Christian alternative to Taoism, while containing within its writings sentiments not dissimilar to these, has, on the whole, followed one of two false paths, both representative solely of the Yang tendency. On the one hand, and predominantly, it has been identified with the capitalist system; on the other, as expressed, for example, by the liberation theologians of Latin America, it has followed the path of communism and the view, expressed by Trotsky, that 'you can't make an omelette without breaking eggs'. One may have greater sympathy for this second way than the first, even though (or especially as) it has received constant criticism from Pope John Paul II throughout his Papacy; but it fails because its ontological perspective – its view, in particular, of human nature – is a false one as is that of Marxism. And before proceeding to reflect further on Taoist perspectives, we must look briefly at the last of the four Ms mentioned earlier.

## MARXISM

Some readers may view my somewhat dismissive statement about Marxism as inapposite, to say the least, in respect to a philosophy which has arguably influenced more people's lives than any other, certainly over the past century. The reason for this dismissal was nothing to do with its aim of sharing the world's resources more equably, for that aim is admirable. Nor am I here reacting, as I was earlier, to the determinism of its historical perspective, which I find both unproven and unrealistic. Rather, I am alienated from Marxism by its lack of any metaphysics and, in particular, of an understanding of ontology. In other words, its understanding of human nature – or, since that is a question-begging word, of human behaviour throughout history – contains some enormous lacunae (or blind spots).

Its fundamental error lies in its interpretation of human beings *en masse*, categorizing them all according to their social class, and commenting on them accordingly. We have on the one side, the capitalistic owners – the 'barons' mentioned earlier – who are viewed, quite simply, as the enemy, representative of an archaic economic system which historical processes are inexorably bringing to an end. On the other side are the exploited millions, waiting only for the removal of these overlords (by evolution or by revolution) in order to be able to give according to their ability. In the new, socialist order, it is proclaimed, there will be no classes, no 'us' and 'them' syndrome, but only, and gloriously, harmonious and benevolent co-operation between all, a universal state of I and thou.

This is an admirable but unfulfilled, and, by the methods it advocates, unfulfillable vision. Granted that there are many people at the lower levels of industrial society who are not contributing, because they are in no position to contribute, as much as they are capable of doing to the general weal; and granted the emergence of a society which enabled everyone, whatever their social backgrounds, to develop their fields of Being more comprehensively: it does not follow that a great many more will actually do so – or, in those countries where this philosophy has been put into practice, are actually doing so – than under the capitalist regimes. Marxism – as expressed by its practitioners – takes it as axiomatic that those who had power in the past achieved this because of privilege rather than on merit, and that those whose contribution was meagre were restricted only by underprivilege. In fact, as any unblinkered reading of social history will confirm, many people under the capitalist system reached the top by merit, and many were at the bottom because they were incapable of maintaining a more demanding position. (In the long run, the designations 'top' and 'bottom' in relation to value as persons are of course irrelevant and meaningless, as we shall see when discussing the Tao and education (p. 256); but that is another matter.) The word 'equal', when used in relation to human worth, as in 'all men are equal' or 'all are born equal', is in fact either verifiably false or so bland a statement that it says nothing, like a political candidate who fights for 'a better deal for all'. That this is the case is illustrated by the fact that in communist countries (which have presumably attempted to practise at least a nuance of Marxism) the old hierarchical differences between classes have not changed *per se*; only the players have changed. Some who previously looked on themselves as having been born to rule have had to think again (if they still had heads to think with), and others who had previously entertained no hope of fulfilling themselves have been given the means of doing this. But differences in status still remain and, with them, variations in the amount of respect accorded to people possessing these statuses. There may be changing opinions about which roles should be highly respected and which not; but categories, and grades, and differentiations between people remain, as one believes they will always remain. In other words, while, in many countries, the cast has been changed on the national stage, the plot remains the same.

What Marxism achieves is to exchange one form of I-it for another. It is difficult to see how things could be otherwise in a philosophical perspective which is ontologically illiterate; and until Marxism recognizes the total inadequacy of a materialist philosophy and begins, however tentatively, to take a few steps towards a metaphysical appreciation of human beings, it will continue, as it always has continued, to speak of people only in terms with which the most die-hard monetarist would agree: in the beginning was avarice; greed rules, OK. Marx led astray all those who swallow his teaching whole because he was blind to one fundamental reality about his fellows: you can, by changing the externals, take people out of the cesspit; but the process by which the cesspit may be taken out of *them* is one which must emanate from within people themselves. Confucius stated this thousands of years before Marx, in an age of greater inequalities and injustices than ever Marx saw. But, more even than Confucius, Lao Tsu recognized this and expressed it in his Taoist philosophy.

## THE ANTIDOTE TO THE FOUR Ms

The prime philosophical consideration for anyone stumbling along the labyrinthine path of the 'brother's keeper' situation (a path which no one can avoid: to be is to be moral) seems to me to be the recognition that everyone is, at least potentially, *a sharer in the Tao*. A remarkable change can occur in a person, once the understanding of this reaches an I-thou, rather than stagnating at an I-it, basis. From the latter perspective one may know *that* this may be the case, and one may even fantasize about how the appreciation of this truth might destroy false images and harmonize relationships within society; but at this level the issue remains largely academic, akin to, and meriting the same rebukes as, Kierkegaard's aesthetes. One may indulge oneself in the most high-flown of fancies about how, under some kind of Taoist umbrella, society might be transformed: and then go home and browbeat one's family, exploit the meek and ignore the poor.

It is possible, however, to go beyond this casual, bemused commitment of oneself to the Tao to one of being totally possessed by the idea on an I-thou basis. When this happens, the image of one's fellows is transformed from that of people 'out there', conveniently labelled for quick identification under such gradings as 'poor', 'unemployed', 'single parent', 'black', 'city type', 'red', 'liberal' and so on, and instead one sees beyond these labels to the person behind them. Many of them may have radically different life-styles from one's own, and may hold values quite at variance with those by which one lives, yet one's relationship with them can be more real – even if this means no more than that *some* kind of relationship is got off the ground – by saying to oneself: whatever the Tao means, or may mean, to me, it means, or may mean, the same to this person.

We have seen how this might work out in relation to the social divisions in our communities. It can also provide the direction whereby other barriers, detrimental to the community's health, happiness, fulfilment, and perhaps even survival, may be broken down. These barriers arise, as the word suggests, even when used metaphorically, through the desire to divide oneself from anyone who is in any way different from oneself; we have seen this in relation to differences of class, but it happens on the basis of language, creed, or colour. It is appallingly easy to participate in what is to the existentialists the greatest of all sins: treating people according to one's image of them, or according to the label one puts on them – *êtres-en-soi* – rather than as authentic persons who are beings-for-themselves. National characteristics, so-called, are a supreme example of the belittling process that thus occurs. Jokes based on these alleged characteristics keep many a comedian in business – the humourless German, the randy Frenchman, the boasting American, the pompous Englishman, the philistine Australian, the cowardly Italian, and so on – but to treat people according to this ingrained national image of them must destroy any possibility of the creation of a real relationship, and help to increase international discord. This is of course especially true in the sphere of race relations; a whole dissertation could in fact be written on the theme 'The Tao and Race'.

## THE TAO AND NATURE

Accepting that all that exists shares with human beings the gift of Being, what, from the Taoist perspective, should be one's attitude to nature? From one perspective, Tennyson's description of it as 'red in tooth and claw' is valid; but the Taoist view looks beyond these surface **phenomena** to the underlying **noumena**, the thing-in-itself. At that level, its view of nature reflects an insight which Newton, in his *Opticks*, was later to express with great precision: 'Nature is very consonant and conformable with herself.' This implies, at the very least, that nature must be accorded the same respect as may be expected by human beings. It must be allowed to be, and this means to be true to its own Being. It is no more to be exploited, treated as a means to an end rather than an end in itself, than are human beings.

Many commonly accepted practices in relation to animals become by this test unacceptable. Caging animals for the pleasure of human spectators, or hunting them in order to indulge the blood lust, using them merely to indulge one's greed or one's vanity: all these practices, and many more, are acts of exploitation of lower species by the highest. And just as among human beings some will attain positions of *responsibility* over and for others which should be wielded, according to the Confucian version of the Tao (and as the word suggests), *responsibly*, that is to say, with due regard to the happiness and self-fulfilment of the many who are thereby dependent on the few: so we, in our relationship with animals, must bear this responsibility in mind. There may be the case for the removal of vermin (because they spread disease, or are a special danger to the lives of others, for example) as there may be the case for the removal of the human equivalent (homicidal maniacs, psychopaths and so on): but to gain pleasure from other creatures' misery must be seen in the same light as its equivalent among human beings, where those who derive pleasure from causing others pain are labelled sadists and locked away in mental asylums.

This may not seem an over-bold statement to make, since I am avoiding the controversial issues of using animals in medical research and breeding them for human consumption. Aren't both of these examples of the kind of exploitation I'm rejecting? To enter fully into this discussion would mean getting into deep water, and would need more space than is either possible or justifiable in this book. I have recorded my continuing questions on these issues in an earlier book, *Living Philosophy* (pp. 302–3), and anyone consulting these pages will recognize that, on the whole, I remain unconvinced by the assertions of animal rights enthusiasts on these issues. From the Taoist perspective, one has to view Being as a whole; within the natural world, the predator–prey syndrome is universal, and I view the eating of animal flesh by human beings as a link-up with that syndrome. (The question of the methods of husbandry for those to be slaughtered, and the methods of slaughtering, are discrete issues with which I should probably agree with most animal rights defenders.) Equally, if it is the case – and I remain to be convinced that it is not – that many human beings have been given extra life, and alleviated frrom suffering, as a direct result of laboratory experiments on animals, this seems to me to be the kind of co-operative harmony which is reflected throughout the whole of nature. Animals, of course, don't suffer willingly in this cause, but I wonder how manyy soldiers fighting the Nazis suffered and died *willingly*. It is with this perspective that I view experiments on animals: as part of the continuous struggle, which continuously requires sacrifices, for the greater good; or, to put it in ontological terms (and because the phrase 'the ggreater good' has regularly been the excuse for gross inhumanity of various sorts), while some fields of Being must be put at risk for the sake of many other fields, Being endures.

The examples I have just discussed concern treatment of living creatures for the benefit of others (meaning meeting other people's needs rather than just satisfying their wants). The type of exploitation which is rightly coming more stringently under the microscope is the exploitation of nature by the use of chemicals, nuclear waste, and other destroyers of both the earth and its atmosphere. Ecologists have for decades been reminding us that this earth should be viewed as a spaceship, an interrelated and interdependent entity, and that the neglect or abuse of a part will ultimately be catastrophic for the whole. The kinds of perspectives offered by these ecologists seem to me basic in our perception of both the validity and the practicality of Taoism. We harm nature at our cost because the Tao is indivisible. Expressed in a different, but parallel, way, our relationship with nature should be at an I-thou, not an I-it, level. This is the oneness of Tao.

## I-THOU AND EDUCATION

There is a school of thought about education which views it as no more than a tool of the rat race (though why rats should be so maligned in this phrase is beyond me) and existing only to further the aims of the great M of materialism. This school's educational philosophy is summed up in terms of qualifications, a tangible substance that can be *possessed* and used in the market-place. If you have education, you will succeed in that arena, and any educational pursuits which don't prepare the student for it must be downgraded, if not totally eliminated.

This is an I-it view of education. It makes of education an objective entity, varying in size and degree (no pun intended) but measurable and assessable in an easily identifiable way.

Against this materialistic approach to education is one which relates to the I-thou perspective. Here, education is viewed not as a commodity but as an essential part of the *becoming* aspect of Being. It is not some *thing* which can be held aloft for all to verify, or an event which can be identified and described as having occurred at a certain time and place; it is an *approach to living* which is one of constantly removing blinkers from a person's field of vision. It is a process of continuous growth, not just (or even primarily) in the academic field but in every facet of Being, including the emotions, the imagination, the feelings, the ability to empathize with others, and so on. From this vantage-point the comment 'She is ignorant' could justly be made of a woman with a string of degrees measuring an arm's length; and a man whose qualifications have taken him to the top of his career ladder and to every quarter of the globe could still be described as small-minded, sexist, or racist. To be educated, in terms of I-thou, is not (as on the I-it perspective) to have 'arrived' but, in the immortal words of Richard Peters, 'to travel with a different view'. Just as on the broader ontological front it is impossible to separate Being from the Ground of Being, Atman from Brahman, the individual from the Tao, so, within these more circumscribed limits, education and the one being educated are one. Such a person would never, in fact, describe him- or herself as being educated because that would be a misrepresentation of a continuous, never-ceasing process. In ontological terms the person might speak of being simply absorbed in the unending journey of exploration and discovery which is Being-becoming. This can be fostered, of course, in educational institutions, but it is no more dependent on these than are the development of the imagination or the emotions. And many of our institutions, as Ivan Illich has forthrightly stated, (*Deschooling Society*) are a positive barrier to this journey.

If there were space, we could reflect on many more social, moral and political issues in the light of the ontological perspective arrived at in this book. (Some other examples are to be found in case studies 22 and 23.) I hope that these few examples indicate the total relevance to practical issues which both the Taoist philosophy and the existentialism of I-thou provide. The realization that they can be guides amid the diverging, baffling claims of the multitude of life's interests can enable anyone willing to commit him- or herself to this approach to pass beyond Kierkegaard's aesthete, through the ethical stance, to that of his religious person making an existentialist commitment to living.

To be is to be involved: and this involvement in no way demands the abandonment of Taoist ontology. What this implies from a more personal angle I wish now finally to explore.

*Case study 26*
*The worship of Mammon*

*Mamona*, from which our English word is derived, was the Aramaic word for riches (Aramaic was the original language of the Hebrews, and the source language of the Old Testament). Most religions and philosophies of the world have uttered warnings about the consequences of making Mammon one's god: that the pursuit of material gain endangers (and, according to some schools, totally destroys) the quest for other, non–monetary and intangible values.

The purpose of this case study is three-fold.

(1) To make some kind of assessment of the extent to which Western culture has become a Mammon-worshipping culture.

(2) To assess the extent to which you have been, or might be, seduced by the lure of possessions. Bear in mind how easy it is to be hyper–critical about this. (I have known many students who have been unequivocal in denouncing material rewards while they were too hard up to buy philosophy textbooks, but who changed their tune years later when they were established and the cash began to flow their way.)

(3) To decide whether the love of money is, in St Paul's words, 'the root of all evil' (1 Timothy 6:10).

Ponder first on the following quotations. The wide range of sentiments about wealth which they express should at least indicate that these are not issues to be glibly resolved.

(1)   Wealth is like sea water; the more we drink, the thirstier we become; and the same is true of fame. (Schopenhauer)

(2)   We have among us a class of Mammon worshippers, whose one test of conservatism or radicalism is the attitude one takes with respect to accumulated wealth. Whatever tends to preserve the wealth of the wealthy is called conservatism, and whatever favours anything else, no matter what, they call socialism. (Richard T. Ely)

(3)   . . . the idea, which is popular with rich men, that industrial disputes would disappear if only the output of wealth were doubled, and everyone were twice as well off, not only is refuted by all practical experience, but is in its very nature founded upon an illusion. For the question is not one of amounts but of proportions. (R.H. Tawney)

(4)   If a rich man is proud of his wealth, he should not be praised until it is known how he employs it. (Socrates)

(5)   I have no complex about wealth. I have worked hard for my money, producing things people need. I believe that the able industrial leader who creates wealth and employment is more worthy of historical notice than politicians or soldiers. (J. Paul Getty)

(6)   The greater the wealth the thicker will be the dirt. This indubitably describes a tendency of our time. (J. K. Galbraith)

(7)   There are few ways in which a man can be more innocently employed than in getting money. (Samuel Johnson)

(8)   Money is the symbol of duty, it is the sacrement of having done for mankind that which mankind wanted. (Samuel Butler)

(9)   If you make money your god, it will plague you like the devil. (Henry Fielding)

(10)  It is physically impossible for a well-educated, intellectual, or brave man to make money the chief object of his thoughts. (John Ruskin)

(11)  If you would know what the Lord God thinks of money, you have only to look at those to whom he gives it. (Maurice Baring)

(12)  It's a kind of spiritual snobbery that makes people think they can be happy without money. (Albert Camus)

(13)  When it is a question of money, everybody is of the same religion. (Voltaire)

(14)  Business, you know, may bring money, but friendship hardly every does. (Jane Austin)

(15)  If possible honestly, if not, somehow, make money. (Horace)

(16)  He must have killed a lot of men to have made so much money. (Moliere)

(17)  We haven't the money so we've got to think. (Lord Rutherford)

(18)  Where large sums of money are concerned, it is advisable to trust nobody. (Agatha Christie)

(19)  Money, it turned out, was exactly like sex , you thought of nothing else if you didn't have it and thought of other things if you did. (James Baldwin)

(20)  If a man runs after money, he's money mad; if he keeps it, he's a capitalist; if he spends it, he's a playboy; if he doesn't get it, he's a ne'er-do-well; if he doesn't try to get it, he lacks ambition. If he gets it without working for it, he's a parasite; and if he accumulates it after a lifetime of hard work, people call him a fool who never got anything out of life. (Vic Oliver)

(21)  Money doesn't always bring happiness. People with ten million dollars are no happier than people with nine million dollars. (Hobart Brown)

Now take a look at these two comments, quoted in the British press, on, in the first place, the increasing use of drugs in Britain and, in the second, the increase in fear of violence among the people (both of them issues which could inspire articles almost anywhere else in the world, one fears).

This pattern will certainly be repeated unless the cause of it all is faced – the incentive to turn to drugs to give lives that have become meaningless a fillip of chemically-induced excitement. The spiritual sickness at the core of our society, which makes drugs so inviting, invades all classes: it is there in the parties of the opulent young and in the street-corner huddles of unemployed youth. The idle black does not know where life is leading nor does the young stock exchange high flier tearing his energies to pieces for an obscenely high salary. Both are caught up in a sense of pointlessness. We are all caught up in this, after years in which our country has stood for nothing more exalted than raw self-interest.

In the Sixties, working people in my town were relatively no worse off than today. They had fridges and washing machines then. They were affluent. Today, they've not changed materially, but their attitudes have. Greed has become acceptable. The sense of community has gone. In those days, you could walk down behind the backs of houses, but now they're barred off with gates. Everyone commutes by day and has got a dog to protect them at night. They're locked in, each within their own fortress.

A lengthier analysis of the way monetary values are overtaking other values even in higher education was made in 1988 by a *Guardian* columnist, Melanie Phillips. The following extracts give the gist of her argument:

The Government is, by its own proud boast, in the business of changing attitudes. It is also wholly committed to the enterprise culture, the flourishing of small businesses and the making of money, objectives which it feels the universities have, in their snobbish, otherworldly way, done their best to frustrate. The universities and polytechnics must perforce mend their ways. Open minds are therefore very much not the flavour of the decade. Approved ideologies are in favour instead, particularly if they promote the pursuit of profit.

Ms Phillips then indicates how in practice this has brought about change in the academic institutions. In particular, it has brought about a massive reduction in the staffing of non-vocational courses, such as the arts and social sciences; high among those to suffer is philosophy, which has seen a reduction of 25 per cent in its teaching staff, despite an increase of over 20 per cent in those applying to study the subject. She continues:

A university without a philosophy department is like a cake without eggs. It exists, but only as an enfeebled version of what it should be, lacking an essential binding element that gives it body and identity. Universities incorporate a wide range of disciplines which are not simply co-terminous but influence or strike sparks off each other. They also embody a commitment to the theoretical dimension of research. Philosophy vitally underpins these two distinctive aspects of a university. It is relevant across the academic spectrum, dealing as it does with reasoning techniques and providing the theoretical underpinning across the range of arts and sciences. More than any other discipline, philosophy binds the disparate elements of a university into a coherent whole.

Ms Phillips then discusses the mixed reactions of differing university departments to this call to be enterprising. Many rejoice in the cash rewards which will follow for those who attain this status; others see it as the abandonment of the true meaning of education, leading to a policy of indoctrination rather than exploration. She concludes:

As philosophers ponder how on earth they are supposed to promote the enterprise economy within their teaching of Plato and Aristotle, they may well conclude that the meaning of meaning no longer means as much as the meaning of money. Or, to paraphrase one of the Conservative Party's greatest sages, Adam Smith, philosophy is now a project altogether unfit for a nation of shopkeepers.

It is tempting to pursue a fuller inquiry into the meaning of education, but our purpose is to assess how highly we rank money in our own chain of hierarchies. The following questions and/or hypotheticals should, if tackled with total honesty, give you some chance of discovering where your own priorities lie.

(1) 'Every man has his price' (and women too, presumably). Is there anything you would not do for money – whatever the amount? For instance:

publicly deny something you believe deeply
give up a job you enjoy for one you know you'll hate
exchange your comfortable home environment for the rat race of an inner city
give up certain friends because you're warned they will hamper your career
tone down any anti-establishment feelings you may hold
betray a secret which will deeply embarrass the person who gave it you in strictest confidence
betray your country
betray your firm
alter your accent because you're told it will be a drawback to material success
give up writing poetry and take up writing Mills & Boon stories
give up philosophy and take up accountancy/estate management/etc.

Don't forget: we're not talking peanuts, but enough money to be secure for the rest of your life.

(2) The British Prime Minister, Mrs Thatcher, on an occasion when she entered the field of biblical interpretation, accepted the view of one of her ministers that the basic virtue of the Good Samaritan was that he had the wherewithal to look after the man fallen among thieves. Even if you reject this as the gravamen of the parable, do you think it is right that there's nothing wrong with money *per se*? ('Better nouveau riche than never riche' as an American friend assured me.)

(3) If you agree that it is the love of money rather than money itself which is the root of all evil, how do you think a rich person sets about not loving money?

(4) The emphases which have come across from the Eastern philosophies reviewed in this book run completely counter to the view that money should be high on anyone's list of priorities. If you agree about this, how do you think other values can be put across to children from an early age? Thinking particularly of the argument put forward by Melanie Phillips, do you think that the sphere of education is losing the means of doing this because, whether by inclination or political

and economic pressure, it is reducing its activities to one solely of
providing the skills which can be turned into money?

(5)  'He knows the cost of everything and the value of nothing' (Oscar
Wilde). What do you think this means? Do you think it is becoming
more, or less, true of people around you today?

(6)  How far do you think the theistic religions in particular have paved
the way to a materialistic philosophy of life? (cf. the historical link
between Christianity and the rise – and continuation – of capitalism;
and, particularly in the United States, the enormous number of very
wealthy business people who belong to fundamentalist religious sects
and denominations; and the fact that Judaism throughout history does
not seem to have discouraged the accumulation and manipulation of
material wealth.)

(7)  In a society increasingly controlled by 'market forces' do you think
it inevitable that compassion will be exploited for monetary gain, as
in the advertisement?

(8)  If people are willing to pay for a particular service, however abhorrent
it may seem to some, is there any conclusive reason why they should
not be allowed to go ahead? For example:
    sex on a commercial basis
    selling a (superfluous) kidney
    becoming a surrogate mother
    selling corpses of loved ones for medical research
    selling sperm for artificial insemination
    selling an eye to pay off the mortgage.

Since no third party is being exploited in any of the above transactions
(is there?) does society need to make them illegal? Could these not
be seen as unusual but praiseworthy examples of the enterprise
culture?

Those who believe that the making of money brings out the best in
a person often quote as their mentor the so-called prophetess of heroic
selfishness, Ayn Rand. She was a Russian émigrée to the United States
(1905–82) who founded the philosophy of objectivism, which expresses
the belief that the aim in life is to rise above one's fellows through strength
of character expressed in undiluted selfishness. Many of President Reagan's
closest advisers admired her, as did the large numbers of business persons
whom she addressed throughout the United States. How far do you
think it inevitable that that administration, representatives of what has
been called the 'Me Decade', should welcome philosophical backing for
the neglect of society's weaker representatives in the name of her style of

heroism? How far do you think that the competition which accompanies the worship of Mammon is nearer the heart of the evolutionary process than is co-operation? Is the all-American dream of 'from rags to riches' a viable philosophy for a large society in which, purely logistically, not all can be successful? What is the Taoist perspective on the philosophy of 'every man (or woman – but one tends to think particularly of the male in this connection, interestingly enough) for himself'?

Here, finally, is part of a letter I wrote to a national newspaper in reply to a suggestion that there was no principle to justify the law whereby childless (perhaps poor) parents should be compelled, through their taxes, to give aid to parents (sometimes rich).

> The basic reason why it is right for childless people to subsidise those who choose to have children (or don't choose, as the case may be) is that the children of any family belong not just to that family but to the nation and ultimately to the race as a whole. Mr G speaks of children as though they fell into the category of special luxuries, like a second home or a third car, rather than the hope for and insurance of the future.

> Of course the example he quotes – poor childless people supporting rich people with children – seems unfair, but it illustrates neither the philosophy that underlies child benefit, nor the general pattern in practice. Maybe the time will come when children will have to fight for their own survival, but meanwhile our species, like every other species on this planet, cares for its young. This is both natural and commonsensical: as a species we are indivisible, and this evolutionary fact requires that adults as a whole care for infants as a whole – including those that are not their personal offspring.

> If Mr G finds this to be unprincipled, let him reflect on this: the children he is presently, however reluctantly, supporting will be those who will be supporting him in his old age with his state pension (unless this has disappeared down the market, along with other state benefits). If his views had dominated the evolutionary process and there had been no co-operation between old and young, strong and weak, the race would not have been started, let alone survived.

(1) How do you react to the suggestion that, in however remote a way, you are responsible for the world's infants?

(2) With overcrowding as a problem of crisis proportions on this planet, should not child benefit apply for, say, only the first two children born in any family?

(3) How far does the final paragraph defeat the earlier argument by suggesting that one only gives now in order to get later?

(4)   Is the co-operation between the generations illustrated in the argument at all akin to the Taoist perspective of the Way, to which we all belong?

(5)   How far does the evolutionary process as a whole support the Taoist view of life, nature and the universe? Taoism speaks of letting things be, but Tennyson describes nature as 'red in tooth and claw': is one of these an unreal perspective?

*Footnote*: if you agree with the view that material possession should not rank highly in the priorities of a worthwhile life, how far do you in practice express this view? In particular, which causes, or needy groups, do you support (or would you support if you had the money) on a regular basis? cf. John Wesley on money:

Earn all you can; save all you can; give all you can.

What would Buddha have said about this? Or Sartre? What do *you* think?

## Case study 27
### Drugs and the Fourth State

In his book *The Doors of Perception*, Aldous Huxley describes his experiences while under the influence of the drug mescalin. This is a hallucinatory drug, like LSD, and, according to Huxley and others, is non-addictive. You may wish to read Huxley's description for yourself, so that you will appreciate how greatly heightened were all his perceptive powers, and how he came to look on ordinary awareness as at a lower level than that of the drug-induced state. As a believer in the doctrines of Advaita Vedanta, he argued that this induced experience was akin to that of the Fourth State, and that this drug provided a speedier way of achieving this state than could be found through, for example, long periods of meditation. (He did not deny the worth of meditation, but simply argued that what meditation was seeking to achieve over – inevitably – a long period of time was readily available through this physically and mentally harmless drug.)

   The use of drugs to produce heightened perception has been a practice for millennia. It seems for instance beyond question that many of the vivid and colourful images of the Old Testament prophets (such as Ezekiel's vision of the valley of dry bones in Chapter 37) were originally spoken in a drug-induced state – perhaps 'the sacred mushroom' as it is often described. The prophecies are none the less valid because of this, and the same is true of Huxley's descriptions of his 'awakened' state. What we need to discuss, then, is the validity not of the goal but of the means of arrival. And on this, another Westerner who embraced the Eastern idea of the awakened state, Arthur Koestler, made an unambiguous statement when interviewed on the matter on BBC television. He expressed his total sympathy with the end that Huxley had in view, but described his proposals as an unnatural attempt to go too far too fast. The insights and experiences that Huxley had gained at the end of a needle were, Koestler suggested, the kind that should be gained only gradually, so that people should learn and grow by intermediate steps, building on what had been previously achieved, and so more comprehensively prepared for the grand awakening if and when this happened. To do otherwise, he suggested, is like taking a plane from Heathrow in the middle of a British winter, and being set down two hours later in the warm luxuriousness of a Mediterranean resort: better to travel slowly, adjust gradually, and thus, so to speak, *grow into* the new climate.

You may wish to debate this issue with friends or colleagues, starting off with general questions such as the following:

(1) Is the inducing of a chemical change in the brain unnatural? What is meant by 'unnatural'?

(2) Is the change brought about by hallucinatory drugs 'artificial'? What do you mean by 'artificial'? Is any art produced under such influence 'artificial'? Are irrational acts of bravery, produced, as we now know, by the excessive (and unnatural?) pumping of adrenalin into the system, artificial?

(3) Do you prefer to approach the issue from a different perspective: that the awakened state, by whatever term it be described, is like a good wine – something to be appreciated and savoured slowly, not gulped rapidly? Or, using a different analogy, that it is a state to be gained only after prolonged effort like appreciating the peaks of (say) Snowdon, the highest mountain in Wales, after the travails of the climb, rather than the easy ascent by rail?

(4) Do you find the whole association between the ontological views we have considered, and the taking of drugs, to be absurd? If so, why?

*Case study 28*
*Yoga*
*(contributed by Ananda Shakti)*

Yoga is an ancient philosophy and a science of life, with its roots way back in the mists of time. It is mentioned in the oldest known literature of mankind, the Vedas, which are full of spiritual wisdom. Archaeological excavations made in Pakistan have unearthed many statues of Lord Shiva and Parvati his wife, performing different yoga postures. These came from the ruins of dwellings of those who lived in the Indus valley in the pre-Vedic age, before the Aryan civilization began to flourish. At this time, when men were reaching out to explore the world around them, there were those who went to live alone in the mountains and forests, and explored the world within themselves. They became the rishis and sages of that time, wandering teachers who passed on to those drawn to them the experiential wisdom they had gained. Yoga means the experience of unity or oneness with your inner being. It was out of their own experience of this unity that the teaching came.

In the Yoga Sutras of Patanjali, written more than 300 years BC, we read:

Yoga is the settling of the mind into silence. When the mind has settled, we are established in our essential nature which is unbounded Consciousness. Our essential nature is usually overshadowed by the activity of the mind.

In order to be able to settle the mind into silence, it was necessary to sit in one position without discomfort for extended lengths of time, as in meditation. It was for this purpose that the physical postures, the asanas, of yoga were developed.

The Yogis who developed the yoga postures and techniques were living very close to nature, not only observing themselves but studying the animals in the forest. Throughout the centuries, the postures they devised have been modified and reduced in number so that there is knowledge of a very natural system for maintaining a supple and healthy body, and effectively preventing and curing disease. In the Svetasvatara Upanishad, it is said that disease and old age do not come to the Yogi whose body is supple and healthy and whose mind has been made pure by the practice of yoga.

During the past twenty years, the benefits of yoga have been increasingly recognized in the West, particularly in relation to management of stress. It is now seen as a practical way to work towards physical well-being, mental balance and clarity, and spiritual growth. There are many paths of yoga. Because it is based on the experience of inner exploration and self-awareness of people of different personalities and temperaments, there is a path to suit every seeker. You can follow your path as far as you choose. *You can never fail at yoga.* Every practice, every experience, is a step on the way. The path takes you from where you are to discover what you are.

Hatha Yoga is the usual starting-place. This is the yoga of physical health, which combines asanas, or postures, with pranayama, the control of the breath. To this are added kriyas, which are movements repeated rhythmically, and mudras, which allow the practitioner to develop awareness of the currents of vital energy within the body, and direct them at will.

The postures work systematically on every part of the body. The spine is kept supple and strong. Through alternate stretching and contracting, the muscles are toned, and so direct vital energy to the organs of the body. Many postures actually massage the internal organs, helping them to perform better. The heart is strengthened and circulation is improved. The glands are stimulated, and the network of nerves branching out from the spinal column is strengthened and activated. In the upside-down postures, blood flows easily back to the heart and nourishes the cells of the brain. The sympathetic and para-sympathetic nervous systems of the body are brought into balance, actively helping the immune system. According to Sanskrit texts, the word *Hatha* is divided into two syllables, *Ha* meaning sun, or positive energy, and *Tha* meaning moon, or negative energy. When the two forces join and work together in harmony, the two currents cause complete equilibrium and balance of body and mind. (See question 3 at the end of this section.)

The yoga postures are also a necessary step on the spiritual path. Apart from giving the body a firm and steady seat from which to withdraw from body awareness and move to meditation and enlightenment, the postures themselves can be used for meditation and psychic purification.

Raja Yoga, the royal path to enlightenment, was outlined by Patanjali in his sutras (see text, pp. 174–5):

There are eight limbs of Yoga.
Yama – the laws of life.
Hiyama – the rules for living.
Asana – the physical postures.
Pranayama – rhythmic control of the breath.
Pratyahara – withdrawal of the mind from the dominion of the senses.
Dharana – concentration, steadiness of mind.
Dhyana – meditation.
Samadhi – the settled mind – enlightenment – the Superconscious state.

Yama – the laws of life – are five:
Non-violence, truthfulness, integrity, spiritual conduct and non-attachment.
These laws are universal. Unaffected by time, place, birth or circumstance, together they constitute the 'Great Law of Life'.

Niyama – the rules for living – are five:
Simplicity, contentment, purification, refinement, surrender to the Lord.

For those whose minds are serene and pure, and who have learnt to concentrate and control their minds, Raja Yoga is the path to take. But for many people this is extremely difficult. For those with aggressively active minds, who cannot withdraw the mind from the sense organs, or bring the mind to a still point, there are other paths to follow. Kriya Yoga could be the way. In Kriya Yoga the practices are designed in such a way that they begin by influencing the body, then the nervous system, and finally consciousness. Yoga Nidra is a systematic method of inducing complete physical, mental and emotional relaxation. During the practice of Yoga Nidra, one appears to be asleep, but the consciousness is functioning at a deeper level of awareness and contact with the subconscious and unconscious dimensions occurs spontaneously.

There are other paths too. Jnana Yoga is the yoga of knowledge, Karma Yoga is the yoga of service, Bhakti Yoga is the yoga of devotion, and Mantra Yoga is the yoga of recitation of sacred words, usually in Sanskrit. Chanting Sanskrit has an extraordinarily powerful effect upon the body and the mind. The vibrations caused by intoning the sounds touch every cell of the body and awaken dormant centres of the brain. In India, young thugs have been given the choice of prison for six months, or Sanskrit classes for a year. They choose the lessons, and after a year of daily chanting they have become totally different people with the characteristics of gentle philosophers.

Yoga teaches that man possesses five bodies: the Physical Body, the Vital Body, the Memory and Conscious Body, the Superconscious Mind Body and the Cosmic Body. If these bodies are not properly aligned with each other, then depression, disease and accidents occur. Slow deep breathing helps the balance to be maintained.

Modern science, with its latest discoveries, helps us to understand that

> the body is really a shimmering sea of energetic movement, an energy dance, a web of interconnection.

These words were written by John Davidson in his book *The Web of Life* in which he aims to establish a synthesis between ancient mystic philosophies and modern science.

Over the centuries, yoga has produced many teachers, who, having turned their awareness inward, have reached the state of Self-Realization. They have left their teachings and their practices for us to follow.

On the first page of his book *Meditations*, Swami Satyananda Saraswati dedicates his book

> To all those who descended and then left, both known and unknown, who have created, developed and mastered the tantric and yogic sciences, thereby giving to mankind the gift of light, the tools which can aid in the task of human evolution.

The list begins with 'Lords Brahma, Vishnu and Shiva' and includes 'Abraham, Moses and the compilers of the Kabbala, Jesus, the Essenes, the Christian saints, Mohammed and the Sufis, the mystical Mayans, Zoroaster, Lord Buddha, Kabir, Patanjali' and ends with Swami Sivananda of Rishikesh – who is still teaching in India today.

Questions for reflection and discussion:

(1) It has been suggested that, in one system or set of practices, yoga brings wholeness to a person in a way not found in other 'health-giving' pursuits. For example, psychoanalysis tackles the subconscious; bodily fitness exercises tackle the physical; academic exercises, the mental: but yoga brings all these together as parallel expressions of the person, none able to be without the others. How sound a view do you take this to be, and what do you think are the implications of accepting it?

(2) Do you think that much of the value of yoga lies in its having no presuppositions about the nature of the numinous – that is, it is non-committal about the existence of God?

(3) What parallels do you recognize in the above outline with the Taoist philosophy of Yin and Yang? How far do you view the two schools of thought as differently expressed but basically similar views on the nature of Being?

(4) Why do you think that both schools originated in the East rather than the West? If they were widely followed or practised in the West, can you name any areas of Western life, culture and beliefs where you would expect changes to occur?

(5) Should yoga be taught in Western schools? If you say yes to this, what other subject should be reduced (or perhaps eliminated) in order to make room for it?

(6) Should men in prison for violence be taught to chant?

Here are two exercises to start you in Yoga.

(A) STAND, BREATHE AND STRETCH

Stand with your feet a little apart, arms by your sides, body well balanced. Breathe through your nose, and for a few moments tune in to yourself, watching the rhythm of your natural breath. Breathe in deeply, drawing life force and vitality into you. Breathe out tension and frustration and anxiety. Relax your tummy muscles and direct the air deep down to the lower part of your lungs. Feel your tummy expand as you breathe in. Tighten your tummy muscles as you breathe out. Concentrate on expelling as much air as possible. Start to move your arms up sideways as you breathe in, and lower them as you breathe out. Become aware of your body and the sensations of movement. As you breathe in, bring the arms up to touch overhead. Hold for a few moments with the lungs full, then slowly lower the arms, palms facing down. The arms should reach your sides as you complete exhalation. Repeat this several times, being aware of the feeling of fullness and the feeling of depletion. See how in the natural rhythm one follows the other. Be aware that life itself consists of the same duality. Happiness and sadness, hope and anxiety, friendship and loneliness, good health and illness, life and death: whatever we experience, deep within it lies the potential for the opposite.

Then lie and relax. Within your mind, be the observer, the witness of your own life, noting the dualities that have been experienced by you over the past few days.

### (B) CANDLE-GAZING

Place a lighted candle approximately a metre (3 feet) in front of you, preferably at eye level. Sit comfortably and close your eyes. Be aware of your body, adjusting your position as you feel steady and still. Open your eyes and gaze directly at the flame for two or three minutes, eyes wide open, but without strain. Close your eyes and put the palms of your hands over them. Visualize the after-image of the flame. Concentrate on the image and do not let it wander or disappear. Fix your mind completely on the image of the flame and let no thoughts distract you. After a couple of minutes, open your eyes and relax. Repeat this procedure for as long as you have time. This exercise develops powers of concentration and memory and prepares the mind for meditation.

# 10 Epilogue:
## living with paradoxes

Life is an amalgam of inconsistencies and those who try to make it otherwise are either foolish or dangerous people. The foolish person tries to avoid inconsistency by wearing blinkers, or, more radically, spectacles which give him or her tunnel vision. Life for such people is simple because they keep it that way, remaining secure with a handful of long-standing friends, a fixed and regular routine, a limited number of ideas and convictions. Not for them are the agonizings of those who have somehow to establish priorities in the fulfilment of differing duties, or contend with rival claimants on their time; more fundamentally, not to them comes the effort of looking new ideas squarely in the face, with the chance of having to endure the pain of discarding old ones. The foolish person's picture of the world is one of whites and blacks, rights and wrongs, goods and bads. His or her moral development ceased at the fairy tale and the American Western. The rut which such a person has dug for him- or herself leads smoothly and painlessly to the grave.

The dangerous person recognizes that there are many possible angles to living, but decides to pursue one of these to the exclusion of others, and do all he or she can to persuade others to do likewise. The motives which underlie this determination vary from person to person. They may spring from the genuine conviction that a particular interpretation of circumstances and events is the right one (good for all) while others are fraught with danger; this seems to be the mainstay of those who associate themselves with such bodies as the 'pro-life' organizations. They may on the other hand spring from the drive for material gain and the power this may be expected to bring to its acquirer, who will view other people as simply pawns to be manipulated to his or her personal ends. This person is dangerous because, whether dealing in ideas and beliefs or in bank balances and profits, he or she will seek to put others into a straitjacket. Thus any potential thou in their lives is transformed into an it – the it of possession.

To accept and live with inconsistencies seems preferable to either the comfortable laziness of the first type above, or the self-congratulatory malice of the second. It also seems more natural, since the whole of life, like the whole of nature, seems to be construed from a union, not just of inconsistencies, but at times of opposites. The days which provide the inescapable context of our living are a union of light and darkness. In our environment we encounter polarity continuously and eternally: positive and negative, summer and winter, heat and cold, male and female, life and death – neither is whole without the other, though they seem to have nothing in common. Even the elemental unity of light is brought about by the individual colours of the spectrum, which, taken in isolation, will seem obviously discordant: what have the colours blue and orange in common except that they are both contained in light? The cycle of existence is throughout, and *in toto*, a composite of discordancies (and the word 'cycle' is apposite: the hub of a wheel is kept in place by numerous spokes, each exerting pressure in a totally different direction from all the others).

These inconsistencies I am summing up under the one term 'paradox', since it is the word that emerges uppermost to characterize the mixture of ideas presented in the foregoing chapters. By this word I am implying that it must seem that if some of the ideas are sound, some of the others are not, with the logical conclusion that if we follow one line we must discard the other, or vice versa. Against this simplistic (however logical) view I am arguing that it is not only *possible* to be paradoxical on these issues, but natural and healthy to be so. It is natural because nature is a vassst universe of paradoxes; it is healthy because (recalling that the word healthy means 'whole') it is comprehensive and complete. So, to try to avoid being paradoxical is either to miss out on much, perhaps most, of life's fullness, or to experience life in a state of imbalance caused by over-using part to the exclusion of the rest, like badly balanced car wheels (though not all expressions of this imbalance are totally undesirable, as is reflected in the advertisement 'twin beds for sale, one as new'). I want to conclude these deliberations by selecting five areas in which an essentially paradoxical situation has presented itself.

## THE NECESSITY BUT INSUFFICIENCY OF REASON

This theme has already been discussed at some length, and needs only brief mention here. The intellect is both the noblest human possession and the most dangerous human plaything. On the one hand, it enables us to reflect on our ways of living and behaving so as to improve on both. And the problem-solver has been a boon not only to him- or herself but to many other forms and expressions of life in the world. On the other hand, left alone this reasoning faculty has overreached itself. We have tried to 'improve' on nature as we have found it but the end product has been not a state of supernature, as we intended, but the elimination of natural resources, the extermination of species and the destruction of the atmosphere.

In terms of ontological exploration, we have been both helped and hindered by our intellectual prowess. There is certainly something almost mystical about a carefully pursued piece of intellectual inquiry. This mystical element was allegedly expressed by Watson as he and Crick gazed in awe at the model of DNA which they had constructed: 'I feel like Pygmalion: it's the nearest we'll ever get to God.' And there is something profoundly rewarding in hearing a carefully researched exposition of a theme demanding deep concentration of the intellect on the parts of both lecturer and listeners. I recall hearing one such lecture by a colleague, Andrew Harrison, on the theme 'What is a work of art?' which left the audience feeling that they had been present at the creation of an example of what he was analysing.

The fact is, however, that the intellect alone will never either create a work of art or provide the sole means of achieving any other experiences of the numinous which I discussed earlier, and which are for many people the peak moments in their lives. Music, for example, is an indefinable, ineffable entity, described by the poet Heine as 'somewhere between thought and phenomenon'; yet music probably does more to keep people sane than all the reasoning in the universe. One wonders whether *homo sapiens*, for all his *sapiens*, could survive at all without art in some form. Henri Bergson (1859–1941) went even further than this in his criticism of intellectualism, arguing that its demarcations in time have created classifications and stratifications which are totally unreal because they are unnatural. He acknowledged the value expressed by the problem-solver, but argued that the insistence on grading and classifying everything in the universe – giving things names and stations – was creating division in what was an essential expression of unity. Furthermore, he argued that dividing time up into hours and minutes, night and and day, was confining one's fellows to the limited perspectives of one's own blinkered existence. If we could leave behind the confines of the earth, which creates day and night every twenty-four hours, and could exist in the wider universe, the difference between 'now' and 'then' would cease to be. He wrote:

> The interval of the *durée* [duration] exists only for us, and because of the mutual penetration of our conscious states; outside us one would find nothing but space, and thus simultaneities, of which one may not even say that they objectively succeed each other.
>
> (*Time and Free Will*)

It was in the East rather than in the West that the weaknesses, even dangers, latent in pure intellectualism were most clearly perceived and outlined, but it is worth acknowledging that here is one Western philosopher who recognized this; perhaps A. N. Whitehead was thinking along these lines when he wrote:

> In formal logic, a contradiction is the signal of defeat: but in the evolution of real knowledge it marks the first step in progress toward a victory.
>
>                                          (*Adventures of Ideas*)

But the crucial exposure of the fallibility of an ontological perspective based solely on the intellect has been made in the East. These words by a recent expositor epitomise the viewpoint of many:

> Thought, intellect, the mental grew to be regarded in the West more and more as the supreme means and even as the supreme goal; in philosophy, the thinking mind is the beginning and the end. Truth must be discovered here through intellectual examination and speculation; even spiritual experience is required to subject itself to the tests of the intellect if it wishes to be declared as valid . . . . Western thought is no longer dynamic, it has sought a theory, not realization . . . it turned into intellectual speculation without any practical method of attaining the truth with the help of spiritual experience, spiritual discoveries, and spiritual transformation . . . . In the process of overintellectualization of the mental realm in Europe, what was lost was the spiritual path, the way that leads past the intellect, the bridge from the outer being to the inmost self.
>
>                                   (Sri Aurobindo *Letters on Yoga*, vol 1)

## MYSELF ALONE AND THE UNIVERSAL THOU

One central ontological affirmation of this book is that, when the question of experience is under consideration, there is, and can be, only *my* experience. I may observe what happens to others – how they relate to their fellows, how they tackle the problem of making awkward, and perhaps fateful, decisions, how they cope with crisis or distress in their lives, and so on. The example that I observe in others may even be the catalyst that directs me in the extension or modification of my own field of Being. But nothing can remove me from my own field and, in the end, whatever experience I may undergo is mine, and mine alone, and whatever direction my life takes depends on my decision. As Tennyson wrote,

> I am a part of all that I have met;
> Yet all experience is an arch wherethro'
> Gleams that untravelled world, whose margin fades
> For ever and for ever when I move.

Thus any authority I may possess in the opinions I express, the style of life I may advocate, or my rejections of values which confront me from others' fields of Being can all be put forward only on the basis of my experience. To engage oneself in any of these processes without having encountered their subjects at first hand is to act without authority and, quite likely, to say and do things one may later regret. Experience is the yardstick of conviction.

But even this apparently incontrovertible statement is fraught with difficulty. Whenever I speak or act on the basis of experience, I am willy-nilly doing so on the basis of my own *interpretation* of that experience. I may conclude that what I have experienced in a particular quarter is typical, and therefore capable of being universalized. Many of the debates between people are directed in this way: 'Blacks are lazy – look at that idle loafer down the street'; 'Blacks are the salt of the earth – look how that nurse works.' Any mistakes in interpreting experience in situations like this result from restrictions on the area of inquiry. But sometimes the misinterpretation is based not on paucity of evidence but on self-delusion. One of my parishioners years ago was quite convinced that her uncle Bob, who at that time had been dead twenty years, sat permanently on top of her wardrobe, from which vantage-point he would give her advice if she requested it. Her interpretation of her experience was that she was then acting and speaking according to uncle Bob's insights. Epistemologically speaking, it is of course impossible to disprove her conviction; but the normal concourse of life would be impossible if such delusions were not recognized and treated as such. As a matter of fact, the advice this lady usually received from 'uncle Bob' was commonsensical, so there seemed no point in trying to disillusion her; but the matter takes on a more ominous note when, say, a man affirms, as one notorious murderer did affirm, that he is under divine instructions to murder young women.

There must clearly be some kind of testing of individual experience by others, lest we reach the impossible situation of having to accept as genuine any kind of crazy notion springing from even the most warped and twisted of minds. Otherwise we should have no answer to the protean newt, whose perceptions are quoted in case study 3. What this means in practice is that we should be constantly seeking to extend the range of our experience, in the hope of reducing elements of prejudice and bigotry in the judgements we make. These will never be totally eliminated since none of us can be omniscient; but we can try.

The paradox of myself alone and the universal thou springs from two different sets of experience which are equally real to different people, and perhaps are both real, at different times, to one and the same person. The first perspective is exemplified by D. H. Lawrence in his *Studies in Classical American Literature*: 'Each soul is alone and the aloneness of each soul is a double barrier to perfect relationships between two beings.' This viewpoint reflects a strong emphasis in existentialist thought, and the experience it describes is, I believe, a major reason why people turn to religion: not everyone either desires to be alone or is capable of sustaining themselves in isolation from others.

Yet equally real in the lives of most people is the experience of I-thou described by Buber, whether in respect to personal relationships or as a sense of harmony with the universe as a whole. It is a simple fact, attested to constantly by people on the basis of their experience, that two lonely souls, in Lawrence's image, may find at least some form of temporary union with each other, and for many people this union is the mainstay of living. To state what seems transparently obvious, this loss of the ego in and with another can occur during a very deep sexual relationship. It would be folly, as Lawrence knew only too well, to suggest that all such encounters involve a genuine union of two souls: this is the area *par excellence* not only of great self-emptying but of greed, rapaciousness and exploitation; but it must be an unfortunate person who has never experienced the shared non-dualism of these moments. Lawrence is right in affirming that the desire for a perfect soul-mate and the unwillingness to accept anything less than this is doomed to bring dissatisfaction, but this is different from saying that *no* kind of relationship is possible. Once again, Aristotle's words hit the nail on the head: the best is the enemy of the good.

The I-thou experience is generally to be found among close friends and sometimes, as in time of war or of some other long period of shared endurance, between people thrown accidentally together. The frustration lies, I suppose, in the fact that many of these relationships don't endure. People change; friends grow apart; and the circumstances which bring people together for a specific purpose alter, often leaving their participants dissatisfied thereafter with what seems a shallower kind of existence. But despite all, the I-thou happens, if only, sometimes, for a brief period.

Is it unrealistic to reflect on the possibilities on a wider scale still? The Taoist philosophy assumes that all Being is, or may be, united ultimately in a harmonious whole. Is this any more than self-delusion or wishful thinking (among those, that is, who are not in any case appalled by the idea)? Maybe we can learn from other species. Observers have for centuries, for instance, wondered at a flock of starlings in flight, apparently circling and swirling, expanding and contracting as one. It is absurd to suggest that they follow their leader, since clearly there is no leader. Their action is more like that of girls in a chorus line, but these are choreographed and trained: who choreographs and trains the starlings? Brian Inglis, writing in the *Guardian*, says: 'The only explanation that makes sense was put forward earlier this century by the great naturalist Edmund Selous. He came to the conclusion that in flocks, the birds were one individual organism, welded together by some form of communication which enabled them to manoeuvre as a unit.' Inglis then discarded Selous's view that some form of thought transference occurred, since 'whatever may be transferred, it can hardly be "thought"'. He concludes: 'Yet his premise is surely valid. Next time you see a flock of starlings cavorting in the sky, ask yourself whether there is any conceivable explanation other than the existence of some group force at work, making them into a single organism – for the endurance of the manoeuvres.'

Is it too far-fetched to suggest that these birds illustrate a faculty which all beings possess, including *homo sapiens*; but that in *homo sapiens* the *sapiens* factor has prevented the species from experiencing this because of its stress on individual reason, and the dominance of logic and rationality? May it not be that the chief harm caused by the exaltation of reason to the exclusion of all other faculties is to divide us from other beings, with whom the reality of the I-thou experience would otherwise be as natural to us as it clearly is to other species? 'There are already too many names,' states the Tao Te Ching; and by the naming of species, and peoples, and parts we create an archipelago out of what might otherwise be a union of Being. Is this the mystery of the Atman finding the ground of its Being in the universal Brahman? Philosophy should not ignore this possibility.

## METAPHYSICS WITHOUT THEOLOGY

The differences in ontological perspectives between East and West are nowhere more stark than in the area of metaphysics. In Western thought, whether in the Thomist/Anselmian tradition, or in the rationalism of Descartes and Spinoza, metaphysics directs itself towards theology. The questions with which any Western student of metaphysics will have to be concerned may well be the same as those introduced in these pages – teleology, immortality, the soul, and so on. But these issues will generally be discussed in relation to the dominating doctrine of belief in God. Thus metaphysics is viewed by most Western expositors as the handmaid of theology, designed to indicate that one can accept the concept of Revelation – the Creator God revealing Himself in some way to some of His creatures – without abandoning one's academic integrity. It is probably for this reason mainly that metaphysics has in recent years occupied a less than significant place in the curricula of Western departments of philosophy: having been battered by Newton, blasted by Darwin and blown up by Freud, God can no longer justify Himself in the minds of Western philosophers sufficiently to merit the expenditure of resources on His behalf.

This viewpoint is quite understandable, provided the reaction stops there. But in turning against all metaphysics because of the apparently ineradicable link it had established with theology it seems to me that Western philosophers have thrown out the gold with the grit. The study of metaphysics involves the consideration of how far our perception of the universe and its multifarious facets is based on logic and how far on intuition (or whatever other word we may choose to describe the non-rational yet ever-active faculty in *homo sapiens*). It compels people to reflect on the problems of ontology – the inner self, the nature of Being, the goal, if any, of Being, the ground of Being – not in order to reach a fixed set of tenets or beliefs, much less to find a divine or supreme source of revelation on these matters, but because, as a simple matter of fact, these ontological issues (by whatever name they're called) have been the concern of human beings since they first gazed at the setting sun.

This whole area has been bedevilled (if that is not an inapt metaphor) by theology and in particular by the concept of revelation. This concept reduces human beings to the role of secondary creatures dependent on divine light, which is offered only on the whim of its originator. The initiative is God's; the response is ours; and if, for whatever reason (and we shall never know the reason) God decides to withhold revelation from any individual or society, so be it. Ours is not to reason why. Against this theological misconception, and divorced from its theological straitjacket, metaphysics can open the doors of perception in ways that can be achieved by no other method of inquiry or exploration. It has been described as 'guided meditation', a means of communication between people regarding experiences which, because they are ineffable and undefinable (and beyond any scientific analysis), are well-nigh impossible to share. Yet by these attempts at communication, however haltingly they be made, some kind of unity and consistency may, perhaps, be sensed in these experiences. Metaphysics encourages the testing of these experiences by comparing them with those described by others throughout the centuries and across the continents. It encourages us to try to make sense of our fields – and this includes our pondering on the question of whether there *is* any sense to be made of it, or whether the whole of existence must simply, as the existentialist Camus affirmed, be treated as absurd.

The broader question of the ground of Being, Brahman, the Tao, are simply an extension of the questions relating to individual fields; and again, God need have no place in the inquiry. It seems totally natural to wonder whether there is any feature of universal Being which cannot be reflected, or even contained, within our own fields, or our fields in it. As the number 1 contains every conceivable fraction *ad infinitum*, may not the ground of Being contain every individual expression of Being? Although this may sound like some kind of theological discussion (theologians would certainly be likely to make this claim) it is not so at all – or, at any rate, it need not be; it is a typically Western attitude to suggest that it is an example of 'God-talk'. In fact, metaphysics as an exploration of the numinous needs to be rescued from the clutch of theology, and it seems at least worth considering that the way forward here is offered by the ontological perspectives of existentialism and the East. Both these approaches are, incidentally, totally devoid of sentimentality, so that neither requires the student, or general explorer, to adopt reverential tones when discussing it. That is no small gain.

## OPTING IN AND OPTING OUT

The supreme paradox which arises from the dichotomy of perspective undertaken in these pages relates to the extent of one's commitment to the world of affairs. The Western emphasis is on the virtue of activity, and existentialism is in this respect a typically Western philosophy. Kierkegaard's religious attitude demands personal commitment in the world of moral and social problems. Nietzsche's *Übermensch* stands on his own feet to combat the limitations in the world brought about by those who look primarily to 'another world' for their personal fulfilment. Sartre's *être-pour-soi* means being immersed in conflict, fighting the forces of injustice and denouncing the faint-hearted who fear to raise their heads above the ramparts. The Westerner, inspired by the vision of a Brave New World, calls for a bow of burning gold, for arrows of desire, for spear and sword, and promises not to lay them down until all has been accomplished (it is an unnerving experience to hear Blake's 'Jerusalem' sung by members of the Women's Institute). 'Life is real, life is earnest, And the grave is not the goal' (or the gaol, either).

The East – or, at any rate, those expressions of it which we have examined – is ambivalent about this urge for commitment. Its emphasis is on passivity and reflection, on exploring the universe of inner Being rather than being overtly concerned about the social and physical environment. The aim according to Buddha is to escape from the continual cycles of experience and to be (or not be) eternally in Nirvana. Buddha was not indifferent to human misery and injustice, but argued that the most fruitful way of encountering them lay in attaining a state of awareness that could not be touched by these wrongs. The Fourth State of Advaita Vedanta is one which is unaffected by the evils of the waking state because the distinction between I and thou which, with their ramifications, are the cause of those evils, has ceased to be. Both Buddha and Advaita therefore advocate a life centred on meditation and contemplation as preferable to one of involvement in the encircling strife because, so they affirm, their way relates more closely than that of the West to the destiny which confronts all men.

This passivity or withdrawal from the worldly scene is expressed even more directly in Taoism. To Lao Tsu, involvement in human affairs was fruitless. His view was that the removal of one injustice would simply create the conditions for the next; the regime that replaces the tyrant itself eventually becomes tyrannical. Reform must therefore take place not in the political arena but within the individual, through a changed perception of priorities.

In the pursuit of learning, every day something is acquired.
In the pursuit of Tao, every day something is dropped.
Less and less is done.
Until non-action is achieved.

When nothing is done, nothing is left undone.
The world is ruled by letting things take their course.
It cannot be ruled by interfering.                    (Tao Te Ching, ch. 48)

'Let things be' is the motto of Tao: the Tao is not to be found in the frenzied desire to change things since, even wearing the shiniest of armour, the knight may have lost his way.

Anyone not torn between these two apparently mutually exclusive philosophies of living must either be so immersed in the one as to be unable to perceive the value of the other, or too obtuse to recognize the problem in the first place. Speaking for myself, I am perpetually torn between the two approaches. There are, as must be apparent to any reader of this book, certain social and political issues about which I feel compelled to speak out and, sometimes, take action. These days I am more reluctant than I was twenty years ago to get out on the streets and express my feelings, but the depth of my convictions about certain gaps, as I see them, in human justice must be quite clear. There are issues about which I cannot avoid opting in, if I am not to be consumed by inner turbulences.

On the other hand (and again I hope this emerges from this book) I have learned over thirty years increasingly to appreciate the value of meditation. For some years (my final years as an ordained minister of the Church) I spent a week annually in retreat at the Taizé Community in France, and habitually spent the occasional day in contemplation in a convenient nearby monastery. Since then my explorations into Eastern philosophy have served to intensify my conviction that periodic withdrawal from the external world, as complete as deep meditation requires, is at least desirable and maybe essential for anyone who wishes to make the maximum possible impact in the world of affairs. The manic dedication of oneself to party politics, in which I was for some years completely involved and which demanded my presence at meeting after meeting seven nights a week, is totally destructive of any value one might help to bring about in the community. The paradox is that through meditation and withdrawal a person develops inner resources strong enough to sustain him or her in the heat of whatever area of strife is the current concern.

I don't wish to give the impression that I am hereby numbering myself among Plato's enlightened philosophers, patronizing those who still mistake the shadow for the substance. For me it is not like that at all. I simply experience the two forces at work within my own field of Being, the one to opt in, the other to opt out. The trick lies in discovering the most fruitful way of exploiting this paradox. A satisfactory solution is found, I think, through the Yin/Yang dichotomy, making of life both commitment and non-commitment, advance and withdrawal. With the inner resources gained in periods of contemplation, one equips oneself to face the noonday heat (or even just the rush–hour crawl); and this in turn creates the need to return to the fount, so to speak, lest the resources are drained away and one's field is left barren. This balance of Yang and Yin can make for a rich and comprehensive existence, meaning that a person whose life moves between these twin poles should make progress towards the achieving of his or her essence, or whatever parallel phrase may be used in this context.

The question that remains is whether this balancing process represents the end of any ontological quest, or whether we should look beyond it to an even higher state. I think this is necessary, though the attaining of it must be rare. It is to unite the two poles, *not by moving back and forth between them but by bringing them together.* This means developing and experiencing inner tranquillity – or whatever term may be chosen to represent the resources built up within one's own field – not by avoiding conflict, but in its midst; recognizing all the delusions involved in committing oneself to social action and change, knowing that heaven will never be established on earth, but realizing that because to be is to be moral, letting things be, in the Taoist phrase, does not mean leading one's life like a pillar saint or a Jainite monk. To co–operate with the Tao means to help to bring harmony out of conflict: and this is most likely to be achieved, if there is any worth at all in the basic perspective of this book, by manifesting one's inner harmony where the conflict is at its height. Harry Truman, when US President, advised his colleagues, 'If you can't stand the heat, stay out of the kitchen.' The East-West synthesis which I am advocating may enable us to stay longer in the kitchen because we are insulated against the heat. It is the yogic state of Sanyama; or, to redirect Wordsworth's description of poetry, it is *tranquillity recollected in emotion.*

An image in my mind which illustrates what I am trying to say is that of Father Damien, working in a South Seas leper colony. Buddha's message to the lepers would no doubt have been to look beyond their suffering and use their time building up good karma; and for many this would have been deeply rewarding. Sartre would no doubt have gone to the authorities and demanded that the living conditions of the area should be improved so that the causes of leprosy might be removed and the disease no longer threaten the inhabitants; and no doubt many would have been glad of this advocacy. Damien had involved himself in both these approaches and the lepers had heard him politely; but it was only when he himself became a leper that they responded openly and positively to him. His remarkable fortitude as he approached his death, born of an I-thou relationship with the disease, created an I-thou relationship with the other sufferers. And this was possible, I think, only because of the expression of the inner resources within a context of total commitment. Damien opted out (of a neutral, even negative, approach to the disease) by opting in: his Being and becoming were one. It illustrates, as I mentioned earlier, what Dietrich

Bonhoeffer was to describe a century later as 'the beyond in the midst', and indicates that even from the theistic perspective of Christianity, of which I have been generally critical, enlightenment has come.

The danger latent in following solely the Yang tendency in this field must be clear for all to perceive who have eyes to see: bellowing with anger and flaying the air, dividing the participants in the struggle into 'us' and 'them', and reducing to the level of an 'it' anyone with whom one is in conflict. Equally, the dangers latent in following only the Yin tendency are equally plain to see: 'evil men prosper while the good do nothing'. This was made vividly real to me in some words that another Christian, Pastor Martin Niemöller, said to me in Frankfurt in 1955 when I was staying with him during a lecture tour of Germany I was making with an international pacifist group. (We were hoping to dissuade the Federal Republic from rearming!) Niemöller had been imprisoned in one of Hitler's concentration camps during most of the war, and his description of how he arrived there has become famous. He said, 'In Germany, the Nazis came for the Communists and I didn't speak up because I was not a Communist. Then they came for the Jews and I didn't speak up because I was not a Jew. Then they came for the trade unionists and I didn't speak up because I was not a trade unionist. Then they came for the Catholics and I was a Protestant so I didn't speak up. Then they came for me . . . By that time there was no one to speak up for anyone.'

## BEING AND BECOMING

For most of us, the best that we can hope for is that in the polarity of Yin and Yang we will never be so committed to the one tendency that we lose sight of the other. In this final expression of paradox, however, the two are by nature in a state of harmony rather than of polarity, because, while Being and becoming are in one sense poles apart, neither can be expressed without the other. The totality of experience is found not solely in the Yin of Being, essential though it of course is *to be* if one is to have any kind of experience at all. Nor can it be found solely in the Yang of *becoming*, essential though this of course is if one is to avoid non-Being. Only in the union of the two opposites can I describe myself. As time is the continuous projection of the now into the not-yet, so I am the me moving continuously into the me-to-be. Charles Wesley expressed this with great felicity in one of his hymns:

Our life is a dream,
Our time, as a stream,
Glides swiftly away;
And the fugitive moment refuses to stay.

It is possible to proceed through life without ever reflecting on this truth, and adopting the kind of simplistic philosophy already referred to: 'plus ça change, plus ça la même chose'. And in one sense this is the case: the entire universe is contained in the molecule DNA, and, while its potentiality for change and development may appear to be infinite, the universe remains none the less, in Wittgenstein's words, 'all that is the case'. But it is a dynamic universe, never the same from one moment to the next, even if it will return to the state of *this* moment at some remote point in the future. Perhaps the situation is summed up in the words of my eldest son apropos of a friend of his whom we needed to consult: 'I know where he'll be if he's not where he is.'

You who are reading these words are not the same person who started this book (or chapter, or sentence): every department of your being – physical, mental, emotional, social – has become, in however small and unnoticeable a way (even to yourself, perhaps especially to yourself) different; as I have become different in the writing. More and more I am gripped by this ontological mystery; I am not, and never was, the person I was; and I am not, and never will be, the person I am to be. Sometimes this truth becomes startlingly real to me, such as when I by change look at old photographs or letters. Is there anything in life so capable of bringing instant depression so surely as looking at last year's diary of engagements? There is a dead world, infinitely hollower, gloomier and more shadowy than any family vault in an Edgar Allan Poe story.

Thus our experience of Being is, on the one hand, looking forward to (or dreading, or viewing with indifference) the next event, and looking back on events (with pleasure, or disgust, or with an indifference that instantly allows it to be erased from the consciousness): this is the realization that the *now* can no more be static, is no more capable of being held still, than can electrons round the nucleus of an atom. Yet, on the other hand, amid this perpetual process of change there remains a single constancy: my Being, and the field which I create by bringing together all the events, the encounters, the conflicts, the habits, the hopes and fears, the drudgery and delights which remain perpetually mine, real to me if to no one else. The sum total may be an infinitesimal fraction of the universal expression of Being: but in that tiny fraction is contained, so far as my Being is concerned, the entire universe, as wheat is contained within a grain, and all the civilizations of the world were contained within the first man and women. To be is to possess all that the universe exists for. Billions of other beings preceded me, and billions more will succeed me. But this consideration is incidental to the realization that *my* experience of Being – mine and not theirs – is for me all that is the case. Dust and ashes I may, therefore, on the one hand be: but for my sake the universe exists.

I do not know what is ultimately to ensue in the process of becoming. In these reflections I have speculated here and there along Taoist lines. I hope that the position I have tentatively arrived at will not be written off – as numerous Western philosophers write such views off – as merely yet another attempt to justify a belief in personal immortality, since, as I have indicated, this concept seems to me to be meaningless. The fact is, quite simply, that in a universe where *everything* dies, life persists; in a universe where everything grows old, the old continuously gives birth to the new. Even those totally uninterested in metaphysical inquiry might do well to reflect on the implications of that.

This syndrome I know on an I–it basis. From the perspective of I–thou, however, this knowledge is simply an aspect of my field, which is eternally with me. And I can offer this field, so to speak, to the universal Yin and Yang, constantly changing moving away and returning, illustrating what is at the ground of all Being, and reflecting what I know to be the case from within my own Being. After that, it seems enough to wait and see.

We have thus (I hope) thrown into relief in all these examples of paradox the one supreme paradox of existence which, more than any other factor, illustrates the fundamental difference between the Western and Eastern approaches to philosophy: their view of man. In the West, the human race is, quite literally, *homo sapiens*, analysing, classifying, the subject of rational thought. In the East, the subjectivity of human reflections is subsumed in what is conceived to be a wider, and perhaps infinitely wide, experience of Being. Western empiricism encourages each of us to fight against the forces of ignorance; Eastern ontology suggests that these forces will be transformed by merging with them, as a touch of sugar transforms the flavour of a drink.

The Yang side of the paradox – aggressive, assertive, committed, initiating and, if need be, acting alone – is illustrated in these words from the autobiography of Gary Kasparov, the world chess champion. Having described his years of struggle with the Soviet chess authorities, he writes:

> For some time my personal motto has been a Soviet saying which translates roughly as 'If not you, who else?' What it means is that if you don't take responsibility for your own life, nobody else will. I have this slogan on my wall wherever I go. . .
>
> I believe I am engaged in a battle for universal principles that should apply equally in East and West. That is a long and lonely crusade. It is bound sometimes to make a young man of 24 seem naïve and self-important. So be it. When I look back over the battles I have fought since the age of 18, both on and off the chess board, at the mental, physical, and nervous energy I have expended to become world champion, I wonder what good or harm it has done me. I have forced my way down a long, dark tunnel, scarcely looking to

left or right. My childhood vanished somewhere in that tunnel. I have
become a creature in a Vissotsky poem:

> You can take an easier route,
> But we chose the one that is the most difficult
> And dangerous like a path of war.

I can enthuse over these sentiments: they epitomize the existentialist
approach to living, and Kierkegaard, Nietzsche and – perhaps most of
all – Sartre would have approved wholeheartedly.

In contradistinction to this heroic Yang image, these words by Christmas
Humphries, from his book *Zen Buddhism*, illustrate the Eastern, Yin side of
the paradox:

> There is a harmony called Tao which blends all events in each moment
> of the universe into a perfect chord. The whole situation in and around
> you at this instant is a harmony with which you have to find your own
> union if you are to be in accord with Tao. The right life, therefore, is
> the natural life, and he who has found and lives in Zen lives naturally.
> To what extent his newfound harmony affects his outward life, to bring
> his outward mode of living into accord with his inner awareness, is a
> matter of time and the individual, but just as the direct drive of an
> engine is sweet and without discordant tension, so the right use of
> action, direct action, is sweet and frictionless. Only self, the desire
> of self for self, intervenes and pulls the machine out of alignment.
> Alignment becomes the operative word. From the 'power-house of
> the universe'. . .to the individual self the power is direct, and the
> right means used in the right way at the right time and place makes
> up increasingly the perfect act.
>
> (quoted in *From Darkness to Light*)

There will always be those, I suppose, who feel no need for a metaphyscial
perspective in their lives, and for them these words will seem out of
place in relation to those of Gary Kasparov. But those who view things
differently will recognize that this is the heart of life's paradox, and the
key to understanding the central problems posed in this book: who are
we, and why are we here?

It may seem illogical to follow, or attempt to follow, the way of Tao,
or of Zen, or of yoga, at the same time as following the way of the
reforming prophets in the style of the existentialists. But I believe that
to attempt either path to the exclusion of the other must lead to a life
of less than total fulfilment, producing a field of Being that is less than
comprehensively fertile. To be is to become, and to become is to be: therein
lies the supreme mystery, paradoxical and contradictory, yet startling in

both its simplicity and its completeness: 'all we know on earth, and all we need to know'.

## Case Study 29
### The place of reason

Logic and critical thinking rank highly among Western values, and philosophers from Plato to Russell have eulogized their importance. The analytical approach to philosophy seeks to establish these two qualities as the means, above all others, of reaching an understanding of any issue, complex or otherwise. So in the State University of California, for instance, the only compulsory course for all students is a credit in this subject.

However, one of the themes of this book has been that, while reason is *necessary* in life, it is not *sufficient* to sustain us in many of its facets; that we need to be 'irrational' in the sense that reason is recognized as being only one – the most important one, perhaps, but still only one – of the human resources which enable us to make up our minds (itself a question-begging phrase!) on a host of issues.

In this case study a wide range of common (or fairly common) issues or situations are suggested. Your task is to reflect on these with the following questions in mind:

1    Can I resolve this entirely by reason?

2    How far are other factors contributory: feelings, instinct, 'common' sense, or simply because I have been told (through the media, by parents, by an expert, etc.)?

What is the meaning of 'knowing that . . .' in the following:

*Knowing that*    (1)    Your partner has no wish to harm you.
    (2)    Your partner loves/is faithful to you.
    (3)    God exists/you have a soul.
    (4)    Orange is between red and green in the spectrum.
    (5)    Your local car dealer is a crook.
    (6)    Mozart was a great composer.
    (7)    Plastic ducks are not works of art.
    (8)    The sun is 92 million miles from the earth.
    (9)    The ozone layer is being destroyed.
    (10)    Eating meat is wrong.
    (11)    Cigarette-smoking is bad for your health.
    (12)    Drinking alcohol in moderation is good for your health.
    (13)    You have a subconscious mind.
    (14)    Dreams are/are not indicators of the future.

(15)  No race is inferior/superior to another.
(16)  Any male person is capable of rape.
(17)  The female of the species is stronger than the male.
(18)  The Pythagorus theorem is true.
(19)  The cube of 9 is 729.
(20)  *In vino veritas.*
(21)  Walking under a ladder brings bad luck.
(22)  Your star sign is an indicator of your personality.
(23)  Peace is possible for your country only with strong defensive forces.
(24)  Russia/the USA/Iran/Japan would like to conquer the world.
(25)  Born-again Christians have been visited by the Holy Spirit.
(26)  The end justifies the means.
(27)  President Nixon was a crook.
(28)  President Reagan was a nice chap/a phoney.
(29)  Winston Churchill was a great leader.
(30)  Cannibalism/abortion/adultery/homosexuality is wrong.
(31)  Kindness is a desirable human quality.
(32)  Animal intelligence is a contradiction in terms.
(33)  Matter is neither created nor destroyed in the course of a chemical reaction.
(34)  The universe was intended.
(35)  Malory and Irving were the first men to climb Everest.
(36)  In some respects you are sometimes free.
(37)  The age of the earth is 4 $1/2$ billion years.
(38)  *Homo sapiens* is descended from the ape.
(39)  Selfishness is natural.
(40)  Every event has a cause.
(41)  There is no such thing as coincidence.
(42)  Violence depicted on TV causes an increase in violence among viewers.
(43)  The problem of Ireland is/is not the British.
(44)  Gravity is a law of nature.
(45)  Apples are good for you.
(46)  The *Mona Lisa* in the Louvre is genuine.
(47)  The sun will rise tomorrow.
(48)  The future looks hopeful.
(49)  A vase of flowers should be arranged in a certain way.
(50)  Exercises like this should end at a round figure.

*Case study 30*
*Expressions of Eastern philosophical thought*

Quoted below are statements made by Eastern thinkers on some of the
issues discussed in this book. It will be helpful to turn back to the first case
study (pp. 12–13) and apply the same four questions to these statements.
See also the further questions at the end.

(1)   The Vedas have the three Strands (of matter) as their scope;
      Be thou free from the three Strands, Arjuna,
      Free from the pairs (of opposites), eternally fixed in goodness,
      Free from acquisition and possession, self-possessed.

      As much profit as there is in a water-tank
      When on all sides there is a flood of water,
      No more is there in all the Vedas
      For a brahman who (truly) understands.

                                                    (The Bhagavad-gita)

(2)   'A Yoga of integral perfection regards man as a divine spiritual being
      involved in mind, life and body; it aims therefore at a liberation
      and a perfection of his divine nature. . .It seeks to go beyond
      mind to the supramental knowledge, will, sense, feeling, intuition,
      dynamic initiation of vital and physical action, all that makes the
      native working of the spiritual being. . .The integral Yoga meets
      the religious ideal at several points, but goes beyond it in the sense
      of a greater wideness. The religious ideal looks, not only beyond
      this earth, but away from it to a heaven or even beyond all heavens
      to some kind of Nirvana. . .But the integral Yoga founds itself on
      a conception of the spiritual being as an omnipresent existence, the
      fullness of which comes not essentially by a transference to other
      worlds or a cosmic self-extinction, but by a growth out of what
      we now are phenomenally into the consciousness of the omnipresent
      reality which we always are in the essence of our being.'
                                              (Sri Aurobindo, 1872–1950)

(3)   'Do not think that good and evil are two, are two separate essences,
      for they are one and the same thing appearing in different degrees
      and in different guises and producing differences of feeling in the
      same mind.'
                                                       (The Vedanta)

(4)   'With everything, whether it is above or below, remote or near,
      visible or invisible, thou shalt preserve a relation of unlimited love

without any animosity or without a desire to kill. To live in such a consciousness while standing or walking, sitting or lying down till you are asleep, is Brahma vihara, or, in other words, is living and moving and having your joy in the spirit of Brahma.'

(The Buddha)

(5) 'Truly, this seer, toucher, hearer, smeller, taster, thinker, conceiver, doer, the conscious self [*vijnanatman*], the person – his resort is in the supreme imperishable Self [*Atman*].

(Prasna Upanishad)

(6) 'This "I and mine" causes the whole misery. With the sense of possession comes selfishness, and selfishness brings on misery. Every act of selfishness or thought of selfishness makes us attached to something, and immediately we are made slaves. Each wave in the Chitta that says "I and mine" immediately puts a chain round us and makes us slaves; and the more we say "I and mine" the more slavery grows, the more misery increases. Therefore, Karma–Yoga tells us to enjoy the beauty of all the pictures in the world but not to identify ourselves with any of them.'

(Swami Vivekananda, 1863–1902)

(7) The Koan (enigmas as meditation-topics):
(a) If I have nothing, what should I do? Throw it away!
(b) You are not allowed to travel at night, but You must arrive before daybreak.
(c) The bridge flows, the water does not.
(d) What is the sound of ONE hand clapping?
(e) If You run away from the Void, You can never be free of it. If You search for the Void, You can never reach it.

(C. T. Chang: *Original Teachings of Ch'an Buddhism*)

(8) 'I shrink to give up my life, and thus do not plunge into the great waters of life.'

(Rabindranath Tagore, 1861–1941)

(9) 'Lao Tsu said: "Human nature is like rushing water, which flows east or west according as an outlet is made for it. For human nature makes indifferently for good or for evil, precisely as water makes indifferently for the east or for the west." Mencius replied: "Water will indeed flow indifferently towards the east or west but will it flow indifferently up and down? It will not; and the tendency of human nature towards good is like the tendency of water to flow down. Every man has this bias towards good, just as all water flows naturally downwards. By splashing water, you may indeed cause it to fly over your head; and by turning its course you may

keep it for use on the hillside; but you would hardly speak of such results as the nature of water. They are the results, of course, of a *force majeure*. And so it is when the nature of man is diverted towards evil."'

(Mencius, third century BC)

(10) 'Master K'ung said, There are three things that a gentleman fears: he fears the will of Heaven, he fears (morally) great men, he fears the words of the Divine Sages. The small man does not know the will of Heaven and so does not fear it. He treats great men with contempt, and scoffs at the words of the Divine Sages.'

(Confucius: *Analects*)

(11) 'In ancient China there were five theories about destiny or the Mandate of Heaven. The first was fatalism: the Mandate of Heaven is fixed and unchangeable. The second was moral determinism: Heaven always encourages virtue and punishes evil; therefore, man can determine his reward and punishment through moral deeds. The third was anti-fatalism. . .The fourth was naturalistic fatalism, which means that destiny is not controlled by Heaven in the sense of an anthropomorphic God but by Nature and works automatically. Lastly, there was the Confucian theory of "waiting for destiny". According to this doctrine, man should exert his utmost in moral endeavour and leave whatever is beyond our control to fate. It frankly admits that there are things beyond our control but that is no reason why one should relax in his moral endeavour. The tendency was definitely one of moralism and humanism. The Confucian theory represents the conviction of enlightened Chinese in general.'

(Wing-Tsit Chan: *A Source Book in Chinese Philosophy*)

(12) When the best student hears about the way
He practises it assiduously;
When the average student hears about the way
It seems to him one moment there and gone the next;
When the worst student hears about the way
He laughs out loud.
If he did not laugh
It would be unworthy of being the way.

(Tao Te Ching, ch. 41, trans. D. C. Lau)

Further questions are as follows:

1    Do you think that the philosophical perspectives represented above can coexist in the same person with those represented in case study 1? How would *you* aim to bring them together?

2 Looking back at the quotations in case study 1, do you interpret them any differently in the light of your understanding of Eastern philosophy?

3 If you read the above quotations before tackling the book, do you feel more able to appreciate their emphases now than you were then? Could you summarize the issues on which you are clearer?

# Glossary of terms

## Proper names

**Aquinas**, St Thomas (1224–74): aimed to reconcile Greek philosophy with Christianity. His philosophy, based on that of Aristotle (q.v.) whom he called 'the philosopher', is known as Thomism.

**Aristotle** (384–322 BC): pupil of Plato, tutor to Alexander the Great. Founded the Lyceum in Athens – a grove in which he taught, beside the temple of Apollo. Expounded on virtually every known subject – philosophy, science, logic, politics, poetry, etc.

**Augustine**, St (354–430): converted to Christianity in his thirties, became Bishhop of Hippo in North Africa. A predestinarian in theology, he tried to express the nature of man in a Christian framework. Basically Platonic in outlook.

**Ayer**, A. J. (1910–89): British philosopher. Visited the Vienna Circle of philosophers in 1932 (school of logical positivism). Wrote *Language, Truth, and Logic* as an antimetaphysical treatise.

**Bergson**, Henri (1859–1941): French philosopher. Originated the concept of the 'Life force' – *élan vital* – which he believed caused variations in the species as they developed; hence his doctrine of 'creative evolution'. Had a double view of time, as outlined in the text.

**Berkeley**, George (1685–1753): Irish bishop and idealist philosopher. Argued that the material world exists only in being perceived by the mind.

**Bradley**, F. H. (1846–1924): British Idealist, developed a system of monism (q.v.) Anti-utilitarian (q.v.) in his ethics (q.v.); e.g. *My Station and its Duties*. Influenced Russell (q.v.) and, indirectly, Wittgenstein (q.v.).

**Feuerbach**, Ludwig (1804–72): German philosopher; wrote against immortality, etc., in his *Das Wesen des Christentums* (translated into English by George Eliot as *The Essence of Christianity*). Believed that all authority above human beings is a delusion; man creates the image of ideal humanity and worships this as God. German communists applied this idea to their attacks on their political masters, not just to a God who was spiritually above human beings.

**Fox**, George (1624–91): founder of the Quakers (Society of Friends). Pacifist; egalitarian, anti-ecclesiastic. Taught the presence of the 'inner light'. His *Journal* is a classic.

**Hobbes**, Thomas (1588–1679): English philosopher; primarily a political philosopher: expressed the need for an absolute sovereign to control the natural selfishness of his subjects. *Leviathan* (1651) was his main political/philosophical work.

**Hume**, David (1711–76): Scottish philosopher, one of the British empiricists. Sceptical about the powers of the reason, causation and necessity. Kant stated that Hume 'aroused him from his dogmatic slumbers'.

**Huxley**, Aldous (1894–1963): grandson of T. H. Huxley, protagonist of Darwinism and evolution, and brother of Julian (q.v.). Novelist, e.g. *Brave New World*, depicting people bred only for their status in life. Took refuge in mysticism (q.v.), which he wrote about in *Eyeless in Gaza* and *The Perennial Philosophy*.

**Huxley**, Sir Julian (1887–1975): biologist; formulated a pragmatic (q.v.) ethical theory based on the principle of natural selection. First Secretary-General of UNESCO.

**Isherwood**, Christopher (1904–): English novelist (e.g. *Goodbye to Berlin*). Made the Bhagavad-gita (q.v.) more well-known to the British and Western public, working with Swami Prakhavananda.

**James**, William (1842–1910): American psychologist and philosopher, brother of Henry, novelist. Leading exponent of the school of pragmatism (q.v.) Books include *The Varieties of Religious Experience* (1902), and *Pragmatism* (1907).

**Jung**, C. G. (1875–1961): Swiss psychologist; coined the term 'complex' as in 'inferiority complex'. Collaborated with Freud, but came to question his exclusively sexual definition of libido. Developed the understanding of types, such as extrovert and introvert, and what he termed 'the collective unconscious' with its 'archetypes'.

**Kant**, Immanuel (1724–1804): German philosopher; asked what it is possible for any mind like the human mind to know. Tried to derive morality from reason alone. Believed in the freedom of the will, and that a person should be treated as an end in him(her)self alone, never as a means to an end. A deontologist, i.e. duty seen as the guide to moral decisions and behaviour.

**Locke**, John (1632–1704): English epistemological (q.v.) philosopher, linked with Hume in the school of empiricists. Wrote on political theory from a liberal perspective. Opposed to the Stuarts, his writings formed a basis for the American Declaration of Human Rights.

**Luther**, Martin (1483–1546): German Protestant, led the Reformation with his Ninety-Five Theses against the sale of indulgences (1517). Theologian, biblical scholar, translator, musician, hymn-writer, liturgiologist, polemicist. Founder of the church which bears his name.

**Marcus Aurelius** (Antoninus) (121–80): Roman emperor, adopted at the age of 17 by Antoninus Pius, Hadrian's successor. Stoic philosopher (i.e. live with self-control and minimum display of the emotions). His classic work was *Meditations*. Treated in awe by his people, he persecuted Christians for their fanaticism and what he saw as their superstitions.

**Marx**, Karl (1818–83): German philosopher who settled in London. Applied his philosophy primarily to the spheres of economics and politics. Starting from the dialectics of the philosopher Hegel, he founded the doctrine of dialectical materialism and developed a system of economic determinism (communism). Books include *Communist Party Manifesto* (1845) and *Das Kapital* (*Capitalism*) (1867).

**Mencken**, H. L. (1880–1956): American philologist, journalist and literary critic. Satirical, iconoclastic. Autobiography, *Days of H. L. Mencken* (1947).

**Mill**, John Stuart (1806–73): British philosopher, pioneer of utilitarianism (q.v.). Author of *Utilitarianism* and *On Liberty*, etc. Defended the rights of the minority in a democracy.

**Nietzsche**, Friedrich (1844–1900): German philosopher, linked with the existentialists. Wrote on (in particular) aesthetics and ethics (q.v.): opposed 'master-and-slave' mentality: against utilitarianism and Christian ethics. Taught of the 'will to power' and the 'overman' (usually mistranslated 'superman').

**Popper**, Karl (1902– ): Austrian philosopher of science and political philosopher. Taught that for a statement to be scientific rather than metaphysical it must be falsifiable; cf. his *Refutations and Conjectures*: scientific research involves the researcher in first devising a theory and then attempting to disprove it. As in politics, he believed that in science one should attempt to eliminate the bad rather than establish the good.

**Radhakrishnan**, Sir Sarvepalli (1888–1975): Indian philosopher and statesman. Professor of Eastern Religions and Ethics at Oxford University. First Indian ambassador to the USSR. Author of *Eastern Religion and Western Thought* and *Indian Philosophy*.

**Rand**, Ayn (1905–82): Russian-born American novelist and philosopher. Author of *The Fountainhead* and *Atlas Shrugged*. Promulgated her theory of objectivism (q.v.).

**Russell**, Bertrand, Earl (1872–1970): English philosopher of logic and mathematics. Taught Wittgenstein at Cambridge. Involved in pacifism in the First World War and in the Campaign for Nuclear Disarmament in the 1950s and 1960s. His *The Problems of Philosophy* is a readable introduction to the subject, though his *Principia Mathematica* (with A. N. Whitehead) is his most original work.

**Ryle**, Gilbert (1900–73): British philosopher, early exponent of linguistic analysis in philosophy. Wrote mainly on epistemology and philosophical logic.

**Samkara** (*Shankara*) Swami (? 788–820): Indian teacher, founded doctrine of non-dualism (Advaita, q.v. in Eastern glossary). Of Brahman stock, he lived a controversial life.

**Savonarola**, Girolamo (1452–98): Italian Dominican religious and political reformer. Preached against the sinfulness of both religious and political leaders and fell foul of the Medicis in Florence. Known as the Puritan of Catholicism. Hanged and burned at the stake. In morals and religion a forerunner of the Reformation.

**Schopenhauer**, Arthur (1788–1860): German philosopher, emphasized the role of the will, including unconscious willing (which predated Freud). His pessimistic philosophy of resignation was influenced by Indian thought (karma, etc.).

**Schweitzer**, Albert (1875–1965): German doctor of medicine, music, theology and philosophy. World-famous organist and exponent of J. S. Bach. Spent most of his life as a missionary doctor in the Belgian Congo. In his most famous book, *The Quest of the Historical Jesus* (1910), he argued that Jesus's ministry and teaching took place under the mistaken conviction that the world was about to come to an end.

**Shankara**: see Samkara

**Skinner**, B. F. (1904– ): American psychologist, leading proponent of behaviourism. Taught that *homo sapiens* is controlled by external factors, and that autonomy and free will do not exist. Has attempted to show how his principles could be applied to create an ideal society. Has influenced educationists with his theories of programmed learning.

**Spinoza**, Baruch (1632–77): Dutch philosopher. Though of Jewish stock, became a Christian; earned his living as a lens-grinder. Influenced by Descartes, but parted from him by stating that he saw no distinction between God, mind and matter. Believed that God, the universe, nature, are one (pantheism). Disbelieved in the freedom of the will; taught that man must understand the processes at work within him and find joy in union with God (or harmony with nature). Major work: *Ethics*.

**Vivekananda**, Swami (1863–1902): Hindu philosopher, studied Western thought and science. Aimed to link Western science and materialism (q.v.) with Eastern spirituality. Founded Vedanta (q.v.) movement in the West. Disciple of Ramakrishna (1836–86) who taught the essential unity of all religions. He died while in samadhi (q.v.).

**Whitehead**, Alfred North (1861–1947): mathematician and philosopher. Became Professor of Applied Mathematics at Imperial College, London, and of Philosophy at Harvard. Collaborated with his former pupil, Russell (q.v.) in the *Principia Mathematica*, described as 'the greatest single contribution to logic since Aristotle'. Awarded the Order of Merit in 1947.

**Wittgenstein**, Ludwig (1889–1951): arguably the greatest philosophical genius of the twentieth century, who in his lifetime produced two distinctive philosophies. The first is contained in the *Tractatus-logico-philosophicus* (1921) and expresses, in sentences which are intensely complicated in their structure, the view that the structure of reality determines the structure of language. In his later years, in writings which are not so systematically presented as those in the Tractatus but are more accessible to the interested reader, he explored the view that it is, on the contrary, our language that gives us our concept of reality. cf. *Philosophical Investigations* trans. G. E. M. Anscombe, Blackwell, Oxford 1953.

## General terms

**absolutism**: in ethics (q.v.) absolutism is the view that particular forms of behaviour are right or wrong in all circumstances. *Relativism* is the view that the rightness or wrongness of an action depends on the time, the place, the circumstances and the people involved, or any combination of these.

**agape**: one of four Greek words for 'love'. The others are: *eros*, or sensual love; *storge*, or family affection; *philia*, or liking (friendship). Agape is deeper than feelings; it involves sympathy, understanding, empathy: action conducted with the best good of the other person(s) or species in mind. There can be agape even where there is no philia.

**analytical**: in logic, a statement that is true in all possible worlds, independent of any additional facts. If a statement is analytically true, it is true by definition, e.g. 'All bachelors are male.'

**animism**: the primitive belief that every form of reality – stones, trees, thunderstorms, etc. – has its own indwelling spirit; it often includes the belief in the continued existence of individual disembodied spirits exercising a benign or (more frequently) malign influence.

**Cistercians**: an order of monks founded in 1098 by St Robert of Molesme (*c.* 1027–1111) as a stricter offshoot of the Benedictine order. Named after the mother house at Cîteaux in France. St Bernard of Clairvaux brought them great prestige. In the seventeenth century, further reform brought about the community known as Trappists.

**Cosmos**: the universe; seen as an orderly and harmonious system.

**descriptive**: see *prescriptive*.

**dynamism**: Greek *dunamis*, 'power'. A quality of restless drive or movement.

**elitism**: belief in leadership or rule by a section or group regarded as socially superior (with Plato, the intellectuals).

**Epicureanism**: the philosophy of Epicurus, who taught a hedonistic ethic; that is, that the aim of moral choice is to bring about pleasure, intellectual pleasures being the highest good; and advocated the aim of imperturbability.

**epistemology**: the theory of knowledge, with reference to its limits and validity.

**ethics**: the theory of right and wrong conduct.

**etymology**: the study of the history of a word, tracing the modifications in its meaning over the centuries and from one language to another.

**immanent**: belief in God as an indwelling presence in the world (see also *transcendent*).

**immaterialism**: the belief that external objects exist essentially only in the mind.

**linguistics**: the scientific study of language. In the nineteenth century this study was termed philology (q.v.) and mainly related to the classical, or Indo-European languages. Modern linguistics, under the influence of (in particular) Ferdinand de Saussure, Leonard Bloomfield, and Noam Chomsky, has three main branches, corresponding to the three main components of language: semantics (q.v.), grammar, and phonetics (the study of the production and perception of sounds in languages). *Comparative linguistics* compares languages either to establish the history of and relationships among related languages (e.g. the Semitic languages), or to test whether there are universal characteristics in language by comparing unrelated languages.

**materialism**: the theory that physical matter is the only reality, and the reality through which all being and processes and phenomena (q.v.) can be explained.

**Mechanism**: a doctrine that natural processes, especially the processes of life, are mechanically determined and capable of complete explanation by the laws of physics and chemistry. (See also *teleology, vitalism.*)

**monism**: the metaphysical view that there is only one kind of substance or ultimate reality: opposed to *dualism*; and that reality is one united whole with no independent parts: opposed to *pluralism*.

**mysterium fascinans**: the sense of awe brought about through the belief in God's love and mercy.

**mysterium tremendens**: the sense of awe brought about through the belief in God's omnipotence and judgement.

**mysticism**: the experience of mystical union or direct communion with ultimate reality, reported by mystics. Frequently associated with the belief that direct knowledge of God, Ground of Being, Tao or other parallel concepts is attainable through immediate intuition, insight, or illumination, without recourse to reason or perception through the senses.

**noumenon**: in Kant's writings, the underlying reality of an object: the 'thing-in-itself'.

**objectivism**: in this book, the philosophy associated with *Ayn Rand* (q.v.) in which self-interest is exalted to the highest good, and government, religion and other forms of control are viewed as destructive of this good.

**pathetic fallacy**: the ascription of human traits or feelings to inanimate nature, as in 'the harsh face of the mountain', 'blushing rose' or 'this liquid is kind to your hands'.

**phenomenon**: the form or appearance of a thing as received by the senses.

**philistinism**: the views of a modern Philistine (the Philistines were enemies of the Jews in Old Testament days): indifference to aesthetics (appreciation of beauty), being uninformed, lacking specialist knowledge.

**philology**: the term given to the scientific study of language before the advent of modern linguistics (q.v.). Originally concerned with the study of classical languages and literatures, it came to be applied to what we now term comparative linguistics (q.v. under linguistics).

**pragmatism**: the philosophical view, associated with William James (q.v.), that the meaning and value of ideas and concepts is to be found in their practical consequences; the effects of this belief or idea on the believer or holder of the viewpoint. 'By their fruits shall ye know them' is a pragmatic statement if applied to ideas.

**prescriptive**: laying down rules, suggestions and implications of events; drawing out a moral, or message, from these events. Opposed to *descriptive*, which is to state the course of events without drawing out any moral or implication from it. A descriptive statement might be: 'He preached for twenty minutes'; a prescriptive statement: 'Although the hour was late, he still preached for fully twenty minutes.'

**relativism**: see *absolutism*.

**semantics**: the study of meanings in relation to words and signs: a branch of semiotics.

**semiotics**: literally, theory of signs: the philosophical theory that deals with the function of signs and symbols.

**social Darwinism**: the application of Darwin's theory of evolution to society, and the belief that social and cultural advantage is brought about through inter-group conflict and competition, and that the social elite (such as the wealthy and powerful) have a biological superiority in the struggle for existence: thus 'the survival of the fittest'.

**spiritism/spiritualism**: the belief that departed spirits (of dead people) commune with living people, usually through a medium.

**teleology**: purposiveness: the explanation of events by final causes, the end which they are seeking. In nature, events viewed as having these final causes are often seen as under the control of divine Providence: opposite of mechanism (q.v.). In utilitarianism (q.v.) the utility of happiness is seen as the end of human moral choices.

**transcendent**: the view of God as above material existence and/or existing apart from the universe. Contrasted with *immanent* (q.v.).

**utilitarianism**: the philosophical view, pioneered by Jeremy Bentham and pursued in a modified form by John Stuart Mill (q.v.), that the aim of human moral decision-making (that is, the factor that determines whether moral decisions are right or wrong) is happiness: 'the greatest happiness of the greatest number'. Opposed to Kant, who believed that moral choices should be based on principles, utilitarianism bases its values on consequences.

**vitalism**: the doctrine that living organisms function as they do because of a vital principle (cf. Bergson's *élan vital*, or life force) and not because of physiochemical factors. Opposed to mechanism (q.v.). For the human being, the belief that life is self-determining, not mechanistically determined.

**Zoroastrianism**: a dualistic pre-Islamic religion, founded in Persia by the prophet Zoroaster *c.*700 BC. He taught the worship of the one God, Ahura Mazda, as the source of all good, requiring from His worshippers the practice of good thoughts, words and deeds, and the combating of evil, which is personified as Ahriman. Zoroaster was commended by Nietzsche (q.v.) in his *Thus spake Zarathustra* (the Persian transliteration of his name) because of the purity of his moral teaching. Regarded by some scholars as the first theist, predating the Old Testament prophets in this respect.

# Eastern words and ideas

**Advaita** (*dvaita*, 'dualism', *a-*, 'negative', hence non-dualism). The doctrine of monism (q.v.) advocated by Samkara (q.v.) which contends that only Brahman (q.v.), the Ultimate Principle, has any actual existence, and that all else is illusion (maya, q.v.).

**Analects**: translated in 1938 as *The Analects of Confucius*. Compiled in the fifth and fourth centuries BC. A collection of sayings of Confucius, and of anecdotes about him and his disciples. Comments on ethics, government, ritual, etc., a fundamental part of education in traditional China.

**anatta** (*natta*, 'self' *a-*, 'negative', hence 'no self'). The doctrine that there is no soul. One of the three Buddhist marks of existence.

**anicca** (*nicca*, 'person', *a-*, 'negative', hence 'no permanence'). One of the three Buddhist marks of existence. Everything is in a state of flux. (Also anitya.)

**astika**: literally 'orthodox': a description of those systems in Indian thought which acknowledge the validity of the Vedas (q.v.).

**Atman**: the soul, self, principle of life and sensation. Etymology (q.v.) doubtful; cf. German *Atem* 'breath'.

**avatar**: the descent of a deity (often Vishnu); an incarnation. Literally 'to pass across, through, or over'.

**Bhagavad-gita**: Literally 'the song of God' (i.e. Krishna). A philosophical epic poem, date uncertain, which indicates the relationship between morality and absolute ethical values in Hindu philosophy of action (karma, yoga).

**Bodhisattva**: literally 'being of wisdom'. In Buddhism, one who has attained the status of Buddha, but who postpones his/her entry to Nirvana in order to assist others in their quest for truth.

**Brahman**: in Hinduism, the ultimate indefinable power of the universe, the 'Ground of Being'. In the Upanishads (q.v.) and after, Brahman is identified with Atman (q.v.). Not generally an object of worship, but of meditation. Not to be confused with Brahmin, which is a member of the priestly caste.

**carvaka**: an adherent of the school of materialism in Hindu philosophy, named after its founder.

**chi** (*or ch'i*): in China: energy, life force.

**Chuang tzu**: literally 'Master Chuang'; traditional dates 369–286 BC. Author of the Taoist text which expresses the primacy of nature over man and governments, and the relativity (q.v. under *absolutism*) of good and evil.

**Dharma**: literally that which binds, supports, sustains. In Buddhism, the law of Buddha, the basic doctrine of the Four Noble Truths. One of the three 'Jewels of the faith', the other two being the person of Buddha and the Sangha (q.v.). In Hinduism, dharma is the form of conduct befitting one's station in life.

**Dharmkaya**: literally 'embodied law' in Mahayana Buddhism (q.v.). It teaches the reality of an Absolute, and the Buddha as the personification of the law.

**dhyana**: One of the states of yogic meditation leading to siddis (q.v.) lit. 'perfection', the gateway to enlightenment. The other states are dharma and samadhi (q.v.) which together bring about sanyana (coherence).

**duhkha**: suffering; the unsatisfactoriness of existence as we encounter it. According to Buddha, one of the three Marks of Existence.

**guru**: literally 'heavy', 'venerable'. A personal religious teacher and spiritual guide in Hinduism.

**Hinayana**: literally 'lesser vehicle'. The orthodox branch of Buddhism which remained faithful to the original teaching of Buddha. Contrasted with Mahayana (q.v.). Established in Ceylon, Burma and Thailand.

**I Ching**: 'Book of Changes'; one of five Chinese classics. By throwing coins or casting yarrow stalks a petitioner chooses one, or two, out of sixty-four hexagrams by lot. The corresponding text reveals the petitioner's prospects or provides guidance in what to do.

**Jainism**: Indian religion, originated *c*. sixth century BC. Teaches that, while gods control time and matter, any human being is capable of achieving divine status. Jainites practise extreme asceticism, are strict vegetarians, avoid killing any living creature, eschew agriculture. They have scriptures, temples, strong ritual and a monastic order. Associated with the sage Mahavira, they are divided into those who accept nudity (the 'skyclad') like their founder and those who wear simple white clothing (the 'white-clad').

**jen**: the cardinal Confucian virtue of benevolence towards one's fellows.

**jnana**: knowledge, especially the knowledge derived from meditating on the Universal Spirit – Universal Knowledge.

**koan**: a paradox, used in Zen (q.v.) Buddhism as an instrument of meditation in training monks not to depend on reason; aimed to direct them into sudden intuitive enlightenment.

**Lao Tsu**: literally 'Great Teacher'. Supposedly an older contemporary of Confucius, sixth century BC. Revered as the founder of Taoism, and author of the Tao Te Ching (q.v.).

**li**: Confucian concept of propriety, proper conduct; virtue seen as an outward expression of an inner harmony with the ethical principles of nature.

**Mahayana**: 'Greater Vehicle' Buddhism, which expresses the belief that the spirit of the doctrine is more important than its original formulation. It broadened out the strict orthodox (and conservative) ideas of the chances of achieving Nirvana in this lifetime (or round of experience) as taught by Buddha and, after his death, by Hinayana Buddhism (q.v.). Established in China, Japan, Tibet, Nepal and Korea.

**maya**: delusion. In the Vedanta (q.v.) the obscuring force of nature, displaying universal consciousness as duality, thus producing error and illusion.

**moksa**: emancipation; release from worldly, finite existence; liberation from *samsara* (q.v.).

**Nirvana** (*nis*, 'out', *vana*, 'blown', hence extinction of the flame of life): final emancipation from karma. In Buddhism, a state from which no further birth is needed.

**Prakriti** (*pra*, 'before', *kar*, 'to make'): Cosmic Substance, Primal Nature, the primeval source of all things according to the Sankhya system. In Vedanta (q.v.) known as maya (q.v.). See also Purusha.

**Purusha**: Cosmic Spirit. According to the Sankhya system, the ultimate principle that directs the process of cosmic evolution.

**samadhi**: Sanskrit, literally 'establish', 'make firm'. The fourth state of consciousness, beyond deep sleep, dreaming and waking. It is total absorption in the object of meditation. If the object is Brahman (q.v.), the ground of Being, the result is union. Samadhi is a non-dualistic state of consciousness in which the mind is not directed from here (subject) to there (object), which would be a dualistic mode of experience, but one in which the consciousness of the experiencing 'subject' becomes one with the experiencing 'object'; thus samadhi is only experiential content. In Mahayana Buddhism (q.v.) the attainment of the state of samadhi is a precondition of dhyana (absorption) (q.v.). Any type of samadhi which does not have this emptiness as a goal is viewed, even at its highest stage, as worldly.

**samsara** (*sam*, 'together', *sara*, 'flowing', hence 'going about'): the passage of the soul in the cycle of births and deaths. Transmigration, birth and rebirth.

**sandhya bhasya** (*sandhya*, 'state of dreaming', *bhasya*, 'commentary'): a description of the dreaming state, the second state of Advaita Vedanta.

**Sangha**: in Buddhism, the community of monks. One of the 'three Jewels' (*tri-ratna*). One may become a monk temporarily, or for life.

**Sat-Chit-Ananda**: 'Being-consciousness-bliss'; in Vedanta (q.v.) the three attributes of Brahman (q.v.). Ananda is the Absolute Joy experienced in the Fourth State. Sat-Chit means the unaffected absolute bliss of Brahman experienced only in the state of samadhi (q.v.) or total absorption in the Absolute.

**siddhis**: from *siddhi*, 'to purify', hence 'pure categories': pure, because the dual relationship of subject and object is a single unit; i.e. the object is seen as part of the subject. Siddhis are supernatural or psychic abilities which can be developed through Tantric or Yogic practices, but the greatest teachers have warned that they do not aid spiritual progress and should not be developed for their own sake.

**sutra**: literally 'thread': aphorisms, precepts, or collection of brief rules, originating generally from the period 500–200 BC.

**T'ai Chi'-T'u** (*T'ai*, 'supreme'; *Chi*, 'ultimate'; *T'u*, 'diagram'): the Yin-Yang symbol.

**Tao Te Ching** (*Tao*, 'Way'; *Te*, 'virtue' or 'power'; *Ching*, 'treatise' or 'book'): treatise on the virtue of the Way (or Treatise of the Way and Virtue).

**Tat tuam asi** literally 'Thou art that'; 'that' = Brahman (q.v.); 'thou' = the individual self. The Hindu expression of the union of Atman (q.v.) with Brahman. The individual self also has Brahman for its Self because Brahman has entered into it.

**Theravada** literally 'teaching of the Elders'; the form of Hinayana (q.v.) Buddhism which is found in Sri Lanka and South-East Asia.

**Upanishads** (*upa*, 'near to', 'towards'; *ni*, 'down'; *sidati*, 'he sits'): by implication, a secret session, sitting opposite (the teachers). One of the late series of Vedic (q.v.) treatises dealing with such philosophical problems as the nature of ultimate reality, man and the universe. There are over 100 Upanishads, but the thirteen oldest are Chandogya, Brhadaranyaka, Aitareya, Taittiriya, Katha, Isa, Munda, Kausitaki, Kena, Prasna, Svetasvatara, Mandukya and Maitri. They date probably from the eighth century BC.

**Veda**: literally 'to know'. Generic name for the most ancient literature of the Hindus, classified as revealed literature. Estimated to date from 1500–1000 BC.

**Vedanta**: literally 'the end of the Vedas', the consummation of Indian thought because the central topic is the ultimate principle, Brahman (q.v.).

**Vedic**: the divisions of the Vedas; each is divided into two parts, or broad divisions: (1) mantra, or hymns, and (2) Brahmana, or precepts, which include (a) Aranyakas, theology, and (b) Upanishads, philosophy.

**Yin Yang**: literally the dark and the light sides of a mountain; so the negative and positive forces in the universe.

**Zen**: the branch of Buddhism introduced from China to Japan in the twelfth century. Emphasizes meditation and physical work as a means of gaining enlightenment, or *sartori*. A special feature is reflection on the koan (q.v.). Has influenced much of Japanese culture, including No drama, martial arts and the tea ceremony. Introduced into the West largely through the writings of Daisteg Suzuki (1870–1966).

## Foreign words and phrases used

**deus ex machina**: literally 'God (let down upon the stage) by machine'; hence the artificial introduction of the idea of (for example) God to 'prove' an argument which would otherwise remain unresolved. In fiction, a forced (artificial) incident which allows the story to end (happily), such as the intervention of the woodcutter in *Little Red Riding Hood*.

**faute de mieux**: for lack of anything better.

**in extremis**: in desperate circumstances (often used as at the point of death).

**in toto**: entirely.

**modus operandi**: mode of operation; way of working; procedure, 'plan of campaign'.

**modus vivendi**: literally 'way of life', or of living; often used in the sense of a compromise – a working relationship by which people with many differences can get on, at least for a time. The modern word is 'package', or 'deal'. The cynic might say that most marriages represent a *modus vivendi*.

**par excellence**: superior to all others of the same sort.

**sine qua non**: essential ingredient, indispensable condition. Oxygen is a *sine qua non* of life on this planet; the Pope is a *sine qua non* of Roman Catholicism; music is a *sine qua non* of opera.

# Works referred to
# in the text

Aeschyllus (1937), *Prometheus Bound* (Oxford: Oxford Classical Texts).

Altizer, T. (1966), *The Gospel of Christian Atheism* (New York: Westminster).

Aquinas, St Thomas (1963–80), *Summa Theologiae* in 61 vols. (London: Eyre and Spottiswood).

Aristotle (1908–52), *Nichomachean Ethics* in W. D. Ross (ed.) *Works of Aristotle* in 12 vols. (Oxford: OUP).

Aristotle (1908–52), *Poetics* in W. D. Ross (ed.), op. cit.

Augustine, St., of Hippo (1953–5), *Enchiridon* in M. Dods (ed.), *The Works of Augustinus Aurelius* (Edinburgh: T & T Clarke).

Aurobindo, S. (1948), *The Synthesis of Yoga* (Madras: Sri Aurobindo Library).

Ayer, A. J. (1936), *Language, Truth and Logic* (Harmondsworth: Penguin).

Bacon, F. (1968), *Essays* (London: Dent).

Barrett, W. (1961), *Irrational Man* (London: Heinemann).

Bergson, H. ([1889]1971), *Time and Free Will* tr. F. Pogson (London: Allen & Unwin).

Berkeley, G. ([1710]1962), *The Principles of Human Knowledge* G. Warnock (ed.) (London: Collins).

Bernard of Clairvaux, St. (1943), *Rule of St Benedict (499–543)* Extracts in Bettenson. Documents of the Christian Church (Oxford: OUP).

Bhagvad–gita (1957), in S Radhakrishnan and C. A. Moore *A Sourcebook in Indian Philosophy* (Princeton NJ: Princeton University Press).

Billington, R. J. (1971), *The Christian Outsider* (London: Epworth).

Billington, R. J. (1988), *Living Philosophy* (London: Routledge).

Bonhoffer, D. (1953), *Letters and Papers from Prison* (London: Collins).

Buber, M. (1937), *I and Thou* (Edinburgh: T & T Clarke).

Buber, M. (1947), *Between Man and Man* (Edinburgh: T & T Clarke).

Buber, M. ([1946]1988), *Moses* (Oxford: OUP).

Capra, F. (1975), *The Tao of Physics* (London: Wildwood House).

Chang, C. C. (1978), *Practice of Zen* (London: Greenwood Press).

Chang, J. (1977), *The Tao of Love and Sex* (London: Wildwood House).

Chopin, K. (1989), *The Awakening* (London: Women's Press).

Collins, S. (1982), *Selfless Persons* (Cambridge: CUP).

Confucius (1988), *Analects* tr. and annotated by Arthur Waley (London: Unwin Hyman).

Chuang–Tzu (1968), *Complete Works* tr. B. Watson (Columbia: Columbia University Press).

Churchill, W. S. ([1930]1989), *My Early Life* (London: C. Cooper).

Darwin, C. ([1867]1968), *Origin of Species* (Harmondsworth: Penguin).

Darwin, C. ([1871]1987), 'The Descent of Man' in M. Ridley (ed.) *Essential Darwin* (London: Unwin Hyman).

Davidson, J. (1988), *Web of Life* (London: C. W. Daniel).

Eddy, M. B. (1875), *The Science of Health* (Boston: First Church of Christ Scientist).

Edwards, D. (ed.) (1964), *The Honest to God Debate* (London: SCH).

Freud, S. (1986), 'The Origin and Development of Psychoanalysis' in *Essentials of Psychoanalysis* tr. Anna Freud (Harmondsworth: Penguin).

Goethe, J. W. von (1952), *Poetical Works* in *Oxford Book of German Verse* (Oxford: OUP).

Gollancz, V. (ed.) (1956), *From Darkness to Light* (London: Gollancz).

Hamilton, W. (1965), 'The Death of God' in *Playboy*, December 1965.

Hamilton, W., and T. Altizer (1968), *Radical Theology and the Death of God* (Harmondsworth: Penguin).

Hegel, G. W. F. (1956), *Lectures on the Philosophy of History* tr. J. Sibree (New York: Dover).

Heidegger, M. (1927), *Being and Time* tr. W. Brock (Oxford: Blackwell).

Hobbes, T. ([1651]1962), *Leviathan* (Harmondsworth: Penguin).

Hobbes, T. ([1656]1962), 'Of Liberty and Necessity' in R. S. Peters *Body, Man and Citizen* (London: Collier–Macmillan).

Hospers, J. (1956), *An Introduction to Philosophical Analysis* (London: Routledge and Kegan Paul).

Hoyle, F. (1950), *The Nature of the Universe* (Oxford: Blackwell).

Hume, D. ([1737]1978), *Enquiry Concerning Human Understanding* L. A. Selby–Bigg (ed.) (Oxford: OUP).

Humphries, C. (1974), *Exploring Buddhism* (London, Allen & Unwin).

Huxley, A. (1932), *Brave New World* (London: Chatto & Windus).

Huxley, A. (1954), *The Doors of Perception* (London: Granada Panther Books).

Huxley, A. (1958), *The Perennial Philosophy* (London: Collins).

Huxley, J. (1943), *Evolutionary Ethics* (London: Greenwood Press).

*I Ching* (1984), tr. J. Blofeld (London: Unwin Hyman).

Illich, I. (1971), *Deschooling Society* (Harmondsworth: Penguin).

James, E. (ed.) (1988), *God's Truth* (London: SCM).

James, W. ([1897]1984), *The Will to Believe* (London: Longman).

Kafka, F. (1953), *The Trial* (Harmondsworth: Penguin).

Kant, I. (1781), *Critique of Pure Reason* tr. N. Kemp Smith (1933) (London: Macmillan).

Kant, I. (1788), *Critique of Analytical Reason* tr. L. Beck (1849) (Chicago: Chicago University Press).

Kasparov, G. (1986), *The Test of Time* (Oxford: Pergamon).

Kierkegaard, S. (1843), *Either/Or* in 2 vols. tr. Hong and Hong (1987) (Princeton NJ: Princeton University Press).

Kierkegaard, S. (1946), *Journal* in *A Kierkegaard Anthology*, R. Bretall (ed.) (Princeton NJ: Princeton University Press).

*Koran, The* (1976), M. M. Pickthall (ed.) tr. A. J. Arberry (London: Allen & Unwin).

Lao Tzu (1973), *Tao Te Ching* tr. Gia Fu–Feng and Jane English (London: Wildwood House).

Lawrence, D. H. (1960) *Lady Chatterley's Lover* (unexpurgated edn) (Harmondsworth: Penguin).

Lawrence, D. H. (1955), *Phoenix* (London: Heinemann).

Lawrence, D. H. (1983), *St Mawr* (London: Heinemann).

Lawrence, D. H. (1971), *Studies in Classical American Literature* (Harmondsworth: Penguin).

Lawrence, T. E. (1955), *The Mint* (London: Cape).

Leibniz, G. W. ([1686]1961), *Discourse on Metaphysics* tr. P. Lucas and L. Grint (Manchester: Manchester University Press).

Locke, J. ([1690]1979), *An Essay Concerning Human Understanding* P. H. Nidditch (ed.) (Oxford: OUP).

Lodge, D. (1984), *Changing Places* (London: Secker & Warburg).

Lorenz, K. (1950), *King Solomon's Ring* (London: Methuen).

Lorenz, K. (1966), *On Aggression* (London: Methuen).

Magee, B. (1978), *Men of Ideas* (Oxford: OUP).

Marx, K. ([1867]1963), *Das Kapital* in *Karl Marx: Selected Writings* in *Sociology in Social Philosophy* tr. T. B. Bottomore (Harmondsworth: Penguin).

Mencius (Mang Tzu) (1960), *The Sayings of Mencius* tr. J. Lang (New York: New American Library).

Mencken, H. L. (1973), *Prejudices and Notebooks* in A. Cooke (ed.) *Vintage Mencken* (New York: Vintage Books).

Mill, J. S. ([1861]1972), *Utilitarianism* (London: Dent).

Morris, D. (1967), *The Naked Ape* (London: Pan Books).

Nietzsche, F. ([1886]1967), *Beyond Good and Evil* tr. W. Kaufmann (New York: Vintage Books).

Nietzsche, F. (1974), *Ecce Homo* tr. R. J. Hollingdale (Harmondsworth: Penguin).

Nietzsche, F. ([1882]1974), *The Gay Science* tr. W. Kaufmann (New York: Random House).

Nietzsche, F. ([1883–5]1954), *Thus Spake Zarathustra* tr. W. Kaufmann (New York: The Viking Press).

Otto, R. (1923), *The Idea of the Holy* (Oxford: OUP).

Peters, R. S. (1973), *The Concept of Education* (London: Macmillan).

Plato (1967), *Republic* (London: Heinemann).

Prabhpada B. S. (1968), *Bhagavad–gita As It Is* (Watford: Society for Krishna Consciousness).

Rawson, P. (1981), *Oriental Erotic Art* (London: Quartet Books).

Robinson, R. (1964), *Seventeen Come Sunday* (private publication).

Robinson, J. A. T. R. (1963), *Honest to God* (London: SCM).

Robinson, J. A. T. R. (1967), *Explorations into God* (London: SCM).

Russell, B. (1961), *Has Man A Future?* (Harmondsworth: Penguin).

Russell, B. (1943), *History of Western Philosophy* (London: Allen & Unwin).

Russell, B. (1910), *Mysticism and Logic* (London: Allen & Unwin).

Russell, B. ([1912]1973), *The Problems of Philosophy* (Oxford: OUP).

Ryle, G. ([1949]1967), *The Concept of Mind* (London: Hutchinson).

Sarawati, S. K. (1984), *The Bhagavadgita in Day to Day Life* (London: Element Books).

Sartre, J.-P. ([1943]1958), *Being and Nothingness* tr. P. Mairet (London: Methuen).

Sartre, J.-P. ([1946]1948), *Existentialism and Humanism* tr. P. Mairet (London: Methuen).

Sartre, J.-P. ([1944]1987), *No Exit* Eng. trans. 1947 (London: Methuen).

Schopenhauer, A. ([1841]1960), *On the Freedom of the Will* (Oxford: Blackwell).

Schopenhauer, A. ([1851]1960), *Parerga and Paralipomena* 2 vols. tr. K. Kolenda (New York: Bobbs–Merill).

Schweitzer, A. (1910), *The Quest of the Historical Jesus* (London: A & C Black).

Schanker, S. G. (ed.) (1986), *Philosophy in Britain Today* (Beckenham: Croom Helm).

Shearer, A. (1985), *Effortless Being* (London: Wildwood House).

Skinner, B. F. (1973), *Beyond Freedom and Dignity* (Harmondsworth: Penguin).

Skinner, B. F. (1953), *Science and Human Behaviour* (New York: Macmillan).

Smith, H. D. (1948), *One Hundred and Ten Upanishads* (Bombay: n.p.)

Smith, H. D. (1968), *Selections from Vedic Hymns* (Berkeley: n.p.)

Spark, M. (1961), *The Prime of Miss Jean Brodie* (London: Macmillan).

Spinoza, B. ([1677]1963), *Ethics* tr. A. Bogle (London: Dent).

Spencer, H. ([1879–93]1967), *Principles of Sociology* (Chicago: Chicago University Press).

Stevenson, L. (1974), *Seven Theories of Human Nature* (Oxford: OUP).

Stevenson, L. (1981), *The Study of Human Nature* (Oxford: OUP).

Thomas, D. A. T. (n.d.), *East and West: A Mirror of Divine Duality* (to be published).

Tillich, P. J. (1948), *The Shaking of the Foundations* (London: SCM).

Watson, L. (1986), *Supernature* (London: Hodder & Stoughton).

Watson, L. (1987), *Supernature II* (New York: Sceptre Books).

Weil, S. ([1952]1987), *The Need for Roots* (London: Arle Publications).

Wesley, C. (1966), *Hymns* arranged by H. A. Hodges and A. M. Allchin (London: Hodder & Stoughton).

Wesley, J. (1985–8), *Sermons* 4 vols., A. C. Outler (ed.) (Nashville: Abingdon).

Whitehead, A. N. ([1933]1967), *Adventures of Ideas* (New York: Free Press).

Whiteley, C. (1963), *Introduction to Metaphysics* (London: Harvester).

Wilson, M. M. (ed.) (1969), *The Essential Descartes* (New York: Mentor Books).

Wittgenstein, L. ([1921]1960), *Tractatus Logico–Philosophicus* tr. D. F. Pears and B. F. McGuiness (London: Routledge and Kegan Paul).

Wittgenstein, L. (1969), *On Certainty* tr. D. Paul and G. E. M. Anscombe (Oxford: Blackwell).

# Suggestions for further reading

Most of the books recommended for following up the Western elements discussed in this book are listed separately (pp. 304–7).

**Books which include material relevant to a study of Eastern philosophy as a whole are:**

Foy, W. (ed.) (1978), *Man's Religious Quest* (London: Croom Helm) (readings in the world's religions).

James, W. (1902, 12th impression 1985), *The Varieties of Religious Experience* (London: Collins, Fontana pbk).

Smart, N. (1969, 3rd edn 1984), *The Religious Experience of Mankind* (New York: Scrivener).

**Books on, or related to, Buddhism are:**

Conze, E. (trans.) (1959), *Buddhist Scriptures* (Harmondsworth: Penguin).

Keightley, A. (1986), *Into Every Life a Little Zen Must Fall* (London: Wisdom Publications).

Watts, A. (1962), *The Way of Zen* (Harmondsworth: Penguin).

**Books on Hinduism are:**

Hiriyanna, M. (1932), *Outlines of Indian Philosophy* (London: Allen & Unwin).

Isherwood, C. (ed.) (1948), *Vedanta for the Western World* (London: Allen & Unwin).

Radhakrishnan, S. (1929), *An Idealist View of Life* (London: Allen & Unwin).

Radhakrishnan, S. (1940, 2nd edn), *Eastern Religions and Western Thought* (Oxford: Oxford University Press).

Radhakrishnan, S. and Moore, C. A. (eds) (1973), *A Sourcebook in Indian Philosophy* (Princeton, NJ: Princeton University Press).

Vivekananda, S. (1955) *Jnana Yoga* (Calcutta: Advaita Asram).

Zimmer, H. (ed. Campbell, J.) (1951), *Philosophies of India* (Princeton, NJ: Princeton University Press).

Those interested could write to the Ramakrishna Vedanta Centre, Bourne End, Bucks, England SL8 5LG for details of other literature and relevant material on Advaita Vedanta.

## Books on China are:

Blofeld, J. (trans.) (1965), *I Ching, The Book of Changes* (London: Allen & Unwin).

Chan, W. (1963), *A Source Book in Chinese Philosophy* (Princeton, NJ: Princeton University Press).

Fung Yu-lan (1953), *A History of Chinese Philosophy* (2 vols) (Princeton, NJ: Princeton University Press).

Needham, J. (1956) *Science and Civilisation in China* (7 vols) (Cambridge: Cambridge University Press).

Waley, A. (trans.) (1938), *The Analects of Confucius* (London: Allen & Unwin).

Watson, B. (trans.) (1968), *The Complete Works of Chuang Tzu* (New York: Columbia University Press).

# Index of names

# Index of subjects